Domesticating the World

THE CALIFORNIA WORLD HISTORY LIBRARY

Edited by Edmund Burke III, Kenneth Pomeranz, and Patricia Seed

Domesticating the World

African Consumerism and
the Genealogies of Globalization

Jeremy Prestholdt

UNIVERSITY OF CALIFORNIA PRESS
Berkeley · Los Angeles · London

University of California Press, one of the most
distinguished university presses in the United States,
enriches lives around the world by advancing scholarship in the humanities, social sciences, and natural
sciences. Its activities are supported by the UC Press
Foundation and by philanthropic contributions from
individuals and institutions. For more information,
visit www.ucpress.edu.

Chapter 1 previously appeared as "Similitude and
Empire: On Comorian Strategies of Englishness,"
Journal of World History 8, no. 2 (2007): 113–40.
Chapter 3 appeared as "On the Global Repercussions
of East African Consumerism," *American Historical
Review* 109, no. 3 (2004): 755–81. Chapter 4
appeared as "Mirroring Modernity: On Consumerism
in Nineteenth Century Zanzibar," Boston University
Center for African Studies Working Paper Series,
January 2006.

University of California Press
Berkeley and Los Angeles, California

University of California Press, Ltd.
London, England

Library of Congress Cataloging-in-Publication Data

Prestholdt, Jeremy.
    Domesticating the world : African consumerism and
the genealogies of globalization / Jeremy Prestholdt.
        p.   cm. — (The California world history
library ; 6)
    Includes bibliographical references and index.
    ISBN 978-0-520-25424-4 (cloth : alk. paper)
    ISBN 978-0-520-25423-7 (pbk. : alk. paper)
    1. Consumer behavior—Africa, Eastern.
2. Globalization—Africa, Eastern.   I. Title.

HF5415.33.A354P74   2008
339.4'709676—dc22   2007011567

Manufactured in the United States of America

17   16   15   14   13   12   11   10   09   08
10   9   8   7   6   5   4   3   2   1

This book is printed on New Leaf EcoBook 50, a 100%
recycled fiber of which 50% is de-inked post-consumer
waste, processed chlorine-free. EcoBook 50 is acid-free
and meets the minimum requirements of ANSI/ASTM
D5634-01 *(Permanence of Paper)*.

For my grandfather, Olaf Ofstad,
who first taught me to imagine

Contents

Illustrations

Acknowledgments

The experience of researching and writing this book has shown me how to see the world differently. I thank everyone who has contributed to that shift of vision. Long before any of these ideas took shape my parents, Cynthia and Perry, and my sister, Jennifer, lovingly nurtured my interests. My parents also made my first visit to East Africa possible, for which I am still grateful. Kianga Ford, who shared all the experiences of that visit, supported me through every moment of researching and writing this book. I can never repay her time, intellectual energy, and care. My first East African history course with Isaria N. Kimambo, as well as the encouragement of Jamie Monson, Mary Jo Arnoldi, and Christine Mullen Kreamer, offered me the tools to seed this work.

Jonathon Glassman gave far more of his time and attention to this project than should be expected of an advisor. I am deeply grateful to him, and I hope this book stands as a humble tribute to his guidance. Ned Alpers has supported every aspect of this project from start to finish. He gave selflessly when he had no obligation, and I greatly appreciate the myriad investments he has made in me. David Schoenbrun has been a mentor from his first day at Northwestern, giving his attention to this project and my incessant questions. For his advice and direction I am most grateful. Even after her last day at Northwestern, Jane Guyer enthusiastically offered her energies and ideas to this project. Indrani Chatterjee, Adam Green, Laura Hein, A. G. Hopkins, John Hunwick, and Tessie Liu all guided my intellectual trajectory. Jim Brennan has been a true friend. He has shared his home and ideas with me from Chicago to Dar es Salaam to London. Chris Hayden likewise put me up countless times and generously supplied me with important documents from French archives. Chap Kusimba not only offered endless hospitality in Chicago and Kenya, but he also introduced me to new ways of seeing the East African coast. Jake Dorman has somehow never tired of my ideas, always offered many more in return, and provided unceasing inspiration. Matt Hopper, who heard these arguments over and again, has always offered new insight and critiques, to say nothing of much-needed Arabic translations.

As long as this project has existed it has benefited from the scholarship and friendship of Abdul Sheriff. Ann Biersteker refined my Swahili and supported my research even when I had only a vague sense of what I was doing. Bruce McKim showed me much about Zanzibar that I had not seen and taught me, by example, the skill of listening. Richard Roberts generously offered his time as well as incisive critiques when I most needed them. Ilham Makdisi has been a supportive colleague and an even greater friend. Anne Bang treated me as if I were family and has been equally generous with her thoughts and ideas. Without the aid of Sean O'Fahey I would have never made connections in Norway nor so many in Mombasa. Pedro Machado went far out of his way to introduce me to archives essential to my research and put a roof over my head in London. John Middleton saw the potential of this work long ago and offered constant encouragement. Engseng Ho gave his time and keen eye to this manuscript and guided it towards what I believe is a much better book.

I owe a tremendous debt to all teachers, friends, and neighbors in Tanzania and Kenya. Humoud Said Seif and his family made me feel at home in Zanzibar. The staff at the National Archives, Zanzibar, gave me access to the collection and assisted me with my work at a very difficult time. On the eve of elections, Khamis S. Khamis, Hamad Hassan Omar, and many other members of the staff ensured that I completed my research in Zanzibar. None of my work in Kenya would have been possible without the intellectual and logistical assistance of Athman Lali Omar. He could have been neither more supportive nor more integral to the completion of my research. Also infinitely helpful, both before and after my arrival in Kenya, were George and Lorna Abungu. All of the staff at the Fort Jesus Museum, Mombasa, aided me in untold ways, particularly Ali Abubakr, Mohammed Mchulla, and Jimbi Katana. Sheikh Ahmed

Nabahani offered his great insight into the history and complexity of the Swahili language. I benefited from the wonderful generosity of the late Sayyid Abdulrahman Ahmed Badawy Jamalilyl (Sharif Khitamy) and his extended family, Ustadh Zein l'Abdin Ahmed al Moody, and Mohamed Perryman, who always offered food, observations, and Internet access. I owe the greatest debt to Habib Kassim Habib and his family: Mwana Hawa, Muhammad, Hassan, Zakiya, Nuru, and Fatuma. They unreservedly accepted me (and all of my ways) and continually offer their unbounded generosity.

This book has benefited immensely from comments by participants at scores of conferences, workshops, roundtables, and lectures. I am particularly grateful to people and institutions that offered the time and space to put these thoughts on paper and then rethink them. At UC Santa Cruz I am especially indebted to Terry Burke, Jim Clifford, Chris Connery, Gail Hershatter, Anna Lowenhaupt Tsing, and fellow scholar-in-residence Liz DeLoughrey, who heard my ideas and offered their thoughtful criticism. At the Department of History and Centre for Middle East and Islamic Studies, University of Bergen, I offer a special thanks to Anders Bjørkelo, who made my stay in Bergen possible. He gave so much of his energy to create time for me to finish this manuscript that I can only hope the final product was worth his investment.

This project would not have been possible without support provided by many institutions and foundations, including the Social Science Research Council with funds from the Andrew W. Mellon Foundation, the Woodrow Wilson Foundation, the Center for Cultural Studies at UC Santa Cruz through a grant from the Rockefeller Foundation, the American Historical Association, the Fulbright Institute for International Education, the Fulbright Council for the International Exchange of Scholars, Northwestern University, Northwestern's Program of African Studies, Northeastern University, and the University of California, San Diego. A special thanks to librarians at the Fort Jesus Museum, Northwestern University, the British Library, SOAS, the Phillips Library at the Peabody-Essex Museum, UC Los Angeles, and UC San Diego. A heartfelt thanks to the director of the Africana collection at Northwestern University, David Easterbrook, for making possible the publication of so many early images of East Africa. Michael DiBlasi and anonymous readers for the *American Historical Review* and *Journal of World History* offered trenchant critiques and polished essays adapted for this book. Nick Murray further smoothed the rough edges of my thoughts and words. Finally, I could not have asked for more from UC Press. Niels Hooper, Chalon Emmons, and Rachel Lockman were patient beyond all expectation.

At one hundred years my grandfather continually encourages my curiosity and empathy. With love, respect, and gratitude I dedicate this book to him.

Introduction

While some boundaries seem as impassable as ever, many people feel as if the spatial divisions of the world are fast disappearing. Though these perspectives reflect different experiences, they both are predicated on presumptions of historical insularity. Attempts to describe the myriad ways that people, ideas, and objects either transcend spatial barriers or are restricted by them are important. But we should be mindful of the ways our analyses confirm the all-too-common presumption that human history has been typified by bounded geographical and cultural spheres. The aim of this book is to challenge notions of discrete sociocultural spaces and limited interactions that shape our understanding of the past and give rise to our wonder at a "globalized" present. Specifically, this book offers a reflection on the seemingly out of place, on the social lives of people and objects well beyond the boundaries of nation, continent, or sea that we regularly imagine to have been historically restrictive. Forgetting historical circumstances of interconnectivity and the reciprocity they entailed weakens our appreciation of how humans have historically affected and been affected by others, both far and near. Remembering histories of a relentlessly interdependent world can challenge contemporary fantasies of past isolation and our obsession with independent local or regional historical trajectories. Most importantly, histories of transsocietal interrelation remind us of how individual actions have often had long-term and distant consequences.

HISTORIES AND GLOBALITY

Contemporary globalization rhetoric regularly obscures pasts that never easily conformed to the distances, dichotomies, and differences that we often imagine to have constrained human relationships across space. Michel-Rolph Trouillot suggests that the wonder implicit in contemporary global reflection reveals a perceptual frame that is the result of both a forgetting and silencing of histories of interrelation. "For Muslim veils in France to seem out of place," he contends; "we need to forget that Charles Martel stopped 'Abd-al-Raman only 300 miles south of Paris, two reigns before Charlemagne."[1] In making this observation Trouillot does not deny that things around us—cultures, economies, ideas—are changing, that capital now moves at breakneck speed, or that people acutely feel an impinging world. Instead, what Trouillot points up are the conceptual principles of a contemporary global consciousness that allow us to see the present as wholly unprecedented. The fact of a historical Muslim presence in Western Europe is perhaps more relevant than ever, and so the fiction of historical isolation and global disjuncture that appears commonly in globalization discourse and spurs the revival of such nineteenth-century abstractions as *hybridity* is a conceptual inheritance of modernity that deserves challenge.[2]

Many analysts of global relationships posit that the contending forces of our world hinge on incommensurate differences bound to separate historical trajectories: Western and Sinic civilizations clash, the Lexus uproots the olive tree, jihad and McWorld battle, Islam struggles to come to terms with the influence of the West, tradition faces the modern world.[3] Like their nineteenth-century conceptual antecedents, these juxtapositions of difference fail to appreciate the ways in which people relentlessly incorporate seemingly conflicting ideas and forces. Only our failure to recognize people's ability to amalgamate foreign ideas, things, and people into their everyday existence makes the picture of a veiled woman drinking a Pepsi on the cover of Benjamin Barber's *Jihad vs. McWorld* seem paradoxical. The visceral sense of paradox prompted by the juxtaposition of such seemingly discordant signs as Pepsi and the veil has become a staple of popular reflections on globalization. Yet this sense of paradox is not born of simple novelty. Instead, it has blossomed in the field of repressed mutuality and inattentiveness to the bricolage of human history. Historical silences, maintained by enduring notions of difference, bind us to a sensibility in which, to use a postcard sold in Zanzibar as an example, a Zanzibari man wearing "traditional" clothes but talking on a mobile phone is ironic. What must be silenced to make the card ironic is the fact that Zanzibaris began buying telephones almost immediately after their invention well over a century ago.

Reflections on globalization in the popular media as well as in academia still too commonly assume that until very recently the world was constituted by discrete spheres (continents, nations, cultures) whose minimal interactions ensured internal consistencies.[4] Many of these assumptions are the legacies of nineteenth-century Western analysts who reshaped and operationalized sophisticated classificatory regimes, or hierarchies of humanity, grounded in the belief that distinct types of things existed in the world, each with its essential qualities. Many scholars have traced how these concepts and categories affected human actions. The questions that drive this book are therefore somewhat different: What did these classificatory regimes obscure, and how did they silence other histories of global relation? The essentialization of difference allowed and allows views of global integration to appear as vignettes of unprecedented, even paradoxical, contrasts of traditions, religions, economies, and racial, national, or social groups. The fascination and wonder occasioned by hybridity suggests that our inherited modalities of difference have concealed profoundly entangled relationships just below the surfaces of difference. This is why I find Trouillot's insight so appealing; he suggests that, beyond the superficiality of "encounter," the archive of our interdependent past harbors stories that complicate modern sensibilities. Though we may create bounded identities, shore up exclusivist genealogies, and create borders that we enforce physically and discursively, our interdependent past reveals that creolization has no pure antecedents. Humanity, across its profoundly social history, has restlessly engaged in an inter-networking of networks across space, for better and for worse.

One virtue of historical reflection during a time charged with the discourse of globalization is that it allows us to reconsider the myriad and conflicting processes by which the world around us has come into being. History and Foucauldian genealogy—a Nietzsche-inspired critical framing of changing human relationships that highlights the discourses that have obscured or shaped such relationships—enable us to see the worlds we have forgotten and, just as important, how they were lost to historical memory.[5] Historical reflection can remind us that the past does not always offer clear patterns, that it is confusing, vast, incalculable as a totality, that we are not always who we are for the reasons we assume. Genealogies of globalization, both as narratives of inter-networking and reflections on the discourses that have defined how we perceive, or fail to perceive, global interconnectivity, are vital in our times. We should be cognizant of forgotten routes of human connectivity and understand how we have come to see the world as we do.[6] In this book I offer vignettes of intra- and transregional relations in an attempt to resuscitate visions of globality that were eroded by silencing and forgetting—other ways of interpreting and knowing the world that, for Western analysts in the nineteenth and twentieth centuries, seemed incommensurate with modern knowledge systems. Considering the world in the terms and through the ideas of actors marginalized in the historical record allows us to imagine how the world was—and can be—different than it appears from our contemporary vantage points. Forgotten histories of mutuality in global encounter can, moreover, re-member patterns of global interdependence, which, while seemingly counterintuitive in hindsight, are nevertheless our inheritance.

In an attempt to re-member one section of the vast archive of our interconnected past, this book examines the complex relationships among economies, cultures, and the translocal networks they affect by considering the importance of African consumer desires to nineteenth-century processes of global integration. This is a history of trans-societal relationships projected through the lens of eastern Africa during a period of dramatically increasing regional and transoceanic connectivity. Specifically, the book addresses the cultural rationales for East African consumer desires, the symbolic uses of imported things and people, the global repercussions of African consumer demand, and interpretations of consumerism in East Africa. I focus on consumer goods and their circulation because they are uniquely able to help us perceive routes of interrelation. They channel and expose desires, they connect, affect, are affected by people, and they transcend political and social boundaries. By focusing on the demand for globally circulating commodities, we can better perceive (1) the cumulative agency of individual choices, and (2) connections between the contingent realms of economy, social relations, cultural translation, travel, and changing perception. My aim is to offer insights into how objects, symbols, and people were remade through their movement and through the movement of others.[7] My plea is that the theorization of global integration should not lose sight of the predecessors of contemporary globalization, the repercussions of everyday choices, the interests in transregional integration on the part of Africans before colonialism, or the historiographic dislocation of Africa from the rest of the world. Through the narratives and the narrative method I offer in the pages ahead, I intend to demonstrate the importance and mutuality of many forgotten routes of global interconnectivity through and beyond East Africa.

AFRICA AS PART OF THE WORLD

Narratives of Africa's relation to global processes have yet to take full account of mutuality in Africa's global exchanges.[8] One of the most complicated questions analysts of African pasts have faced is how African interests figure into an equation of global interfaces historiographically weighted toward the effects of outsiders' actions.[9] The slave trade, imperialism, colonialism, and neocolonialism have all severely constricted African possibilities and potentials. Since Africa's global relationships have often been inequitable, scholars have concentrated on exploitative processes of African production for foreign markets and imbalances of trade. In the era of decolonization, such emphasis was a necessary response to assumptions of Africa's perennial backwardness, the positivism of modernization theory, and colonial administrations' refusals to acknowledge the long-term economic traumas wrought by their policies. But while the constraints of interaction engineered by the colonial powers affected African futures, the colonialist presumption that the interests of others have by and large steered the continent's past, even before colonialism, leaves a crucial question insufficiently explored: What did Africans seek in precolonial global exchanges? If, as many would agree, the importation of consumer goods has been a destructive process that entailed the slave trade and ensured underdevelopment by decimating African manufacturing,[10] then it is critical that we understand why imports were so important to African societies.[11] This question has been difficult to tackle in systematic ways because African demands and corresponding sociocultural foundations of need have received relatively limited attention in analyses of Africa's global economic relationships.[12] And since questions of what Africans wanted have not been thoroughly addressed, we have not seriously considered the possibility that African demands had effects on societies beyond Africa. By considering the demand for imports before colonialism, we can gain a perspective on economic relationships that complicates, as I demonstrate below, some baseline assumptions about Africa's relationships to other parts of the world.

To undermine common assumptions about Africa's interfaces, this book addresses thorny cultural questions that have not figured prominently in analyses of precolonial global relationships, such as rationales for exchange and the complex meanings of imports in "peripheral" societies. Perhaps more important, the perspective of consumer demand offers an alternative way of considering the differing conditions that have affected Africa's profile in the world economy. A focus on East African consumerism in the nineteenth century reveals that as East Africans became more deeply affected by contemporary movements of goods, ideas, and people, they also influenced patterns of global trade and foreign production. The mutuality inherent in this trade was not a function of equity or symmetry over the long term, but it did entail reciprocal effects that reshaped extra-African locales even as non-African images, desires, and strategies changed East Africa. I believe that by reclaiming a sense of African material interests in the field of global relations we can address why global trade came to be important to East Africans long before most were compelled to produce for the world market.

Scholars have demonstrated that processes of commodification were extending deeply into African social relationships in the nineteenth century and that imported commodities and currencies at certain moments, and in many locales, became important to local social and political relations.[13] These processes of commodification were not only crucial to the remaking of East Africa in the nineteenth century, but they also pose challenges to the conceptual dichotomy between the cultural-symbolic emphasis in analyses of everyday experience and the economic-material focus of political economy. For instance, in order to appreciate the economic circumstances of commodification, we must be vigilant about the kinds of complicated questions anthropologists, sociologists, and cultural studies theorists frequently pose: How were imports integrated into specific social environments? What meanings did imported commodities acquire in African societies? How did these meanings converge with or diverge from those given them by their manufacturers?[14] I address these questions in the chapters that follow, but I wish to suggest here that histories of globality must always bear such questions in mind. East Africa's global economic relationships, for instance, were inextricable from the cultural and social dynamics of regional societies that gave rise to the demands articulated in interregional trade.

Many historians of Africa have suggested that African consumer demand deserves attention.[15] In fact, the potential of my approach to Africa's global relationships has already been demonstrated. David Richardson's work, which I consider in greater detail in chapter 3, suggests ways of thinking about the global repercussions of African consumer demand on British trade and manufacturing. He shows that during the era of the transatlantic slave trade the requirements of satisfying the tastes of West African consumers affected suppliers, prices, and even the networks on which Liverpool merchants relied. Liverpool firms were forced to depend, in part, on foreign producers of iron, beads, and textiles since British manufacturers had mixed success in producing the consumer goods that West Africans wanted. More than a third of Liverpool's exports to West Africa in the mid-1780s had to be procured from non-English sources, primarily in the Indian Ocean region. Richardson argues that both the structure and profitability of the English slave trade were contingent, to a significant degree, on African patterns of demand and English abilities to adapt to this demand.[16]

Philip Curtin, Joseph Inikori, Joseph Miller, John Thornton, and others have also highlighted the importance of African demand in shaping global economic relationships.[17] Curtin, for example, argues that at the height of the external slave trade in Senegambia the terms of trade were in West Africans' favor. Thus, French manufacturers had to go to great lengths to appeal to the tastes of West Africans. African consumer demand has, at times, had more extreme effects on trade. For instance, whole shipments of goods sent to East Africa had to be returned if particular items did not suit African tastes (see chapter 3). African boycotts of imports affected trade as well. Igbo traders, for instance, boycotted the Lagos palm oil market for five months in 1855 to protest substandard guns brought for sale.[18] But the relation of African consumer demands to global exchange was not always so obvious. As we will see, manufacturers all over the world, in dialogue with people in East Africa, developed goods over time that accommodated the regularly changing consumer desires of East Africans. This attention to changing African desires points up the centrality of African cultural, social, and political dynamics to the making of Africa's global economic relationships.[19] If, as Jane Guyer suggests, histories of exchange and histories of social relationships deeply permeate one another, then we can gain important insights into the dynamics of global economic systems by exploring the social lives of people—even those, like East Africans, who may seem marginal to global trends.

This study proposes a simple postulation that has significant ramifications: if demand for commodities shapes commercial systems, and demand is a social product, then the minutiae of social and cultural interests are deeply intertwined with global economic systems. In order to understand the complexity of economic relationships, we need to appreciate not only patterns of trade and modes of production, but also rationales for need and the social relations that engender them. Since the late 1970s, a rich body of cross-disciplinary literature has demonstrated that consumer goods are primary mediators of human relationships and give substance to social claims.[20] Literature spanning the humanities and social sciences has emphasized the symbolic rhetoric of consumer goods, the ability of things to constitute personhood by representing aspirations publicly, and the importance of commodities to strategies of distinction.[21] Much of this literature further suggests that consumer goods often receive new social meanings beyond the cultural boundaries of their regions of production, and that these meanings can diverge dramatically from those given by their producers.[22] Yet accounts of historical as well as contemporary global integration still too easily discount the important ways in which people who are labeled the victims of global cultural homogenization conceptually transform imported goods and symbols.[23]

In the chapters that follow, I draw on consumption studies to address rationales for African demand in the nineteenth century. I also build on interdisciplinary approaches to the social meanings of commodities by outlining the reception and remaking of globally circulating goods—a process that I refer to as *domestication*—as a strategy for understanding the deeper histories of an interconnected world.[24] *Domestication* is a particularly useful term because it carries multiple, complementary connotations: the process of making familiar or usable, controlling, and bringing into intimate spaces. Thus, in using this term I mean to imply not only the localization of foreign goods, but also something of the gendered intimacies East Africans developed with and through them. By considering East African domestications of globally circulating goods I outline the cultural logics of consumer demand that shaped Africans' global relationships.

ORGANIZATION

This book is composed of a series of essays that address overlapping themes. Since the issues and places that concern me could easily drive a project much larger than this work, I have chosen to look at specific themes in particular temporal circumstances. The themes include consumer desire, the repercussions of demand, cosmopolitanism, the transformation of global symbols, the symbolic uses of people and things, and the interpretation of cultural change. Because of this structure, the narrative does not strive for a total history of economy, consumption, or cul ture. Instead, it reflects on their interface. It offers analyses of the ways that specific people in specific places, primarily Mutsamudu, Mombasa, and Zanzibar, related to each other and the larger world through imported goods. Thus, the arguments that I make for each locale must be understood as limited to those locales. Certain insights may be helpful in conceptualizing relationships elsewhere, but for the purposes of this study I only aspire to bring to light sufficient lines of connection to frame a picture of how concepts, desires, exchanges, and images all came into dynamic tension in one part of the world. The advantage of this organization is that it traces the minutiae of everyday life while remaining mindful of the larger processes that constituted them and which they, in turn, affected.

The first chapter demonstrates the potency and limits of certain acts of self-representation in the spaces of global relation. It asks how the domestication of English symbols—a strategy of reflecting similarity that I call *similitude*—affected Mutsamudu's (Comoros Islands) relationship with the British Empire in the late eighteenth and early nineteenth centuries. Through a close reading of the adoption of English material culture, social etiquette, and the English language in Mutsamudu town, I show how some East Africans used things that signified Englishness to convince the British to provide them with special economic and military assistance. As a prelude to many of the themes discussed in later sections, the chapter focuses on the role of cultural practice in developing and maintaining material relationships. It also offers a view of East African relations with the British Empire that contrast with those I outline in later chapters.

Chapter 2 looks at Mombasa, the second largest city on the East African coast, during the 1840s and 1850s, when a great variety of imported consumer goods were becoming available. It asks how people conceived of needs for imported goods in Mombasa during a period of rapid integration into changing commercial systems. To answer this question I offer an ethnography of consumer demand that stresses the *social logics of economy*, or the psychological creation of needs before possession and how culturally defined imported goods, when used to aid in the constitution of certain kinds of personhood, became fundamental to social relationships. The chapter seeks to anchor East Africa's trade connections in the minutiae of local social circumstances by first examining the rhetoric and idioms of material desire in Mombasa's public culture. It then focuses on several contemporaneous reflections that address the centrality of imports in Mombasan social relationships. These reflections on consumer demand in Mombasa offer examples of how people in one place developed relationships bound to imported goods.

The third chapter moves outward from the social spaces of interaction in East Africa to consider the effects of East African consumer demand elsewhere. It asks how East Africa's new engagements with other parts of the world changed those distant locales. The chapter begins with the supposition that the terms of trade were often in East Africa's favor during the nineteenth century. Merchants from the United States to India competed for limited African products like ivory, cloves, hides, and gum copal. In this economic climate, East Africans had enormous liberties of choice. This meant that foreign manufacturers and traders had to be aware of and appeal to the rapidly changing consumer demands of East Africans or else founder in the Zanzibari market. East African consumer demand directly affected the region's ties to New England and India. I argue that in the cases of both Salem, Massachusetts, and Bombay, East African demand not only shaped foreign production, since manufacturers were keenly interested in appealing to East African consumers, but also provided important stimuli to the industrialization of both cities' textile industries.

Chapter 4 develops an image of East African cosmopolitanism and its relation to Western concepts of modernity. It asks how goods from and new engagements with distant locales affected Zanzibar. I show that Zanzibaris used consumer goods such as American clocks, British handkerchiefs, and Indian umbrellas to create as well as challenge new social and material sensibilities in the second half of the nineteenth century. Zanzibari cosmopolitanism represents one form of social reconstitution stimulated by global integration in the nineteenth century. It also represents a material vision of global relations that was discounted by nineteenth-century theorizations of Western modernity. In focusing on the rise of a new materiality in Zanzibar, I excavate precolonial visions of global relation and cultural domestications of global symbols. I argue that East African desires for goods produced all over the globe represented not simply a Westernization, Indicization, or Arabization of Zanzibar, but a configuration of a standardized set of imported materials deployed to address or contest specific local circumstances.

Chapter 5 examines how slaves of African, Indian, and European origin were used to represent the self-images of Zanzibaris and how enslaved people resisted resignification. My focus is on the symbolic uses of urban slaves as well as their social value to both slave-owners and antislavery activists. *Symbolic subjection*—the use of people to represent the abilities of their possessors—was not only important to the construction of social personas in Zanzibari society. The notion of slaves as blank slates onto which the interests of others could be written was also taken up in a British imperial rhetoric that affected the entire region. The enslaved, however, often had very different interests. Slaves used imported goods to fashion their own social projects. Slaves and freed slaves often desired greater social mobility within Zanzibari society, and they attempted to attain such mobility by consuming imported items of personal adornment and acquiring slaves themselves, abilities that signified an ideal public persona.

The final chapter examines how Anglophone analysts interpreted East Africans and their desire for imported goods, as well as the relation of these interpretations to the spirit of intervention. It asks how East African consumerism in the late nineteenth century complicated Western analyses of the region. Expanding on themes addressed in chapters 4 and 5, the chapter focuses on the efforts of Anglophone authors, illustrators, and photographers to create a coherent picture of East Africa through explicit reference to material life. Attempts to make East African sociocultural complexities understandable by bundling a variety of material and physical traits crystallized in material-racial figures such as the turbaned Arab, the richly robed Hindu, and the naked African slave. At the same time, East Africans' consumption of European goods troubled the notions of material difference that Westerners brought to East Africa. In the second half of the nineteenth century, British analysts began to think of East Africans as "semi-civilized" because of their material engagement with Western modernity. The mixing of ostensibly bounded and distinct cultures, bloodlines, and material goods in East Africa signified to Anglophone writers an internal contradiction and East Africans' inability to adjust to modernity. In their perception of many Western goods as incommensurate with East Africans, and their presumption of the necessity of British intervention to guide Zanzibar into the modern era, analysts discounted the meanings that East Africans gave to the objects of their domestication.

CHAPTER I

Similitude and Global Relationships

Self-Representation in Mutsamudu

A town on a small island in the Indian Ocean once acquired a voracious appetite for English things. It was not a British colony, and it hosted neither an English Consulate nor a permanent English resident until the 1850s—fully two centuries after islanders began their relationship with the English. By consuming English goods, speaking English, and asserting an affiliation with Britain, the people of Mutsamudu town on Nzwani (Anjouan) Island in the Mozambique Channel created an intimacy with a global power and parlayed their claims to a special, at times familial, relationship with Britain into economic and political support. Through various strategies of representation, Mutsamuduans claimed a moral proximity and similarity to the English that convinced Britons to view them differently, to imagine them as people in some way akin to themselves. For at least a century Mutsamuduans were largely successful at using things that signified Englishness to direct imperial means to local ends.

This chapter seeks to reveal the efficacy of cross-cultural performances of similarity—a strategy of appeal that I call *similitude*—on the stage of global relation. It demonstrates how the strategic uses of imported symbols affected the producers of those symbols and ultimately their relation to Nzwanians. Nzwanians relied on similitude to affect relations with diverse foreigners, including Arab, French, and American visitors. But by exploring the extreme case of Nzwanian appropriations of Englishness, we can more clearly discern how the cultural appropriation of symbols in even seemingly marginal locales has affected patterns of global interrelation.

STRATEGY AND GLOBALITY

One of the most important questions that analysts of global integration have addressed is how people who are too easily labeled the victims of global cultural homogenization conceptually transform imported materials, symbols, and ideas.[1] Aviad Raz describes this analytical impulse as an attempt to augment scholarly focus on cultural imperialism with a consideration of the "reception" of global symbols.[2] The entrance of such terms as *domestication, hybridization, localization,* and even the orthographically unwieldy *glocalization* into vocabularies of analysis reveal the increasing attention given to *re*interpretation in the global circulation of signs.[3] Expanding on Michel de Certeau's insight that the masses always renegotiate the meanings offered them, many analysts of reception have convincingly shown that meanings are rarely as transferable as their objects. The work of Aviad Raz, Mark Alfino and his colleagues, and Joseph Tobin, among others, suggests that even when such symbolically laden products as McDonald's hamburgers or Hollywood movies circulate globally, their uses and social relevance can diverge dramatically among national, cultural, and gendered spaces.[4] As James Watson has illustrated for McDonald's in East Asia, things as simple as processed fast foods can easily lose both their associations with their place of origin as well as the cultural meanings given them in their home society.[5] The strength of reception literature thus lies in its demonstration that symbols circulating beyond the boundaries of their places of origin are rarely simple copies. Instead, imported things are often socially and culturally reconstituted, and given compound local meanings and associations that are sometimes directly related to foreign meanings and sometimes quite distinct from them.

In its stress on the internal dynamics of cultural domestication, reception literature has yet to adequately address the possibility that cultural incorporations can be directed back at the source of their perceived fabrication and can even affect that perceived source, a phenomenon Michael Taussig referred to as the ability of the copy to influence that which it copies.[6] While rationales for domestication are born of diverse, specific social circumstances, the effects of domestication need never be solely local. In championing the integrity of local interpretations, it is too easy to neglect the fact that incorporation is at times expressly desired to develop a new kind of relation with the sources of such symbols. This chapter expands on reception literature by addressing the ways in which domestications of goods, etiquette, and ideas can work toward multiple, translocal, and reciprocal ends. Further, the Nzwani example points up an increasingly important topic in the analysis of global integration: the function of cultural domestication in fashioning global relations. In Nzwani we are confronted with a marginal, noncolonial polity that incorporated English symbols and, in turn, affected its relationship to an emerging superpower through a mastery of those symbols. By reflecting on the historical relation of Mutsamuduans to Englishness, we can perceive some of the ways in which (1) the simulation of sameness has worked on a global stage to accomplish specific ends and (2) how symbolic discourse has produced material dividends.

THE SIMILITUDE OF PRINCES

In early 1858, the British Political Resident at Aden, Yemen, received word of the arrival of an unexpected visitor, a man who would for almost a decade travel the world at the expense of the British Empire. The man's name was Prince Abudin of Nzwani Island in the Comoros Archipelago. He claimed to be the son of the Sultan of Nzwani and was traveling to London in order to offer Nzwani to the British Government. As he had very little money, and arrived without slaves or retainers, the British agent offered to host him as an official guest of the British government. The agent spent a large sum to support Abudin during his stay and gave him transportation to Muscat, Oman, where the prince could find a vessel to return home. While he was in Muscat, the British agent there allocated additional monies for the prince's expenses. Though he claimed to be heading home, the prince soon arrived in Bombay. There he was again put up at the British government's expense. But he did not stay long. From Bombay he traveled to Karachi, where the British administration gave him a stipend, even though he lived in the house of an exiled relative. After Karachi, near the end of 1859, the prince returned to Muscat. There he collected yet another official stipend and, according a government memo, "amused himself" by sending official telegraphs to various people in Karachi. After some time, he returned to Karachi, staying only briefly before arranging transport back to Muscat. Once there, Prince Abudin petitioned the administration to find him passage home.[7] Instead of returning to the Comoros in 1859, Prince Abudin sailed from Muscat to Zanzibar. There he became well known and respected by the

European residents and claimed to be the King of Nzwani. As a result of
the high regard in which Westerners in Zanzibar held the prince, the
British consul offered him free passage back to Nzwani.[8] In late 1860,
Abudin was in Madras. In the interim, he had traveled to Réunion and
then Mauritius, where he defrauded a friend of the British consul. In
Madras he changed his name to Colonel Abudin and offered a formal
cession of the Comoros Islands to the British government. By March he
was in Sri Lanka, where he appealed to the British administration, claiming that all his resources were expended. The Colombo Government gave
him money to settle his local debts and then paid for his passage to
Aden.[9]

   In September of 1863, Prince Abudin, accompanied by his uncle Prince
Muhammad (a.k.a. Mahmud Abdullah), finally made it to London.
Prince Abudin (alias Colonel Abudin) was now Prince Abdullah.[10] He
and his uncle had found free transport to Paris via Madagascar and Cape
Town. On their arrival in Paris, they were put up at the Grand Hotel and
granted interviews with Lord Cowley, a senior agent of the British government. After a short time, they concluded their interviews and the government covered the bill. But the two princes were dissatisfied with their
meetings and remained intent on traveling to London, presumably to
offer Nzwani to the British government again. They applied to the Turkish ambassador in Paris for the sums necessary to continue to London
and were soon on their way.[11] Abdullah's correspondence with Lord
Palmerston of the Foreign Office while the two princes were in London
makes it clear that the Nzwanians relied entirely on the assistance of the
British government during their visit. The letters also reveal that the
prince's command of English was superb. The form, word-choice, and
tone were typical of British official correspondence. These letters give
insight into why British government agents around the world had been
so accommodating of the prince: he used British social etiquette and a
command of the written and spoken language to fashion an utterly convincing persona.[12] Having failed to cede Nzwani to the British government, the two traveled from London to Cairo, where they offered
Nzwani to the Egyptian government—again to no avail. Though
Abdullah's subsequent travels are obscure, Prince Muhammad arrived in
Aden in late 1866.[13] There he claimed to be the Nzwanian ambassador
from Istanbul en route to Bombay to conclude a treaty of commerce. He
reported that he had been robbed in Egypt and had lost all his possessions. As with Prince Abdullah eight years earlier, the consulate gave him
free passage to Bombay.[14]

Abdullah's story is remarkable, in no small part because of his success in winning the sympathies of so many British officials. But as fantastic as his story is, the prince's exploits are representative of a more common dexterity in self-presentation developed by Mutsamuduans to foster a variety of beneficial relationships with outsiders, and Britons in particular. The prince's actual name was Abdullah bin Alawi, son of a deposed sultan, and he had once represented his father as an ambassador to Mauritius.[15] His multiple offers of Nzwani to the British were, no doubt, a ploy to unseat the reigning sultan. Prince Abdullah's successes, however, cannot be attributed to his royal birth, since none of the government representatives with whom he had contact knew anything of Nzwanian politics, much less that he was no longer a prince and had no authority to offer the island to the British. Instead, Abdullah's successes were attributable to his ability to replicate English etiquette and convince British administrators across the globe that he deserved certain privileges. Colonel Rigby, the British consul at Zanzibar, described Abdullah's success as the result of his mastery of three persuasive modes of self-representation: he spoke English "remarkably well," had a very "plausible" manner, and dressed in richly embroidered clothes.[16] Consuls, agents, and individuals gave him money, accommodation, and transport simply because he was convincing, the validity of his claims evidenced in expensive clothing as well as "superior [social] attainments."[17] Moreover, he never failed to present himself as a friend of the British Empire. By affecting a social image that reflected British etiquette back to Britons, Abdullah convinced myriad British agents that he was a political leader and ambassador. This gave him access to the submarine cable, stipends, free transportation across the Indian Ocean, the Eastern Atlantic, and the Mediterranean, and several months stay in Europe, part of that time in one of Paris' finest hotels. The prince, it seems, used his cultural dexterity to live an extraordinary life while pursuing his own political agenda.

Speaking English and appearing materially "plausible" was key to Mutsamuduan relationships with the English in the eighteenth and nineteenth centuries. Through a signification of Englishness, Nzwanians forged alliances, expanded the island's economy, and ensured their own political sovereignty. For most Mutsamuduans, things English, be they words or objects, were signs that reproduced for those who adopted them some of the qualities of what they signified: English "civility." By taking on the signs of an English elsewhere, Nzwanians like Abdullah reflected the perceived abilities of, and equated themselves with, the English. On Nzwani, English goods, in conjunction with nonmaterial signifiers, were employed not only to affect local relationships (a topic that I address in chapters 2 and 4),[18] but also to shape the way Britons perceived and related to Nzwanians. By superficially approximating Englishness, Nzwanians, rather than challenging the structure of imperial power, instead used the English for the economic, political, and military benefits they could offer.

By the time Prince Abdullah explored the British Empire, Nzwanians had long circulated in British circles. Though there seemed to be no institutional memory of them in Britain, Nzwanian diplomatic missions to London preceded Abdullah by almost two centuries. Further, Mutsamuduans had long used the codes and language of empire for their own ends. Mutsamudu became part of the English realm as neither a colony nor protectorate but as a sovereign state that aggressively appealed to the sensibilities of Britons. While Prince Abdullah was particularly dexterous, his successes exemplify the long-practiced Nzwanian strategy of similitude: a conscious self-presentation in interpersonal and political relationships that stresses likeness. As strategic replication, similitude bears a close resemblance to Homi Bhabha's notion of colonial *mimesis*.[19] But whereas Bhabha outlines mimicry as a strategy of replication that confronts and disrupts the authority of colonial symbolic discourse, similitude is a more general strategic *appeal* in the space of global interrelation that, through a claim to sameness, seeks to affect the perceptions and policies of more powerful agents. Moreover, similitude need not be subversive, confrontational, or limited to the colonial environment. Similitude is more commonly employed in circumstances of asymmetrical power beyond the boundaries of colonialism, often as an attempt to manipulate imperial representatives without necessarily challenging broad hierarchies of global relation. The cases of Hawaiian, Siamese, and Malagasy official relationships with Euro-American powers in the nineteenth century, to say nothing of Cold War and post–Cold War international relations, offer examples that resemble the Nzwanian strategies I describe below. As a mode of self-representation, similitude links symbols and claims to sameness in order to leverage relationships with the more powerful. Thus, similitude, like mimicry, is a strategy of the political margins.

ARTICULATIONS OF GLOBALITY

One might not immediately imagine a small island in the Mozambique Channel, roughly equidistant from the East African mainland and

Madagascar, as a cosmopolitan locus of cultural and economic interchanges stitching together Africa, Asia, Europe, and the Americas. But the fact that a man like Prince Abdullah, with little formal education and few resources, could have such a strong command of the English language, be so well versed in the politics of the British Empire, and have such a nuanced understanding of the imperial administrative system of which he was not a subject suggests that Nzwanians were not isolated. Many European travel accounts relate that in the town of Mutsamudu a "curious" experiment in Anglo-global integration commenced in the seventeenth century. Actually, Nzwani's particular cultural bricolage had much greater historical precedent.

Centuries before and for centuries after the first English vessel visited the island, Nzwanians were well integrated into the Indian Ocean's economic and cultural flows. Almost everything on the island had traceable provenance outside of it: the African, American, and Asian crops cultivated, the language spoken (Shinzwani—closely related to Swahili, with heavy borrowings from Arabic, Malagasy, Gujarati, and Persian, as well as Makua, Yao, and other East African languages), and the ancestors of Nzwanians themselves, who arrived from places as distant as Southeast Asia, southern Arabia, and Central Africa. They used Indian, Mediterranean, and American currencies. They were Muslims living at the southern reaches of the *dar al-Islam,* well integrated into networks of Islamic scholarship, and many performed the hajj.[20] In addition to Shinzwani, many islanders spoke Arabic, Malagasy, Swahili, and multiple East African languages. They imported clothing and other consumer goods from Madagascar, India, and the Persian Gulf. When English visitors began describing Nzwanian globality, they noted that islanders regularly traveled to Madagascar, the East African coast, and India. Nzwani's position between markets in northwestern Madagascar and the East African coast meant that merchants not only transshipped goods, but they also created small emporiums where goods might be perused by visiting western Indian, southern Arabian, Persian Gulf, or East African merchants.[21] Nzwanians depended on the sea, and they wrote their cultural relation to oceanic exchange into the local material environment. J. Ross Browne described a mosque in Mutsamudu whose walls were painted with naval charts. "[F]rom all I could gather from Selim [his guide]," Browne wrote, these, "show the latitude and longitude of the seven heavens, the true bearings of the infernal regions, the rocks, shoals, and sand-bars to be avoided by a soul bound heavenward."[22] Many Mutsamuduans even added an evocative feature to the outside of their homes that referenced

their oceanic connections: on the upper stories of their houses Nzwanians affixed the bows and sterns of ships.[23] Houses themselves could thus
simulate sailing vessels. Added to this translocal sensibility was the
Atlantic trade, which would become particularly important in the eighteenth and nineteenth centuries. By the middle of the nineteenth century,
fifty to sixty European or American vessels visited Mutsamudu each
year.[24]

In the seventeenth century, Nzwani developed a new set of global relations when it became an important refreshing station for European vessels plying the route between India and Western Europe. The political
elites of Nzwani, as well as local farmers and traders, appreciated the
commercial possibilities inherent in the regular arrival of large merchant
vessels searching for provisions. By the middle of the seventeenth century,
Nzwani had begun to exploit its position as a way-station between
Europe and India, finding an increasingly large market for local products, particularly meat, fruits, vegetables, and grains. Nzwanians had
long exported rice as far north as Pate (Kenya), coconut oil to the southern Arabian coast, and they regularly traded with merchants based on
Mozambique Island.[25] But in the European traffic, Nzwanians found an
immediate market for local produce that incurred virtually no transportation expense. Eager to maintain these economic ties, Nzwanians
forged a particularly strong relationship with English visitors in the early
eighteenth century. Capt. H. Cornwall wrote in 1720 that Nzwanians,
"affect[ed] the *English* very much, to whom they shew [sic] an Abundance
of awkward Civilities."[26] For nearly two hundred years, Nzwani-English
relationships would hinge on two factors: convenience and similitude.
For English captains, the island offered an ideal locale to refresh and collect provisions for their onward journeys. For Nzwanians, the regularity
of English visits was a boon to the local economy, giving people across
the island, and wealthy landowners in particular, the opportunity to
exchange produce for cash and sometimes even directly for goods,
though this was increasingly less common by the early nineteenth century. The second factor, similitude, proved to be a lucrative tool for
Nzwanians wishing to expand and solidify narrow English interests in
the island.

In the late eighteenth century, when an English vessel arrived in
Mutsamudu, it was greeted by Prince George, Lord Baltimore, Admiral
Blankett, Lord Rodney, the Duke of Rottinberry, Lord Gloucester, and
many other recognizable British personalities. And yet the famous personalities hardly looked like their namesake dukes and lords. English vis-

itors described them as wearing turbans, long robes, and short jackets
with gold or silver trim. One visitor to Mutsamudu described Nzwanian
title-holders as looking like "all Orientals."[27] Though appearing
"Oriental" to English visitors, Nzwanians signified Englishness in their
names and miscellaneous English apparel. In addition to taking famous
names and titles, like duke, lord, lady, and king, Nzwanians constantly
reminded English visitors of their similarity to Nzwanians, whom the
English called "Johanna-men," Johanna being the unorthographic Anglicization of Nzwani. As early as 1689 the phrase "Johanna-man, Englishman, all one" had become a common dictum among Nzwanians and
would, over the next one hundred and fifty years, appear regularly in
Western accounts of the island.[28] English visitors were constantly told of
their oneness with Mutsamuduans, so that the phrase's use became an
overt reminder of Nzwanian claims to similarity and alliance with the
British.

In 1783, Sir William Jones wrote that Nzwanians spoke English, "and
some appeared vain of titles. . . . We had *Lords, Dukes,* and *Princes* on
board, soliciting our custom, and importuning us for presents." While
they were "too sensible to be proud of empty sounds," Jones concluded,
they "justly imagined, that those ridiculous titles would serve as marks of
distinction, and, by attracting notice, procure for them something substantial."[29] Jones deduced what seems more obvious in hindsight: that
many Nzwanians received real dividends from this strategy of presentation. One of the most telling indicators of this is the fact that people with
such titles became well known among English travelers. English visitors
who had heard of the Duke of Gloucester or the Prince of Wales often
asked for them on their arrival in Mutsamudu. The English traveler
J. Richards, for example, was disheartened when he arrived at Mutsamudu nearly seventy years after Jones and asked for Lords Rodney and
Nelson, only to be informed that those names had gone out of fashion.[30]
At the height of their popularity near the end of the eighteenth century,
English titles were a key means of fostering recognition. To enhance this
effect, Nzwanian title-bearers often had their names engraved in gorgets
of copper or brass worn around their necks, sometimes complimented by
English epaulets on their shoulders.[31]

Those who introduced themselves with recognizable names, like Duke
Drummond or General Martin, were usually businessmen seeking clients
among the crew of an English vessel. They acted as hoteliers or contractors, offering accommodation, provisions, meals, and laundry services.[32]
Though some visitors assumed that the famous personalities performed

the tasks themselves, and were thus highly amused by such ludicrous titles for menial laborers, the famously titled men usually farmed out the work. For example, they might contract with English vessels for certain quantities of produce or livestock, which they would then supply from their own estates or buy from the estates of others.[33] Jones describes these contractors as "Banas," or men of significant standing in Mutsamudu. "Bana Gibu," for example, was a vegetable and egg wholesaler who, because of his business dealings with English visitors, had taken the title "Lord."[34] Other visitors confirmed that Mutsamuduan appropriations of English titles of rank were not random. Anton Hove wrote that English title-holders were "such enthusiasts of these [titles]" that "if perchance one of them was called a captain, and had a title of a general, he took it as a great disgrace to his class, and replied, with displeasure, that he had a higher dignity."[35] Nzwanians depended on such titles to convey a certain image to Europeans and to other Mutsamuduans, though the extent to which such titles were important in intra-Nzwani social relations is unclear. An indicator of the way in which titles were employed to impress an image of Nzwanian similitude on Britons is a letter sent to Earl Russell from the Nzwani court. Though the signers' names are recorded similarly in the Arabic and English drafts, the author—possibly the famous Prince Abdullah—gave the titles of each signer in English and translated these as Minister, Member of Parliament, Chief Justice, Commissioner of Police, and Magistrate.[36]

Another essential strategy for Mutsamuduan self-presentation was that each contractor kept numerous letters of recommendation written by previous visitors to the island. Though Mutsamuduans could not always read these, they usually pressured captains, crews, and ships' passengers to write letters on their behalf. Such attestations to the good services of particular contractors could be instrumental in drawing the attention of a prospective client. For example, the English visitor Sir James Prior was impressed when Mr. Pitt and the Duke of Portland came on board his vessel and presented papers written by several previous customers that praised the men for their services. So important could these letters be to the livelihoods of Mutsamuduans that some Nzwanians insisted on them. Bombay Jack, who served as pilot and interpreter on many English vessels, refused gifts from the crew of an English vessel and instead wanted only, in addition to his fees, a written testimony of the services he performed while aboard. Such letters of recommendation— thousands of which were collected between the seventeenth century and the 1870s—were kept for decades, even centuries.[37]

Nzwanian claims to similarity with the English were also given weight as early as the mid-eighteenth century by competence in the English language. Early European reports of the island mention interpreters, but by the middle of the eighteenth century, visitors commented that Mutsamuduans generally understood English "very well" and spoke it intelligibly.[38] William Jones was surprised at Nzwanian competency in English, especially when he showed an Arabic manuscript in his possession to a cousin of the king, who proceeded to explain it in English. En route to Zanzibar in 1864, Bishop Tozer was amazed to find everyone on Nzwani Island so "wild" to learn to read and write English. Nzwanians deepened this intimacy of relation by, Captain Rooke explained, never failing to ask about the health of the English king. In the early nineteenth century, this was the signature greeting of Nzwanians. When an English survey party was presented to the Sultan of Nzwani in 1823, the sultan's first question was, "How is King George and my good friends in England?" On the street, people greeted English visitors with diverse pleasantries. A visitor to the island in 1812 wrote that people followed him eagerly asking "innumerable questions respecting our health, welfare, appetite, slumbers, and [a] variety of others, equally friendly and unmeaning," and asked "after the health of their good friend King George." By the mid-nineteenth century, not only was English widely spoken, but Nzwanians were writing in English using Arabic characters. In 1849, Richards wrote that, "almost everyone I met with wished me a "good morning" and wished to shake hands with me." Prior wrote that some who had taken the names of famous Britons "inquired affectionately after their name-sakes in England, begged their compliments on our return, and promised the best reception should they at any time visit Johanna."[39]

THE VALUE OF LIKENESS

Nzwanian similitude was not haphazard replication. It was a strategy born of Mutsamudu's particular political economy. The Owen nautical survey party sponsored by the British government reported that after greetings and reminders of likeness, Mutsamuduans regularly interjected requests for business relations or donations that played on sentiments of reciprocity and comraderie.[40] For example, Prior was approached by Bakamadi, a man well versed in English matters who had spent time in Cape Town. Bakamadi's knowledge and questions reveal the dividends of similitude for Mutsamuduans. After talking with the crew about English concerns and stunning them with his understanding of English affairs, he requested to be retained as a merchant "in preference to others." Moreover, he invited the crew to his house, wishing them to meet his wife and to serve them, "as good roast-beef as any in England."[41] Bakamadi used his cultural knowledge to create individual economic relationships with Englishmen, winning preference through his cultural faculty.[42]

The Nzwanian court developed even more elaborate appeals to English visitors. Over decades of rigorous questioning, close observation, and travel in the British realm, the elites of Mutsamudu amassed detailed information about England, its military power, economic expanses, and colonial possessions. The eighteenth-century English traveler Henry Grose wrote that the sultan insisted on visiting all the European ships that put in at Mutsamudu. "[H]e always expresses a great desire of knowing the name of everything that is new to him," Grose recalled, "and as he has a tolerable smattering of the English tongue, is very inquisitive concerning our wars in Europe."[43] This compilation of information about the British Empire allowed Mutsamuduans to impress English visitors. Jones was astonished by the questions Alawi, a cousin of the king (and possibly Prince Abdullah's father), asked regarding the independence of the United States, "the powers and resources of *Britain, France, Spain,* and *Holland,* the character and supposed view of the Emperor; the comparative strength of the *Russian,* Imperial, and *Othman* armies; and their respective modes of bringing their forces to action."[44] On his arrival in Mutsamudu in the early nineteenth century, Prior was met by Nzwanians who hoped for peace in Europe, "abusing Bonaparte with as much cordiality as if they had been tutored by some of the London editors." "One of the most inquisitive," Prior recalled of Bakamadi, "expressed his joy, that his Royal Highness the Prince Regent made so good a governor . . . and to our utter astonishment, asked whether an *illustrious reconciliation* had yet taken place."[45]

In 1821, Prince Ali invited an English reverend to what the reverend described as an English-style dinner. The prince met him with his usual "urbanity of manners," and the guest found the table set with knives, forks, plates, other English tableware, and roast beef. Though Nzwanians generally ate with their hands out of large, communal wooden trays, the prince, following British etiquette, took up the utensils.[46] When William Jones met the king, they spoke for some time about English matters. Immediately thereafter the king attempted to convince Jones of the profitability for the Bombay Government of annually sending a merchantman to Mutsamudu to trade, emphasizing the cheapness of local commodities. The request surprised Jones. He wrote of the "enlarge-ment of mind" such a proposition evidenced, which he could have hardly expected "from a petty African chief."[47] Since Jones had already learned of the enormously complex economic relationships Nzwani maintained with neighboring islands, mainland ports, southern Arabia, and western India, his surprise to find an "African chief" interested in soliciting a stronger commercial relationship with Bombay suggests something of both Jones' preconceived image of East Africa and the strong impression Nzwanian similitude made on English visitors in consequence of such preconceptions.

While the strategy of similitude employed by Mutsamuduan political elites mirrored that of merchants, the stakes of Britons' personal interest in the sultanate often could be much greater than simple economic exchanges—they could entail the safety and sovereignty of the state. When Prior first met Sultan Alawi, the monarch immediately "praised his friend, good King George, Sir John Cradock, Captain Beaver, and the whole English nation abundantly; in fact, everything English was admirable," according to Prior's report.[48] Sultan Alawi, on receiving the officers of the infamous British man-of-war *Nemesis* in the early 1840s, asked about the Queen and Prince Albert, "and whether an heir to the throne had yet been born." According to William Bernard, the captain of the *Nemesis,* the sultan was "not a little curious to know if the Thames Tunnel was finished." In Bernard's eyes, Sultan Alawi, as a result of his knowledge, amenity, and inquisitiveness, "appeared to be a very well-bred and courteous young man."[49] Much like local businessmen, the sul-tan used his intimacy with things English for specific ends. After asking these questions, Sultan Alawi "alluded painfully" to the distressed state of the island.[50] He would later appeal to the English for pecuniary and military assistance, and such petitions became increasingly common dur-ing the nineteenth century. The sultan's attendants also solicited passen-gers aboard visiting English ships to contribute something toward improving Nzwanian navigation, and, Grose reported, "by way of per-suasive example, [they] produce several lists of persons who have sub-scribed to that purpose."[51] Such appeals could yield as much as 30–40 Maria Teresa dollars (MT$, standard currency in the western Indian Ocean) per ship for the government coffers.

More important, sultans regularly appealed to the English for military aid. As early as the late seventeenth century, Nzwanians were asking English captains to intervene in inter-Comoros conflicts. After a conver-sation with the prince and brother of the king, who spoke English well, the English visitor John Ovington remembered, "When he had a while considered the strength and power of the English arms, and the native valour of our [English] puissant prince, he heartily wished he had been in a nearer neighborhood to his dominions, that by securing an alliance with him, he might engage his arms in crushing a troublesome offensive enemy [the sultan of neighboring Mwali Island]."[52] Such subtle appeals for support became stronger as Nzwani-English relations grew more intimate, and in the eighteenth century the English gave military assistance to Mutsamudu on multiple occasions. Grose wrote that the English were treated "cordially and fraternally" because of English aid in Nzwani's campaigns against its neighbors. It is equally likely that such cordiality and fraternity motivated English intervention in the first place.[53]

The English expanded the Nzwanian sultans' military capacities by constantly providing gifts. In the late eighteenth century the established "custom" of the king from each English vessel was two barrels of gunpowder, plus cash.[54] The sultan kept letters from the British Admirals Renier and Blankett, who had visited the town in the 1790s, requesting captains of warships to give powder and arms to the local government. The island's most consistent supplier, however, was the Governor and Council of Bombay who, for example, in 1808 sent powder, muskets, flints, musket-balls, and even cannons to Nzwani.[55] In the early nineteenth century, the Government of Bombay sent biennial presents of arms and ammunition in acknowledgment of assistance given by the Mutsamuduan government to East India Company ships.[56] As an example of the windfall of armaments a single vessel could bring the sultanate, when the *Nisus* arrived at Mutsamudu, it gave the king muskets, powder, musket cartridges, brass swivels, ball, and flint. The captain, moreover, distributed muskets and ammunition among the elite men of the town, "according to their rank."[57]

The Sultanate of Nzwani was at times dependent on this assistance. It is no coincidence that when munitions were most needed, Nzwanians both claimed their greatest affinity for the British and made the greatest gestures to evince friendship. For example, most of Nzwani's cattle were killed by Malagasy raiders in the first decade of the nineteenth century, and the ones that survived were for a time earmarked by the sultan to provision English East India Company ships. An English captain wrote that Nzwanians did not kill cattle for their own consumption, "it being expressly prohibited by the King, who looks up to the Company as his only friends."[58] While the sultan no doubt promulgated the sumptuary law to ensure both British interest in the island and Nzwani's economic stability in a time of distress, the captain's interpretation of the action—that it was born only of great admiration and friendship—indicates the persuasiveness of Nzwanian strategies of similitude. When Sultan Alawi was faced in 1839 with a rebellion led by a Malagasy refugee resettled on neighboring Mwali Island, he wrote to Mauritius, the Cape, and Bombay requesting assistance. His letter to the Governor of the Cape appealed to British generosity "in return for the faithful adhesion of his family to Great Britain, and the hospitality of his people towards all British subjects."[59]

In addition to stressing reciprocity, Sultan Alawi traveled to Calcutta to address the Governor-General in hopes that the East India Company would take possession of the islands, "which," a visiting English captain wrote, "he felt [he] could no longer hold without assistance." It seems Alawi was willing to hand over the administration of the island, merely asking for himself an annual stipend out of the island's revenues.[60] As Captain Bernard put it, the king would, "rather give up the island altogether to the English," than see it lost to the rebel. This kind of action greatly impressed the commander of the British warship Nemesis, W. H. Hall.[61] And such impression, as with names, breastplates, and stockings, had consequences. Without a mandate to interfere, Hall nevertheless decided that the Nemesis must in some way aid the sultan. The solution was to give Mutsamudu an English flag to fly over its citadel which, once raised, would be saluted by the Nemesis. The Nemesis commanders, moreover, drafted a threatening letter to the rebel leader explaining that the sultan was an old ally of the English and that they would not allow the taking up of arms against him.[62]

THE AESTHETICS OF APPEAL

Through similitude, Nzwanians appealed not only to British strategic or economic interests, but also to the sensibilities and moral sympathies of Britons. In many conversations with Britons, Mutsamuduans explained their ideas and actions using metaphors and comparisons they imagined British visitors might know well. When Major Rooke asked about the rebellion on Mayotte Island (which had been a tributary of the Sultan of Nzwani) in the 1780s, Mutsamuduans told him that Mayotte was simply "like America," an analogy sufficiently explanatory for the visitor.[63] During a series of Malagasy raids in the 1810s, which devastated Mutsamudu and threatened the mainland, an English visitor asked why Nzwanians chose not to face the invaders in the field. Bombay Jack, a well-traveled pilot and broker, replied, "Why do not the English march

to Paris?—Why does not Bonaparte go to London?"[64] The travel writer
J. Ross Browne was annoyed by the fact that Mutsamuduan women
rarely entered male public spaces when visitors were present. He decided
to see what Mutsamuduan women were "made of" and in the process
badgered an old man with questions about Nzwanian purdah. After
Ross Browne insulted Mutsamuduan women several times, the old man
lost his patience, "Got damn! de devil you, sir! We great people; we all de
same as English. Syed Mohammed [the sultan] all de same as King
George. Suppose I go to your country, I no talk so. I no want to see your
d—d women! If it de fashon of de country, very good; I like to see, very
well. If it no de fashon, what for I want to see your women?"[65] Offended
by Browne's insistence on breaking a local social code, and in order to
both defuse the situation and force Browne to be more respectful, the old
man reminded the sailor of the likeness of Nzwani to Europe. At a
moment when the cultural differences between the West and Nzwani
were most evident—that is, in contrasting forms of gendered seclusion—
the Mutsamuduan man claimed an equality with and similarity to the
American (whom he thought was British) that simultaneously acknowledged difference and claimed likeness.

Investments in the material environment of Mutsamudu were often
the result of strategies of similitude. It was common for Mutsamuduans
across social status lines to ask for a great variety of things from visitors,
like shoes and stockings, hats, a sword, a uniform coat, or other English
signifiers. Prior claimed that such objects were "productive of no slight
degree of envy to the possessors," though he did not qualify this conclusion.[66] At the very least, such iconic goods contributed to the images of
similitude Mutsamuduans wished to project for their English guests.
Stockings and hats could act much like gorgets or letters of recommendation to draw the attention of English visitors who might assume that
the possessor had some particular relation to other Englishmen. It seems
Mutsamuduans used English clothing to achieve commercial ends,
attracting customers by evidencing cultural similarity. Much as with language and clothing, Mutsamuduan home decor reflected, created, and
reinforced a variety of socioeconomic relationships. When foreign visitors were invited into the homes of Nzwanians, they were generally only
given access to the semipublic, male-only reception rooms. Among the
wealthy, these rooms were often furnished with sofas, couches, high-
backed chairs, pillows, sometimes even chintz or satin mattresses. But
English material culture was prominently displayed, at least when
English people visited. Prince Ali placed an English bedstead and an oak

table in his reception room. This duly impressed English visitors.[67] Mutsamuduans often lined the walls of their reception rooms with arms and small mirrors. In the 1820s, Prince Ali's reception room boasted more than one hundred looking glasses in gilt frames. His guest, Rev. Elliot, also described "Round pieces of time, many of which were gilt," "nailed to the walls and ceiling, and several china basins were stuck in, bottom upwards." Interspersed between these were prints "daubed over with the brightest and most gaudy colours, which served to fill up every vacancy throughout the walls and ceiling, so that it was impossible to distinguish what the latter consisted of, but upon the whole it gave the room an air of comfort."[68]

Elliot wrote that many other houses were furnished in the same manner as Ali's, including a profusion of Chinese pictures, which homeowners were very keen to praise.[69] Browne visited the house of Muhammad Deshari, a Nzwanian businessman living at Majunga (Madagascar), and found the house, though built of bamboo, whitewashed like the houses of Mutsamudu. The walls were covered with Chinese plates, American-looking glasses, Arabian fans, flags of other nations, Chinese pictures, copper plates with inscriptions, and Egyptian "relics."[70] The conglomeration of so many objects from across the globe, things that had rich symbolic potential—to represent connections with distant places and to incorporate images of China, England, America, and Arabia into individual personalities—impressed visitors. Even though Britons often considered such decor gaudy, there was something about the accumulation of familiar exotic objects (British consumers likewise collected Chinese plates, Oriental "curios," and Egyptian "relics") that gave English visitors like Rev. Elliott "an air of comfort" in an unfamiliar locale.

This was not entirely coincidental. Mutsamuduans both impressed their neighbors with "exotic" objects and used such imports to create familiar comforts for their English guests. On visiting Prince Ali's house, members of the Owen survey party were served refreshments with silver sugar-tongs, spoons, and a "handsome display" of cut-glass tumblers. While they enjoyed refreshments, the prince called in a man who sang "God Save the King" for the guests.[71] The sultan filled his reception room with the porcelain common to other urban homes and added to this festoons of English bottles.[72] Such goods were important to Mutsamuduan self-images, both in their representation to outsiders and to their neighbors. When Americans began trading at Nzwani in the 1830s, they found local tastes more diverse than they had imagined. Chairs, glass lamps, plates, cups and saucers, mirrors, and clocks all found buyers in

Mutsamudu.[73] When the British government approved the establishment of a British Consulate on the island in 1858, the sultan requested not just English arms, but also British soldier's coats. The sultan soon had hundreds of men armed and clothed, according to the consul, "after the European fashion."[74] The sultan did not simply want to defend himself; he wanted symbols of British military power to represent his own ability. In the future, this mimesis of English military culture would duly impress English visitors.

The desire to capture symbols of Englishness reached such an extreme that some Nzwanians even attempted to possess English women. A wealthy Mutsamuduan was once so intrigued by a young Englishwoman on board a vessel that he sought to purchase her. He offered MT$5,000 to the crew for the woman—nearly ten times the price of an expensive Ethiopian concubine—but was informed that, "she would fetch at least 20 times that sum in India."[75] The wealthy Mutsamuduan yielded, lamenting that such a high price was much more than he could offer. The possession of an Englishwoman would have been unique in eighteenth-century Mutsamudu, even though Mutsamuduans regularly purchased concubines, sometimes eastern European women exported from the Ottoman sphere. But the commodification of the young woman, both by Englishmen (though they were perhaps having fun with the wealthy man) and an Nzwanian, suggests that signifiers of Britishness were indeed more exchangeable than we might imagine in hindsight—that, with certain means, Nzwanians believed that even English people could be incorporated into the Nzwani social environment. Subsequent English travelers probably would have been offended to see a Mutsamuduan man with an English concubine, and the attempt to acquire an English-woman was therefore probably a social strategy intended to impress other Nzwanians, but the wealthy man's attempt reveals the breadth of Nzwanian desires to command Englishness.

Mutsamuduans were masters of cultural dexterity and sometimes relied simultaneously on languages of equality and clientage in their appeals to the British. Though they reminded English visitors that they were "one" with them, they also proclaimed themselves vassals, unofficial subjects of Britain. When the sultan attempted to supply Captain Beaver with provisions at public expense in recognition of British efforts on his behalf, the captain declined the offer. At this, Bombay Jack, according to Prior, "fell on his knees, . . . declaring he would not rise till permitted to supply our wants. . . . 'Englishman,' said he, 'give me everything, now me give to the English.'" Though Prior's account may seem indulgent of

British self-importance, the performance of clientage had a dramatic effect on the English. Moved by the incident, Prior believed that "[t]he most laboured effusion of eloquence could not express more."[76] The twin claims of equality and clientage reached seemingly paradoxical extremes when several sultans offered Nzwani to British representatives as a colony. In 1839, when Mwalian rebels threatened Mutsamudu (see above), Sultan Alawi, perhaps through Prince Abdullah, appealed to Sir William Nicolay, the governor of Mauritius, in a way that simultaneously employed many of the well-established Mutsamuduan tropes of clientage and friendship:

> The Sultans of Johanna consider themselves as under the contract of the King of England, and they have so considered themselves from the time of their forefathers until the present time. Everybody knows that we are the Allies of the English, and that we are, of old, the subject[s] of the King of England. We are unable to repay you for the favors you bestow on us, but God will repay you for your goodness, next to God. We Pray for you as our best friends. Do not leave us, and do not forget us, for if you abandon us, we perish; our lives, our families, our property.[77]

The Foreign Office did not take Sultan Alawi up on his offer. In fact, even though several sultans offered the island as a colony, Nzwanians never became subjects of Britain. Perhaps such offerings of the island as a colony were meant as only symbolic tokens of Nzwanian alliance with the British. Or perhaps Mutsamudu's political elites sought to use the British to ensure their own political longevity, albeit under a protectorate. Either way, the simulation of likeness, and at times even clientage, was a significant strategy. For Mutsamuduans, minor investments in material culture, language, and etiquette paid vital dividends until the latter nineteenth century.

CONCLUSION

Mutsamuduans appealed to the British by domesticating and projecting fragments of Britishness. They obtained symbols of a significant global power that both embodied and represented an intimate relationship with empire.[78] Thus, while English things were on the one hand locally relevant signs of particular access to an iconic power, they also reproduced images of Englishness for British consumption. In order to symbolically neutralize their significant religious, cultural, and social differences from English visitors, Mutsamuduans claimed to be *like* the English in limited ways. To this end, they used what they knew of Britons to appeal to British senses of reciprocity and morality. Mutsamuduans sought simultaneously to understand and, through the projection of certain self-images, manipulate British perceptions. By wearing English clothes, putting English furnishings in their homes, and serving English meals with English crockery to English visitors, Mutsamuduans reconfigured, at least in limited ways, English cultural geographies of the world and attracted significant English interest. The small island, so far from civilization in the mind of Britons, somehow became proximate for English visitors. Nonetheless, metropolitan British policymakers who had never visited the island took little interest in Nzwani. Individual Britons sympathized and allied themselves with Nzwanians, but official policies rarely addressed the island directly, despite its importance as a refreshing station and the fact that several sultans offered the island to Britain as a colony. British policymakers had no desire to claim a protectorate in Nzwani precisely because its political leadership already demonstrated an affinity for Britain. In the wake of the 1858 Indian Mutiny, Prince Abdullah's appeals to British officials attracted little interest. A friendly sultanate was far more appealing to the Foreign Office than administering the island as a colony.

Even Britons who visited the island were sometimes conflicted in their attitudes toward Nzwanians. The juxtaposition of the familiar and the exotic drew diverse responses. British visitors at times disparaged Mutsamuduans, though they showed an affinity for them and were quite concerned with maintaining Britain's positive image in Mutsamudu. Some, like Sir William Jones, who recognized this duality of British perception, attempted to reconcile seemingly contradictory reactions to East African provision-brokers wearing English military symbols. The resulting justifications for affection toward Nzwanians reveal the power of similitude. Despite their criticism of Mutsamuduans, Britons accepted that they generally relished things English and took pride in, as one visitor wrote, "that unstained ensign": the British flag.[79] Britons might not have agreed that "Johanna-men" and Englishmen were one, but they privileged Nzwanians like Prince Abdullah in many ways, believing that the islanders were loyal to British interests and faithful to the empire in ways few others were. British captains, crews, and even administrators were often sufficiently enamored of Mutsamuduans to make their town a primary port of call for English vessels and to regularly supply Nzwanians with arms. What is important to recognize in these transactions is that most English representatives who assisted Nzwanians did not refer to the strategic or economic importance of Nzwani to Britain as a rationale for intervention. Instead, they justified their actions by recalling the long friendship between England and Nzwani. Though a seemingly superficial reason for intervention, the moral economy of reciprocity was continually cited as the rationale for action by British visitors until the latter nineteenth century, when Nzwani seemed of little import to British foreign policy and was claimed by France.[80] Even though Britons were hesitant to accept Nzwanians as clients, they regularly allowed Nzwanians to claim them as patrons.

Nzwanian similitude resonates with contemporary reflections on the reception of global symbols. In eighteenth-century Mutsamudu, cultural domestication was not reducible to simple coercion or cultural imperialism. Nzwanian desires for symbols of Englishness were in no way determined by the pressures of a colonial state. Nzwanians had their own particular interests in global symbols, and islanders used their collections of cultural signifiers strategically for specific ends. Contemporary popular as well as academic analyses of globalization too easily overlook the logics and effects of such actions.[81] The Nzwani case additionally suggests that even when totalization or cultural homogenization seems evident, domestications may be working toward diverse ends, and the desires of minor players on the global stage may alter global relations. On Nzwani, a strategy of similitude used cultural symbols to gain material returns and cultivated a relationship with the more powerful by claiming to be in some ways like them. This is the concealed potency of similitude in the spaces of global interrelation: an ability to affect the powerful by appealing to their self-image.

Nzwani's unique relationship with the British Empire highlights some of the ways goods and symbols have been used as a means of appeal in trans-societal relationships. But my reflections so far have not done justice to the complex, local, social meanings of imported goods. The next chapter uses the example of Mombasa in the 1840s and 1850s to consider how people in one town drew imported goods into local social relationships and broader concepts of morality. More specifically, my frame is the social and psychological longings that stimulated demands for consumer goods and the community mores that restricted these longings. By scrutinizing the concept of desire in Mombasa at a time when diverse imported goods were becoming increasingly available, we can better understand the intimate dimensions of choice as well as the morality of desiring. It is to these social logics of consumer need in mid-nineteenth-century Mombasa that we now turn.

CHAPTER 2

The Social Logics of Need

Consumer Desire in Mombasa

As we have seen in the case of Mutsamudu, a full appreciation of the changing dynamics of translocal relationships requires an examination of the logics that shape them on all sides. In the seventeenth and eighteenth centuries, Mutsamuduans tapped dramatically expanding global networks. Though East Africans had maintained connections across the Indian Ocean region for at least two thousand years, in the nineteenth century many cities along the East African coast accessed new interoceanic commercial circuits that linked them with more of the world than ever before. The configurations of these connections were determined both by foreign demands for East African commodities and reciprocal East African demands for imported consumer goods (as we will see in chapter 3), as well as by new patterns of migration and proselytization. Because demand was firmly rooted in local definitions of the self and social needs, an appreciation of the circumstances that generated consumer demand is essential for understanding how East Africans affected global networks. Further, since on the coast these desires were often negotiated in majority Muslim towns, outlining local definitions of self and society through relationships to goods can shed light on the confluence of two spheres of relation: the world economy and a complex moral system shaped by Islamic tenets.

This chapter seeks to outline the social logics of East African consumer demand by exploring attitudes toward and rationales for demand in Mombasa—East Africa's second most important commercial center—

during a period of rapid integration into both Zanzibari and broader
transoceanic commercial systems. It offers an ethnography of material
needs in one locale by analyzing both their conception in and importance
to its particular social environment. My focus, then, is on the symbolic
rhetoric of objects and the ability of commodities to shape personhood
by representing the self publicly in reference to moral norms. By studying
consumption in this way we can access the *social logics of economy,* or
the ideas about merchandise that were fashioned before purchase and the
ways in which culturally defined imported goods, when used to aid in the
constitution of personhood and status, were fundamental to Mombasan
social relationships.[1] I begin by outlining the context of a rapidly changing Mombasan socioeconomic environment. I then address Swahili concepts of desire and their relation to three overarching, metaphysical agencies of the self: *moyo* (heart), *nia* (conscience), and *roho* (soul).[2] Finally,
I take up the importance of objects in projecting notions of personhood
as circumscribed by local and translocal moral discourses. By these
means, we can perceive the ways in which economic realities, through
consumer demand, were deeply embedded in social relationships.

ANALYSES OF A NEW MOMBASA

In Mombasa, the first half of the nineteenth century—particularly the
years leading up to Busaidi-Zanzibari acquisition in 1837 and following
into the 1850s—was an era of rapid change. It was a period of passage
from sovereignty to political control of the city by Sultan Seyyid Said al-
Busaidi of Zanzibar and Mombasa's more complete integration into the
Zanzibari cultural-economic zone. The Busaidi acquisition of Mombasa
ended more than a decade of resistance by Mombasa's Mazrui leaders
who, after the fall of the city in 1837, found themselves in exile as their
former capital became the second most important city in Seyyid Said's
East African dominion.[3] For many Mombasans, it was an era of an
inverted world order, a sentiment that the city's most celebrated poet,
Muyaka bin Haji al-Ghassany, captured in the popular refrain, "Those
who once called the assembly are those who are now called."[4] Busaidi
rule had great economic repercussions. The government instituted new
currencies, guaranteed protection to creditors and foreign merchants,
and, perhaps most important, through these measures the Busaidis
bound the Mombasa market to Zanzibar.[5]

The Busaidi government altered the conditions of business in Mombasa. They encouraged Zanzibari-based merchants to trade in Mombasa

by offering lenders better enforcement of creditors' rights. With an economic environment that was more attractive to lenders, the Busaidis
were able to attract capital to Mombasa for local businesses, landowners, and the traders who brought ivory and other commodities from the
interior.[6] The Busaidis also diversified Mombasa's monetary system.
Mombasans continued to use the widely circulating Austrian dollar
(MT$) and Spanish quarter-dollar, but after 1845 the copper East Indian
pice replaced Mazrui-minted coins (which had been pegged to a measure
of maize), and by the 1860s American dollars coming through Zanzibar
served along with the Austrian dollar as a regional currency.[7] Using these
flexible global currencies, the Busaidi government encouraged the greater
monetization of a variety of social transactions in Mombasa—even criminal punishments. For example, under the Mazrui the punishment for
murder was death, since it was thought a disgrace to take money in
return for the life of a family member. The Busaidis instituted a fixed fine
for murder: a *kisasi,* or standardized revenge-payment. A free person
who killed another free person now had to pay between MT$600 and
MT$1,200; if the murdered person was a slave, the free person paid
MT$60.[8]

By the 1840s, increased access to credit through Zanzibari-based firms
fueled the expansion of trading ventures to the interior, encouraged
greater agricultural production for export, and brought more cash into
circulation.[9] Credit enabled people to spend more immediately, regularly,
and at higher levels. An expanding economy and access to credit opened
for renegotiation the sign-qualities of goods by enabling some previously
excluded people to engage more fully in the signifying system of public
consumption.[10] With the greater integration of Mombasa into the Zanzibar zone and increased revenue from regional exchange circuits, by the
1840s Mombasans were consuming an increasing variety of Indian,
American, and European goods, most of which came through Zanzibar.[11]
In this new environment of cash availability and decline of the old political elite, sumptuary restrictions quickly lost their catalyst. The symbols
of status, while often still limited in circulation, were becoming more
accessible to a greater diversity of Mombasans.[12] For example, before
Busaidi subjugation, *viti vya enzi,* or chairs of "power" and "authority,"
were common physical and figurative symbols of political authority in
many coastal societies. Many of the holders of such chairs were either
overthrown or co-opted by Seyyid Said in the first two decades of the
nineteenth century. Accordingly, by the 1840s, the term *viti vya enzi,* and
the chairs themselves, had become something different in Mombasa.

Instead of symbols of political position held by a few, they were now simply the chairs of the wealthy, symbols of "power or dignity," imported from India, the United States, and Europe and owned by many. *Viti vya enzi* were no longer strictly part of the political iconography, but chairs of fashion—still exclusive, but no longer the possessions of only the most politically powerful. Much like chairs, certain items of clothing were appropriated beyond their previously limited circles of use. The *mtawanda*, a wooden shoe once available only to the very wealthy, was in demand by the larger public in the 1840s.[13]

By the 1880s, two monumental projects addressing the social, cultural, and economic conditions of mid-nineteenth century Mombasa came to fruition. These were meticulous compilations of language and verse spanning the mid-century period of transformation in Mombasa. Taken together, they are the most extensive reflections on social life in any East African city before the 1860s. The first project collected the verse of Mombasa's most celebrated poet, Muyaka bin Haji, a propagandist, satirist, and humorist remembered for his penetrating insight.[14] Critical of social norms, certain cultural practices, and many people, his captious verses were designed for public recital. They are moral critiques intended for vocal performance, delivered in a coded language translated by his listeners. Muyaka was a poet who, because of his social liminality as a celebrated but chronically poor public figure, was obsessed with the social and material distinctions between wealth and poverty. His work constitutes the largest surviving body of poetry by a Swahili composer in the early nineteenth century, and his reflections on the themes of wealth, poverty, and materiality were important references in Mombasan public discourse from the 1830s until at least the 1880s. His verses were so important as both art and social commentary that many East Africans committed them to memory and repeated them for decades after Muyaka's death.[15]

The second project was the compilation of a monumental Swahili-English dictionary in the Mombasa dialect (Kimvita) completed by a long-time resident of the city, Johann Ludwig Krapf, a missionary of the London Missionary Society. Krapf's dictionary—whose orthography I will retain as a reminder of the particularities of nineteenth-century Kimvita—is a critical supplement to Muyaka's poetry in its capacity as (to borrow Umberto Eco's term) "a disguised encyclopedia" of mid-nineteenth century Mombasa.[16] Both collections are philosophical, concerned with faith and wealth;[17] both at once detail and critique the cultural environments of mid-century Mombasa; both are distinctly male in perspective; both reflect their authors' religio-cultural attitudes. Taken

together, these collections are unique reflections on life in Mombasa from
the 1830s to the 1850s. Though these works were not published until
several decades after their production, they remain the most detailed surviving interpretations of a key moment in the history of Mombasa's integration into expanding global networks.[18] They are particularly useful
for this study because they offer cultural and linguistic interpretations of
Mombasan concepts of need and highlight the social complexity of consumer choice in Mombasa.

   In the changing political, cultural, and economic landscape of mid-
nineteenth-century Mombasa, an era of greater consumption, increasing
wealth from trade and production, and easier access to credit, Mombasans conceptualized desire as originating in the many overlapping agencies
of the self. To understand how desire directed economy, we should begin
with a consideration of Mombasan notions of desire's psycho-social
provenance.

DESIRE AND THE AGENCIES OF THE SELF

In *A Dictionary of the Suahili Language* (hereafter *D*), Johann Krapf
identified several mental agencies that Mombasans believed every person
to possess. Three overlapping metaphysical agencies in particular—the
moyo, nia, and *roho*—are important for our purposes because they were
imagined to mold desire and project it into the material world as needs
for specific things.[19] These were cohesive within a person, but each
agency had its own particular functions and directions. Among the three
agencies, Mombasans believed that the roho and a sub-agency of the
moyo—the *kijoyo*—gave birth to desires, while both the nia and the
larger apparatus of the moyo articulated (or suppressed the articulation of)
desire as needs. Only the moyo had a dual physical form and metaphysical
existence: it was the actual as well as the figurative heart.[20] It could both
articulate and control needs for objects. The moyo was the epicenter of
emotional longing, of love, both for people and objects. The poetry of
Muyaka bin Haji outlined the place of the moyo in Mombasan concepts
of desire. In his verses, Muyaka references the moyo as a receptacle and
projector of emotions, particularly of the longing for people and material
things. When Muyaka spoke of emotion, he invoked the moyo. Though
the larger apparatus of the moyo expressed need and was a container for
emotion, one's *kijoyo* produced acute wants.[21] The kijoyo was covetous;
it identified the things it wanted and forced the moyo into an emotional
bond with those things. To refuse the demands of the kijoyo (*sebu sebu*

kijoyo kimúmo, "to refuse that which the little heart would like to have or to possess") was difficult indeed. Yet if one denied a craving of the kijoyo, Mombasans believed that one would have a gratified heart: *moyo umekunduka,* an ideal state of being. The gratified heart was serene, a moyo that, if we take the phrase literally, was "unfolded, expansive, which grew large" (*D,* 325, 179).[22] Such a state, however, was only the ideal. Generally, the pressures of the kijoyo led a person to pine for and strategize about how to acquire a material thing.

In common usage, moyo could also mean the "mind," "will," and sometimes even the "soul," at least in a very loose sense. To entirely devote oneself to a thing, one would *tia moyoni sana:* "put spirit/effort into it," or be diligent in working toward its fruition (*D,* 333). In the senses of mind or will, the moyo could restrict desires. It could have agency over the kijoyo's longings. Muyaka mused about the tussling within the moyo between desire and social conscience. For Muyaka, the ironies of the moyo were that

> The moyo says, "[Speak out] but don't speak of others' business."
> The moyo says, "Pray [or beg], but don't beg for that which belongs to others."
> The moyo says, "Lick, but don't lick a spark."
> The moyo desires tusks of ivory, but they are on the heads of elephants.[23]

The heart fomented endless wants, no matter how unattainable, like the tusks of an elephant. Because of the infinity of needs and the moyo's affinity for extremes, many Mombasans believed that the moyo should be bridled. The drives of the heart could be dangerous if acted upon carelessly. For example, the heart craved ivory—an item of great exchange-value, a sign of wealth, prosperity, and success in trade—but taking it from the elephant was perilous. There is no solution, Muyaka contends, except the control of the moyo. Calming the self came only through action to control the moyo: *ku tuza moyo,* "to make the heart well [as after sickness]" (*D,* 388).

Indicative of the relationship of the moyo to both the material world and the public realm was a kind of cloth that was in fashion in Mombasa and along several caravan routes in the 1840s: the *passúa moyo,* or "tearing of the heart." Its exorbitant price of MT$3 per piece meant that its suitor was either wealthy, in debt, or willing to forgo other needs to purchase the fabric (*D,* 90). Mimetically reflecting the longings of the heart, the *passúa moyo* brought into relief the emotional relationships among people, objects, and an agency that articulated material need. As with love for a person, people felt in the moyo emotion for an object. If a thing was agreeable, like a gift or some purchased object, it pleased the moyo (*D*, 301). So when the moyo expressed hunger for things, its relationship to those objects was often emotional. This hunger could be more or less motivating, depending on an individual's self-control. The moyo was not the principal generator of desires, however. As we will see, the roho held that position. Instead, the primary role of the moyo was to continually express needs for objects and articulate the self's emotional relationship to things and people.

Like the moyo, the *nia* had no existence outside of the body. The nia was the mind, or more precisely, the conscience. Nia fashioned character, the qualities of a person's self and its manifestation in behavior. A *nia suafi* was a clean conscience or positive character, while a *nia batili* was a bad—or corrupted—conscience. The nia was a person's disposition, their interest, intention and/or diligence to undertake something (*D*, 280).[24] Thus, to change the nia was to change one's mind.[25] The nia and moyo overlapped in their abilities to control behavior. The nia as conscience could, like the moyo itself, regulate longings that required restraint. The conscience could suppress desire in the sense that it could convince the self not to succumb to its urges, though even the nia was often overcome by longings. A semblance of the nia's control was socially important because when the nia was corrupted by desire, the self could never be content; that is, when desire forced one to act against one's conscience, the conscience became worthless and the self was no longer whole (*D*, 280).

Because material goods were implicated in social relationships, the attempt to prescribe their appropriate, even morally right, uses was a central concern in Mombasan public rhetoric. Mombasan notions of how to affect and control the projections of desire are, moreover, instructive for the study of economy because they shed revealing light on consumer decision making. If a person constantly gave in to the cravings that desire produced, they found little satisfaction. Instead, they became socially and spiritually self-destructive as well as morally impaired. Such people of bad conscience were vehemently condemned. Muyaka satirized those whose cravings entirely dictated their actions. Of Tima, Ima, Mwaniya, and Mwanakombo—women who, spurning social norms, were notorious for their drinking—Muyaka says,

> They're like palm-wine tappers, loving their drink.
> If we say to them, "It's not good [what you're doing, as] in the grave there
>   will be trouble,"
> they reply, "Never mind [all that], when will we be there?"[26]

A song of the 1840s warned against over-indulgence in attempts to satiate longings. Like Muyaka's verse, it proclaimed that the world deceives those who follow it as palm wine deceives the drunkard. Overindulgence, like total self-reliance in place of accepting the assistance and advice of others, was a deplorable personality trait because it removed the person from the realm of normal social relations. Moreover, Krapf wrote that in Mombasan philosophy self-reliance distanced a person from God since dependence on oneself was a reliance on materiality instead of God, what Mombasans termed an act of "loving the world more than God" (D, 251, 282).

Though the moyo, nia, and roho were all connected,[27] there were crucial differences between them. For example, the moyo and nia were not divisible from the body. On the other hand, the roho, or at least part of it, was extricable from the physical person and could continue to live after the expiration of the body. The roho was both central to the constitution of the self and potentially independent of the person. Further, the roho, unlike the other agencies, could act directly on things and people, even though it took no tactile form. It could enter into the consciousness of others and, distinct from all the other agencies of the self, it was mobile. Most important, whereas the kijoyo created some desires, the roho was the principal source for the most deeply entrenched of motivations. While roho could be translated as "soul" in the sense of its transcendence of the physical body, it was, however, more motivating than the Western-defined soul because, in producing desires, it fashioned material needs. The moyo was primarily a consolidator of thoughts and emotions, the nia acted as the agencies' conscience, but the roho was the most significant engine of desire that dictated a person's actions. In short, the roho created cravings and forced the person, consciously and unconsciously, to seek ways to satiate them.

Where it appears in his dictionary, Krapf defines the roho variously as the "soul," "spirit," "essence of life," "breath," and "greed." According to Krapf, the roho was desirous, voracious, covetous, greedy, and insatiable. Because of the roho's aggressiveness, Mombasans struggled to control it. But, as evidenced by the phrase rokho ime-m-piga nia, "the roho defeated [the person's] nia," people were not always successful. The roho gave the conglomerate self direction (D, 316, 303). For example, to the question of where a person intended to spend the night, the answer could be "my roho directs me" to such and such place. To direct someone else's actions was metaphorically described as acting on, or "changing," his roho. Cash paid to a judge before a ruling was called "secret money to clean [the judge's] roho,"[28] or a bribe to ensure a favorable outcome.

Kimvita and its metaphors suggest that the condition of one's roho defined the person. Figuratively speaking, to have a small roho meant that one was dissatisfied, fainthearted, hasty. To have a white roho meant that a person was honest and candid (*D*, 89, 169, 355, 281). A *roho makini* was a mild, placid soul, one that was not, in Krapf's words, "inordinately desirous." The roho also had sensory capacities that went beyond the body. For example, if someone had heart palpitations with no known cause, they could assume that their roho sensed that they were the topic of someone else's conversation (*D*, 197, 85). The roho stood as a signifier for the body's material longings, exemplified by two entries from Krapf's dictionary:

> *rokho yangu imekaúka, nadáka maji*
> My soul has dried up, I want water.

> *ni-pa maji kidogo, ni stiri rokhoyangu*
> Give me a little water so that I may take my soul out of distress. (*D*, 162, 345, 31)

Satisfying the body's longing for water also satiated and calmed the roho. To give the body what it craved was also to relieve the roho of figurative pain. So, while the roho and body were distinct, the satiation of the body affected the roho. The relationship between the roho and body was not balanced, however, as the roho was more strongly positioned. The roho pressed the body to do its bidding, and only the nia could limit the exertions of the roho.

The desire of the roho was the most powerful force of longing, stronger, for instance, than that of the kijoyo. Mombasans said that to want with the roho, *ku daka kua roho*, was the greatest longing of all (*D*, 356). If not contained, the power of the roho could destroy a person, send them into poverty, or even kill them. Therefore, to allow the longings of the soul to direct all actions was a sin. The thief exemplified resignation to the roho's covetousness: *muivi ana-i-pa roho mbelle, kisha yuwaiba kua wazi*, "the thief puts the wants of the roho in front of all other considerations," and as a result finds no moral obstacle to stealing. Without a conscience to limit their indulgence of the roho, thieves stole with impunity.[29] Perhaps the most extreme, and dangerous, examples of longing were those with a *kijito*, or "little eye" of the roho. Not everyone had a *kijito*, but for those who did, it made them want all they saw, like the beautiful clothing, fine furniture, or jewelry of a neighbor (*D*, 143).[30]

So intense could this longing become that without satiation the *kijito* might make one weep out of envy. The same phrase used to describe one weeping for grief was used to describe someone weeping out of envy upon seeing someone else receive something that they themselves were denied.[31] The poor were said to direct such avaricious cries toward God: *mtu asie mali yuwalia uifu kua Mungu*, "the person without possessions weeps with envy to God," so that, as Krapf explained, "God may destroy the property of the rich" (D, 396).

The roho was forceful and insensitive. It put its cravings before all else.[32] It did not consider the socio-spiritual consequences of the actions it proposed. It wanted satiation, even though such satiation was never more than temporary. Those who ate quickly or ravenously were said to follow their roho and thus have a "ravenously hungry soul" (D, 185). Mombasans believed that when the roho was not restrained, the end was dissatisfaction and social alienation: *lafúka*, or gluttony. The glutton was a symbol of social transgression in his or her disregard for manners. The proverb went: "He eats today, he ate yesterday, and what was it that he ate?" The answer was that for the glutton it did not matter. In their haste, gluttons only concentrated on the food in front of them or their next meal; all previous meals were long forgotten in their ravenousness.[33] In their extreme, the gluttons' wants had physical effects. They could manifest, for example, in heart palpitations if a glutton concluded that the quantity of food presented at a meal would not suffice. In Mombasan formulations, the glutton's loss of control over his roho resulted not only in social ostracism but also in physical adversity. Muyaka satirized the material glutton as a desirous son who asks his mother for more money after squandering his inheritance. Through the voice of the mother, Muyaka expressed indignation toward the person with uncontrollable longings:

> . . . you turned into a moth and ate all of your clothes
> with uncontrollable appetite, leaving nothing.
> Now you stink, the girls run from you.
> Go away, go with your wretchedness[34]

Similarly, in his lampoon of a high-status woman whose needs were so great that she had forgotten the social consequences of insatiable desire, Muyaka explained that she found no sympathy for the pain of desire: "Even without wealth I do not long for the things of others / covet without means, let her sit and long."[35]

As we might imagine from the above, people who did not harness their cravings lost respect. The records of their condemnation in contemporaneous language attest to the ubiquity of needs as well as the social and spiritual pressures to control the insatiability of desire. The verb *ku niéta* meant "to have all that one could wish . . . but never to be satisfied," as well as, "to be proud or arrogant," or "to be without good breeding" (D, 282, 84). In a searing indictment of unbridled lust for consumer objects, Muyaka again criticized the glutton of objects:

> You grasp for this and that, "that's it," "no, it's not [that]";
> you can't leave a single thing alone, how could we know what you want?
> You're not afraid of doing wrong, can't you restrain your moyo?
> The bad you chose to leave is gone, and the good has deserted you.[36]

Muyaka both elucidated and lamented the perpetuity of desire.[37] He often underscored the point that satiation is fleeting because there are never enough objects to satisfy people's craving to represent and differentiate themselves publicly. In effect, more things will always be needed because they are compared to the constantly changing possessions of others.

Complicating control over the roho was a component of the agency that was beyond all restraint: the *kifuli* (also spelled *kivúli*), or "shade" of the roho.[38] This was the essential element of consciousness. Much of the roho, like the moyo and nia, died with a person.[39] The shade of the roho did not. Upon death, the shade departed the body and left the remainder of the roho to rot (D, 316, 163).[40] In life, the larger roho remained in people while they slept. It contributed to the pulsation of the heart and enabled breathing. As long as the roho stayed in the body, pulsation continued. The kifuli, however, was free to travel during sleep. It was the agent that showed a person images while they slept, producing dreams. As a person dreamed, the kifuli went far afield and communicated with the *koma* (the kifuli of a dead person)[41] of others, with which it would exchange news and information. The kifuli could also enter into any object it liked. A woman's kifuli, for example, once entered a kettle, and she was presumed dead since, with her shade gone, she could not regain consciousness. But when the kettle was upset, the kifuli returned to her body and the woman revived. There could be much more serious consequences to the roaming of the kifuli. Krapf offers this story of the kifuli with a horrifying end: "A husband one night trode upon a peeled bark of sugar-cane. In the morning he found his wife dead in consequence of his mistake."[42] In its appetite to inhabit the sugarcane, the woman's shade, in effect, sacrificed her body.

The relation of the roho to desire and consciousness reveals the inter-dependency of needs and the self. The roho fashioned desires and did so relationally, creating envy, jealousy, and greed as emotions of the moyo. At the same time, the shade of the soul could both escape the body and inhabit the very objects it wanted. It could exist inside objects, though to stay within a thing was to jeopardize the body, and destruction of the object with the kifuli inside meant the death of the body and all its agen-cies, except for the subagency of the shade itself. The body could not exist in a conscious state without the kifuli. When the shade of the soul was gone from a person, that person was like any other object: he or she had no self-recognition. By producing desire, the roho and its shade also attempted to assert the self's existence by projecting cravings for things that might attract the attention of others. By generating desire for things that created relationships between people, the roho constantly reassured the self of its existence. It would seem that the longing for material things was thus a critical component of personhood. To want was to imagine oneself socially, to aspire to the social position or cultural ideal that an object reflected.

OBJECTS AND THE CALCULUS OF PERSONHOOD

Wanting material things was integral to Mombasan social life because desire was always relational. "To want" was a concept with a seemingly infinite vocabulary. In everyday use, most words for *want* could accom-modate multiple meanings.[43] *Haja* implied nonmaterial wants, like the pressing need to do something, such as to urinate or get to a place. Yet it could also mean physical property, a thing that one would like to possess. *Mapenzi,* a word now commonly used to reference romantic love, had material connotations in mid-nineteenth-century Mombasa. For exam-ple, *mapenzi ya kupena kitu kuliko mtu* or *ku shiriki kitu kua ku penda kuliko mtu,* meant to give one's self over to craving a thing more than a person. The term *pendo la mali* meant the love of wealth, consecrated in the act of giving one's self over to the longing for possessions (D, 93, 202).[44] Other words were more extreme in their connotations. *Ku ipa* meant to want everything that one sees, or to covet excessively. More complicated, *utúmi* meant wanting as well as the process of making a profit. It could even refer to the act of physically consuming food or drink. *Utáshi* meant both demand itself and, by extension, the object of demand. For example, before betrothal, a man would send gifts to the parents of his prospective bride (cash and clothing valued at about

MT$1.50). Asking to marry their daughter without first giving these was foolish, and such an attempt might only draw this response from her parents: "Empty hands are worthless, arrive with *utáshi*." With *utáshi*, the very word for "wants" was metonymic, referring back to the specific objects wanted (*D*, 108, 416, 413).[45] The most emphatic verb for objectival want was *ku t'amáa*: "to crave or covet."[46] Using the noun *t'ámani*, Mombasans said that *t'áamani mali yegni t'áamani ku,* or "the craving for wealth is that most extreme of cravings." The word *tamásha,* another noun derived from *t'amáa,* meant an object of interest. This was, however, no regular object of demand, but a spectacle, a new, strange, or startling thing—something of great interest, like a new design of cloth or jewelry.[47] To have resolute longing for a thing was to crave it with the roho, which, by emphasizing desire born of the roho, stressed the gravity of the longing. To long for a thing with one's roho was not redundant but emphatic (*D,* 387).

Though needs were articulated through complex psychical realms, they were defused in just two manners: satisfaction or unfulfillment. As far as the latter is concerned, the loss of a certain craving was usually passive. If, for example, an anticipated object never arrived, the want for it often slackened. Resolution less regularly came through satiation. Though Mombasans usually regarded covetousness and greediness as lifelong states, there could be temporary relief. This relief, when it did come, always directly affected the mental agencies of the self. For example, in the 1840s there was a certain kind of need, the word for which seems to have fallen into disuse: *kuiu,* a greediness for meat, particularly after a long abstinence from it. This longing could only be extinguished when one ate enough meat that it "struck the moyo," or pained one to eat any more.[48] After arriving at this threshold of saturation, the glutton might announce, *sidaki tena, nimekinaisha roho:* "I don't want any more, I've satiated my roho" (*D,* 176, 149).[49] However, as we have seen, this satisfaction was only fleeting, since the larger infrastructure of desire remained to produce needs. The following day, as the proverb said, the glutton would not even remember what it was that satiated him.

As a result of the condition of desire, need was not just the drive to possess objects in private, but the urge to incorporate things into one's persona, to use objects to project a public self. There were enormous social stakes in having and presenting material things. In order to better appreciate this, we might consider Mombasan notions of personhood as defined between two referential axes of social division: wealth and poverty. Wealth and poverty were relational social conditions assessed in reference to material things and to each other. Since needs were always pegged to the comparative material scale of wealth-poverty, to understand the role of consumption in constructing personhood we might first consider how Mombasans imagined these poles as well as the ways in which objects related to positions on this scale of social comparison. Unbridled desire could be a person's social downfall, but respectability and the "pleasures of the moyo" were, nonetheless, directly related to wealth and possessions. For the wealthy, the self found its greatest satisfaction in *némsi*, a particularly masculine ideal of good reputation or name. Though some of the "respectability" of this condition could be inherited, it was proven by its accoutrements: fine adornments for the person and his environment, servants, and slaves. With strong Orientalist overtones, Johann Krapf described what he imagined to be the *némsi* ideal in material terms: fine dress, money, good food, two women who fan a man, "whilst he keeps a small stick in this hand, and sits cross-legged in his chair with a fine dagger on his side" (D, 277).

Wealth, whether granted by God, gained as a result of success in business, or obtained through unscrupulous means, could grant its possessor power. In Mombasan concepts of wealth, the ability to convert desires into material things was linguistically inscribed in the things themselves. For example, from the noun *uwézo*,[50] "ability," came the concept in home furnishing, *uwézo wa niumba*, "the ability or power of the house." The "ability" of the house referred to the delicate and expensive plaster-work designs carved into the walls and the imported mirrors, as well as English, Dutch, French, and Chinese porcelain fixed into the plaster of the walls.[51] More broadly, *uwézo* could mean the process of interior design or the perceptual effect produced by configuring furniture and objects in a particular fashion. Aligned with this was the notion of *mapambo ya niumba*, or the furniture displayed in a room as well as the variety of things placed in wall niches: objects such as European porcelain, glasses, Indian brass, and English silver vessels. Krapf wrote that, "[t]he natives like to display all their finery by putting it up in their rooms, so that people may see their plates, coffee-cups, trinkets, baskets, and many other things" (D, 152).[52] The *uwézo* of a house, by reflecting the attributes of the owner, signified a family's ability. To say that a house "has no ornaments"—*niumba hi heina kipambo*—implied that its owners were poor indeed. Similarly, the abilities of the body were evidenced in its physical appearance. According to Krapf, Mombasans believed that "[t]he ability of the body is the beauty of the body" (D, 270, 417).

Mombasans conceived of the exercise of power as inextricable from having wealth and possessions. For example, the word *bádiri* had two interdependent meanings: (1) "to spend money in order to marry" and (2) "power" (*D*, 18). Marriage, at least for men, was a part of acquiring full personhood, and so the marriage process was centrally focused on ability, wealth, control, and gifting. A groom would deliver a constellation of objects to the bride before the wedding, things like furniture (the *malazi*, or marriage bed, the most costly imported from India and Basra), clothes made of expensive Indian or American cloth, jewelry from Muscat, cash, and cooking utensils. According to Krapf, the "wealthy and honourable ladies" required MT$60 or more for the standard jewelry set, accessories equivalent to the price of eight hundred yards of American cloth (*D*, 198, 78).[53] Weddings, while forums for displaying a groom's ability, were also scenes of his material depletion. An entry from Krapf's dictionary records such a complaint: *mke huyu ame-ni-tia hasara nengi = ame-ni-ishia mali nengi, kua harusi kua ku pamba na kua kula, kua ku nunua manukato na godoro na mido,* "This woman has caused me enormous loss. She's finished off a lot of money/property for the wedding [in the form of] ornamentation, food, to buy the perfumes, and for the mattress and pillows" (*D*, 97, 390).

Though marriage required a great investment, it was dangerous to let a man of increasing prosperity live unmarried. People feared that he might expend his wealth in unacceptable ways, perhaps through what Krapf calls, "illicit intercourse with women" (*D*, 20). While a young man might groan about the impoverishing costs of a wedding, his family could be equally uneasy with his continued bachelorhood, since this lifestyle offered few socially appropriate avenues for wealth investment. The cultural ideal of great, concentrated spending on socially acceptable objects, such as the proper outlay for a wedding, carried over into all manner of public performance. For example, there was a ceremony for announcing one's ability and wealth that mirrored wedding rituals. As part of most wedding festivities, the bridegroom was ferried around town on his friends' shoulders.[54] Likewise, when a newly enriched man wanted to show his "wealth and greatness," he arranged to be carried around Mombasa on someone's shoulders (*D*, 117).[55]

The proper social use of wealth was to consume it, not to store it up for future use. People who had wealth were expected to spend it, *ku ji-lisha,* to enjoy it, or to euphemistically "feed" themselves. *Kujilisha maliyakwe,* "to enjoy one's property," or "[lit.] to feed one's self their own wealth," was to transform money into objects and relationships.[56] The practices of Hindu businesspeople in Mombasa were often stereotyped as examples of what respectable people should not do with their wealth. They were said to hoard their money. Krapf quotes Mombasans as saying, "Banians [Hindus] don't eat good things, they don't feed themselves their own money; they're people of great avarice. They're misers" (*D*, 117).[57] This contrast, one that comes up often in nineteenth-century Mombasan reflections, between the practices of Hindus (or others from the Indian subcontinent) and the Swahili community is instructive in that it sets up an opposing set of cultural norms that more clearly defines Swahili ideals. For Swahili Mombasans, "miserly" Hindu businesspeople who did not spend in public performances offered alien points of contrast that reified popular Swahili notions of normalcy—in this case the importance of expending wealth through public consumption (*D*, 98). According to a Mombasan aphorism, "The property of the miser (*báhili*) is eaten by worms." Someone who profited from business or other ventures but did not translate his wealth into material things that signified position and reflected cultural norms was despised as a miser. The standard measures for such practice were Hindu merchants and a wealthy Swahili named Famau, "who from avarice sold the meat which he had boiled, himself only using the broth. He feasted at the table of other people, while the eatables of his own were left to rot, and then thrown into the sea" (*D*, 19). If someone was a miser in the extreme, Mombasans said that they were "a *báhili* like Famau."[58] Such narcissism was an abomination, since the miser chose none of the socially appropriate means of wealth use: he neither fed himself his wealth nor spent it on clients or family. By not spending, misers did not socially represent themselves as wealthy and thus sought no more respect than the poor. To disregard these acceptable uses of wealth was to waste money and show contempt for one's neighbors. Though the miser acted differently, Mombasans imagined him as akin to the gluttonous over-spender who became so obsessed with procuring that he too forgot about social conventions. Both were greedy, and in Mombasa there was a conflation of all forms of "excessive incorporation of value," to borrow Alfred Gell's phrase, whether they were evidenced in distended purses or distended bellies.[59]

An alternative to miserliness was the spending of wealth to secure clients who might support a patron. Using wealth to attract followers who, like objects, reflected the status of their patron was a good investment, though not without complications. Investing too much in clients could destroy one's wealth. Wealthy elites secured a client by making some person dependent: *ku fathilisha*. Similarly, the verb *ku fuatia* meant to make one follow, to bring a person under one's patronage. Krapf used it in a sentence that gave causality to the relationship and action of client making: "Abdalla induced my servant to follow or join him by giving him property or flattering words." Here, to gain followers, one had to make overtures to prospective clients, such as offering them gifts or promises. This practice is summed up by the phrase: *ku afia mali, ku wapata watu,* "to spend property/money for getting people" (D, 64, 71, 3). Those most receptive to the propositions of wealthy patrons were unmarried men without houses, often the most politically weak men in town. These clients, particularly during Ramadan, feasted at their patron's houses, and through this, Krapf tells us, "the followers are kept attached to the interests of the chief, who gives them no fixed wages, and who reckons on their support in every case of emergency" (D, 56).

Dependents were by definition weak in property, and so their actions and relationships were more easily directed by the proper deployment of gifts than were those of the wealthy. Yet to rhetorically overdetermine clients as entirely passive was dangerous. In fact, there was a very precise phrase for a situation in which a rich person was divested of his wealth by clients: *ku-m-komba mtu,* "to draw away all the money or property of a person by begging, and by showing apparent attachment to him, but when he has spent all his property and has become destitute, to leave him to his fate." Krapf wrote that the demands of clients often impoverished patrons and that there were "many Suahili who were once wealthy people, but who lost all their riches by aspiring after greatness, influence, and a large retinue." Of such people, Mombasans said, *watu wame-m-komba maliyakwe pía iote,* "the people got all his/her wealth" (D, 168).[60]

Even outside of patron-client relationships, Mombasans put great emphasis on public spending and the everyday distribution of wealth as a socially correct alternative to miserliness. "To get a haul of fish is nothing," Muyaka charged, "the real problem is dividing the catch." To store wealth, Muyaka reminded those whom he satirized, is contemptible.[61] Muyaka's sentiment is here reminiscent of the tale of the greedy scholar. As the parable goes, a particular learned man would receive a loaf of bread and a cup of water from God each day. One day, the scholar was visited by a stranger who asked to stay the night. The following morning the scholar found two loaves and two cups of water in place of his usual one loaf and one cup. Instead of giving a full loaf and one cup to the guest, he divided one loaf and one cup of water and shared it with the stranger, hiding the other serving. The stranger, as it turned out, was an angel. When it revealed its identity to the learned man he, not understanding the gravity of his deceit, asked it, "Will you greet our Lord, *mkuawetu* [our Provider], and ask him to make ready the *pepo* ["wind" in this context] to convey me to Paradise?" Promising to convey the message, the angel departed and, after meeting with others on the road, returned to heaven to relay the scholar's words to God. Shortly thereafter, God summoned the angel and sent it back to earth with messages for all it had visited. The angel returned to the learned man. On meeting him it said, "The Lord ordered me to tell you that the pits of fire are ready for you." Dumbfounded, the scholar listened as the angel explained how, after taking leave of him, it passed a palm-wine tapper on the road. Though perceived as morally bankrupt in Muslim Mombasa, the drunkard, unlike the scholar, invited the angel to share his drink, offering him palm-wine in profusion. On hearing of the tapper's generosity, God sent a message to him, informing him that the pepo would bring him up to Paradise on account of his hospitality. After hearing all this, the learned man took his books, tore them apart, and left the solitude of his studies to become a palm-wine tapper. The moral: Receiving comes with the burden of sharing, regardless of one's social standing. Distribution was God's intent, and all things given by God were to be shared. Miserly people created the conditions of their own social and material undoing (D, 207).

There is a paradox in this socioeconomic morality, at least as far as the wealthy were concerned: distribution was socially necessary but pared away those things that signified wealth, prosperity, and némsi. To distribute was to be acclaimed, but to give away all of one's possessions was to lose the means of gaining acclaim. Thus, no matter how important clients were, to redistribute all of one's objects in order to gain them was a zero-sum game. The answer was to give out just enough to keep "the people" from getting it all and still not incur the wrath of either God or one's neighbors, while investing in objects that reflected the condition to which one aspired. Muyaka's longest meditation on wealth explores this paradox of distribution and material possessions.

Ai, gold and silver, such proverbial things.
People don't lend them out, not even to a friend.
Those that distribute are few, and these go too far.
Ai, ghee and flour, when the two meet.

Ai, flour and ghee, the choicest foods,
things of distant lands, Portugal and Baunagar [in northwestern India].
He who gives a little of them to a friend, God fills with joy.
Ai, milk and sugar, when the two meet.

Ai, sugar and milk, which give people strength,
with them a sick person recovers and goes about again
and walks with confident steps, flaunting his colorful garments.[62]

God gives joy to the generous; human giving, Muyaka tells his listeners, creates more wealth. The gifts allow others—the poor in particular—to "recover," to become social beings again, given confidence by their new clothes. Muyaka suggests that God's gift of wealth in possessions brings elation, and possessions bring strength, as to the sick. Wealth gives confidence and puts one in the position to flaunt possessions, to curry envy. Because people were defined by what they possessed, objects given to the poor made them whole social beings.

Defining wealth as confidence, strength, and the ability to publicly represent one's self through objects is also to define poverty as a lack of these conditions. People actively lost wealth through their incorrect use of it and their own blundering. A song current in the 1840–50s encapsulates Mombasan perceptions of the impermanence of wealth, the contempt for those who lose their wealth, and the typologies of those with limited "ability": *ulimengu mdauili wasinga mbelle na niuma, ya utukuni Mguame wausa kapo kua mia*, "the world is round, it turns in front and behind [i.e., all things are susceptible to change]; see there, Mgwame [who was once a wealthy and respected man] in the market, he sells baskets [receiving in return only] the strips [used to make them]" (*D*, 256). The story of Mgwame's fall from affluence had enormous currency in Mombasa because it so effectively played on fears of the loss of prosperity—and with it position and respect. Before becoming poor, Mgwame was the Sultan of Vumba, a town to the south of Mombasa. Through the treachery of a friend whom he invited into his sultanate, Mgwame was forced to abdicate his throne and leave Vumba without his possessions or slaves. In desperation, he moved to Mombasa, where he was only able to sustain himself by hawking baskets in the market. Soon he was a failure even at this, since the only compensation he ever received was more of the strips used to make the baskets.[63] By foolishly inviting a foreigner into Vumba, Mgwame was unseated, relegated to poverty, and hopelessly trapped within its cycle. According to the story, Mgwame created this condition himself. He was rich, but he made himself poor. So potent was the Mgwame trope of property loss that Mombasans employed it to address the social condition of poverty more generally. Songs about Mgwame were used to mock the poor: "You, Mgwame, were once a man of great possessions, and good luck followed you; you sent out your people at pleasure like a king, but now you have become poor, of no use in the town" (*D*, 256).[64] The only thing worse than being born into poverty was to willfully do something to become poor. The story of Mgwame was a strong rhetorical statement because it allegorically illustrated the common notion that to have and to lose was catastrophic, since in losing things, one also lost one's reputation and sense of self.[65] In the parable, Mgwame was despised for what he represented: someone who was given much but foolishly cast it away.[66] In common language, Mgwame did not simply become despised, but "caused himself to be despised" (*D*, 382).[67]

As important as it was to "feed" oneself wealth, the common sin of entirely giving in to the whims of desire was an overdependence on objects represented in Swahili literature as ending in God's retribution (*D*, 337). Indeed, so important was the overindulgence trope that it transcended the glutton and became part of historical explanation. Abdulla ibn Ali ibn Nassir's treatise on the collapse of the city of Pate as a regional power, *Al-Inkishafi*, is a widely known meditation on how the overindulgence of desire led, through God's damnation, to one city's poverty.[68] Similar to Nassir's reflection, the history of the people of Ungama, another parable repeated by Mombasans, depicted divine retribution as the result of overindulgence in material things. At Ungama people freely reveled in the abundance of things. They washed themselves with milk. They cleaned their anuses with bread. Because of these transgressions, God destroyed Ungama; the town was swallowed by the sea, and its inhabitants drowned (*D*, 405). Having goods and not using them brought the wrath of neighbors, but having luxuries and using them indiscriminately (cleaning oneself with bread and milk, the most expensive of foods) invoked divine retribution.

Stories like those about Pate and Ungama were moving moral tales, partly because they played on the fear of losing those possessions that signified certain kinds of personhood.[69] Poverty, or the absence of valuable property, was the condition of a lack of respectability and its signifying objects. If objects signified personhood, their absence suggested a failed or valueless person. To be without possessions was to be without strength, without power. To be poor was to be weak. Of the *mdílifu*—a poor person—Mombasans said: *hana kitu wala hana ngúvu*, "he/she has nothing [in the material sense of no possessions], nor does he/she have strength" (*D*, 337, 218). In popular idiom, the poor were never free from thirst and hunger. They had no friends, and their relatives retreated from them. In their weakness, the poor never brought things to fruition. According to Krapf, the meaning of the word for poverty, *uniónge*, connoted both "weakness in point of property" and weakness in "influence among men." The concept of becoming impoverished was synonymous with decay, dying away, wasting (*D*, 382, 337, 407, 388).

Quite simply, to be poor was to want. A *muhitaji*, or poor person, was literally a "wanter," someone without possessions. To make matters worse, the wanters of things, because of their weakness and social liminality, were tormented by others. To the poor person who wore tattered old clothes, children derisively sang: *mtu mfifu awa mitambara yasiokua usima* [or] *misima, ya ku nianiuka, mikia kana ya puesa,* "a lazy person wears bits of cloth, all tattered, in tails like the octopus" (*D,* 264, 392, 226). Clothing, while reflecting position, also signified health, well-being, abilities, all the conditions of the person. Being full, whole, healthy was reflected in nice clothing. To be without a constellation of objects—those attributes of the wealthy, like imported clothes and jewelry—was to be lazy, without ability.

Muyaka's verses frequently return to the theme of poverty since he was himself chronically poor. He personified many of the stereotypes of the poor: he was dirty, a bad dresser, and dependent on his patrons, relatives, and friends (whom he often ridiculed for their miserliness).[70] Like other nineteenth-century poets, Ali Koti and Muhammad Kijumwa among them, he was what people often called a *mkó,* or an unkempt person who washed neither his clothes nor his body, and who, instead of adorning his house with beautiful, imported ornaments, left it bare. In his position as a poverty-stricken public figure, Muyaka offers important reflections on the tensions between wealth and poverty and the hardships that the poor suffer, both in their lack of possessions and status. Complaining of his position, Muyaka speaks of poverty as if it were a ravenous vulture searching out its victims.

> When poverty went roaming and reached the island [Mombasa],
> that's where it came to stay, satisfying itself.
> Its canopy is made of straw matting, so miserable it looks over the bed,
> and [yet] if you speak out against them, they accuse you of the wrong.[71]

Through the striking metaphor of the bed, Muyaka illustrates the social stigma of being without signifiers of respectability. A respectable, comfortable bed had a canopy of imported fabric, usually red printed cloth called *msudu* (*D,* 250).[72] To use straw matting—the cheapest material available—was laughable. Poverty negated the social self because its objects, like straw matting over a bed, attracted negative attention to the subject; instead of drawing the positive attention of others, poverty incited scorn. To be perceived as poor was, for Muyaka, more painful than the physical state of having few possessions.

In his longing for wealth, Muyaka at once resented the prosperous and envied their position of respectability and their "pleasures of the moyo" gained through possessions.

> I wish I could cut a smart dash
> so that wherever I go I'd look prosperous.
> I long to throw off this poverty since all the slandering against me started
> that my clothes are full of lice and make me scratch all over.[73]

It is the duality of Muyaka's moyo, on the one hand embracing the lifestyle of the prosperous, even fetishizing it, and on the other hand begrudging the wealthy, that shows the stakes in having respectable possessions. In imagining what it might be like to be among the wealthy, Muyaka made two propositions: (1) that the pain of his poverty stemmed from the castigation he suffered at the hands of those better off than him, and (2) that looking prosperous was a solution to the agony of poverty. If he could appear fashionable, he would no longer be subject to the torments of others since, after all, his poverty was perceptible in his dirty, infested clothes—a public synonym for his character. He wished to *look prosperous*. He longed for the signifiers of elevated personhood, particularly since he imagined these to reflect his inner self, while his dirty clothes masked the respectability he thought he deserved. These public objects could bear the social weight that the poor sought to unload. In these verses, Muyaka did not desire success to mediate his social relationships or bring elation. Instead, he looked to the signifying abilities of clothes.

Muyaka cited the efficacy of clothing to project respectability, desirability, and all varieties of character traits into the social field. He also, in frustration, called this projection deceit, at least as far as many of his neighbors were concerned. About a group of women who teased him, maybe even rejected his advances, because of his old clothing, he offered this revelation:

> If you see them from afar with their bracelets and ringing jewelry,
> you would think they were real women able to satisfy men's needs.
> Ah, but it's all make-believe; they are no different from us.
> They are not women to concern us; it's only that they have beautiful
>   clothes.[74]

Here Muyaka directs his listeners to see through the signifying qualities of clothes in order to recognize what is being figuratively obscured by them. Clothes do not signify *real* respectability; they do not represent the reality of the women's characters. The women are not who they appear to be; they have only masked themselves in the signs of desirability. For

Muyaka, Mombasans gave far too much credence to the signifying qualities of things. Finery was the mask for a charade of respectability. Nonetheless, Muyaka longed for the ability to wear such a mask.

Using the mask of objects to conceal himself, Muyaka imagined what it might be like to occupy the position of the wealthy, to become the object of envy and admiration. By inverting his social position, he might demonstrate to the wealthy the absurdity of their pride and the deceitfulness of their clothing.

> If I could strut around in beautiful clothes [of] the latest fashions,
> you would all weep enviously as I pass,
> your moyos would admire me when I took up my folds [of clothing].
> When you punch the wall, you only hurt your knuckles.
>
> What do I wait for, why shouldn't I strut my fashions
> trailing my folds, so that they billow over the ground?
> So when I go out everybody knows,
> walking proudly at leisure with my eyes hardly open.
>
> When the fashionable of Mombasa pass by, they show their style.
> They come out [like they're asleep with their eyes hardly open] not even
>   deigning to recognize their friends.
> When they're in the street, you would think the whole world belongs
>   to them,
> and if the moyo were a book, I'd give it to you so that you might read.[75]

For Muyaka, the wealthy concealed themselves in their folds of cloth, masking their characters in the signs of enviability. Muyaka believed that if he could show his audience the hearts of the affluent, this thin veneer of finery would be spoiled, because they were not better people; they only had expensive objects that, Muyaka argues, could magnify anyone. He himself could appear respectable if he only had access to objects of acclaim. To attract the envy of the rich by wearing nice clothes would be a sweet victory for Muyaka. Using finery to turn the scorn of the rich into envy would prove to the wealthy their self-deception.

> Ai, let me dress up in finery and strut about town.
> You'll see how good I look, in my rare and wonderful attire.
> It's among his own people that a person gains status/recognition.
> Look at the outcast today surpassing all of those around him.

This sentiment appears again in other verses:

> All these fashionable people are of high status,
> and their status has corrupted them, their finery should be removed,

they have overdone their fashions.
How astonished might they be [to see me] that I have turned their ridicule
on them.[76]

Muyaka argues that objects are deceptive. He may masquerade in attractive clothes, but he has not changed anything other than his material appearance. Muyaka suggests that in the single act of changing clothes, he might become their social equal, even without modifying his character or genealogy.

According to Muyaka, the wealthy of Mombasa had harnessed the ability to represent themselves in an ideal manner. The wealthy had objects, and with those objects came respect. Yet, in Muyaka's eyes, the prosperous became contemptible for their pride in their possessions and so were unworthy of them. For Muyaka, clothing had become a sign without anchor, and this meant that Mombasans were continually deceived by the finery of the rich. Muyaka believed that commodities had gained such symbolic power that Mombasans accepted the visual signs of respectability as the true representation of a person's character, putting more emphasis on the projected self than the actual character of the person. Muyaka's critique is poignant. Mombasans had invested enormous social capital in the signifying qualities of consumer goods. Thus, items of public consumption were essential to social relationships, and social relations were dependent on the representational abilities of objects.

In his reflections on the signifying abilities of clothes, Muyaka reveals the common denominator of consumer demand for many Mombasans: the ability of clothes to bring recognition and envy. What Muyaka wished for was beautiful clothing that would cause those who strutted around in the latest fashions to "weep enviously" as he passed. He imagined that with beautiful clothes he could be remade into a self-validating object of others' respect and envy, that he might use the means of specific consumer goods to reach the end of a respectable and envied persona. Since the symbolic qualities of objects were their most important faculty in Mombasa—they needed to signify relation to or distinction from others in order to bring positive recognition to their owners—needs were regenerated when objects no longer afforded their owners distinction or character in relation to other consumers.[77] Perceived in this way, the economic actions of Mombasans were to a great degree shaped by the finiteness of objects' signifying life-spans. And since Mombasans imagined that the satiation of the roho and moyo came through consumer goods that could bring positive recognition to the self, economy could not be divorced from the impulses of the soul and heart.

CONCLUSION

The consumer goods that Mombasans received through trade were neither inconsequential nor randomly chosen. Instead, they were selected to meet the social necessity of representing the self in the public realm. This chapter has outlined attitudes toward and rationales for consumer demand in Mombasa at a time when Mombasans were drawing more deeply on flows of foreign consumer goods and becoming fully integrated into Zanzibari economic, political, and cultural spheres. This reflection has taken us first to the psychical agencies that generated, regulated, and articulated desires: the moyo, nia, and roho. From there we traced needs into the spaces of the overtly relational, or the social discourses and metaphors of display to which needs were directed. In considering the social relations of consumption, I suggested ways in which concepts of personhood were configured in relation to objects. I argued that what was sought in Mombasan consumption was not any actual object by itself, but the imagined condition signified by the object (wealth, respectability, taste).[78] Commodity needs were thus the conscious manifestations of the longing for a certain kind of personhood, that is, respectability, némsi, "goodness."

The economy that such needs in part produced was a result of the dialectic between local social relations and the transregional circulation of consumer goods. Indeed, through demand for imported commodities, the local social environment shaped East Africa's regional as well as global economic relationships. By the 1860s the economy of the East African region was becoming more profoundly connected to distant world regions, from China to South Asia and North America. As direct trade with distant world regions intensified between the 1860s and 1880s, not only was East Africa increasingly at the mercy of global markets, but East Africans were also affecting patterns of global trade and production in important ways. I consider this commercial dialogue, and the global repercussions of East African demand in particular, in the next chapter.

CHAPTER 3

The Global Repercussions of Consumerism

East African Consumers and Industrialization

Analysts of global integration have been rightfully concerned with eluci-
dating global inequalities. But increasing interconnectivity has also created possibilities for seemingly marginal people to affect larger patterns
of interrelation. By concentrating on how economic power is deployed
by dominant global actors, analysts of globalizing processes have largely
overlooked how quotidian acts such as consumer demand across the
globe influence economic relations, however asymmetrical those relationships may be. Highlighting instances of direct reciprocity in global
networks, this chapter recovers some of the ways that East African consumers shaped the global economy in the nineteenth century. East
Africans used imported commodities to affect social and political relations across the region, and their demand for imports transformed overseas locales of production—places as distant as Salem (Massachusetts)
and Bombay. By tracing courses of global integration through the complexities of global circulation and negotiated transaction, this chapter
contributes to an alternative genealogy of globalization that takes into
account the local contingencies of intercontinental relationships and the
interests of historically under-considered populations.

OBJECTS, ECONOMY, RELATION

Global economic systems are to a great degree influenced by the cultural
logics of consumer demand. Thus, reflection on the effects of consumer

desire within networks of relation—even effects that seem to contradict dominant power relations—sheds critical light on processes of global economic integration, past and present. For instance, the recognition that the social calculi shaping consumer desire are both local and transcend the local, and that global economies regularly accommodate changing desire, makes it less probable that the forms taken by transregional systems are reducible to a singular logic such as that of capital accumulation, important as it is. Attention to "peripheral" cultures of demand, or any local interests that produce long-range reverberations, brings to historical analyses of global processes an appreciation of plural causality. Yet reciprocities, however uneven, have rarely gained critical attention in the most developed paradigms of global economic integration, such as the dependency, world-system, and neoliberal approaches. To their great credit, theorists of the global economy employing these models have long debated the ways in which the non-West has been important to the West's economic buoyancy, but neither they nor many other analysts of globalization phenomena have fully appreciated how the *interests* of the "periphery" have affected distant societies. This is particularly surprising considering that world-system theory,[1] one of the most rigorous market-based models of global interaction, implies ways for thinking about the repercussions of "peripheral" interests in its basic conceptualization.[2]

The very notion of interconnectivity on which theories of the world-system are predicated suggests possibilities beyond the deterministic language of core/periphery relations, a language that is now frequently employed in analyses of globalization.[3] If any part of a system has the potential to affect other parts, we should accept the possibility that seemingly marginal actors can, at times, significantly affect seemingly powerful ones.[4] Indeed, a largely forgotten aspect of Immanuel Wallerstein's theorization of global interrelation revealed ways for thinking beyond the monocausality of a world-system determined by Western (i.e., "core") interests. In his analysis of Africa's integration into the world economy, Wallerstein stressed that people act for their own particular purposes under conditions constrained by larger structures, but he added the critical caveat that, "each actor opting for a given alternative in fact alters the framework of the whole."[5] It is this often neglected insight—individual actors are not autonomous, yet they are capable of altering larger frameworks—that deserves particular attention at a time when globalization rhetoric provokes historians to contest monocausal narratives of global integration.[6] What Wallerstein's qualification leaves ripe for consideration are the negotiations and interests brought to bear on transactions the

world over, no matter how insignificant they might appear on the sur-
face.[7] Transactions may be severely circumscribed, but as negotiations of
demand they can both determine the shape of trans-societal dynamics
and, at times, challenge the assumed power of systemic interactions.

Over the last twenty-five years, African historiography has provided
signposts for moving beyond the restrictive analytical logic of an always-
dominant "core" that underwrites many models of historical integration.
One of the ways it has done so is by reconsidering the terms of trade manifest in Africa's transactions of global significance. For example, David
Richardson's work on West African consumption patterns challenged the
notion that the West simply imposed its economic will on Africans by
highlighting how West African demand shaped the parameters of African-
British economic relations at the height of the Atlantic slave trade.[8]
Richardson showed that consumer interests across West Africa were
divergent and locally contingent, which suggested a complexity in Euro-
African commercial relations unexplored in most accounts of precolonial
exchange. More important, Richardson's work demonstrated that African
consumers directly affected the shape of British trade in West Africa and
globally. Africans negotiated the terms of trade by refusing all undesired
goods, and the failure of British manufacturers to replicate the kinds of
items in demand—certain Indian textiles, for instance—forced English
merchants to depend on particular Indian manufacturers.[9] These findings
led Richardson to conclude that we can only fully understand the changing parameters of the eighteenth-century Atlantic slave trade through an
appreciation of regional variations in West African demand.[10] Richard
Roberts's work also illustrates how African interests affected global systems of exchange and production. Roberts reveals that the first industrial
textile mill in India was founded (by French manufacturers) to produce
cloth for the Senegalese market.[11] In the case of Central Africa, Joseph
Miller has suggested that demand for certain Indian textiles shaped
Lusophone trade both in Africa and Asia.[12] What such examples demonstrate is that when activities like consumption in the "periphery" are rein-
serted into systemic analysis, we can develop multidimensional perspectives on economic relationships that amend unilinear models of the
consolidation of economic power in a "core."

The study of precolonial East African consumerism offers another
way to assess the effects of "peripheral" interests on global economic
trends. Through demand, as much as through production, East Africans
leveraged nineteenth-century global commercial relationships. For example, assumptions of the dominance of external market forces in East

Africa are immediately thrown into question by the fact that throughout the nineteenth century foreign firms doing business in Zanzibar were, to their consternation, subject to local trading partners and the whims of regional producers. The records of foreign traders are replete with references to their inability to spur production or even regulate the prices of their own goods. Moreover, the intense competition between foreign merchants, combined with the Sultan of Zanzibar's economic egalitarianism and the relatively buoyant prices of many East African exports, assured favorable terms of trade for both African producers and the marketers of African commodities. From the East African case, an image of global relation emerges that suggests that the shape of world markets has been determined not only by Western interests, but also through a matrix of shifting accommodation and, lest we forget, by the dynamics of non-Western exchanges.

Drawing inspiration from the work of Richardson, Roberts, and Miller, as well as a growing body of interdisciplinary literature that highlights the fact that the West's global relations have rarely been unilaterally determined,[13] this chapter addresses not only the particularities of exchange in East Africa but, following Frederick Cooper's appeal, the courses of global interrelation that Africans affected.[14] The profile of global relations that I present is one of reciprocal determination, inequitable in the long run, and increasingly so from beginning of the East African colonial era in the 1880s, but reciprocal nonetheless. This dialectic constricted possibility without foreclosing a variety of actions, choices, or potentials. Global circuits of exchange fixed the parameters of activity, and yet both East African consumer demands and cultures of production forced outsiders into certain relationships with African producers. By paying more attention to reciprocities among actors in macronetworks, we can better appreciate how historically marginalized people have affected distant societies and world systems of relation. Finally, attention to reciprocities complements market-based analyses, as well as institutional, encounter, and other approaches to global interaction by highlighting—much as Richard White did in his analysis of the "middle ground" of intercultural relationships—dimensions of circularity and accommodation that further temper our genealogies of globality.[15]

THE PLACES OF CONSUMER DESIRE

To demonstrate how East African consumers affected distant societies, I trace the repercussions of East African consumer demand to two distant locales: Salem, Massachusetts, and Bombay. In order to perceive the relationships between places of production and consumption with greater clarity, I first highlight links in the chains that connected East Africa to other world regions. Such links included the consumers and retailers who purchased goods in mainland East African societies; the caravan porters who carried loads of goods across eastern Africa; the caravan leaders who bought and arranged for the transport of goods into the interior, foreign agents and local buyers in Zanzibar and elsewhere on the East African coast; the ships that delivered cargoes; the firms, brokers, and consignors in Asian, American, and European ports; the manufacturers of various consumer goods for domestic consumption and export; and consumers in Europe, the Americas, and Asia. Along these chains of relation, we can see precisely how consumer demand came to drive the system, how demand was translated and relayed, and how, through such translation, the production of certain goods was organized and executed. Of these links between East African consumers and foreign producers, two were particularly important: (1) foreign agents in Zanzibar—East Africa's commercial hub—and (2) the caravan leaders who traded directly with consumers throughout mainland East Africa.

The correspondences of Westerners operating in East Africa reveal the local contingencies of global exchange, such as regional cycles of production and changing regional tastes. Letters from American merchants in East Africa are replete with frustrated remarks about contaminated copal (a resin used for making furniture varnish), producers' unwillingness to collect it during the planting or harvesting seasons, the lack of caravans during the planting season, and the slowing of business during Ramadan.[16] None of the Americans' efforts affected these patterns of production and exchange. Americans could, at best, attempt to control the volume of their national goods in the market; but they were largely unsuccessful even at this since there were so many firms in competition. To complicate matters, while East African demand constantly changed, foreign traders in East Africa could rarely afford to be fickle in their demands. Instead, they had to take, or compete for, what was available and trust that the prices of East African copal, ivory, and cloves remained steady at home. Western agents and travelers, who out of necessity became familiar with East African methods of exchange, were equally frustrated by the complexity of African demand and their utter inability to circumvent it. Joseph Thomson, who fit out a caravan for Lake Tanganyika in the 1870s, wrote that, "fashion was as dominant among Central African tribes as among the *belles* of Paris or London."

"Each tribe," he explained, "must have its own particular class of cotton, and its own chosen tint, colour, and size among beads." Indicative of the importance of sensitivity to local tastes, Thomson continued, "The absence of the required article at any particular point, might mean nothing less than disaster and failure to the expedition, as people will have nothing but the cloth or bead that happens to be in fashion. Everything else is of no value, and will hardly be accepted as a present." Venting his dissatisfaction with the terms of exchange, he added, "Worse still, the fashions are just as changeable [as in England]. . . . In one year a tribe goes mad for a particular bead; but the trader having supplied himself with the fashionable article, according to latest news, might, if his journey was long, arrive to find the fashion changed, and his stock just so much unmarketable rubbish."[17] Speaking directly to the popular myth of African satisfaction with baubles, Richard Burton commented that the "Birmingham trinkets and knickknacks, of which travellers take large outfits to savage and barbarous countries, would in East Africa be accepted by women and children as presents, but . . . would not procure a pound of grain."[18] Burton and Thomson, like countless caravan leaders before them, learned this lesson the hard way. Thomson, for example, took the advice of a caravan leader who had visited the Lake Tanganyika region a full two years earlier and on his recommendation bought, "a great amount of beads of a certain size, composition, and color," which he found to be out of fashion on his arrival. The beads, carefully chosen and carried halfway across the continent, were now of little value.[19]

As European travelers would only be the latest to discover, demand was not easy to predict, nor was it necessarily definable by cultural-linguistic group. Individual consumers often sought out particular goods in order to differentiate themselves from their neighbors. Harry Johnston, who traveled to Mount Kilimanjaro, described the desires of people he came into contact with as "most varied and capricious," adding that, "scarcely two villages concur in their canons of taste." The solution that East African caravan leaders devised to address the contingencies of fashion was to carry various sizes and shapes of, for instance, a bead that had been reported to be in style in a particular locale. Using the *maji ya bahari* (literally "sea water" in Swahili) beads as an example, Johnston advised potential travelers to carry multiple sizes since, "an entire tribe may affect one shade of blue in their bead necklaces, yet each individual will have special opinion as to the correct size of the bead."[20] To put the complex nature of demand into perspective, there were at least four hundred varieties of beads current during Burton's sojourn across central East Africa in

1857, each with a different value, name, and particular locale of preference. Red beads, for instance, were the only kind salable in Unyamwezi, whereas black beads were currency in Ugogo, though worthless everywhere else. "Egg" beads were valuable in Ujiji and Uguha, but refused elsewhere. White beads were popular in Ufipa and parts of Usagara and Ugogo, but disliked in Uzigua and Ukonongo. The bright yellow *samuli* (Swahili: "ghee") was in demand among Chagga and Maasai consumers, but found no market further south.[21] Such drastic divergence in preference meant that merchants had to buy amounts appropriate for the length of travel and the regions passed so that they would not be left with stocks of valueless goods.[22] If a caravan found itself overstocked with a particular variety of bead, its only chance to dispose of the surplus would be at commercial centers like Ujiji (on Lake Tanganyika), where bead-changers converted hundreds of varieties.[23]

Perhaps more indicative of the importance of appealing to East African tastes is the fact that American merchants at Zanzibar had to return entire cargoes when particular goods, like a certain kind of cloth or gun, found no market in East Africa.[24] In order to gauge the market so that time and money were not lost in sending the wrong kinds of things to Zanzibar, manufactures in the United States, England, Germany, France, and India sent samples ahead of cargoes.[25] When firms did not follow this practice, they could incur heavy losses. For example, after receiving a shipment of glassware and crockery, an American agent in Zanzibar wrote to his firm that these were both selling very slowly and that, in the future, the firm should be careful not to ship goods before testing samples in the market.[26] Another American agent, William Jelly, wrote angrily to his firm in 1845 that the wrong kind of muskets had been sent to Zanzibar. After giving a detailed explanation of why the particular variety sent would find no buyers in Zanzibar, Jelly added, with great irritation, that the consignor in Salem had spent enough time in Zanzibar, "to know the kind wanted for the Zanzibar market."[27]

Brass wire, the third most common import after cloth and beads, was a particularly troublesome commodity to the Americans because its width, shape, length of coil, packaging, and weight all determined the wire's value in East Africa. At mid-century, Zanzibari purchasers would only buy certain gauges that they knew to be in demand for making jewelry in the interior.[28] Indian and European merchants also imported American brass wire, and when an American firm wrote to its agent in Zanzibar that the wire was becoming too expensive in the United States, the Zanzibar agent warned the firm that if it ordered wire from England, it must not only be the right gauge but also look exactly like the American variety.[29] The form was particularly important. Pieces had to be of a standard size, in coils nine to twelve inches in diameter, with each coil consisting of either ten or twenty rings. And they had to be wrapped in brown paper so that they would not oxidize. Its "bright appearance," as one American merchant described it, was essential to the wire's sale in the East African interior.[30] Because of its importance to trade—foreign merchants often likened brass wire's exchange-value to that of gold—and the attention necessary to produce the right product and packaging, American manufacturers began making brass coils conforming exactly to East African specifications. One agent described the American brass wire made for East Africa as "a superior article," calibrated for the market.[31]

There was no way for foreign traders to circumvent the exigencies of African demand. In the 1850s, for instance, English chintz did not sell very well in the interior because people across the region preferred French and Hamburg varieties, despite the fact that their price was three times that of English chintz.[32] Imitations were also rarely successful. Lewis Pelly, the British vice-consul at Zanzibar and later the acting political resident and consul general in the Persian Gulf, wrote of several incidents in which foreign merchants attempted substitutions of regional favorites to no avail. In one case a Hamburg firm tried to copy a popular, blue-checked turban cloth made in Muscat (Oman). The firm began to import a knockoff from Hamburg that they imagined to be equally attractive and sold it at a price lower than the Muscati-made variety. But Zanzibari consumers found the colors overly bright, and, accordingly, it was "gossamer to a beaver": valueless. Pelly wrote of the similar plight of various textiles that arrived with a stripe too narrow or a line too broad. Such things were, according to Pelly, "sufficient to make the conservative ladies of the Negro races doubt quality, and stick to the original Surat, Broach or Bengal."[33] East Africans developed both highly differentiated tastes and sophisticated ways of assessing quality. Foreign merchants had to produce goods that fit these parameters if they wished to be successful in East Africa. For example, despite considerable British political influence at Zanzibar, British merchants were virtually frozen out of the direct trade with East Africa because they offered few consumer goods that appealed to East Africans. A British consul wrote in the early 1850s that English manufacturers simply could not replicate the American cloths that had become so popular in East Africa. "Many have tried," Hamerton explained, but they failed to produce the "proper article."[34] Yet, British cloth did find its way to East Africa. Bombay exporters first broke into the East African market by remaking cheap English textiles with added colors and stamped designs.[35] For example, the *kisutu,* a cloth popular across East Africa, was a plain English cotton that had been dyed in Bombay.[36] What Bombay-based firms, like all those who would succeed in the East African market, recognized was that their success was dependent on their agents' abilities to recognize African fashion trends and relay information about these trends to manufacturers at home.

Perhaps the most important figure at the interface of global exchange and local consumers was not the urban import-exporter, but, because of his (these were almost invariably men) intimate knowledge of consumer markets, the merchant in the East African interior. On the East African mainland imported goods were often sold directly to consumers. Therefore, caravan leaders—the primary negotiators of the caravan trade— were lynchpins in the system of global exchange. Without navigable rivers to connect the coast and the interior, caravans of hundreds or even thousands of porters carried goods into the interior, traded, and then collected goods for export. These caravans, and particularly their leaders, faced the immediacy of local demand, its unpredictability, rapid changes in style, and the political environments of each locale. Caravan headmen, whether of coastal or interior birth, had to know the languages and fashion exigencies of all the peoples with whom they wanted to trade or through whose territory they simply wished to travel. If headmen did not possess such knowledge, the journey might be not only unsuccessful, but also extremely dangerous. The caravan leader thus had to gauge the right amounts of each commodity needed in each region. This was a complex process, drawing on experience, recent reports, and knowledge of trade equivalencies between local produce and imported goods. Before setting out for Kilimanjaro, the adventurers Richard Thornton and Baron von der Decken solicited information from Kapitau, a Mombasan caravan leader with a particular knowledge of Chagga country, who informed them of the goods necessary for their journey.[37] Burton's chief advice to those who wished to travel on the mainland was to seek out such *viongozi* (Swahili: "caravan leaders") who knew the route one wished to take, and to inquire as to the "varieties [of trade goods] requisite" for the particular road. "Any neglect in choosing beads," Burton wrote, "might arrest an expedition on the very threshold of success."[38] As an example of this, James Grant wrote that in southern Unyamwezi *gulabi* (Swahili: "rose") beads were, "great favorites; and when exhausted, the price of everything rose to double." The *maji ya bahari* beads, so highly regarded in the Kilimanjaro area, were utterly refused in Unyamwezi, as were white and red beads, even though red beads had been acceptable just four years earlier. Only when the *ukuti wa mnazi* (Swahili: "coconut palm leaf") beads were offered was the caravan able to buy basic provisions.[39]

Even more importantly, viongozi had to stock unique gifts for the political elites through whose territory they wished to pass. These often mirrored the consumer tastes of coastal elites and included things such as music boxes, silk cloth, musical instruments, European or Asian prints, and the latest firearms.[40] East African discrimination among varieties of imported goods became extremely refined over the course of the century, particularly as trade with the coast, travel to coastal cities, and the sheer volume of imports increased. As Jonathon Glassman has shown, by the 1880s political elites like Mandara of Moshi derisively labeled all but the most recent European imports "Zanzibari-made." Much as in coastal cities, the value of certain imported commodities in the interior was rarely stable because elites were constantly looking for objects that could serve to differentiate them from non-elites. Mandara, like his nephew Miriali, sought out the most unique or technologically sophisticated goods from traders in order to set himself off from his subjects—perhaps even to use such privileged access as a way of maintaining his authority—who were by the 1870s accessing a great variety of imports. When offered cloths and other standard gifts by the Bostonian traveler May French-Sheldon, Miriali requested instead her music box, an object highly coveted in the region.[41] The choice of gifts was crucial to the caravan's progress because inadequate tributes paid to rulers or their appointees could stall a caravan and even force it to find another route to its destination.

To complicate matters further, caravan leaders often shouldered responsibility for directing the remaking of consumer goods in their charge. Since fashions changed quickly, it often was necessary to redesign pieces of cloth or restring beads on the road. Caravan leaders purchased the kinds of cloth or beads they thought to be in demand in a particular locale, and, just outside the area where they intended to trade, they would stop and redesign cloth in a way that appealed to local consumers. For example, in the late 1800s Maasai only accepted two kinds of cloth, both of which were syntheses of imported materials. Younger Maasai men wanted what was termed *naibere*. This was a cloth made of about two yards of *ulayti mfupi*, a kind of narrow, unbleached cotton, onto which was sewn a strip of red calico six to eight inches wide. After the strip was sewn on, the edges of the cloth would be frayed about four inches, and this fringe would be bound with a red or dark purple fabric. Older, married Maasai wanted a cloth of similar make, though a little wider and about an eighth longer. This cloth

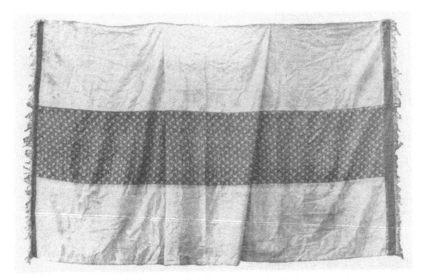

Figure 1. A Maasai *naibere,* colorful Indian dyed cloth sewn onto unbleached cloth with added fringes, ca. 1890. (Photograph from M. French-Sheldon, *Sultan to Sultan: Adventures among the Masai and Other Tribes of East Africa.* London: Saxon and Co., 1892.)

was left without the broad stripe in the middle but was given larger fringes. Before entering Maasai country, the Teleki expedition produced nearly twelve hundred of these cloths. This remaking of cloth occupied the members of the caravan for several days, even with nearly one hundred people engaged in the task.[42] Strings of beads also had to be reconfigured for Maasai consumers. Before entering Maasai country, caravan porters had to rethread beads in lengths of twenty-one or twenty-two inches because beads would not be accepted unless in this form.[43] Similarly, at Taveta (eastern Kenya), Joseph Thomson's caravan had to restring what added up to sixty thousand measures of beads. The remaking of imported goods points up a common fallacy in African economic analysis: the assumption of an asymmetrical exchange of finished imported products for African raw materials.[44] Though we tend to think of cloth, beads, and brass wire as finished manufactured goods distinct from the "raw" materials Africans exported, it is more appropriate to think of them as only partially manufactured, since they often had to be radically redesigned in India, East African centers of trade, or on caravan trails before they could be sold in local markets. Such was the case in Unyanyembe, where coastal artisans purchased imported English broadcloth and tailored it into the *kizibao,* or short, coastal-style coat sought by wealthy men.[45] In Unyanyembe, brass

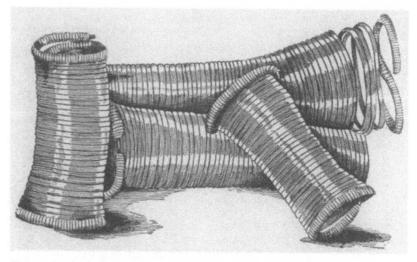

Figure 2. A drawing of imported brass wire formed into arm decorations, ca. 1890. (Illustration from M. French-Sheldon, *Sultan to Sultan: Adventures among the Masai and Other Tribes of East Africa.* London: Saxon and Co., 1892.)

and iron wire was reconfigured before it was sold to consumers; local artisans converted imported wire into armlets, leg bracelets, bells, necklace beads, and rings, as well as inlays for gunstocks and knife hilts.[46]

Much of the remaking of imports took place in East Africa's coastal cities. Artisans in Zanzibar altered cloth designs, added prints and colors, and cut and reshaped textiles according to information provided by caravan leaders and porters. In coastal cities from Mogadishu to Zanzibar one could find artisans who specialized in weaving colored borders onto imported cloth.[47] This value-adding was essential to the mainland trade because consumers, like many in Chagga country, would not buy longcloth without *taraza*, or fringes. The Chagga *taraza* functioned stylistically much like the center strip of a Maasai *naibere*. It gave a measure of American, unbleached cloth vibrant color and, because of the elaborate patterns of its stitching, an ornate, personalized aesthetic.[48] Zanzibaris worked varieties of thread into imported cloth in order to make them more appealing and to drive up their prices. For example, the *uzar*, or silk-cotton wrappers worn by the moderately wealthy on the coast, were often sewn with gold thread at Zanzibar as a way of attracting local consumers and increasing the fabric's value.[49] The value added was extreme for the Surati (western Indian) silk *dewli*, which was embellished with a border of gold thread at Zanzibar. Without a fringe, three and a half

Figure 3. Sewing a large *kikoi,* Zanzibar, ca. 1890. (Photograph by J. Sturtz, from J. Sturtz & J. Wangemann, *Land und Leute in Deutsch-Ost-Afrika. Erinnerungen aus der ersten Zeit des Aufstandes und der Blokade.* Berlin: Ernst Siegfried Mittler und Sohn, 1890. Courtesy of the Winterton Collection of East African Photographs, Melville J. Herskovits Library of African Studies, Northwestern University.)

yards of dewli cost around seven Maria Theresa dollars (MT$) in 1857; when any fringe was added, the price increased by almost 30 percent; when Zanzibari tailors added a gold fringe, the price reached as high as MT$80. In the 1850s, Zanzibaris stumbled on a hit in Unyamwezi with the *kitambi banyani,* or white Indian-made cloth stamped in Zanzibar (or less often in India) with a narrow, red border. Common Surati white cotton loincloths were given broad border stripes of indigo, red, and yellow for interior markets. Different colored borders on the same type of cloth often reflected the desires of its target market. The Kutchi-made *taujiri,* or indigo cotton cloth, was in demand in both Yao and Nyamwezi country, though Yao consumers only bought it if it had a red border, while Nyamwezi only accepted the cloth with a yellow border.[50] Coastal artisans also wove cloth for local consumption and export. Weavers in Zanzibar made a popular turban cloth worn by coastal elites and manufactured coarser cotton cloths for the mainland market.[51] Weavers in several northern coastal cities fashioned the *lemali,* a kind of coarse cotton particularly favored in Oromo territory.[52] Zanzibaris even wove and dyed their own *kaniki,* or indigo cloth, and *kikoi,* or waistcloth, though the volume of production was relatively low.[53] By manipulating imports and manufacturing for market niches, regional artisans could respond quickly to East Africa's shifts in consumer demand.

REMAKING SALEM

For the entire nineteenth century, cloth was at the center of East Africa's global exchanges. East African demand for cloth would shape most of the region's trade relationships and draw economies around the world into dynamic relation with African consumers. Until the U.S. Civil War, American trade with Zanzibar hinged on East African demand for New England cloth. This demand was initially met by the famous Lowell mills of Massachusetts. But increasing competition for Lowell cottons and the introduction of a rail system between the mills and Boston forced Salem merchants to invest in their own mill—the first entirely steam-powered textile factory in the Western Hemisphere. Where American merchants had once staked their East African investments on simple unbleached sheeting from Lowell, between the 1840s and the 1880s they exported a variety of cloths to Zanzibar, including bleached and unbleached sheeting, brown shirting, "common" shirting, "superior" shirting, unbleached and bleached drills, linen, red broadcloth, and handkerchiefs. In the years leading up to the Civil War, demand for American cloth not only provided a commercial staple for East African merchants, but it also assured a primary export market for America's largest textile mill.

In the late eighteenth century, Boston-area merchants sought new markets in the Indian and Pacific Oceans. They exchanged New England–made consumer goods for Chinese porcelain, Indian textiles, Mochan coffee, Muscati dates, and Sumatran pepper. By the end of the first decade of the nineteenth century, Salem and Boston monopolized American trade with Indian Ocean and Pacific ports. However, the War of 1812 initiated the decline of Salem's mercantile power in the Pacific and Eastern Indian Oceans. British hostility kept Americans out of these regions during the war, and as soon as the war was over Salemites faced an equally difficult challenge: competition from New York firms. After 1815, merchants in many New England port cities began to gravitate toward the growing entrepôts of Boston, New York, and Philadelphia, all cities with better port facilities than Salem. Moreover, capital investment within New England was now shifting from mercantilism to industrial production. By the 1830s, American trade with many of the world's most lucrative commercial ports—across the Atlantic, in India, China, and Southeast Asia— was controlled by firms based in the larger port cities. As a result, Salemites began to concentrate on a variety of alternative ports of trade outside the long-standing trade routes. Of the new markets Salemites entered in the Indian Ocean, Zanzibar would prove one of the most important.[54] The East African market was attractive to Salemites because it supplied two commodities essential to New England industries: hides for regional leatherworks and high-quality gum copal, a resin necessary for the varnishes used in the regional furniture industry.[55] In the early nineteenth century Salem's tanneries were its most lucrative industry, and East African hides constituted a large proportion of Salem's imported supplies. More important to Salem's economy over the longer term was the fact that the finest copal in the world came from East Africa. In the nineteenth century, high-quality copal was dug on the *mrima*, or mainland coastal strip just opposite Zanzibar. Serving furniture manufacturers across the Eastern seaboard, the Whipple Gum Copal Factory in Salem became one of the city's largest employers as a result of its access to East African copal. Fortunately for American merchants, people in the copal-producing region and across East Africa took a great interest in Lowell's unbleached calicos (called *merekani;* "American," in Swahili). Salemites thus gained a distinct advantage over others desirous of East African copal. This unique access to copal would frustrate British manufacturers. British furniture manufacturers expressed their interests in circumventing the American copal monopoly in a letter that Richard Burton received before embarking on his "exploration" of East Africa. The letter-writer asserted that any suggestions for increasing British access to East African varnish would, "entitle Captain Burton to a larger share of the gratitude of his countrymen than the measurement of the elevation of the Mountains of the Moon or the Determination of the Sources of the Nile."[56] In the face of fierce competition from New York and Boston, Salem merchants were able to insure their city's prosperity by turning, at least in part, to trade with Zanzibar, a port that promised access to markets for American manufactures and important materials for Salem's industries. The profits derived from the sale of copal, cloves, ivory, and hides, moreover, provided capital for the shift from mercantilism to industrial manufacturing in the Salem area.[57] The relation of East Africa to the vitality of Salem is even clearer if we consider that many of the merchants invested in the Zanzibar trade became key members of boards at Salem banks, insurance companies, and factories. And East African demand for various products such as cloth, furniture, shoes, and glass gave new life to an array of Salem's industries. The repercussions created by Salem's fiscal dependence on markets like that of Zanzibar even had perceptual dimensions: the mother of Richard Waters, one of the most important American traders in Zanzibar, was said to know more about Zanzibar's surroundings than the outskirts of Salem, even though she had never visited East Africa.[58]

East Africans consumed a great diversity of American manufactures. Salem's exports found markets throughout the region and across socioeconomic categories. Most of the *merekani,* brass coil, and beads were sold to caravans heading into the interior, while furniture, clocks, and agricultural goods appealed to coastal consumers. A typical cargo of American goods illustrates the kind of diversification that allowed Salemites to hold an important position in the Zanzibari market: cargoes generally included cloth, brass wire, specie, gunpowder, loaf sugar, muskets, and flour.[59] Yet the cargo manifests of Salem vessels reveal that most ships brought much more than these staple articles. For example, the Salem-based ship *Rolla* sold many of the above products at Zanzibar, but also discharged cedar shingles, two hundred chairs, two hundred boxes of soap (4,000 lbs.), rocking chairs, almost three thousand lustre plates, gold watches, and a diversity of less expensive time-pieces.[60] Other cargoes included things such as lumber (11,226 ft. in one shipment), clapboard, bread, ice, and even ham—a surprising import for Muslim Zanzibar.

Of course, America's greatest trade staple was merekani cloth. By the mid-1830s, the popularity of American unbleached cottons had begun to challenge the dominance of indigos from Kutch (northwestern India). British manufacturers had no luck replicating the American fabric, even though they attempted to counterfeit it by stamping English cloths with American marks. This strategy was unsuccessful, according to one American in Zanzibar, because, "the people say, the strength and wear of the American goods are so superior"; and he added that, "lest they be deceived, [Zanzibaris] will no longer even purchase from Englishmen."[61] In 1847, the British Consul wrote that merekani had come into "universal use" in Arabia and East Africa, in no small measure because of its durability. He wrote to his superiors in Bombay that even the most extreme measures—such as pressing the Sultan of Zanzibar to change his treaty with Britain in order to favor the importation of British cloth— would still not allow British merchandise to compete with American cloth.[62] So successful was the American unbleached calico by the early 1860s that an American merchant compared the merekani domination of the market to another American victory over Britain: "Zanzibar," he proudly proclaimed, "is the Saratoga of the East."[63] More important, in the late 1840s, merekani supplanted Indian manufactures as the most common article of imported clothing for all East Africans. Within just ten years of its introduction, merekani was more commonly used than the Surati- and Kutchi-made indigo kaniki, the cloth with the longest history in the East African market.

From the 1830s until around 1847, the vast majority of unbleached shirting and sheeting that arrived East Africa was manufactured at the Lowell mills.[64] Echoing his predecessor, the American consul wrote in 1851 that the demand for merekani in East Africa seemed infinite, since people across the region preferred them to all other imports.[65] As we have seen, merekani cloth was remanufactured into all manner of clothing by stitching other material onto it, dying it, or tailoring it. It was also used for making burial cloth, it was durable enough to use as sail cloth, and it was used as a form of currency across East Africa.[66] In some societies, even the stamps that the mills printed on the textiles became fashionable. James Grant wrote that at Ukuni (in southern Unyamwezi, Tanzania), when people acquired a piece of merekani bearing the blue stamp "Massachusetts Sheeting" they would wrap the cloth around their bodies in such a way as to ensure that the words appeared clearly across the front of the garment. According to Grant, anyone who could afford this particular length of merekani was thought "a considerable swell."[67] American cloth was authenticated by its stamp, and the stamp itself became not only a signifier of quality but also a fashion item.

The steady increase of elephant hunting, copal digging, intraregional slave trading, and slave production of grain as well as cloves for export led to a greater commodification of economic and social relationships in East Africa. The tendency by mid-century to consider the exchange-values—not simply the use-values—of both people and produce, and the increasing ease with which people could sell commodities to the market, meant that imported cloth was more accessible to more people than ever before.[68] By the 1840s, it was no longer only the elite who could access imported goods but anyone with produce valued by passing caravans, or who were willing to carry produce to regional markets. The enormous demand for American cloth was directly affected by the increasing commodification of produce and people across East Africa as well as the buoyant prices of East African exports. Increasing African demand was soon reflected in New England. Demand for Lowell cloths domestically, in East Africa, and in other export markets strained the supply of Massachusetts' cotton mills in the late 1830s and early 1840s. In 1843, a Salem consignor wrote to the American merchant Richard Waters in Zanzibar to inform him that merekani was scarce because Lowell could simply not stay apace of demand.[69] The strain on Lowell's production led to a rapid inflation in the prices of cloth, and soon Salem merchants were forced to contract for future consignments at prices to be determined at the time of delivery. These conditions were disastrous for Salem exporters because the cost of Lowell cottons was now raised above the projected returns from the East African trade.[70] It was this crisis of the Salem trade, and the possibilities of increased profits from manufacturing in a moment of great consumer demand, that, as P. H. Northway first argued in his treatise on Zanzibar-Salem relations, encouraged Salemites to invest in the Naumkeag Steam Cotton Company.[71] The opening of Naumkeag would be a landmark in Salem as well as in American history.

Founded by a former shipmaster in 1847, the Naumkeag Steam Cotton Company was both the first fully steam-powered textile mill in the United States and the largest mill in the hemisphere. Richard Waters, a long-time agent in Zanzibar and probably the American most knowledgeable of the East African market, became the director and later president of Naumkeag.[72] In the late 1840s, Naumkeag's output was not only greater than that of its competitors, but the quality of its manufacturers was among the best in the nation. During its first year of production, Naumkeag textiles won national acclaim.[73] Though the factory made twills as well as various other cloths, it focused production on the sheeting that underwrote the East African trade.[74] From its opening, the mill was fantastically successful, and between the late 1840s and the early 1860s the growing East African market was one of the most important export outlets for Naumkeag.[75] In the 1850s and early 1860s Salemites finally had significant control over the variety, designs, and availability of the cloth they exported. As a result, the volume of merekani exports to Zanzibar grew exponentially, and Americans soon dominated Zanzibar's trade with the Atlantic.[76] From 1855 to 1859, British, Hamburg, French, Portuguese, Prussian, Spanish, Danish, and Hanoverian ships visited Zanzibar, but the number of American vessels and their total tonnage consistently surpassed those of all other Atlantic nations. In most years, Americans shipped at least twice the tonnage of Hamburg vessels, their closest European competitor.[77] In 1859, for instance, Americans imported all of the cotton piece goods brought directly from Atlantic ports (most English cottons came through Bombay); this added up to almost five million yards of merekani.[78] In the same year, Americans exported almost one thousand clocks and three thousand chairs to Zanzibar, while Hamburg merchants, since they had difficulty finding consumer goods for the East African market, were forced to export bullion to Zanzibar.[79] In the six years leading up to the American Civil War, East Africans consumed more than twenty-nine million yards of merekani cloth.[80]

Yet America's dominance of the textile import trade in East Africa would prove short-lived. Soon after the U.S. Civil War began, Salem's cotton supplies were cut off. American merchants in Zanzibar stayed on during the war but became hopelessly dependent on imported specie, a dependence that severely cut their margins of profit. The merekani once dominant in the market was now far too rare and expensive to sell in East Africa. American imports fell to a fraction of what they had been, and Bombay firms began flooding Zanzibar with English-made merekani knockoff cloth—likely bearing the fake stamp of a New England textile mill, as was the practice of some English manufactures in the 1870s—in an attempt to gain market-share.[81] Unfortunately for the Americans, the volume of ivory exported from Zanzibar increased steadily over the war years, as did the demand for imported goods in East Africa. As a result of the expanding purchasing power of East Africans, the total value of beads and brass wire imported more than doubled in a short four-year span, while the total value of textiles imported nearly doubled as well.[82] Indian-exported textiles, both Indian and British-made, filled the enormous gap in the market created by the exit of the merekani and widened by rising ivory prices.[83] Though East African consumers initially showed little interest in merekani-style Indian textiles, as the Civil War drew to a close, cloth exports from India—exported from both Kutch and Bombay—accounted for the vast majority of the total Zanzibari textile import trade.

By the end of the Civil War, Americans had lost the battle for East African consumers. Moreover, the cost of postwar American labor forced the prices of cottons well above those of their competitors, Indian as well as British. For much of the rest of the century, Americans were reduced to buying East African produce with gold.[84] Moreover, Salem firms that had once been important to the Zanzibar trade were coming under increasing pressure from Boston merchants who were now aware of the commercial prospects in East Africa. New York and Providence merchants soon followed, and by the 1880s Salem firms had taken a back seat to other Americans in Zanzibar. Even though East African consumers continued to show an interest in the American unbleached cloths well into the 1880s, their high prices, compared to the affordability of Bombay copies, made it extremely difficult for Americans to regain the sizable share of the market lost during the war.[85] The situation of American merchants became dire in the early 1880s. In 1884 the American Consul Edward Ropes Jr. wrote angrily about Bombay merekani knockoffs that were meticulously folded, stamped, and packaged to look like real American cloths, yet were sold for far less.[86] Writing three years later, the American consul lamented the retreat of American cloth from Zanzibar: "Immense quantities of Brown sheetings, the production of the many Bombay mills," Seth A. Pratt explained, were now the staples of the Zanzibar economic system. "Their merit," he remarked bitterly, "is their extreme cheapness."[87] While East Africa had been important to Salem's economy in an era of intense competition from larger Boston and New York firms, its greatest importance to Salem was in the transition from mercantile capitalism to industrialization. Not only was the first steam-powered mill in North America built in part to accommodate the East African trade, but Zanzibar was essential to the expansion of several local industries. Salem's most important industries were all linked to East Africa, and what was perhaps the largest industry for much of the 1840s—varnish making—was entirely dependent on African copal producers. Finally, the returns from the East African trade in part allowed Salem to remain a viable commercial center despite its crippling lack of competitive port facilities.

REMAKING BOMBAY

For centuries, Indian manufacturers produced textiles and other consumer goods for the East African market. Varieties of Gujarati indigo-dyed cottons, for example, had been essential components of East African exchange systems since at least the fifteenth century.[88] In the early nineteenth century Kutch became the center of Indian textile manufacturing for East Africa.[89] By the 1820s Zanzibar was the single most important market for the Mandvi (Kutch's metropole) export trade, and weaving constituted the city's largest industry.[90] Mohamed Reda Bhacker suggests that from 1800 until about 1840, Mandvi exported three times as much cotton cloth to Zanzibar than did Surat or Bombay, and it imported at least twice as much African ivory.[91] In turn, capital investments and credit from Kutchi and Kutchi-born Bombay businessmen helped fuel the expansion of the East African regional economy. Indian merchants at Zanzibar acted as intermediaries between East African consumers and Indian as well as British, American, German, and French firms. The role of Indian merchants, financiers, and small business operators in the nineteenth-century East African commercial boom cannot be underestimated. The majority of Zanzibar's largest retailers at mid-century were either western Indian or of Indian descent.[92] In fact, by 1863 at least four-fifths of the entire trade of Zanzibar passed through the hands of British Indian subjects, most of whom were either from Kutch or Bombay.[93] Western Indians had long been important to East Africa's global relationships, but after the American Civil War their response to the consumer demands of East Africans had enormous consequences for the industrialization of the western Indian Ocean's emerging commercial center: Bombay.

Two shifts in the Zanzibar market during the early 1860s drew East Africa and Bombay more closely together. First, the American Civil War took the popular merekani cloth out of circulation. Second, the total value of East African ivory exports increased dramatically. Though the volume of ivory on the coast had been increasing since 1857, the rise in ivory demand in Europe, India, and China put a premium on East African ivory. This, combined with the sudden removal of merekani cloth, provided an ideal market opportunity for Bombay exporters interested in selling Indian cloth in the Zanzibar trade. Bombay exporters moved quickly to flood the market with Indian consumer goods.[94] The immediate success of Bombay goods in East Africa is exemplified by the fact that before the war Zanzibar was an insignificant consumer of Indian-made cloth exported from Bombay, whereas by 1863 it had already become the second most important export destination for Bombay-made cloth.[95] This trend continued, and in 1866–67 the number of Indian-made cloths exported to East Africa increased ninefold.[96] To put this trade in perspective, the only Indian product of more importance to Bombay exporters was opium.

Initially, however, it was neither Indian-made cloth nor dyed, printed, and otherwise remade British cloth that became an important item of export to East Africa; instead it was unbleached English cloth, the closest match to the merekani available in sufficient quantities at the outbreak of the U.S. Civil War. The volume of this cloth exported to East Africa in 1863–64 was more than twice that of Bombay-dyed English cloth.[97] English unbleached cloth coming through Bombay picked up where the merekani left off, and this meant a windfall for Bombay merchants and their British suppliers. It also made the Bombay export sector more dependent on East African consumers than it had ever been. The volume of East African cloth consumption continued to increase throughout the 1860s. After the end of the American Civil War, ivory production and prices remained high, and Bombay textile exporters invested heavily in

Figure 4. The ivory market in Zanzibar, ca. 1890–92. (Photograph from Paul
Prencke, "Erinnerung an Deutsch-Ost-Afrika." Courtesy of the Winterton
Collection of East African Photographs, Melville J. Herskovits Library of
African Studies, Northwestern University.)

the Zanzibar market. In the short four years between 1866 and 1870,
East African consumption of Bombay-exported, English unbleached
cloth quadrupled. With the increasing price of ivory and African production of a greater variety of commodities for the world market, Bombay's new relationship with Zanzibar would change Bombay as much as
East Africa in the early years of the 1870s.

In the first half of the 1870s, the exportation of Bombay-manufactured,
unbleached cottons to East Africa increased, while the volume of British
unbleached cotton sent to East Africa declined proportionally. By 1878,
Bombay exports of locally made cloth to Zanzibar reached a volume of
2.8 million yards annually, surpassing the volume of British-manufactured,
unbleached cloth exported to East Africa. Another telling sign of the increased volume of the Indian cloth trade was that by 1878 the East African
region had become the most important importer of Indian-manufactured
soap, which was used to wash and soften stiff new cloth. In aggregate, the
volume of cloth exported to East Africa from Bombay increased many
times over in the late 1870s, even though the Bombay trade in British cloth

decreased by 15 percent.[98] The changes in Bombay's relationship to Zanzibar were, much like similar changes in Salem production forty years earlier, directly related to local production for the East African market. As Bombay merchants and financiers began to invest heavily in expensive European industrial machinery, they appealed to East African tastes in order to secure a growing foreign market. In the 1880s, East Africans would be Bombay's most important overseas consumers for its single most important manufactured export: unbleached cotton cloth.

The first textile mills in Bombay were built in the 1850s, and their number increased rapidly in the 1860s and 1870s, reaching almost seventy by the mid-1890s. What is particularly important about these mills from the perspective of the western Indian regional economy and colonial India's history, is that they were founded almost entirely by investments of Indian, not British, capital.[99] Bhatia (a Hindu social group) merchants, many of whom relocated to Bombay from Kutch, built up the Bombay overseas trade and invested tremendous amounts of capital in the new mill industry at the very moment that the exit of American cloth left a consumer vacuum in the western Indian Ocean region.[100] Bhatia firms, along with many Parsi houses based in Bombay, expanded their operations and came to command much of the export trade of western India, which was concentrated on cotton, opium, rice, and diverse manufactures.

It was these firms that had the greatest interest, and seemingly the most to gain, from the establishment of Bombay as western India's industrial center. Mills that could both spin cotton and manufacture cloth provided ideal investments for Bombay-based houses, as they allowed Bhatia and Parsi cotton-traders flexibility in a volatile global cotton economy. With the option to either export cotton thread or manufacture cloth at home, firms could export raw and spun cotton when prices were high or produce their own textiles when cotton prices were depressed. The ubiquity of Indian firms in East Africa ideally positioned Bombay's textile industry to produce for the East African market. Moreover, in the 1870s, the establishment of a telegraph station at Zanzibar allowed immediate communication between Bombay firms and their Zanzibar agents. Perhaps most important, expanded steamship service between Zanzibar and Bombay substantially lowered transportation costs and, in turn, reduced the retail price of Bombay cloth in East Africa.

In the late 1870s, Sultan Barghash of Zanzibar, as part of his vision for the commercial preeminence of his sultanate, introduced a line of six steamships to run between Bombay, Zanzibar, and Madagascar. Though the British Indian Steam Navigation Company already covered the route between Bombay and East Africa, Barghash was dissatisfied with the company's service. The sultan bought several large steamers from German and Scottish manufacturers and offered cargo space at low rates.[101] Since most of his revenue would come from duties, which increased with the introduction of the line, this investment was based on long-term fiscal reasoning. Bombay firms quickly began consigning thousands of tons of cargo to each voyage. American residents reported, with great dissatisfaction, that these vessels increased the business between Bombay and Zanzibar exponentially. In the early 1880s, trade in Zanzibar expanded so significantly that Barghash was forced to enlarge the Zanzibari customs house to accommodate the new volume.[102] With lower shipping rates, firms based in both Zanzibar and Bombay began to saturate East Africa with unbleached, merekani look-alike sheeting, kaniki (usually English cottons indigo-dyed in India), as well as rice, wheat, sugar, furniture, and wood—all products that would become essential to the Bombay export trade in the 1880s and contribute to Bombay's position as the premier entrepôt in the western Indian Ocean.[103]

By replicating American cloth and capitalizing on low-cost shipping to Zanzibar, Bombay could continue to lower its cloth prices and appeal to an even wider market. Assuming the place American exports had once held in the East African market, the inexpensive, Bombay-manufactured, unbleached cloths sold well, and the repercussions were immediately felt in Bombay. In 1881, the annual volume of Indian-manufactured, unbleached cloth exported to Zanzibar reached 5.5 million yards, far outpacing British cloth exported from Bombay.[104] Over the course of the 1880s this trend intensified, so that in 1887–88 Zanzibar imported almost all of the unbleached drills, more than half of the unbleached, Indian-manufactured sheeting, as well as nearly one quarter of all *dhoti* (a lighter loincloth material) exported from Bombay. In terms of value, these cottons comprised the most important category of Indian-manufactured Bombay exports. By 1888, Bombay exports of unbleached and English cloth to Zanzibar had reached the astonishing amount of more than fifteen million yards a year.[105] Reflecting the increasing buying power of East Africans, the decreasing costs of consumer goods, and the revolution in Bombay manufacturing, the volume of imported Indian unbleached cloth alone was now 30 percent higher than the American export trade had been at its apex. East African consumers were also becoming essential to Bombay's other manufacturing sectors. They were now buying Indian carriages and carts, cabinet-ware, furniture, boots, shoes, stationary, rice, ghee, and even fresh vegetables.[106] While the Bombay export economy as a whole was still focused on un- or semi-manufactured exports like rice, opium, raw cotton, and thread, Bombay manufacturing for export received critical stimulus from East Africa. At the same time, convergent price curves meant a windfall for African consumers.

If we track the aggregate Bombay trade with Zanzibar up to the creation of the British protectorate in Zanzibar (1890), we can see that in just five years (1885–1890) the total value of Indian-produced exports to Zanzibar more than doubled. What is noteworthy about this statistic is the fact that although the total volume of the export trade of Bombay had not increased significantly, Zanzibar's share of that trade had increased dramatically. In 1890, Zanzibar imported almost thirteen million yards of unbleached cotton cloth—India's most important manufactured item—amounting to nearly *half* of the total unbleached cloth exported from Bombay.[107] By the date of the Sultan of Zanzibar's acquiescence to protectorate status, East Africa was importing 10 percent of the total of all Indian manufactured goods and produce exported from Bombay, which less than fifty years earlier had only accounted for 10–15 percent of Bombay's trade, but now accounted for the vast majority of the commercial hub's exports.[108] Zanzibar's share of India's trade would further increase in the 1890s and only plateau after the turn of the century.

Bombay had become the Indian Ocean's most important commercial and industrial center, and its success was related, in part, to East African demand for a constellation of consumer goods. On the eve of colonial imposition in Zanzibar, Bombay had not only overtaken its American and Kutchi competitors, but it had supplanted their manufactures by developing its own textile industry, one which likewise catered to the tastes of East Africans. As a result, unbleached cottons became the central focus of the Bombay export trade in manufactured goods. Between the 1860s and the early 1890s, Bombay had effected a radical economic change, drastically increasing its export and manufacturing capacities. When the British government appropriated Zanzibar in 1890, East African consumers were crucial to both the export trade in Bombay-manufactured goods and the external commerce of South Asia's commercial hub generally.[109] This new relationship was clear in East Africa as well. Imported cloth had become ubiquitous throughout the region, and wearing an abundance of cloth was by no means uncommon. For instance, when French-Sheldon visited Taveta (eastern Kenya) in the late 1880s, she wrote that the elders with whom she met wore up to fifteen yards of cloth at a time.[110]

Figure 5. Young women wearing dyed and printed Indian cloth, Zanzibar, ca. late 1890s. (Photograph from large album labeled "South Africa to Egypt via the East African Coast, Zanzibar and Aden." Courtesy of the Winterton Collection of East African Photographs, Melville J. Herskovits Library of African Studies, Northwestern University.)

It is difficult to assess the myriad, long-term ways in which East African consumers affected India's export economy, but the figures I have considered here, combined with Bombay's trajectory as the British empire's second city and most important colonial capital, suggest the significance of East African consumer demand to Indian industrialization and British Indian interests. When East African consumption of Bombay goods peaked at the turn of the twentieth century, Bombay was India's most important port for foreign trade. The mills were Bombay's primary industry and the city's largest employer. Textile production was the foundation of the city's prosperity and rapid economic growth. The industry shaped the nature of the regional labor market, along with patterns of rural-urban migration, and made Bombay one of Asia's most important manufacturing centers.[111] Under pressure from cheap English textiles— what Marx famously called the "heavy artillery" of capitalism—the Bombay export industry appealed to East African consumers. English

merchants flooded Indian markets with British cloth, and Indian merchants both remade this British cloth to meet African standards and cultivated a market for Bombay-manufactured textiles by replicating the
American varieties popular in the western Indian Ocean region. In choosing to buy immense amounts of Indian cloth, East African consumers in
turn stimulated Bombay's industrialization.

CONCLUSION

This chapter has sought to examine the complex relationships among
economies, cultures, and the global systems they affect by considering the
importance of East African consumer desires to the nineteenth-century
global economy. Significant international competition for East African
commodities—such as ivory and cloves—assured East Africans favorable terms of trade. As a result of this commercial position, East Africans
had great leverage in defining their relationships to other world regions.
American, Indian, and European producers learned that they had to
appeal to African tastes and often found no market for goods that did
not meet Africans' shifting aesthetic standards. Since fashions changed so
quickly in East Africa, overseas manufacturers could not always stay
abreast of fashion trends. Thus, many trade goods had to be refinished or
remade in Zanzibar, other coastal cities, at inland centers of trade, or
even on the caravan trail. Despite the complexities of East African trade,
manufacturers in America and India produced inexpensive cloth that
appealed to East African consumer interests. In the process, Salemites
built the first steam-powered textile mill in the United States, while western Indian financiers and manufacturers made Bombay the industrial
center of the Indian Ocean region. For two cities on opposite sides of the
world, manufacturing for the East African market offered new economic
opportunities and provided important stimuli to industrialization at
crucial moments in their histories. What we can discern from these
vignettes of transregional engagement is that negotiated transaction and
consumer desire on the part of people considered marginal to global systems have, at times, been just as important to patterns of global integration as "peripheral" adjustments to the demands of international capital
have been. More specifically, we can conclude that (1) the terms of trade
in the southwestern Indian Ocean were constantly being negotiated
before colonialism, and (2) that these terms were never wholly determined by the interests of Americans, Indians, or Europeans.[112] The direct
reciprocities evident in these exchanges were not a function of equity or

symmetry over the long term—Europeans colonized Africa after all—but they did entail a dialectic that reshaped extra-African locales at the same time that foreign interests, ideas, and strategies were transforming East Africa.

The global repercussions of East African consumerism also point up an epistemological concern that transcends the networks I outlined above. By not recognizing the kinds of histories of interdetermination evident in East Africa's global relationships, we indulge a mode of thinking that imagines the world as a conglomeration of historically disjointed spheres only brought into relation by the interests of Westerners. Such a divisive ideology, nurtured by the nineteenth-century imperial imagination, dispossesses "peripheries" of global historical relevance beyond production for a world market and obscures the ways in which societies have always constituted themselves in relation to others across the globe. It is my belief that interconnected pasts such as those outlined above have the potential to challenge modern fantasies of historical isolation and contest notions of discrete national or continental historical trajectories inherent in contemporary globalization rhetoric.[113] The archive of an interdependent past, of which the repercussions of East African consumerism are only a small part, offers myriad stories that complicate assumptions of hermetic pasts. A reconsideration of global interrelation from a multidimensional, historical perspective allows us to see contemporary globalization processes as overlaying and drawing on, as well as departing from, past moments of integration. Vignettes of relation like those offered above can resuscitate visions of globality that have fallen prey to a process of forgetting integral to imperial, colonial, and nationalist knowledge production.[114]

The global effects of East African consumer demand demonstrate that accounts of globalization that posit a singular historical trajectory are untenable. While we should not discount the constraints on choice faced by people around the world, the evidence I offered above suggests that seemingly marginal individuals have been able to affect larger frameworks. Thus, I believe that the frames of reference and strategies for self-definition that many people outside of the "core" employ in their everyday lives deserve greater attention in the development of an inclusive genealogy of globalization. By considering trajectories of global integration from the standpoint of "peripheral" interests, we can reinsert multicausality into narratives of globalization and thus offer perspectives on global relationships that do not assume the primacy of any unmitigated globalizing dynamic. The evidence I have offered here suggests that we can ascribe systemic changes not only to the interests of the "core" but also to consumer desires across the globe and myriad transactions as seemingly inconsequential as the purchase of a length of cloth.

Imported consumer goods were an important catalyst for East Africa's new economic relationships, and how East Africans gave meaning to things like imported cloth offers insight into how they perceived distant societies as well as their own place in the world. I suggested in chapter 1 that imported goods and symbols had translocal strategic utility: they could be used to shape foreigners' interpretations of, and relationships with, Mutsamuduans. In chapter 2 I suggested that Mombasans formulated socially important relationships with consumer goods because their use was an important aspect of local public and private self-presentation. With the preeminence of Zanzibar as the region's commercial hub from the 1840s through the imposition of a British Protectorate in 1890, consumer goods increasingly became essential means for staking claims to social position and challenging the boundaries of local social hierarchies. Just as important, the uses of consumer goods evidenced changing forms of corporate self-definition in Zanzibar. The next chapter addresses the question of how Zanzibaris used the consumer goods they imported and how, in the process of making them socially and politically relevant, Zanzibaris gave imported goods meanings that linked local social circumstances with shifts in consciousness that were affecting the entire planet.

CHAPTER 4

Cosmopolitanism and Cultural Domestication

Consumer Imports in Zanzibar

The dialectics of global integration and social change that produced the Western concept of modernity likewise gave rise to new social, cultural, and material realities in East Africa. Modernity, as a mode of perception, was ideologically forged at a moment when the world was becoming deeply interconnected. Yet nineteenth-century Western analysts tended to discredit other modes of self-perception, material relation, and economic change by theorizing modernity as a bounded temporal form dependent on exclusionary definitions of historical progression and essential difference. Through the tropes of progression and civilization, proponents of a quintessentially Western modernity denied "coevalness" in time and imagined global spatial distinctions as firm and immutable.[1] Concurrently, in Zanzibar, people refashioned their city out of diverse transcontinental materials. Though excluded from any Western definitions of modernity, change in Zanzibar was as radical as contemporaneous change in Europe. Reconsidering Zanzibar's nineteenth-century remaking offers an opportunity to revisit the relativism implicit in the idea of modernity. More important, changes in Zanzibar highlight new *cosmopolitanisms*—ways of seeing and acting beyond local environments— that affected Western modes of self-perception but were transforming the entire world in the nineteenth century. By focusing on the domestication of imported consumer goods in urban Zanzibar, this chapter excavates visions of globality that mirrored modernity in some ways, but simultaneously cultivated their own singularities that, like Western concepts of modernity, inflected the experience of intense global interconnectivity. In the sections below, I focus on the role of new consumer goods in the articulation of changing social relations and cosmopolitan visions from the 1840s to the apogee of Zanzibar's precolonial remaking in the 1880s.

MODERNITY AND ITS RELATIVES

For many nineteenth-century Westerners, the state of being modern entailed a self-conscious alteration of perceptions of time, space, and relation. Modernity was a redefinition of society theorized as the end of a long historical progression. Because of its comparative nature, Westerners defined modernity on a stage of global interaction through travel, new communication technologies, changing forms of production, consumption, and social as well as political identification. Edward Tylor, one of late nineteenth-century Britain's most celebrated anthropologists, attempted to explain what separated "civilised moderns" from the rest of the world by stressing the crucial role Western knowledge of the world played in the new consciousness. "Acquainted with events and their consequences far and wide over the world," he concluded, "we [moderns] are able to direct our own course with more confidence toward improvement."[2] Modernity was also theorized in dramatic contrast to what Westerners imagined as its opposite. In using the word *modern*, its negative, the *primitive*, was simultaneously defined.[3] Modernity was like the positive of an image. Though the negative is essential to the creation of the positive, it is at once implied and obscured in the positive's appearance. Thus, Western notions of the modern, civilized, and progressive were given meaning through implicit reference to the savage, uncivilized, and regressive.[4] From the eighteenth century, Westerners developed new characteristics of, to borrow Mary Louise Pratt's phrase, a "planetary consciousness" that would provide the foundation for the conceptualization of the modern. In effect, new Western subjectivities were formed in direct relation to confrontations with, and images of, others.[5] In the early nineteenth century, the idea of "the modern" was no longer simply temporal but had become comparative, cultural, and exclusive. Elite ideologues of Anglophone modernity categorized and then ranked populations against the standards of western European upper classes, basing assessments on populations' abilities, objects, and practices, summed up neatly by the words *virtues* and *vices*.[6] As taxonomies of humanity became more complex, physicality, materiality, and belief all came into use in the calculus of civilization.

Recent work has attempted to challenge these Victorian parameters of modernity by reconceptualizing the modern as no single form, but rather as a diversity of configurations called "alternative," "parallel," "vernacular," or simply "multiple" modernities. Such reconceptualizations of modernity stress heterogeneity in place of the West's singular historical narrative of generation and diffusion, recognizing that modernity was theorized in the West only through a diversity of global encounters.[7] This body of work has moved toward a non-isolationist and multicausal definition of the modern, and its scope and emphasis on the ramifications of global interconnectivity are invaluable, particularly as a critique of colonial discourse.[8] To think of modernity "at large" in terms of the relationships and nodes of interconnectivity that have affected new permutations in consciousness as well as their accompanying material forms disrupts the binary nature of received theories of global history. Moreover, these approaches offer an important challenge to the recent popularization of the "clash of civilizations" rhetorical dichotomization of the world by acknowledging the West's history of interdependence with other world regions.

Such redefinitions must, however, contend with the Manichean connotations that the idea of the modern still maintains. I share an interest in recognizing the importance of diverse localities in the material and conceptual histories of modernity, but the universal deployment and projection back in time of the term *modern* has the potential to further decontextualize the discursive creation and comparative connotations of the idea that provide its value-laden temporal and cultural comparative basis. In appropriating this term of difference and applying it to those it excluded, at least before people chose to use this term to refer to themselves, we run the risk of naturalizing the modern as a global phase of human history instead of a bundle of specific cultural and ideological forms ingrained in the practices of imperialism and colonization. The idea of "multiple modernities" risks affirming the cultural and temporal singularity Westerners saw as their biological virtue, posing other visions as divergence from *the* (Western) norm, and reifying the Victorian notion of time as progressing in an evolutionary order.[9] To echo Arif Dirlik's critique of the naturalization of capitalism in world-system, neoliberal, and postcolonial historiography, it seems the universalization of modernity has the potential to obscure the historical desires of those who did not share Western visions of globality by allowing only "multiple modernities," not divergent, though interconnected, strategies of global relation.[10] Finally, championing an infinity of modernities rewrites the global processes that produced Western modernity from the perspective of

Western self-perceptions rather than locating Western modernity within larger patterns of global change.[11] Though the West became in some ways the "centering axis" of an interconnected world, modernity itself was born of this increasing interdependence.[12]

Precolonial Zanzibar offers an illuminating example of the conceptual differences between parallel Western and Zanzibari cosmopolitanisms. Zanzibari self-perceptions were informed by engagements with other parts of the world, yet they did not entail an acceptance of the ideologies of the West, such as Western science, liberal democracy, and the notion of the past as an evolutionary course. Very few East Africans shared Western, bourgeois assumptions of historical progress and political culture, even though they incorporated a diversity of Western goods and technologies into their everyday lives. For instance, Zanzibaris incorporated European and American clocks into the cityscape, but did not regulate their day by the clock. Changes in Zanzibari material life, therefore, mirrored changes in the West, but Zanzibaris did not share the basic conceptual underpinnings of Western modernity. Only under colonialism would Zanzibaris adopt certain assumptions about political culture, social norms, and historical teleology drawn from the ideological canon of Western modernity. As opposed to an alternative modernity, Zanzibar's unique remaking was a form of cosmopolitanism typified by what Homi Bhabha, Carol Breckenridge, Dipesh Chakrabarty, and Sheldon Pollock summarize as the ability to see "the larger picture [of the world] stereoscopically with the smaller."[13] If cosmopolitanism implies an ability to think and act beyond the local, Zanzibari cosmopolitanism represented one way of incorporating the symbols of myriad places without importing the values of those places. Zanzibari bricolage grew out of impressions and firsthand experiences of the world through travel, trade, and access to information flows. Thus, Zanzibar's cosmopolitanism was a particular vision of the world that referenced transoceanic trends but made them relevant to the Zanzibari social environment, much as the notion of modernity did for Western analysts. Zanzibaris superficially reflected aspects of contemporaneous Western societies but engaged in a process of change that addressed the particularities of the western Indian Ocean region and its myriad social environments.

OBJECTS OF COSMOPOLITAN ZANZIBAR

In April of 1840, the Sultan of Zanzibar's bark, the *Sultana*, arrived in New York. It was the first vessel of either an African or Arabian state to travel to

America, and it carried the first Arab emissary to visit the United States. Yet, the *Sultana*'s diplomatic mission was secondary. The envoys did not visit Washington, D.C. Instead, the *Sultana* sailed to America's commercial center. Accordingly, the envoys doubled as traders, buyers of American consumer goods, and sellers of western Indian Ocean products. The crew was representative of Zanzibar's maritime culture, made up of enslaved Africans, Indian sailors from across the subcontinent, an Arab-Swahili diplomatic party, a Portuguese (probably Goan) cook, a Swahili captain, an English navigator, two French passengers, and two Englishwomen. The chief envoy, al Hajj Ahmad bin Na'aman bin Mushin bin Abdulla el Kaabi el Bahrani, secretary to Sultan Seyyid Said, boasted a career equally emblematic of the new Zanzibar. Born in the Persian Gulf, he took up residence in Zanzibar, made the hajj, and, in the service of Seyyid Said, traveled to Europe and America as well as to Cairo and Canton.

The *Sultana*'s voyage to New York was, much like later Zanzibari missions to England and France, an experiment. The sultan had always employed ships in the India trade. He even talked of sending vessels to Manila in order to procure cheap sugar.[14] But direct trade with the West had to this point largely been in the hands of Westerners. Seyyid Said attempted to change this. In the years that followed the *Sultana*'s voyage, Seyyid Said sent several vessels to London and Marseilles—one with a cargo totaling MT$100,000, or about twice the value of the average cargo leaving Zanzibar on a European vessel—and they returned with an assortment of consumer goods for local sale.[15] In New York, the sultan's agents purchased diverse American consumer goods and, in accordance with Zanzibar's 1833 commercial treaty with the United States, were given most-favored-nation treatment.[16] The *Sultana* arrived in New York laden with the western Indian Ocean's export mainstays: cloves, gum copal, coffee, ivory, dates, hides, and Persian carpets.[17] The return cargo included the following:

> 88,101 yards of American cloth, or *merekani*[18]
> 550 yards of red *joho* [broadcloth used for the making of overcoats, or *joho*]
> 2 boxes of red beads
> 4 barrels and one box of white beads; some additional blue beads
> 8004 large "china plates"
> 20 dozen boxes of gold leaf or leaf metal
> 300 muskets and powder

Such a manifest was typical of Zanzibar's import trade at mid-century and reflected the consumer tastes of a broad cross-section of East Afri-

cans: plates, gold leaf, and red broadcloth for ornamental and adornment purposes in Zanzibar, beads and American cloth for Zanzibari and
mainland consumption, and firearms and powder for sale across the
region. In addition to selling commodities on behalf of the sultan, Ahmad
bin Na'aman was commissioned to search out special consumer objects,
such as chandeliers, pineapple and orange syrup, confectionery almonds,
glass plates, watches, shotguns, lamps, and mirrors, for some of Zanzibar's wealthiest residents.[19] What is important about this manifest, and
the manifests of most ships which traded at Zanzibar, is that only a very
small proportion of the objects listed could be considered utilitarian. The
staples of the East African import trade, things like the countless varieties
of cloth, beads, brass wire, and home furnishings, were not the stuff of
everyday productive activities, as were hoes or rope. The goods that
made up the vast majority of East African imports were objects destined
for the social realm of display and public communication.

By the mid-nineteenth century, the East African economic system was
increasingly fueled by both foreign interests in East African products
and, just as importantly, diversifying East African consumer tastes. Over
the course of the century, the consumption of imported goods would
increase tenfold, and Zanzibari social relations would become dependent
on diverse commodities as important means of communication in the
public realm: a phenomenon commonly termed *consumerism*.[20] So important had certain consumer goods become to Zanzibari merchants and
consumers that dictums like, "It is always far more easy to dispose of a
cargo at Zanzibar than to procure one," appeared regularly in the correspondences of resident Western merchants.[21] Zanzibari consumerism was
a new engagement with global cultural flows, a deployment of global
symbols in the service of local image-making practices, or what Jean and
John Comaroff have summed up as the incorporation of diverse ways of
seeing and being without negating one's own.[22] This consumer culture
was also deeply interwoven with new perspectives on the world gained
through travel and the circulation of information. In the early part of the
nineteenth century, foreign vessels trading in Zanzibar usually hailed
from ports in the western Indian Ocean region, and to a lesser extent
from the United States, Marseilles, Hamburg, and Britain. By the 1860s,
vessels from all over the world visited Zanzibar. The American consul
wrote in the mid-1860s of not only Indian, Arab, American, French, and
Hanseatic vessels, but also Portuguese, Egyptian, Danish, Sardinian,
Hanoverian, Turkish, Italian, Spanish, and even Argentine merchant
ships in port.

Zanzibaris traveled as widely as their economic connections, and thus the new economy of East Africa directly affected the cultural landscape of Zanzibar. Take for instance the case of Rajab, a well-traveled, English-speaking Zanzibari featured in J. Ross Browne's popular account of Zanzibar in the early 1840s. His time in Zanzibar drawing to a close, Browne, an American sailor and travel writer, began searching for repre-sentational curiosities to take home. An acquaintance of his, Rajab, who had spent some time in New England employed as the groom of Arabian horses, agreed to conduct Browne through the city in search of the desired goods: shells and a spear.[23] After purchasing the shells, Rajab mentioned that a neighbor of his had a very handsome spear and, if Browne accompanied him home, he would try to get it. Browne found Rajab's house, though in the "dirtiest part of town," whitewashed and "neat." Written on the door were the words: "Rajab No. 1". On entering the front room, Browne was "quite struck with the neatness and taste with which it was furnished. A rich carpet, a polished table, and the usual number of chairs, looking-glasses, &c., which make up the furni-ture of a snug Western log-cabin." To Browne, these "evince[d] some-thing of the civilized notions which Rajab had acquired in Salem [Massachusetts]." Rajab entertained his guest with stories of his experi-ences in America, of steamships and locomotives, of Salem and the curiosities of Boston. Rajab compared the houses in Salem and Boston to those of Bombay and Zanzibar. He boasted that a certain Mr. Shepard even painted his portrait during his stay and gave it to him as a gift.[24] However, on Rajab's return to Zanzibar, his mother was enraged by the image and denounced the artist, according to Browne, as a dealer in "evil sciences," adding that Rajab could only regain "the lost flesh, and whatever of his soul he had lost with it, by destroying the painting." This she forced him to do, Browne wrote, "much to his mortification."[25]

Rajab's experiences and Browne's vignette are instructive on two accounts. First, Browne's description highlights the role of consumer goods—particularly Western manufactures—as important new cultural technologies in Zanzibar. Rajab's eagerness to tell of his experiences, demonstrate his taste in furnishings, and prove his command of English to his neighbors and guests represents a mode of domestication in which bold incorporations of foreign things were possible, and accretions of globality offered social leverage. The story also reveals the way in which, beginning in the 1840s, not only were Zanzibaris drawing more deeply on material culture from America, Europe, and India, but Western authors were becoming more keenly focused on consumer objects as criteria for typologizing Zanzibaris. Through the vehicles of imported and stylistically remade goods, Zanzibaris were creating a symbolic logic of culturedness that at times accorded with the sensibilities of foreign commentators. That Browne was enamored of Rajab's furnishings, even likened their configuration to American homes (if mockingly), suggests a Zanzibari familiarity with transcultural domestic signifiers. Yet, despite Rajab's communicative abilities, Browne's denouement, placed as it is immediately following a suggestion of Rajab's civility, privileges myths of African/"Oriental" aversion to change, a vein of analysis that would be canonized in later analyses of Zanzibaris as distinctly unmodern, prisoners of their static past. I return to this point in chapter 6.

Nonetheless, it would be wrong to assume that Rajab's mother's condemnation of the portrait was a rejection of symbols, goods, and technologies from abroad. In fact, not only was her house full of American objects, but soon after Browne's arrival, she appealed to him for medical assistance. Moreover, such apprehension about portraiture was becoming increasingly rare in Zanzibar by the time of Browne's residency. Though some Zanzibaris thought them un-Islamic, portraits were gaining popularity. Seyyid Said, his sons, and his ambassador, Ahmad bin Na'aman, all sat for portraits about the same time Rajab was forced to torch his likeness. Even photography was well known at mid-century. Immediately after Browne's departure, Charles Guillain, a French captain and Orientalist, took an extensive series of daguerreotypes of Zanzibaris that crossed status and gender lines and included many of Zanzibar's political elite.[26]

By the 1860s, paintings, printed illustrations, and photographs were all fashionable in Zanzibar. While in Zanzibar, the American travel writer Clelia Weeks visited a woman described simply as "Bibi Aisha" who showed her a full-length oil painting of Sultan Majid, and "drew forth from a recess several other portraits of former Sultans [probably relatives of the sultan, not his predecessors]." Bibi Aisha then took her to another room containing more pictures, including one of Ali Pasha and his wife from the *Illustrated London News,* portraits of Queen Victoria, Franz Joseph and his wife, "besides an oil-print just published of a girl in pink seated on a window-ledge kissing a love-bird."[27] Rebecca Wakefield wrote of her visit to Ali bin Suleiman's house, where she "inspected . . . albums; in which were some of the most splendid cartes I ever saw; chiefly of the sovereigns of Europe, and their families," as well as stereographs, piles of which were spread across the table.[28] Images, particularly of distant rulers and panoramic scenes, were by mid-century some of the most vivid examples of what Homi Bhabha termed "certain symbols of the elsewhere" that contributed to Zanzibar's new global consciousness.[29]

Pictures were thus one component of a larger symbolic system. They were only given importance and sign-value through their place in a standard assortment of domestic consumer objects. To take the reception room as an example, the creolized assortment of consumer goods found in a moderately wealthy Zanzibari's home at mid-century included Persian rugs; Chinese pillows; Indian, European, and American tables; American, Indian, European, and Chinese chairs; French mirrors; pictures; American and European clocks; and Asian as well as European porcelain.[30] Wakefield visited the home of an enslaved pilot only identified as "Bukhett," where she found his reception room full of a variety of familiar "ornaments," including vases, glassware, china, pictures, and mirrors.[31] Sayyida Salme, daughter of Sultan Seyyid Said and one of the only Zanzibaris of the time to write for Western audiences, described wealthy people's homes as having all the above accoutrements, adding that in wall recesses, "the choicest and most expensive objects of glass and china are symmetrically arranged. . . . A handsomely cut glass, a beautiful painted plate, an elegant jug may cost any price: if it only looks pretty, it is sure to be purchased." Between these recesses a family might place mirrors, "expressly ordered from Europe," reaching from floor to ceiling. Clocks, she continued, were particularly desirable items of interior decor, and "often the richest collection is found in one single house." These were juxtaposed with the mirrors, either placed in front of them so that the clocks were reproduced in the reflection, or on either side so that they highlighted the mirrors. Finally, according to Salme, the walls of men's rooms were decorated with "trophies": inlaid and expensive weaponry from Persia, Turkey, Arabia, Europe, and the United States.[32]

Objects acted in concert to signify the new urban culturedness of Zanzibar. Nineteenth-century descriptions of Zanzibar interior design evidence what cultural theorist Jean Baudrillard called the *object system* of consumer societies. By using the word *system*, Baudrillard suggested that individual objects do not function on their own but instead depend on a system that relates the larger meaning of the whole. In this logic, consumer objects can be incorporated as signs entirely divorced from the function intended by their manufacturers. Consumer choices need not respond to the demands of comfort or function as long as they address a social logic in which specific objects are desired for their abilities to contribute to a conglomerate social meaning.[33] While a porcelain vase by itself could have been interpreted in infinite ways depending on context, its placement with clocks, mirrors, and chairs in Zanzibari homes shaped it into a reflection of cultural refinement.[34] In Zanzibar, even the most seemingly functional object was at times valued for its sign qualities. Sayyida Salme described her father's enormous collection of European furniture as including sofas, chairs, tables, even a wardrobe, that served "more as show-pieces than for real use."[35] Elizabeth Jacob wrote of the European carved chairs and bedsteads in one of her host's reception rooms, but added that she was told these were never used.[36] The European (or Indo-European) chair even became a poetic metaphor for material luxury in nineteenth-century Swahili verse, a meaning quite divorced from the chair as an instrument of physical comfort.[37]

PLACE AND MOTION

As the examples of Rajab and "Bukhett" suggest, the new cultural-material codes of Zanzibari social relations were born of Zanzibari travel to, experience, and imagination of various global locales. Zanzibari consumerism was in constant dialogue with cultural trends in Muscat, Bombay, Paris, New York, and London. When Richard Waters, the American consul in Zanzibar, first moved into his residence, he was entirely unprepared for the attention the house received. He wrote that people were continually calling at the consulate out of curiosity to see it, "made up," as it was, "in an American fashion."[38] A few years later, Browne, along with several other American residents, was invited to the *shamba* [Swahili: "plantation, farm, or country estate"] of "Hadji Mouchad" to celebrate the anniversary of the Battle of Bunker Hill. When they were called to dinner they found a long table set in the middle of the room with a white cloth, knives, plates, and spoons all arranged, "as near in the American style as could have been expected from an Arab." After dinner came dessert and coffee, and Mouchad entertained the group with a narrative of his journey to Mecca. "When he . . . concluded," Browne wrote, "we had several patriotic sentiments in commemoration of the battle of Bunker's Hill."[39] Elizabeth Jacobs wrote of a similar experience. She was invited to the house of Bibi Suleiman, a relative of Sultan Majid's, who, after entertaining, brought in English coffee, "or what she called 'English' in great glee—that is, coffee with milk and sugar and also in English cups."[40] An American described the accomplished Captain Hassan bin Ibrahim's house as furnished with Windsor chairs, a table, a bureau, an American clock, and several English prints of rural scenes. But the visitor was particularly impressed when Hassan welcomed him into his receiving room with offers of brandy and wine.[41] Born in Muscat, Hassan had studied in Bombay and Calcutta, made several voyages to Canton, Mauritius, and between the Persian Gulf and East Africa, spoke English with "but little accent," and thoroughly understood Western codes of civility. Hassan had traveled the world, seen diverse elsewheres, and materially evoked these at home.[42] These anecdotes suggest two related trends: the phenomenon of culture constituted through travel and time-space compression—what James Clifford calls "traveling culture"—and place-specific cultural trends constituted in the collection of filtered and creolized global flows.[43] At times hardly differentiable, and always closely related, these trends were the products of activities by people of diverse social categories.

Though I have perhaps not made the point forcefully enough, traveling cultures affected and were affected by Zanzibaris of all socioeconomic positions, not simply captains or diplomatic envoys. For example, most Zanzibari travelers to Arabia, India, Europe, and within the East African region were not elites. Sailors, small-business owners, and slaves of all statuses constituted the vast majority of Zanzibar's travelers.[44] The English Consulate records of freed slave sailors and travelers reveals that hundreds of Zanzibari contract workers were traveling to Arabia, India, and elsewhere in any given year, and a sizable proportion of them were women.[45] Slaves, according to British Consul John Kirk, were, "sufficiently free to go [more precisely, to be sent] to India and return to Zanzibar."[46] Such people often relied heavily on their experiences abroad for the articulation of a desired public image in Zanzibar.

One such cosmopolitan—the leader of the Count Samuel Teleki expedition across what is now Kenya—was Qurrah Idris [called "Qualla" or "Dualla Idris" in contemporaneous literature], a Somali who by the age of twenty-four had spent time in America, been with the Stanley expedition in Central Africa for six years, traveled with Stanley in Europe, and spoke Swahili, Somali, Arabic, Hindi, and English.[47] J. Ross Browne wrote that many young Zanzibaris studied at European colleges and seminaries, and that these educational experiences were "a matter of pride," causing other Zanzibaris to consider them "persons of consequence."[48] Jacob Wainwright, a freed slave assistant to David Livingstone and convert to Christianity, traveled extensively in Eastern Africa, studied in England and Bombay, and was the first East African to publish a journal of his caravan experiences.[49] After returning to Zanzibar from his sojourn in England, he was hired by English missionaries on the mainland. Soon thereafter he was dismissed. According to the travel-writer Joseph Thomson, Wainwright was "in the habit of twitting his

European masters with the fact that they had never, like him, had the honour of being presented to her Majesty Queen Victoria."[50] In this case, Wainwright employed the British adulation of Queen Victoria to gain the respect of his employers. Wainwright's story reveals both the experience of Zanzibaris in a globalizing moment and the increasing permeability of status in Zanzibar. The life of Muhammad bin Khamis bears further testimony to this. Son of Khamisi wa Tini—who was described as "Swahili"—"he has certainly something to boast of," Browne wrote, juxtaposing a racial taxonomy with the actuality of ability, "for, although as black as the ace of spades . . . and of low descent, he got himself into notice by his own natural talent and his perseverance." Browne was "greatly amused" both to hear of Muhammad's travels, having, "on various occasions, dined with the queen [of England]," and by the "tone of familiar freedom with which he alluded to his friends Lord—, the Duke of—, Sir Thomas or Sir John—, &c."[51] While in England, Muhammad even approached the Royal Geographical Society with his own proposal for the exploration of the lakes region of Central Africa. Though he was certainly more qualified than Richard Burton, who would later lead such an expedition, the Society did not select Muhammad as a member of its exploratory parties. He was too incongruous with the developing Victorian image of the explorer.[52]

People like Muhammad bin Khamis were essential to the constitution of Zanzibar as a "traveling culture," and their ubiquity makes my second point—the role of people who did not travel in forging new cultural forms—more difficult to address. The vast majority of Zanzibar's residents had experienced significant dislocation. At mid-century more than half of Zanzibar City's population were slaves or freed slaves, and it is likely that most enslaved Zanzibaris were born on the African mainland. In addition to the enslaved population, Zanzibar absorbed immigrant groups from southern Arabia, India, the Comoros, and Madagascar. In fact, most residents of the city had experienced significant travel or dislocation. While not everyone in Zanzibar was mobile, the experiences of those who traveled affected those who did not. For example, an American in Zanzibar wrote of a young man who had learned English from his Zanzibari father.[53] Such instances of creolization in stasis abound, particularly when we move from the linguistic to the material realm. This suggests not a dissonance between two distinct cultural experiences, or travel versus stasis, but their inextricable relation.[54]

In the acceleration of interconnectivity fueled by travel, forced migration, trade, and a polyglot population, a dynamic nexus of creole con-

sumerism took shape in Zanzibar. Though it might be easy to relegate
Zanzibari interest in foreign objects to an obsession with other cultures,
such an analysis quickly arrives at an impasse, leading us to the conclusion drawn by most nineteenth-century analysts: Zanzibaris fetishized
manufactured goods.[55] A more lucrative analytical strategy is to think of
consumerism as, following Clifford, a way of localizing "symbols of the
elsewhere" for purposes of specific action. Desire and symbolic function
should not be separated here.[56] Wealth, master-slave relationships, and
gender relations functioned as social barriers, but Zanzibaris of all backgrounds found themselves on two common planes of interaction: (1) language, or the use of Swahili as a lingua franca,[57] and (2) consumerism, or
an emphasis on objects to communicate social ideas. Consumer goods
such as mirrors, watches, jewelry, porcelain, and clothes proved to be
communication devices as important as the spoken word. Consumerism
became a catalyst for sociocultural grounding, a strategy for representing
the self in the social and cultural diversity of Zanzibar's population. In
the transience of nineteenth-century Zanzibar, consumerism created a
relatively grounded mode of social communication. Freedmen, for
example, appropriated the *kanzu* (long shirt made of imported cloth) to
mark local affiliation and a transcendence of slavery. In doing so, they
laid claim to Zanzibar's creole cultural forms. Imported cloth, when fashioned into kanzus, was a vehicle for the relocation and grounding of
identity; it signified a cultural elsewhere distinct from freed slaves' home
societies and a social elsewhere beyond slavery.

Because of the rapid expansion of Zanzibar's economy in the early
nineteenth century and its political dominance by immigrant Busaidis,
"patina"—a mode of social relation anchored to notions of historical
distinction, such as existed in Lamu and Pate—was in many ways undermined by "fashion"—a mode of social relation relatively unbound from
sumptuary regulations and other historical restrictions.[58] The increasing
volume and diversity of consumer goods offered modes of self-expression
now largely unfettered by prerequisite genealogies or long histories of
residence in the coastal region, distinctions that had once been the basis
for sumptuary restrictions.[59] Any Zanzibaris could ostensibly wear any
cloth they purchased, even though price and availability restricted many
items to relatively small groups. The weakening of patina in Zanzibar
was the result of the Busaidi destabilization of older political and social
relationships. In Zanzibar City, Busaidi political power was established
not through violence against the local population, as it had been in
Mombasa and Lamu, but through the delegitimization of an older polit-

ical system represented by the Mwinyi Mkuu, the pre-Omani ruler of Zanzibar. Yet, in relegating the old political elite to the periphery of the commercial capital—and in the process successfully undermining older status symbols like the Mwinyi Mkuu's drums, horns, and other state regalia—the Busaidis were faced with the project of establishing new symbols of authority. Sultan Seyyid Said turned to new consumer technologies that drew deeply on contemporaneous global material culture.

In the early nineteenth century, Seyyid Said attempted to create status codes that signified both his own abilities and those of his administration. In the 1840s and 1850s, he concentrated on a variety of objects to demonstrate his authority. In addition to decorating his palaces with clocks, mirrors, and all variety of imported furniture, he also purchased an eleven-hundred-ton frigate manufactured at Bombay and christened it *King of the World (Shah Allum)*.[60] Liberalizing much of Zanzibar's trade and concentrating on foreign objects to represent his authority—which, in part, prompted him to send ships to America, Europe, India, and Mauritius to procure such goods—the sultan released new consumer goods from their prior sumptuary restrictions. With the rapid dissolution of sumptuary regulations historically common in Swahili city-states, the centrality of consumerism to new social relations became a hallmark of Zanzibar's cosmopolitanism. The movement of population, free-floating cultural materials of distant origin, and the opportunity for many to accumulate modest, if not significant, fortunes meant that forms of status presentation in the material realm were constantly open to challenge. Even a person of relatively meager means, like Rajab, could travel abroad and accumulate signs of distinction.

In this conjuncture, social signs rendered by consumer objects were unstable; they were being continually negotiated in the public realm and in relationship to their own abundance. A prominent example of this is the umbrella, once reserved for the very wealthy, which became fashionable among those of meager means in the 1870s. Likewise, the *kizibao*, or embroidered jacket of European broadcloth, once popular among free men of means, became one of the greatest investments for freedmen of lesser means.[61] For most Zanzibaris consumerism offered a technology that Nicholas Thomas has described as enabling people "to act in novel ways, and have novel relations imposed upon them."[62] But for the wealthy, fashion allowed for new extremes of material accumulation. One of Seyyid Said's sons, Khalid, indulged a predilection for everything French and assembled a collection of French objects that awed the visitor. His sister, Sayyida Salme, wrote of his plantation, *Marseille:*

Except in the rooms set apart for prayer, the walls were all covered with mirrors. . . . The floors of the rooms were paved with white and black marble slabs, the coolness of which cannot be estimated highly enough in the south. An artfully worked clock, from which upon the striking hours playing and dancing figures stepped out, round toilet-mirrors which reflected the forms in the most various distortions, large round quicksilver balls which can be seen here [in Germany, where she was writing her account] now and again in gardens, and other works of art made the palace *Marseille* into a real museum for the simple people who had been introduced only a little to civilization, especially for our relatives from Omân.[63]

This extreme of cultural domestication, the creation of a museum of European curiosities, serves as a stark example of some elites' desire for association with specific symbols of elsewhere.

The apogee of fashion in Zanzibar also put pressure on elites to seek out new symbols of distinction. As freed slaves and the plebeian population claimed forms of culturedness consistent with those of the wealthy, elites pursued new strategies for material definition. What I am suggesting here is something rather more complicated than the poor's aspiration to status, their appropriation of the symbols of the rich. What is equally important systemically is the wealthy's social desire to distinguish themselves from others as a group, a phenomenon that sometimes led to ludicrous extremes.[64] This desire could address two intersecting goals: distinction from other wealthy people, or a desire to "outdo" one's peers, and identification with a social group by publicly distinguishing oneself from people not in that group. Such acts of distinction were particularly evident in apparel, but they also went beyond mere material signifiers. For example, around mid-century, freed slaves appropriated the term *uungwana* for themselves, though it had previously denoted historical prestige, an elite genealogy, and wealth. In response, by the end of the century the elite had championed a new word for themselves, a term that took on the nuances that *uungwana* had now lost: *ustaarabu*, or "culturedness" (lit. "Arabness"; see chapter 5).

For the enslaved and poor of Zanzibari society, fashion could be both a useful and an oppressive tool. It became horribly oppressive to some, since without resources a system of fashion could entirely foreclose social aspiration. With such a great premium on the symbolic qualities of clothing, the lack of resources to purchase certain kinds of dress consigned one to a kind of social alienation, acutely felt but unassailable without financial resources. For much of the population, though, consumerism proved a useful mode of articulating social aspiration. Thus, while slave-

Figure 6. Young woman wearing printed Indian cloth
(*kanga*), Zanzibar, ca. 1900. This woman's cicatriza-
tions suggest she was born on the mainland and so
was likely brought to Zanzibar as a slave. (Photograph
by Gomes & Co. Courtesy of the Winterton Collection
of East African Photographs, Melville J. Herskovits
Library of African Studies, Northwestern University.)

owners attempted to remake slaves by giving them clothes after purchase, one of the primary aspirations of the enslaved was to reclothe
themselves and thereby lay claim to a new social citizenship.[65] For slaves
and poor free people of mainland birth, the acquisition of kanzus, fezes,
and canes for men, and *ukaya* (muslin head covering), *kisutu* (English
square cloth dyed in Bombay), and *leso* (large, colorful cotton handkerchiefs made in Manchester and sewn together in Zanzibar) for women

became signs of an ability to ground oneself in the material relations of urban Zanzibar. Jewelry was so essential to appearances in Zanzibar that, according to Sayyida Salme, even beggar-women were found in the streets "decked out" in various ornaments.[66] Thus, very similar to fashion among the wealthy, the consumption of "Swahili" clothes by the poor at once symbolized integration into a stratum of Zanzibari society and attempted distinction from others. It is this dual movement of claiming similarity to some and simultaneous difference from others that typified the fashion strategies of Zanzibaris of all socioeconomic categories.[67]

The consumer objects that individual Zanzibaris used to define themselves came to define Zanzibar as a whole. One object employed to represent the self that came into such common usage across socioeconomic lines that it became iconic of Zanzibar was the mirror. Zanzibar was the primary emporium for the whole of East Africa, and thus the majority of consumer goods that landed at Zanzibar found their way to the mainland. Most mirrors, however, did not. Indicative of a longer trend, statistics on Zanzibari imports for 1861–62 show that 80 percent of the mirrors imported to Zanzibar stayed on the island, probably in the city itself.[68] Mirrors are unique consumer goods because they give their owners the opportunity to optically reproduce themselves and their surroundings. Clocks placed between opposing mirrors, as Sayyida Salme described, created an infinity of clocks within a circumscribed space. Mirrors, particularly ones spanning the height of the room, but also the smaller looking glasses that lined the walls of the less wealthy, afforded self-indulgence, an opportunity to reproduce one's own image and that of one's possessions.[69] Burton wrote that mirrors were cheap and abundant in late 1850s Zanzibar. One could find "looking glasses" in the market, and these as well as most goods could be obtained, according to an American resident, as cheap if not cheaper than in America or Europe.[70] After the return of one of the sultan's ships from a trading venture, the prices could be driven down even further. For those who could afford larger mirrors, or a greater profusion of them, they became the foundation of interior design. In Custom Master Jairam Sewji's house, mirrors "without number," as one visitor put it, hung on the walls.[71] The value of mirrors was further heightened by the belief that they could project images of their owners even long after their death. The *koma* (Swahili: "soul of a deceased person") of the last Mwinyi Mkuu, for example, remained in his house and was seen reflected in the large mirrors of his reception hall.[72]

Like the Mwinyi Mkuu and Seyyid Said, Sultan Barghash bin Said used massive mirrors to reflect his image. In this way, mirrors became a statement of doubled individual and governmental power. Seated at the upper end of his receiving room, Barghash placed one large mirror directly behind him and hung on either side of it identical, full-length oil paintings of himself.[73] The profusion of mirrors reflected the sultan, his twin paintings, clocks and telescopes, crystal candelabras, gilt chairs and crimson seats, and, as the traveler Harry Johnston remarked, "our persons on every side."[74] In this hall of mirrors Barghash imposed images of himself on others in infinite repetition, even when he was not physically present. It was a sign of the new Zanzibari cultural ideology that, where Barghash's father, Seyyid Said, had once flanked his chair with paintings of sailing ships symbolic of the global integration that he had helped to facilitate in Zanzibar, Barghash now hung portraits of himself next to mirrors that reflected him, his visitors, slaves, and courtiers ad infinitum.[75]

BARGHASH AND THE COSMOPOLITAN IMAGE

Sultan Barghash's reign (1870–88) marked the height of Zanzibar's prosperity and regional economic importance. It also saw the broad diffusion of a recognizable Zanzibari aesthetic across the coastal region and a greater imposition of the state on the daily lives of its subjects.[76] Barghash undertook a variety of social, civic, and commercial projects that included the installation of public clocks, a free public water system, electric lighting, a mint, the institution of a steamship line between Zanzibar and other Indian Ocean ports, the publication of treatises on Ibadhi law,[77] the cultivation of new musical styles, and investment in Zanzibar's transportation infrastructure.[78] Decades before construction began on the Mombasa-Kampala railway, Barghash offered MT$500,000 to any company willing to construct a railroad from the Great Lakes to the coast.[79] With the sole exception of the railroad, Barghash accomplished all of this with his own resources and of his own accord. The aggressiveness with which Barghash pursued these ends radically altered Zanzibar. What is more, this all happened very fast. All of his major projects were completed between the late 1870s and the mid-1880s.[80] On his return to Zanzibar after an eight-year absence, Henry Morton Stanley was surprised to find a telegraph station, a new palace, clock towers, carriages, steamrollers, and streetlights.[81] Barghash both imagined a new role for Zanzibar's government in local social services and encouraged the establishment of a new urban aesthetic. Perhaps more vigorously than before, during Barghash's reign Zanzibaris consciously remade the city in relation

Figure 7. Portrait of Sultan Barghash bin Said taken
at Maull & Co., London, during his 1875 European
tour. (Photograph courtesy of the Winterton Collection
of East African Photographs, Melville J. Herskovits
Library of African Studies, Northwestern University.)

to diverse materials and changing imaginations of Europe, India, and the
wider world.

Unlike his brothers, Barghash lived for an extended time outside of the
Zanzibar-Muscat nexus before coming to power. After a failed coup in
1860, he was sent into exile in Bombay. His experiences in India deeply
affected his worldview and, if the British consuls in Zanzibar are to be

believed, his general disposition.[82] At the very least, he returned with a different strategy for dealing with Westerners. Whereas Barghash previously had been hostile to European influence, he was now willing to accept British consular advice, though he did not follow the consuls blindly.[83] Barghash's exile and subsequent visits to Bombay deeply influenced his ideas about civic services as well. Street lighting, an expanded police force, and even a light tram system were projects culled from his observations in Bombay. Almost immediately after his assumption of the sultancy, Barghash embarked on a concerted project of architectural innovation. One of his rural residences, Chukwani, built in the 1870s and connected to the city by tram, showed particular British Indian influence in its wide verandah, massive columns, French doors, ornate overhangs, and bulbous colored glass lamps. Maruhubi palace, built a few years later, evidenced British Indian accents overlaying an Omani-style structure with a perimeter wall inspired by park walls he had seen in Britain.[84] Moreover, in the 1880s all of his country homes were fitted with telephones.

Barghash constructed a tower at the seafront that evidenced his aspirations for Zanzibar, as well as the wealth and commanding position the city now held in the region. Also Indian in inspiration, the structure was monumental. With eight terraced stories capped by a glass pyramid reminiscent of London's Crystal Palace, it towered over the city, fixing the attention of new arrivals. Fitted with electric lighting, it also functioned as a lighthouse. Even more symbolically, Barghash placed four massive clocks in the tower facing the city and harbor. The institution of state clocks complete with bells was a significant extension of the private amassing of clocks and watches that had begun in the 1830s. Assortments of wall-clocks were by this time a common feature in Zanzibari homes and mosques, and several large clocks had been installed in the steeple of the Anglican cathedral—gifts from Barghash to the church. But as signs of the state, the massive clocks set into the harbor tower were functionally unique. Whether or not people actually regulated their days by their measurements, the sultan's clocks on the waterfront made the timepiece a central material reference of the state and a public icon.

This domestication of the clock was not a conspicuous Europeanization of time, as the proliferation of public clocks on courthouses and in roundabouts would become in colonial capitals. Instead, the tower clocks reflected a self-conscious aesthetic that drew on symbols that were now fully domesticated. Therefore, the sultan's clock punctuated a longer iconographic history of the clock in the city as well as the state's desire to

Figure 8. Zanzibar seafront, ca. 1880, showing the clock tower, the Sultan's palace (center), a public water cistern in the shape of a ship's hull, and street-lights. Also note the umbrella and the clock, which is set to Zanzibari time, that is, 5:50, or 11:50 A.M. (Photograph courtesy of the Winterton Collection of East African Photographs, Melville J. Herskovits Library of African Studies, Northwestern University.)

use it as a symbol. Soon after the tower's completion, Barghash ordered a clock from Germany that contained a mechanized soldier that would step forward, salute the sultan, and return to his abode at the top of every hour.[85] Most telling of Zanzibar's particular domestication of global objects was the fact that the clocks were not set to European time, or a twenty-four hour day beginning at midnight. Instead, the clocks were set to Zanzibari time: the day began with sunrise at one o'clock, or roughly seven A.M. in European time, and the clocks were readjusted every ten days to account for the changing length of the day.[86] Barghash did not Europeanize time in Zanzibar; rather, he adapted the European timepiece to Zanzibari perceptions of time.

Barghash's most impressive creolization of global symbols was the richly iconic Beit al Ajaib, "House of Wonders," completed around 1883. The construction alone was unlike anything undertaken in nineteenth-century East Africa. Its outward appearance was, again, British Indian in inspiration: wide four-sided verandahs, French doors accented by low-

Figure 9. Clock tower and "House of Wonders" (Beit al Ajaib), with fort in foreground, ca. 1880. Note the pyramidal glass on both the tower and the House of Wonders. (Photograph courtesy of the Winterton Collection of East African Photographs, Melville J. Herskovits Library of African Studies, Northwestern University.)

hanging lamps, richly-worked wooden overhangs, a gleaming white finish, and massive carved doors of western Indian design embellished with a pair of lions on the half-circle lintel, at times buttressed by actual lions in nearby cages.[87] Moreover, the external galleries of the Beit al Ajaib were supported by roughly one hundred and forty cast-iron pillars. Considered with other architectural and design innovations of the central city, the Beit al Ajaib, "a babble of [architectural] tongues," signified what Steve Battle has called a "new self-consciousness" about the city's form and a self-consciousness about Zanzibar's relation to the rest of the world.[88] Unlike other buildings of state in Zanzibar, including large storage facilities, the customs house, and accommodations for family members, slaves, and visitors, the Beit al Ajaib was a symbolic space, as evidenced by its narrow rooms but cavernous central auditorium. The auditorium, reaching up three stories from the floor to roof, was covered, unlike the courtyards of many Zanzibari houses, thus allowing free use of the space in any weather. Adding to its versatility, Barghash installed electric lighting in 1886.

Barghash laid the floors of the Beit al Ajaib with the same French black and white marble that had come into common use by wealthy Zanzibaris and filled the building with large chandeliers. The reception room, according to Harry Johnston, was "of Arab shape [rectangular] but later French decoration." It boasted "fine" Persian carpets, red velvet and gilt wood furniture, kitchen clocks, ormolu timepieces, aneroid barometers, thermometers, anemometers, telescopes, opera-glasses, music-boxes, swords, spears, rifles, pistols, toys "of ingenious kinds," photographic albums, portraits of world personalities, and sets of photographs of sites around the world.[89]

Johnston's account of the Beit al Ajaib suggests an aesthetic similar to the Crystal Palace, or London's Hall of the Great Exhibition. Barghash had visited the Great Exhibition in 1875, so it was no coincidence that he similarly arranged an endless variety of objects in his House of Wonders. The Beit al Ajaib was, like the Crystal Palace, ornamented with objects of manufacture representing new technologies, especially tools used for measurement and surveillance.[90] The House of Wonders contained objects of display different from those in Seyyid Said's more simply furnished palaces. But, like his father's residences, Barghash's House of Wonders domesticated new global objects in the service of the state. The House of Wonders was, in effect, a museum of the contemporary world, designed to equate the power of new consumer objects with the person of the monarch and to awe anyone who visited it.

Inspired by the Beit al Ajaib, Tharia Topan, an influential Ismaili businessman, customs master, and member of the sultan's cabinet, announced in 1887 his intent to construct the city's first public hospital. It would honor Queen Victoria's Golden Jubilee and for it, as well as for other services to the crown, he would be knighted.[91] Built just north of the palace complex, the hospital, when paired with the House of Wonders, evidences the materialization of what has been termed the *zeitgeist* of the Barghash court: opulence, display, and a new aesthetic sensibility.[92] Just as the Beit al Ajaib was no house, the hospital was not designed simply to attend to the infirm. Battle's architectural analysis suggests that it was a palace in its own right. The entire structure, inside and out, was replete with intricate carvings and moldings. Its balconies were the most richly worked in the city, and in the patients' wards the balconies featured decorated panels glazed with multicolored glass. A dining room on the second floor was fitted with a chandelier.[93] The building was a structural creole, combining diverse Zanzibari standards like the courtyard, balcony, and the *wikio*, or bridges across the interior of the structure. Its walls were made of coral in a fashion like almost all contemporaneous

Figure 10. The Tharia Topan Jubilee Hospital (left), ca. 1890. Note that the façade is under construction. (Winterton Collection, Northwestern University.)

structures on the East African coast, but they featured moldings of a European neoclassical style.[94] The hospital was a monument to both the cultural aesthetic of Topan and the localization of British Indian design as much as it was to the public good.

As in the contemporaneous houses of Muscat's commercial elite, Indian aesthetics in the built environment were everywhere evident in Barghash's Zanzibar. The increase in Indian immigration to the island and the accumulation of wealth by many Indian merchants during Zanzibar's commercial apogee spurred investment in the embellishment of older Zanzibari houses as well as the building of entirely new structures. Embellishment took the form of richly worked wooden balconies and other carved accents over the earlier, Omani-East African coastal architecture. Doors of Indian design, sometimes even of Indian manufacture, were also common, recognizable by a rounded lintel intricately carved or, in the case of Gujarati styles, vertical and horizontal raised crossbeams. But just as Indian merchants were adding Bombay-inspired accents to Omani-Swahili creole structures, non-Indians were borrowing, as Barghash did, from the aesthetic vocabularies of Bombay, Gujarat, and Kutch.[95] Tippu Tip, the famous Zanzibari trader who carved out a niche of political power for himself in Central Africa, installed an enormous Indian-inspired door on his house. The architecture of religion now also included an Anglican Cathedral and distinctly Indian-inspired structures, including Hindu temples (earlier banned in Zanzibar and Mombasa) as well as Khoja and Bohra mosques.

Barghash was a man infinitely curious about the world and even keener than his predecessors to collect pieces of diverse elsewheres. Like his father, he sent steamships on missions to England, Hamburg, Bombay, Muscat, Mauritius, and Jiddah. He regularly read Egyptian newspapers and informed the British consul at Zanzibar that there were Egyptian soldiers coming to "relieve" David Livingstone long before the consul had received the news through official channels.[96] Barghash was also entirely cognizant of European representations of him. Johnston wrote that if Barghash was mentioned in the *Times* (London), his confidant Pera Dewji would bring him a copy of the article, circled in red chalk, for his perusal.[97] He was particularly curious about the European residents of Zanzibar, perhaps out of suspicion, perhaps because they were exceptionally exotic. With Dewji's assistance, Barghash collected information on all new European arrivals to the city. Barghash's "great pleasure," as Joseph Thomson explained, was "watching the ways of the foreigners from his palace window." Such "social investigations," Thomson wrote, were carried out with a powerful telescope. In this way, the sultan had become "acquainted with facts not intended for his eye. He has more than once revealed knowledge of a kind and extent," Thomson continued, "which has rather unpleasantly taken some Europeans by surprise."[98] During his trip to Europe in 1875, Barghash likewise surprised his hosts with his recognition of many British political figures, such as Benjamin Disraeli and William Gladstone, whom he had never met. According to the *Standard* (London), it seems that among the many photo albums in Barghash's possession were several containing the portraits of important political figures, which he studied before his official engagements.[99]

His telescopic adventures, when combined with his travels and keen interest in European affairs, gave Barghash greater insight into the West than most Western residents possessed of East Africa. This is an important point because it reveals something of his cosmopolitan vision. Through his own travels and diverse means of assembling information about Westerners, Barghash certainly could have been inspired to embark on programs of state-sponsored social reform, the institution of a broader tax system, and any variety of post-Enlightenment projects common to the industrial European metropoles. He did not pursue these Western courses. His projects suggest that he wished to shape a vision of global integration that was in dialectic with the West, as well as

South Asia and the Middle East, but did not follow these in any formulaic way. Instead of instituting a policy of Westernization, Barghash invested in select services, such as the supply of drinking water, new roads, streetlights, waste disposal, and free passage to those making the hajj. Moreover, he invested little in mechanisms of direct social control, the expanded police force notwithstanding. He put most of his resources into (1) services broadly beneficial to Zanzibaris, and (2) the cultural-symbolic: a House of Wonders, electricity, public clocks, publications, and music. In short, his reformation was focused on basic public services and image. His cosmopolitanism did not aspire to replicate Western mores, but instead borrowed from the West (and elsewhere) to service his interests.

Barghash invested much in his state's public image. For example, his new military—which never saw an engagement—dressed in stark white and red European uniforms. Edward Ropes Jr., an American resident of Zanzibar, wrote that two members of the guard dressed "in the most gorgeous uniforms I ever saw."[100] The force was founded in 1877, given trousers, jackets, and Zanzibar's signature fez.[101] The sultan put his military on parade under the direction of a Briton, Lloyd Mathews. They marched to the music of a brass band every Friday in front of the palace compound. The band was rather large, totaling thirty-five pieces, made up of mostly Goan musicians under the direction of a German conductor.[102] Barghash composed his own anthem, usually called "God Save the Sultan" by Westerners, who described it as sounding "Egyptian," and instructed the band to honor all visitors with their own national anthems. By 1882, Barghash was giving concerts every Wednesday evening.[103] For the occasion, he would set up chairs in the palace square where those who wished might, according to an English visitor, "listen to wonderfully well played operatic selections."[104] Barghash also mixed Arabic and European musics. When he entertained American visitors in 1884, he alternated between a band playing European operas and another performing "Arab airs."[105]

Though many of the changes to the Zanzibari cityscape were monumental, the most dramatic symbol of Barghash's Zanzibar was an object that, by the 1880s, had become accessible to most Zanzibaris: the umbrella. As Jonathon Glassman and others have shown, on the nineteenth-century Swahili Coast umbrellas were particular symbols of the state and patrician identity.[106] In early nineteenth-century Zanzibar, umbrellas of British, Indian, Chinese, and American manufacture were common accoutrements of Asian businessmen. Wealthy women likewise

Figure 11. Young women wearing different kanga
styles, one with a parasol, Zanzibar, ca. 1906.
(Photograph possibly by A. C. Gomes or Coutinho.
Courtesy of the Winterton Collection of East African
Photographs, Melville J. Herskovits Library of African
Studies, Northwestern University.)

carried them, but their use in Zanzibar seems to have been largely limited
to these groups.[107] By the 1870s and 1880s, umbrellas had been thoroughly appropriated by Zanzibaris of diverse backgrounds. Their ubiquity in Zanzibar evidences both the new consumerism and the greater
democratization of some objects. Like mirrors, the vast majority of
umbrellas imported into Zanzibar were purchased by Zanzibaris. As evidence of this great desire, between 1878 and 1882, Bombay exports of
umbrellas to Zanzibar doubled, totaling nearly twenty-seven thousand a
year.[108] Zanzibar, in fact, became the single largest market for umbrellas

exported from Bombay. Umbrellas may have possessed some of the same sign values in New York, Bombay, Paris, and Zanzibar, but in Barghash's capital their use was not restricted to a specific class or group as it was in the West. There were myriad other goods, like carriages, silk cloth, and clocks, that underscored the material and social distance between the rich and poor. Yet, marginal groups, including slaves, defied earlier conventions in Zanzibar by carrying umbrellas. In the process umbrellas became associated with Zanzibari society broadly. Through their appropriation, umbrellas were no longer simply elite objects, but common symbols of cosmopolitan Zanzibar.

CONCLUSION

As a mode of social relation in nineteenth-century Zanzibar, consumerism articulated new senses of self that were inextricable from global dialogues. Conglomerations of clothes and interior decorations reflecting transregional aesthetic trends created a cultural code in Zanzibar that was greater than the sum of its parts.[109] This code reflected a way of being in the world that was not only cognizant of larger trends but made them relevant to the Zanzibari social environment. Much like Zanzibari sojourns in New York, Marseilles, Hamburg, and Bombay, the changing global visions of Zanzibaris challenged the uniqueness of Westerners' familiarity with events and their consequences all over the world by far "exceeding the terms" (to borrow Timothy Mitchell's phrase) of Westerner's projections of East African primitiveness.[110]

If we wish to dismantle the concepts of progress and development so critical to Western definitions of essential difference, we should be wary of the self-assured terms born of nineteenth-century high imperialism. The notion of the modern, at least when projected onto people who did not claim it, is still accompanied by the specter of imperial taxonomy and still discounts the possibilities and divergent visions that coexisted in moments of heightened interconnectivity.[111] Thus, in our efforts to recover the modern for postcolonial ends, we should be vigilant not to gloss over the deep cultural and temporal implications of the modern, lest we forget the modernizing impulse to liberate others from their traditions: practices that were often adaptations to a changing world. In looking out at the world in the nineteenth century, many Westerners saw aspects of their societies mirrored abroad, but they erred in translating these proximates as failed replications of the West. If anything should come of the recognition of the complex cultural domestications and global itineraries of Zanzibaris, it should be that they at least trouble the self-perception of moderns as having unique acquaintance with events and their consequences around the world. Zanzibaris were, as much as Westerners, engaged in processes of self-definition and contests over the terms of global integration in an age of profound interconnectivity.[112]

Though the ideological precepts of Western modernity would not shape Zanzibari self-images until the colonial era, Zanzibaris were engaged in social contests that were at once very local and at the same time embedded in translocal networks and debates. More than any other topic, slavery would bring debates at the local and transregional levels into direct tension. As Zanzibaris bought more enslaved people and used them, much like objects, to represent their visions of ideal social relation, the people they purchased sought ways of defining themselves beyond the objectification of their owners. And as many Westerners came to see slavery as antithetical to their visions of the future, the issue of slavery in East Africa became a transcontinental social and moral contest. As we will see in the next chapter, large- and small-scale debates over the future of one of Zanzibar's most valuable imports—enslaved people—became a near obsession for many in Britain and so would become a critical pillar in the discourse of imperial intervention in East Africa.

Colonialism would substantially alter the terms of integration that Zanzibaris negotiated between the 1860s and 1880s. Under colonial rule Zanzibari temporal, social, and political imaginations would reflect notions of the modern, in no small part because the basic conceptual apparatuses brought to bear on everyday choices were increasingly dictated (through schools, courts, and political culture) by Western worldviews.[113] In the late nineteenth and early twentieth centuries, Zanzibaris merged Western political and cultural concepts with the domestications and contests of the precolonial era. Thus, like the image of the late Mwinyi Mkuu in the mirrors of his former palace, the residues of nineteenth-century creolization were often reflected in colonial Zanzibari cosmopolitanisms that continually referenced and reinterpreted Zanzibar's historical relationship to the rest of the world.

CHAPTER 5

Symbolic Subjection and Social Rebirth

Objectification in Urban Zanzibar

People have been used in ways similar to objects. In the second half of the nineteenth century, slavery—a form of subjection in East Africa fixed by negations of self-definition and rooted in forced social dependency[1]—was both a common facet of Zanzibari life and one of the greatest concerns of British imperial policy in the region. Zanzibari slaves were bought and sold like commodities. Just as important, slaves, like commodities, were socially valuable to owners and even anti–slave trade activists for their ability to represent the interests of those who sought to control them. Though at political odds, both slave-owners and anti-slave trade crusaders used slaves for their symbolic social capital and attempted to limit slaves' capacity for self-making.

This chapter examines the confluence of slavery, social relations, and imperialism. It is tempered by a focus on multiple and intersecting processes of rhetorical subjection on the one hand and slaves' own corporeal refashioning on the other. I address (1) how some slaves in late nineteenth-century Zanzibar City were used in ways akin to objects of display, and (2) slaves' strategies for projecting desirable images of themselves within the circumscribed spaces of subjection. My focus is therefore narrow, on urban slaves and their symbolic uses as well as their rhetorical value to slave-owners and antislavery activists. The making of symbols out of people—a process that I call *symbolic subjection*—was essential to Zanzibari social life, and the notion of slaves as nothing more than blank slates onto which the interests of others could be written was a constant thread in British humanitarian discourse concerned with East Africa. It is no surprise that urban slaves, through myriad everyday choices, sought to undermine the representational power of their owners' social domination. Slaves attempted to dress and name themselves, gain economic autonomy from their owners, even own their own slaves, and thereby claim a social identity distinct from that forced on them by their enslavers. Yet the long-term efforts of slaves to redefine themselves and their relation to their owners were complicated by the deployment of a British antislavery ideology that not only infantilized slaves but also explicitly accepted the slave-owner rhetoric of slaves' incapacity for self-definition. For slave-owners and redeemers alike, slaves were screens onto which concepts of civilization were projected. The legacies of this perception were particularly evident in the discourse of colonial intervention in East Africa, where the civilizing mission of the proponents of colonization presumed a childlike East Africa exploited by inept Arab rulers and thus in desperate need of benevolent protection and tutelage.

SYMBOLIC BIRTHS

At the height of the nineteenth-century economic boom, people became the single most valued commodity in the city of Zanzibar. As much as Zanzibaris valued imported manufactures, they wanted imported people more. The increasing demand for and affordability of slaves in Zanzibar in the second half of the nineteenth century changed the social configurations of urban life.[2] By the 1850s, the majority of Zanzibar's population was enslaved or recently freed, and most were probably of mainland birth. Out of a sample of more than three thousand slaves owned by British Indian subjects and emancipated in 1860, 93 percent had been forcibly brought to the island.[3] Most of Zanzibar's enslaved population had experienced capture, pawnage, sale, travel, resale, and a radical social remaking. It was a population that had been painfully subjugated. Slave trading and slave marketing were processes of desocialization and commodification that allowed a slave-purchaser to approach the enslaved in much the same way as he would any other consumer object— with the desire to employ the purchase to further his own social interests. So closely were the symbolic uses of slaves and consumer goods aligned in slave-owning ideologies that Zanzibaris differentiated between slaves and objects with the simple distinction of those "things" that could speak (slaves) versus those that could not (inanimate objects).[4]

In the city of Zanzibar, "raw" slaves were sometimes less desired for their abilities than for the perceived blankness onto which owners might project images of themselves through naming, dressing, and ornamenting. For slave-owners who would not be dependent on their slaves' labor, aesthetics and health counted more than any skill. Slaves who were not destined for the fields or rigorous manual labor were evaluated in relation to the possibilities of what a prospective owner could say of him- or herself through the slave.[5] The value of domestic slaves lay, in part, in their capacity to represent their owners, to draw attention to and accumulate social capital for an owner, as well as to perform their owner's will. It follows that the most physically attractive slaves, girls in particular, were the most expensive and in great demand. And this demand for Ethiopian, Eastern European, or East African concubines as objects of display and sexual gratification was bound to a culturally relative aesthetic and social value that was independent of a woman's abilities. It is the fictive process of creating a person without self-interests—what Suzanne Miers and Igor Kopytoff call a "non-person"—for the use of another that I consider first.[6]

Zanzibari slave-owners cultivated a simple myth about enslavement on the East African mainland that sought to justify slavery in Zanzibar. The American Consul William S. Speer heard the myth so regularly that, though doubting it at first, he came to believe it. "In Africa," he was told, "niggers are poor—grass dies—he has nothing to eat—man sells his son, or wife, or daughter, for food. A trader gives rice, clothing (cottons) to their father or husband for his wife or children. The trader claims the slaves—puts iron round their necks—puts them on his dow [sic., sailing vessel]—lands them at the Customs House—thence to the auction."[7] In contrast to this simple myth, slaves' journeys to Zanzibar were violent and complex processes that entailed separation from kin, multiple sales, circuitous travel, and experiences in diverse societies. A great number of slave narratives provide evidence of this.[8] One of the more complex narratives from mid-century was given by Bahr-Zain, the slave of Muhammad Wazir, a Zanzibari of Surati descent. When she testified against her owner, Bahr-Zain claimed to have been taken while still young from "Amhara" in Abyssinia seven years prior. She was first sold to a merchant from Hudaydah (on the Red Sea coast of Yemen) and brought to Zanzibar by a Shihri (southern Yemeni) man. She was then sold three more times before ending up in the hands of a Persian who again sold her. Her new owner also resold her, and at some point she was sold to a resident of Chole in southern East Africa, where she was purchased by

Muhammad Wazir and brought back to Zanzibar.[9] In nine years, Bahr-Zain had traveled thousands of kilometers, lived in several cities, and been subject to eight owners.

Slave narratives reveal the fiction of the myth of enslavement as a direct transaction between a male family member and a slave trader. Though Muslim Zanzibaris held that those who practiced African religions could be justly enslaved, the myth further validated the slave buyers' devaluation of his purchase and the forced social dependency of the enslaved. As far as most slave-owners were concerned, slaves had, in effect, been justly exchanged and entrusted to traders by those who had the right to sell them: their families. Moreover, the myth maintained that the enslaved valued nothing more than food or clothing, which made the further argument that they were better off in Zanzibar than in their home societies seem tenable.[10] In the myth of exchange, the slave was justly enslaved and traded by those who had the right to do so. This fit nicely with the slave-owner's paternalistic image of himself, since the sale of the slave could then be seen as constituting a direct transferal of rights over the person from biological father to "adopted" father.

A complementary myth of rebirth both infantilized the enslaved and justified the parameters of their objectification. Purchase in this narrative became redemption, a more or less charitable act of taking on a forfeited and neglected person. Ideologically then, slaves were incorporated into Zanzibari households not as junior kin, but as perpetually dependent children whose lives would be entirely directed by those who facilitated their rebirth. This concept of slaves as perpetual children, reborn in purchase, was again neatly fitted into the Zanzibari social environment: slaves could be "things with words" but, like small children, without the capacity to define themselves beyond their fictive parents' wills.[11] Like infants, slaves were dependent on their owners for their identity as much as for their food.

Respectability in Zanzibar was, in part, determined by one's dependents: children, slaves, or spouses. Social position was the product of family history, inanimate possessions, and dependents. Slaves were physical representations of wealth, and they evidenced the ability to create a retinue that would service its possessor's interests in political or personal conflicts. Even in the burgeoning plantation sector in the late 1880s, where economic utility overshadowed the symbolic consumption of slaves, a German visitor to Zanzibar wrote that "[t]he number of slaves one owns is still a criterion of power and reputation."[12] Urban slave-owners depended even more heavily on the symbolic value of slaves than did their counterparts in the country.[13] In an era of increased consumption and public display in urban Zanzibar, slaves were often the objects of a household's greatest investment. Sayyida Salme binti Said wrote that possessing large numbers of slaves was a necessary symbol of social standing.[14] The British Consul Atkins Hamerton was more explicit: "A man's respectability and wealth . . . is always estimated by the number of slaves he is said to possess." Hamerton wrote that the purchase of a slave permitted a certain kind of lifestyle, on the one hand facilitated by the value of a slave's labor, but sometimes through the social position of ownership. Poorer slave-owners—slaves, ex-slaves, Hadrami (southern Yemeni), and Comorian immigrants among them—tended to depend more on their slaves economically than did their wealthy counterparts, sending them out as *vibarua*, "day laborers" and collecting their wages.[15] But Hamerton and others were quick to point out that while poor people dreamed of the wealth a slave might produce for them, it was the image of oneself as possessor, and the social interest accrued from such investment, that was sometimes more desirable than actual revenue. According to Hamerton, when a freed slave saved up enough money to buy his own slave, he "lounge[d] about from place to place with a sword under his arms, calling himself an Arab."[16] Hamerton's picture is laden with standard stereotypes of Zanzibari men—idle, indolent, undirected— but the acquisition of a slave by an ex-slave did often facilitate a new social opportunity. Even for the poorest in urban Zanzibar, the ideal of slave-owners was not to put their slaves out to work, but to keep them in the house. According to Bartle Frere, slaves often spoke of investing windfalls of cash in a slave or two who, if possible, they would keep at home.[17]

Given the paternalism of Zanzibari myths of enslavement, it is not surprising that domestic slaves were publicly displayed in ways similar to children.[18] Wealthy Zanzibaris usually adorned their young girls in particularly ostentatious ways. When a girl was born in Seyyid Said's house, she was given a variety of expensive jewelry to wear while yet an infant. In a strikingly similar manner, immediately after purchase, a new concubine *(suria)* received a set of jewelry, which she was instructed to put on immediately and which she could not take off, even to sleep. In both cases, the jewelry, according to Sayyida Salme, was an indicator of the giver's status, a mark of the giver's ability. For the enslaved, this material remaking was a symbol of her acquiescence to the power of her new owner over her quotidian existence.

In the market, slaves—women in particular—were also subjected to corporeal remaking. They were dressed up in new clothes, expensive jewelry, and beads, and their hair was elaborately plaited.[19] Slaves arrived sick and malnourished, and slave dealers attempted to force their charges to look beautiful, healthy—in a word, desirable. Since a slave-purchaser sought potential in the market, slave dealers worked to evidence the representational uses to which their charges could be put by remaking them for display. The slave market thus became a horrible masquerade in which newly arrived slaves were forced to wear a profusion of gold, beads, expensive cloths, sometimes even flowers in their hair.[20] Their bodies were smeared with coconut oil, and their eyes were highlighted with kohl. They were forced to represent something new, something that bore no relation to the people they once had been. The market was a compulsory performance in which the interests of the enslaved were fully repressed. In the market, the enslaved was stripped of his or her identity and given raiments that sparked the imagination, interest, and desire of potential buyers. In their forced reclothing, slaves were imagined as new things, objects that could speak but would, more importantly, feed their owner's social or physical desires.[21]

In addition to forcing new slaves to wear ornaments, owners gave them new names and clothing after purchase. Girls and women were forced to accept names such as Faida (profit), Bahati (fortune), and Tamasha (spectacle, entertainment, or marvelous thing). Boys and men became Baraka (blessing), Mabruki (blessed), and Heri (happiness).[22] Naming was a profound act of the owner's domination, for it evidenced an ability to deny the enslaved's history and publicly constitute their identity anew. The same could be said of reclothing. When slaves were brought home from the market, they were given an entirely new set of clothes to wear. Relatively poor Zanzibaris, some who were themselves slaves, often reclothed their new purchases with a length of merekani cloth that would be replaced periodically.[23] Likewise, when a new female slave was brought into the sultan's house, she was given three days to lay aside all of her former clothes and redress in the clothes assigned her.[24] There were no exceptions to this reclothing. Further, there developed an entire category of slaves owned by wealthy Zanzibaris—wapambe (pl., "the decorated" or "adorned"; sing., mpambe)—who were especially well dressed and ornamented to signify the wealth and ability of their owners. In redressing, even by an owner of meager means, slaves who had already been radically divested of their own abilities for material self-making were made dependents and representations of their owners through material symbols of subservience, however lavish. Since apparel mediated the relationship of the body to the self and the public sphere, redressing by an owner was a graphic scene of domination.

The slaves of wealthy Zanzibaris were subject to constant redressing.[25] Messengers, dressed in a profusion of gold and silver, exemplified the divestment of the enslaved's abilities to define themselves physically. W. Cope Devereux, a visitor to Zanzibar who served in the British Anti–Slave Trade Squadron, wrote of the arrival of a wealthy Zanzibari's *mpambe* at the British Consulate. Her adornments were so profuse that they symbolically negated the girl herself. Devereux noted the name of her owner (who was not present), but of the enslaved girl he only wrote, "On her neck was a heavy silver chain, of tasteful workmanship, to which were attached sundry articles, the use of which I could not guess. A lighter chain, to which other nick'nacks were attached, also decorated her throat. On each of her arms she had heavy armlets, from the wrist to the elbow; and on her legs, heavier anklets reached from the ankle half-way up to the knee, where the gold was met by a red silk wrapper."[26] The slave's body was sent, but the ornaments as well as the girl represented the abilities of the owner. Sayyida Shewane, of whom Sayyida Salme writes in her memoirs, always used her slaves to reflect her importance. According to Salme, Shewane sought out the most handsome slaves and weighted them with expensive weaponry and jewelry. When she went out, she was always accompanied by a large retinue of her bedecked slaves.[27]

The arming of male slaves aimed at ends similar to the bejeweling of enslaved women. Wealthy slave-owners spent enormous sums on dressing up retinues of male slaves with expensive clothing and armaments—swords, knives, and firearms—inlaid with silver and gold. The public display of ornamented weapons was a primary mode of self-definition for men, and so the adornment of slaves with expensive armaments reflected at once the control over and deployment of possessions "with words" as well as those without.[28] Eunuchs, like wapambe, were elaborately dressed. They were given turbans, embroidered jackets, kanzus, and expensive armaments.[29] Eunuchs and other enslaved men were stationed at the doors and entranceways of houses as richly adorned sentries, the animate property of the home-owner. Yet the fact that the enslaved had their own wants and acted on them ensured that the public image of the enslaved was always a palimpsest. While a slave-owner might purchase expensive and richly worked weapons for his slave, the enslaved regularly challenged this remaking by pawning off the armaments and spending the proceeds.[30] Despite the actions of slaves, slave-owners held tenaciously to the idea that humans could be used like objects. In this sense, slavery as "social death" was part of a process of social repression initiated by the slave trade and followed by reclothing and renaming—"social rebirth" in Zanzibar.[31] By using a bought person to create a public persona, slave-owners converted the enslaved into symbols.

REDEMPTION AND RESUBJECTION

Slave redeemers—be they abolitionists, missionaries, or British policy-makers —were also largely uninterested in the words of the enslaved. They accepted the slave-owner's image of slaves and, like slave-owners, limited the parameters of slaves' self-making. Over the course of the nineteenth century, British analysts transposed the image of the mute, infantile, and degraded slave onto the entirety of East Africa. Slavery came to be a symbol for all of the East African mainland, and Anglophone audiences came to see all mainlanders in ways similar to the ways they saw Zanzibari slaves. Johann Krapf, one of the first missionaries to write a popular travelogue of East Africa, employed caravan porters (who were almost certainly not slaves) as a literary metaphor for the entirety of Africa. Seeing members of a caravan carrying large loads on their heads, Krapf wrote, "Singularly enough they . . . present a figure precisely like that of the massive and monotonous continent of Africa whose children they are, and which, as if in strict harmony with its painful history, wears the appearance of a huge monster-slave bent down by his burden."[32] In British accounts of East African slavery, Africa was presented as diseased, afflicted by the "cancer" of slavery brought by the Arab.[33] As he lay dying, David Livingstone—Britain's great antislavery protagonist—used his fading energy to write that the East African slave trade was the "open sore of the world."[34] In their acceptance of the slave-owner's myth that slaves were incapable of self-making, redeemers imagined themselves as liberators of those who could not rationally speak for themselves. Over the course of the second half of the nineteenth century, redemption moved from a policy of freeing slaves to one of allegorically freeing East Africa from a host of vices: slavery, degeneracy, backwardness, all cancers to be cured by the "civilizing mission." The slave trade, and slavery in Zanzibar in particular, would provide a flashpoint for British popular interest in East Africa. And many Britons who would seek to remake the enslaved used strategies often indistinguishable from those employed by the enslavers.

Efforts at raising humanitarian concern in Britain for the condition of East African slaves were initially spearheaded by missionary groups such as the Church Missionary Society (CMS), the Universities' Mission to Central Africa (UMCA), and, perhaps most important, through the literary successes of David Livingstone. Such efforts roused "so decided an expression of public opinion in England [and elsewhere]," according to an officer in the British Navy, that Britons began to press their government for more direct involvement in East Africa's political economy.[35] So successful were Church-based efforts to educate the British public— Livingstone, for example, became one of the most popular public lecturers of the century—that Parliament and the queen not only became concerned about the East African slave trade, but committed British resources, even an Anti–Slave Trade naval squadron tasked with intercepting slavers, to curtailing it.[36] These efforts laid the groundwork for imperial intervention and colonization by explicitly accepting the slaveowner's image of the enslaved: the idea that the African was a blank slate onto which others' interests could be written. In Western conceptualizations of East Africa, slaves came to stand as a metaphor for the continent—passive and resigned, tableaus for the free play of "Arab" debauchery. Redeemers wrote narratives of African degeneracy, ineptitude, and need for salvation through descriptions of the slave. A paternalistic rhetoric inherited from earlier abolitionist writings and the longer history of Western slaveholding discourse seeped into writings about East African slaves. Redeemers entrusted with freed slaves (called *mateka,* "captives" or "booty," in Swahili) attempted to remake those in their charge as social dependents, representations of both their own values and the possibilities of "civilization." Zanzibaris called freed slaves entrusted to British redeemers *watumwa wa wangereza,* or the "slaves of the British," because freed slaves were dressed and directed according to the interests of those who had custody over them and because the freed slaves' greatest social ties were to the abolitionists.[37] By ignoring the deobjectifying strategies of slaves and adhering to an image of the enslaved African as voiceless, missionaries, travel writers, and administrators used people to symbolize redeemers' interests.

Humanitarian condemnations of slavery and the slave trade made a fundamental distinction between slavery and other forms of exploitation.[38] As David Brion Davis first argued, public attacks on slavery in Britain were often as concerned with championing proletarianization at home as they were with the specifics of slavery abroad.[39] In formulating slavery as simply a question of labor, the discourse of abolition never addressed the master-slave relationships rooted in symbolic subjection and social dependency. As a result, British antislavery activists in Zanzibar and elsewhere on the coast technically freed slaves but employed free people to perform the same kinds of social labor they most likely would have performed for slave-owners. More important, redeemers followed the lead of slave-owners in imagining themselves as the civilizers of those in their charge. For enslaver and redeemer, African slaves were assumed to need the protection, discipline, and civilization of their new possessors.

Frederick Cooper reminds us that nineteenth-century British reformers had an unfailing belief that "the roots of poverty and social dislocation lay more in the hearts of the poor than in society."[40] This ideology was transferred to Africa in a narrative of the slave trade that stressed the internal destruction of the continent occasioned by "Arab" demand for slaves and a lust for foreign consumer goods. Guns and cloth caused people to raid and enslave each other, creating a culture of wanton destruction that only outsiders seemed prepared to suppress. When a slave arrived in Zanzibar, she signified to redeemers the horrors of African self-destructiveness, barbarity, and inhumanity. This was confirmed in much early theorizing about East Africa focused on the Zanzibari slave market. More than any other site, the slave market would come to define East Africa in the minds of the Western public. No place else seemed so thoroughly to capture foreigners' attention, and, because of the spectacle it promised, no single site was more frequented by Anglophone writers.[41] As I have argued, the market was the pinnacle of the slave's objectification, and it consistently reified the presumed blankness of Africans. In the market, Elton wrote, "all the faces [are] marked with that vacant stare common to the slave population."[42] The market provided ample evidence to affirm Livingstone's images of Africans as corrupted and in need of salvation, and thus the market became a metaphor for all of Africa. In the market, the "lascivious Arab" searched for his prey, and Africa represented itself in no uncertain terms as degraded and "without words."[43]

Slave market narratives almost always focused on young women. Men and boys were rarely mentioned, and the entire process of exhibition was usually discussed as if all slaves were young women. Most narratives included descriptions of the enslaved's dress, jewelry, make-up, the way in which their breasts were felt and genitals inspected.[44] Such a narrative structure usually reobjectified the person in the telling.[45] Moreover, many travel writers came to the conclusion that slaves in the market were

Figure 12. "Slave Market, Zanzibar." This lithograph, a fanciful rendering
of the slave market from the journals of Rebecca Wakefield, is a composite
of images inspired by other travel accounts—the cityscape seems to have been
taken from images of North Africa, not Zanzibar—and features many of the
tropes common to descriptions of the slave market: a chaotic scene with nearly
naked African women being inspected by Arab men. (Rebecca Wakefield,
Memoirs of Mrs. Rebecca Wakefield, Wife of the Rev. T. Wakefield. Ed.
R. Brewin. London: Hamilton, Adams, 1879.)

largely indifferent to their condition. The British travel writer J. Frederic
Elton believed that "with delicately painted eyebrows and artificially
darkened, languid, dreamy eyes, decked for sale in bright-coloured garments, heavy silver armlets, necklets of beads and frontlets of brass (lent
for the occasion by the "dalali," or broker) and *artistically grouped to
produce a provocative effect,* [the women] do nòt look in the least
annoyed at their position, but rather on the other hand gratified at the
attention they command from the glancing eyes of the Arab aristocracy"[46]
(emphasis mine). This mixing of disgust with fascination and utter disinterest in the enslaved, an inability to see them as people and the predisposition to imagine them instead as, in Clelia Weeks's words, "scarcely
human," shows the objectifying spell that the market cast on European
observers.[47] In the slave market, Africans could be pitied, but they were
assumed to be indifferent to their subjugation, and this unequivocally
revealed their debased humanity, their need for redemption and remaking. Descriptions of the market, while intent on exhibiting the brutality
of slavery, created an image of Africans as perpetual, helpless victims.
They fashioned or affirmed a rhetorical equation of slavery with Africa

and the enslaved as black. This concern for equating status with physiognomy is a particularly telling example of the increasing importance of
racial taxonomies to Western perceptions of Zanzibar. The figure of the
"white slave" in accounts of Zanzibar brought the conceptual racializa-
tion of slavery into sharp relief. Here the images held by redeemers and
slave-owners diverged. For their part, Zanzibaris did not imagine skin
color as a determining factor of enslaveability, even though color had
much to do with the value and categories of slaves. British images of
slaves, on the other hand, were not only feminine, but also black.
Livingstone, for example, wrote of a "slave spirit" among the freed
slaves that "goes deepest in those who have the darkest skins."[48] Since
British policymakers and redeemers singularly associated Africanness
with slavery, European, Indian, and Persian slaves in Zanzibar became
one of their primary concerns.

   The Zanzibari white slave troubled the Manichaean equation of
"black" physiognomies with slavery and "white" physiognomies with
freedom. European accounts of white and light-skinned slaves, in contrast
to those of dark-skinned slaves, forcefully asserted the humanity of the
enslaved by reference to both their skin color and their intelligence;
indeed, this dyad was central to their rhetorical unmaking as slaves in
Anglophone accounts of Zanzibar. The British Consul John Kirk went to
extremes to undefine light-skinned people as slaves. He concentrated on
the freeing of what he called "white" boys owned by Zanzibaris. When
the daughter of the sultan's ambassador to Bombay—only identified as
the "Lady of Seyd Hamed bin Suliman"—was shipwrecked near Zanzibar, two "white" passengers rescued from the wreckage drew the consul's
attention. The "Lady" had performed the hajj with a large group of
retainers and chartered the British bark *Hyderabad* at Jiddah for the
return voyage to Zanzibar. After a circuitous journey, the ship wrecked in
East African waters. Among the survivors were two boys whom Kirk
described as being "of fair complexion [and] European features," one of
whom spoke Turkish and agreed to be interviewed. Kirk discovered that
the boy had been taken from Georgia and sold off to Mecca, where he,
along with several other Georgians, was purchased by the Lady for an
immense sum: MT$500 to MT$1,000 each.[49] After talking with the boy,
Kirk demanded his immediate release and delivery to the British
Consulate. The sultan deemed Kirk's demand inappropriate and refused
any discussion of the matter since his subjects had full license to import
white, even Christian, slaves into Zanzibar. Kirk strongly disagreed with
this interpretation of the slave trade treaties and again requested the

boys' release. This time, Kirk spelled out the rationale for his insistence
in the matter. He was attempting to "bring again to [the sultan's] notice
that this traffic in European and Asiatic slaves is to us much more revolt-
ing than the negro slave trade."[50] Slavery was not unequivocally revolt-
ing to the sensibilities of redeemers. The enslavement of whites was a far
worse crime than enslaving Africans. Kirk again demanded the Turkish-
speaking boy, citing that the boy had been poorly treated by his captors.
The consul protested that, before his intervention, "[the boy] was left to
pick up food where he might with slaves on board the yacht," though
after the sultan looked into the matter, the boy "was dressed out in gold
lace."[51] Whether redressing the boy had anything to do with the attention he received from the consul is unclear, but the spirit of Kirk's letter
speaks to his preconceived image of the slave as African. The fact that a
white boy had suffered the same conditions as the other slaves on board
the ship was unconscionable.

What Kirk's intervention makes patently clear is that in the redeemer's
mind slavery had come to be equated with certain people, racially
defined. Even the fact that the boy was a Muslim before enslavement
seemed to have nothing to do with Kirk's insistence, though this point
should have made a great difference to his owners. For Kirk, the image of
the slave was disentangled from religion and conceptually aligned with
physical appearance alone. In a letter to Bombay, Kirk expressed his
fears that the trade in Georgian and "other white slaves" through the
Red Sea was increasing. Yet what angered him more was the fact that
white male slaves were not rising to any "post of honor" like the
Georgian and Abyssinian women. Instead, according to Kirk, "they are
to be seen about the doors [of homes]," and "rumour has it [that they]
are used for the vilest of purposes to the indulgence of which His
Highness [Seyyid Majid] is said to be addicted." Not only were white
slave boys an offense to British racial sensibilities, but the rumor of their
sexual subjection made their enslavement even more intolerable to the
British Consul. Whether or not they performed sexual labors similar to
those of their female counterparts, the fact that Kirk was so deeply unset-
tled by the very thought of white boys as concubines of the "Arab" aristocracy reveals the gendered and racialized image of slavery in the
redeeming consciousness. To control the bodies of "negro" women was
one thing; to control those of white men was another.[52]

The redeemers' equation of slavery with a debased Africa is even more
pronounced if we consider that British residents of Zanzibar sought to
free not only European, but also Persian and Indian slaves.[53] Though

there were fewer Indian slaves than eastern Europeans in Zanzibar, the consuls worked hard to liberate them.[54] Hearing of an Indian and several Georgian girls sold in the city, Kirk wrote a letter of protest to the sultan. The sultan secured the Indian girl's manumission and delivered her to the consulate. She told Kirk that her name was Fatima, though she was renamed Mariam in Zanzibar. While still young, she was sold in Bombay to a man who took her to Hyderabad, where she remained for several years. She was later purchased by a Suri who took her to Mukalla, where she was sold to an East African merchant. He took her to Lamu, where she was purchased by a Shihri slave dealer who sold her to a Kadhi in Zanzibar who later sold her to a young Persian man. Apart from the circuitous route of her travels, what her narrative shows is the impossibility of recourse to the slave-trade treaties to secure her freedom. Yet for Kirk, the fact that he imagined her as unenslaveable trumped all other considerations, including the fact that she was unlawfully enslaved as a Muslim. "Whatever the exact law [according to the slave-trade treaties] on such a subject may be," Kirk wrote, he immediately pressed the sultan for her release.[55] To Kirk, physiognomy defined the Indian in Africa as something more than a slave. Indians in Zanzibar represented imperial Britain; thus, enslaved Indians, as far as he was concerned, were an affront to the empire.

In addition to equating blackness with slavery and slavery with Africa, redeemers attempted to remake the slaves in their charge. Much like their slave-owning counterparts, they also infantilized their charges. Regardless of age or experience, one officer in the Anti–Slave Trade Squadron wrote that enslaved Africans were "in fact, all children."[56] After capturing a slave ship, one of the first things the squadron sailors did was name those in their charge. "[A]mong the Gallas," Capt. Sulivan wrote, "we had Peggy, Susan, Sally, Sophy, Mary, Tom, Jim, &c., &c."[57] Like Zanzibari slave-owners, sailors gave their new charges names that obscured their previous identities. W. Cope Devereux, who served in the Anti–Slave Trade Squadron, wrote that his crew-mates had a generic name for all the young slave girls aboard the vessels: "Topsy," inspired by a character in Harriet Beecher Stowe's *Uncle Tom's Cabin*. On Devereux's ship each "Topsy" was taken by what the sailors termed a "sea daddy," who would dress her up in beads and clothe "her black little corpus in gaudy cloths" from the spoils of the captured ships. "Our blue-jackets are forever fondling" the girls, Devereux wrote, and "the little creatures appear to take to the horny tars most affectionately, showing more precocity and fun than one could expect." This was attributable, Devereux believed, to the girls, "becoming women without going through the stages of child and girlhood."[58]

When slaves who had been captured from slave ships landed in Zanzibar, their lives resembled those of the enslaved in many ways. Some British residents of Zanzibar believed that offering unconditional freedom to the enslaved was morally wrong. Captain Philip Colomb of the Anti–Slave Trade Squadron, who was familiar with the desires of slaves taken off of slave vessels, held that while the slave, "like any other ignorant child," wanted unconditional freedom, such a course of action was "strongly opposed to English sentiment, and liable to call down the wrath of public opinion."[59] Since mass emancipation of captured slaves would not have been well-received in slave-owning Zanzibar, redeemers were faced with the problem of what to do with the great number of children seized from slave vessels. From the 1870s, the Squadron delivered freed slaves to a variety of British residents, including missionaries and the consuls. Before this began in earnest, there were several plantations owned by Englishmen that were dependent on slaves rented from local slave-owners. In 1866, the British Consul G. Edward Seward sent a letter to Bombay proposing that slaves freed in the suppression of the slave trade be delivered not to Aden or the Seychelles, as they had been previously, but to these plantations so as to obviate their use of enslaved laborers. Seward wrote that "from the arrest and relegation of some portion of its [the slave trade's] ilicit [sic] outpour we can certainly stock the Sugar Plantations with Lawful Labour." The use of freed slaves, he explained, would depend either on the English planter's interest "or the power of the English Government to compel their employment."[60]

What is ironic about Seward's proposal, which was approved by Bombay, was that he justified the scheme through the promise that such measures would alleviate the need for Englishmen to "quasi if not actual[ly]" possess slaves in Zanzibar. Seward proposed to stop British planters from using slaves by delivering to them a contingent of newly "freed" slaves who would be compelled to work. His paternalistic ideology mirrored precisely the strategies of enslavers. Seward talked of the "benevolent compulsion" needed to convince freed slaves to work and argued that "a large control" should be given to the planters. Echoing local slave-owners, Seward concluded that an "obligation [should] be laid upon the quondam slave to discharge certain duties for a certain term as the price of his liberty and Civil rights and in return for adequate wages, quarters, clothing, food and Medical Care." Though slave-owners rarely guaranteed manumission, their social contract with their purchases was nearly identical. This use of the enslaved would, Seward imagined, demonstrate the possibilities of "free" labor to Zanzibaris. Seward further concluded that freed slaves brought to British plantations would "of course be regarded as British Proteges."[61] In other words, they would be children in the care of a paternal power.

Sir H. Bartle Frere, whom the British government sent on an official mission to collect information regarding the slave trade in East Africa (and who was later appointed consul to Zanzibar), was quite content with the British planters' domestication and "civilization" of freed slaves. The slaves on Fraser's plantation at Kokotoni, many of whom had been sent to him by the sultan, had been unruly, licentious, and uninterested in having children until Fraser was able to "reduce," in Frere's words, "the savage horde . . . to order and discipline." They found themselves, according to Frere, "under the authority of a higher and kindlier intelligence than the slave dealer," and, as a result, they complied with the directions of their masters. According to Frere, they gradually formed a community, "not civilized according to our ideas," he admitted, "but *far* more highly organized than the bestial crowd as at first turned over from the slave-market."[62] Again, it is striking how closely Frere's rhetoric resembles Zanzibari slave-owning ideology. The enslaved Africans were savage and undisciplined, but under British tutelage they became an organized body, represented their owners well, and aspired to their owners' civilization.

Urban redeemers likewise mimicked the slave-owners whom they condemned. John Kirk, for example, liked to dress freed slaves "fancifully," giving them kanzus, fezzes, and canes.[63] Like a slave-owner, Kirk dressed those in his service in ways that would bring recognition to and increase the social profile of the consulate. The Universities' Mission to Central Africa acquired many freed slaves, and the mission's disciplining of those it acquired reveals an even fuller symbolic subjection of emancipated Africans. Bishop Tozer was first given boys captured from a slaver in 1864, and over the course of the next few years the number of his charges increased dramatically. Since he was unable to cull much information from the ex-slaves relating to their enslavement and subsequent traumas, he assumed that they wished to disown their biological families. He charged that slavery was a "very bad" institution but contended that "the slaves are infinitely better off and more cared for" in Zanzibar "than they would be among their own people."[64]

Within days of their arrival, missionaries reclothed freed slaves. Giving freed slaves red fezzes and kanzus, Tozer imagined, "at once stamp[ed] them as something superior."[65] Instead of signifying their high or "free" status, this redressing functioned much like Zanzibari redressings of raw slaves—liberated slaves now represented the abilities of oth-, ers. Tozer refused to allow the ex-slaves to wear English clothes, even though the boys showed great interest in them. Much like a slave-owner, Tozer wanted the boys to represent, but not mimic, him. In this way, he ensured that the social distance between him and his charges remained significant. Tozer wrote of the "dangers" inherent in any project that attempted to make freed slaves into "black Englishmen." He thought it best that they should follow "native customs," that is, Zanzibari styles. In Tozer's mind, the boys were yet uncivilized and therefore unfit to wear English clothing. Exemplifying this, soon after receiving the boys Tozer began to regret recruiting a shoemaker for the Zanzibari mission. To create a desire for shoes among the ex-slave converts, "where their use would deprive the people of what almost amounts to a second set of hands," was, he concluded, "the introduction of the very opposite of civilization." The uncivilized, it seems, were unprepared for civilization and thus Tozer sought to make all representational decisions for his charges: he would control their corporeality; he would decide how they would appear.[66] In the minds of redeemers, ex-slaves were to be remade to represent order.[67] Rebecca Wakefield delighted in the mission's successes with freed girls. She described in glowing terms a scene of all the mission girls redressed in white frocks, with red sashes around their waists, and Turkey-red handkerchiefs on their heads.[68] The girls, like their male counterparts dressed in white kanzus and fezzes, had been remade to represent the values of others. They were now "orderly."

Redeemers, like slave-owners, sought to inculcate their charges with new cultural norms. For example, when the mission children did not wash their hands, the missionary Edward Steere called them to him and, according to Tozer, "first [gave] them an explanation of the meaning of the expression 'Dirty pig.'" He then forced them to repeat six times "I'm a dirty pig"; thereafter he again ordered them to wash.[69] When the Universities' Mission set up a separate mission house outside of the city for redeemed girls, the disciplining was more complete. The girls, Wakefield reported, were "trained to make good wives for the boys when the proper time has arrived." "I was very much pleased indeed," Wakefield wrote, "by their ready obedience and orderly manners during our stay." As the mission residences expanded, each girl was offered to a sponsor in Britain. These were called "godmothers" and were given the honor of naming the mission children. In reward for their generosity, the missions sent reports to the "godmothers" informing them of the "conduct" of their children.[70] Redeemers imposed a strict and limiting regime of "order" on their charges and believed their efforts successful when ex-slaves became conditioned, accepting of, and remade by their humanitarianism. The control that missionaries sought over their charges led John C. Willoughby, who employed many mission freed slaves on his hunting expedition in the 1880s, to write that the "poor mission men . . . had only left one form of servitude to embark in another."[71] When ex-slaves rejected this remaking—when they wore Western clothes or converted to Islam—they directly challenged the desires of their redeemers. To ensure this would not happen, redeemers attempted to build dependence from a young age, so that those in their charge came to see themselves in the image projected by the redeemers. These social-conditioning projects, which drew on larger discourses of social management and colonial rule, attempted to demonstrate how Africans could be remade according to Western ideals. It is no surprise, therefore, that such projects and popular writings appear now as premonitions of colonial order in East Africa. Through the actions of the redeemers, myths of docile, debased, and wretched Africans would remain part of Britain's conceptual tool-kit for understanding East Africa. Indeed, the image of Africa as a monster-slave incapable of freeing, much less civilizing, itself gained currency among British consuls and policymakers, who would come to believe that only Britain could free Africans and bring them order.

REMAKING THE SELF

Despite the efforts of slave-owners and redeemers, slaves and ex-slaves did not imagine themselves as vessels for the interests of others. Their words and actions reveal a host of quotidian efforts to distinguish themselves from things and to remake themselves within the parameters of subjection. One of the most visible ways slaves sought to reclaim a personhood suppressed by symbolic subjection was by taking command over things, by socially redefining themselves through available objects, particularly those denied them by their owners. As many scholars have recognized, the idea of "freedom" did not carry the same meanings in most African societies as it did in Atlantic plantation societies. Leaving one's master and total self-support were not necessarily ideal social conditions. In Suzanne Miers and Igor Kopytoff's formulation, slaves in African societies often recognized total autonomy as impractical and instead desired social belonging in their new societies.[72] Yet, as Glassman argues, slaves and freed people did not always desire simple social inclusion and often flatly rejected certain forms of belonging. Instead, slaves in East Africa and elsewhere more often sought to define the terms of their belonging and to choose the kinds of relationships of which they would be a part.[73] What enslaved and freed people seemed to desire, regardless of their relationship to their (ex-)owners, was to define their own place in the social order, to represent their own political and social interests, sometimes in contradiction and sometimes in accordance with the interests of their (ex-)owners. A direct response to the processes of subjection, self-definition often first took form through renaming and reclothing, taking on symbols that signified inclusion in a group other than the enslaved.

When freed, slaves in Zanzibar took names that were more respectable than those they had been assigned after purchase. They dropped demeaning names like Baraka and Bahati and claimed standard Muslim ones like Musa, Rashid, Fatima, and Aisha as testaments to their integration into a Muslim society. They also created new names that evidenced desirable associations with certain elsewheres. Sidi Bombay, the accomplished caravan leader who brought Burton and Speke to the lakes and led Stanley to Livingstone, claimed association with India, the place where he was freed and where he hoped one day to retire.[74] Likewise, Mabruki, a slave who had escaped from Zanzibar and lived as a free man in Calcutta, only to be reenslaved on his return, dropped the name his owner gave him and began calling himself "Calcutta" to claim his affiliation with a personally transformative elsewhere.[75] Freed slaves in the possession of the missions also renamed themselves in ways that helped forge entirely new identities. Many, in fact, insisted on English surnames, much to the consternation of the missionaries.

Dressing, like renaming, became a social practice that, as Georg Simmel first outlined and the Comaroffs reasserted, while rendering a kind of social obedience, operated at the same time as a form of individual differentiation.[76] Both names and clothing offered the possibility of new personas, of corporate as well as individual differentiation following the social grammars of Zanzibar City. When slaves were manumitted, some relied on one ornament in particular as a material symbol of their new self-ownership: their deed of freedom, which was placed in a small silver box and worn around the neck. The box became much like the *hirizi*, or amulets given to small children to protect them from harmful agents. As long as the ex-slave wore the "writing," as it was called, she could not be reenslaved.[77] Redressing in "respectable" clothing was another common desire of Zanzibari slaves. Of the slaves called to testify against their owners in the trials of British Indian subjects, it is striking that many of those who were asked of their plans after manumission replied that they, like seventeen-year-old "Suedi," would work in order to be able to obtain "good food and clothing."[78]

On being freed, most former slaves invested considerable resources in clothing. Women aspired to the styles popular in Zanzibar, which, as I suggested in chapter 4, included the *ukaya* (head covering), *kisutu* (English square cloth dyed in Bombay), *leso* (large, colorful cotton hand-kerchiefs sewn together in Zanzibar), and, by the end of the century, the *kanga* (dyed and printed Indian cloth).[79] Men bought kanzus, jackets, and even swords or knives when they could afford them. This consumption of what would come to be known as "Swahili" clothes at once symbolized integration into a stratum of Zanzibari society and announced distinction from both slavery and the denial of self-representation effected by enslavement. In this way, slaves seeking to remake themselves adopted and then manipulated, as Laura Fair has shown, the material codes of Zanzibar society for their own particular social ends.[80]

Since the radical displacement caused by the slave trade often created a profound psychological break from their homes, slaves developed an acute interest in staking out a social place in Zanzibar.[81] Though most slaves engaged in symbolic acts like saving to buy their own clothes or stealing certain kinds of clothing, their resistance to owners' attempts to resignify slaves was sometimes more confrontational.[82] Burton wrote of a king from "somewhere about the great Central African Lakes" who had been captured in war and sold off to Zanzibar. The king resisted all attempts at subjection and insisted on carrying a staff representing his position. What was most troubling to his owner and other slave-owners in Zanzibar was that as he walked through the city, those who appreci-ated his or the staff's power would prostrate themselves in front of him and beg to be touched by the staff. Once his owner recognized that he could do nothing with the man, he sent him to Sultan Seyyid Said. In the sultan's court, the king delivered a speech that, reminiscent of the Mgwame parable in chapter 2, warned of the unpredictability of the world and how, like him, the sultan could one day be brought low. Soon thereafter Seyyid Said manumitted the king.[83] By holding to the symbol of his former identity, the king forced his own self-image and a powerful material cultural symbol of his society on his owner. Through both his own actions and the acknowledgment of others, he successfully resisted symbolic subjugation. Few slaves, however, had the social leverage of a king and so most had to employ more subtle means.

Figure 13. Maasai women in Zanzibar, presumably
taken from the mainland as slaves, wearing coastal
fashions, ca. 1895–98. (Photograph courtesy of the
Winterton Collection of East African Photographs,
Melville J. Herskovits Library of African Studies,
Northwestern University.)

Some slaves, particularly those who worked outside of the house and
kept a portion of their wages, purchased clothing similar to that of their
owners. One such slave who turns up in many accounts of Zanzibar was a
pilot and interpreter who served in the Anti–Slave Trade Squadron called
"Bukhett" or "Buckett" by Anglophone writers. He made a high wage as
an interpreter and always dressed in expensive crimsons and linens.
Curiously, Bukhett seemed to have no desire to free himself from his
owner, who was described only as "some old Arab woman" who exacted
very little from him. Many Europeans found it remarkable that slaves like

Bukhett would not free themselves, given the opportunity. Yet Bukhett's situation suggests that when the owner's efforts to remake the slave were neutralized by the enslaved, the social ties to an owner were imagined to be less onerous, and the legal ties less material.[84] Bukhett had acquired a certain autonomy in his everyday self-making and had, in effect, freed himself of symbolic subjection as a result of his efforts and skills.

It is conceivable too that Bukhett found it advantageous to continue to depend on his owner's prestige or influence. Such seems to have been the case with other slaves who won economic independence. Rashid bin Hassani (a.k.a. Kibuli bin Mchubiri), for example, achieved significant self-definition. He moved into his own house and kept the wages that he earned. He imagined himself to still be under the "protection" of his owner, even though he seemed to have very little relation to her and did not seek manumission. While his economic severance from his owner was complete, his social dependence probably ran much deeper and may have been of even greater benefit to him than distance from his owner.[85] In a similar way, Circassian self-distancing from other slaves—refusing to share certain social spaces with their African counterparts—suggests a competitive social reconstitution among slaves drawn from their owners' values.[86] A process of self-identification in reference to the values of one's possessors was common among the redeemed. Of the boys at the Universities' Mission station in the Mkunazini quarter of Zanzibar, Mabruki was described by Tozer as a "great beau about his dress." Tozer related a story of his demanding new clothing from Bishop Steere. Mabruki complained bitterly of having nothing fit to wear for Sunday, remarking that everything had "come to an end": he had holes in his clothing, and his fez was faded. He informed his redeemers that he desperately needed new clothes. The missionaries bought new fezzes, which Mabruki distributed, fitting them on the heads of his fellow freed slaves and arranging their tassels.[87]

Affecting an even more complete remaking than that which his redeemers desired, Jacob Wainwright always chose to wear European clothing in public. Taken from a slaver as a young child, Wainwright had been given to the African Asylum of the Church Missionary Society's Industrial Mission in the city of Nasik, northeast of Bombay. There he had taken an English name, in spite of his baptism with an East African name, and later returned to Africa with an expedition that searched for Livingstone.[88] Wainwright was with Livingstone when he died and became a minor celebrity in Britain after escorting Livingstone's remains to London. Returning from England, Wainwright helped found the CMS settlement

Figure 14. Jacob Wainwright at Aden, en route to London. Wainwright became a minor celebrity in Europe through both his own writings and those of David Livingstone. This lithograph, printed in *The Last Journals of David Livingstone*, depicts Wainwright bringing Livingstone's remains to London. (From Horace Waller, ed. *The Last Journals of David Livingstone, in Central Africa, from 1865 to His Death*. Hartford, CT: R. W. Bliss, 1875.)

for freed slaves near Mombasa (named Frere Town), and later relocated to Zanzibar. Like other "Bombay Africans," as the CMS freed slaves were called in Zanzibar and Mombasa, Wainwright not only chose an English name, but wore European pants, a coat, wool suits, felt hats, boots, and English ties. "Bombay African" women who emigrated to Zanzibar and Mombasa from India also dressed distinctly in reference to their redeemers; they wore ankle-length dresses, long sleeves, collars, and combed their hair straight—practices that were not discouraged at the Indian missions.[89] Wearing English clothes and speaking English, Wainwright and other "Bombay Africans" provided a contrast with the other mission ex-slaves in Zanzibar, engaging in two modes of self-presentation largely discouraged by local missionaries.[90] Bishop Tozer imagined the wearing of English clothing to be an inappropriate approximation of the redeemer's culture, but "Bombay Africans" in Zanzibar insisted on wearing clothing that defined them as distinct, clothes that invested them with some of the perceived qualities of Europeans. Western clothes, like the wearing of manumission papers around the neck, signified the ex-slaves' transcendence of slavery. Perhaps an even more extreme gesture of self-definition was that of two other famous "Bombay Africans" in Zanzibar, Edward Gardiner and Nathaniel Gumba. Though they won acclaim in Britain for accompanying Livingstone's body to the East African coast, they rejected social reconstitution by the CMS missionaries of the African Asylum and asserted their capability for self-definition by converting to Islam.[91]

Religious conversion, whether to Islam or Christianity, was usually a kind of social renaming that, to some extent, was forced on both slaves and the redeemed. But, as Cooper, Glassman, El Zein, and Nimtz have shown, slaves also manipulated religion to critique slave-owning ideology.[92] Self-naming functioned in a very similar way to the manipulation of religious concepts. What was most politically striking about the self-naming of slaves and ex-slaves was their corporate appropriation of an appellation previously reserved for only the elite of coastal society: *waungwana*, or free people of respectable backgrounds. Once an exclusive term of self-identification among the elite, it became the corporate term used by many freed slaves of mainland birth (though not all who took this corporate title were free). From about mid-century, the term acted as a counterweight to the renaming forced on slaves by their owners and, as such, it was enormously popular. Indeed, *waungwana* became the favorite corporate term used by freed slaves or slaves who had integrated into Zanzibari society.[93]

Johann Krapf was the first to translate the root concept of *waungwana*, or *uungwana*, into English, and his rendering demonstrates the remaking of the term accomplished by freed slaves. While *uungwana* meant a free person in Krapf's translation—that is, one who was not a slave (Swahili: *mtumwa;* literally, "one who is sent")—it also implied a person with a "civilized" constitution and political freedom. It was, in both Mombasa and Zanzibar, "the state of being a free and civilized man," as Steere, the first compiler of a Swahili-English dictionary in the Zanzibari dialect, put it.[94] A *mwungwana* (sing.) was neither subject to nor dependent on any other person.[95] Yet *uungwana* meant more than a state of freedom; it connoted a state of free birth, the ability to influence others and own property. *Muana mke wa kiunguana*, or a woman of *uungwana* status, was not simply free, but, according to Krapf, someone of a "free and noble kind, a 'lady.' "[96] This elite idea of *uungwana* was directly related to lineage and the social prestige that accrued to those with freeborn ancestors on both their maternal and paternal sides. A person's *uungwana* was reduced, for example, if his or her mother was a concubine. In this social arithmetic, if a free woman's father was *mw-*

ungwana and her mother was a freed slave, the very fact that her mother had once been a slave was sufficient to greatly reduce her *uungwana,* leaving the free woman with what Krapf translates as a social "defect."[97] When slaves in Zanzibar began to appropriate the name *waungwana,* they would both reference these strict meanings and ultimately divest the word of its genealogical connotations by redefining it to mean simply a free person familiar with local culture.

On John H. Speke's arrival in Zanzibar in the 1860s, he recorded *waungwana* as meaning free men, born in the interior, enslaved, and then later freed.[98] For ex-slaves in Zanzibar, the title of *hur* (Ar.), or "freed person," was not sufficient for the kind of social labor their self-definition entailed. General social position was constructed in Zanzibar between the two poles of *utumwa* and *uungwana,* or objectification and self-determination, dependency and maintaining dependents, and, as such, the terms were as much mutually defining as mutually reinforcing. Seeking to deobjectify themselves, ex-slaves challenged the definitions of certain kinds of personhood implicit in the use of the word *uungwana.* Though the word *Swahili* also came into common use among ex-slaves and their children as an identity marker, the term *waungwana* implied a cultural claim to Zanzibar and local status that *Swahili* did not. Freed slave caravan porters, for example, accepted the term *Swahili* but, according to Joseph Thomson, "rejoiced . . . in the proud title of Wangwana *[sic]*." For caravan porters, the word *waungwana* referenced a desirable cultural association, an affiliation with free society and coastal culturedness.[99] Freed slaves used the term *waungwana* to define themselves as something different from slaves, but even some slaves appropriated the title *mwungwana* to claim a place in Zanzibari society and a coastal identity when traveling. Despite her condition as a slave forced to work in construction, "Simia Unguana" claimed *uungwana*-ness both in reference to, and in defiance of, the term's history.[100]

The appropriation of the term *waungwana* by ex-slaves who were no longer *watumwa,* but not *waungwana* by the elite's definition, created a profound tension in the grammar of cultural ideals, one that would be answered by the elites' employment of words like *ustaarabu* (Arabness) and *utamaduni* (culturedness) to reassert a semantics of social superiority.[101] As *waungwana* became a common term of self-definition among freed slaves in the second half of the nineteenth century, *ustaarabu* gained popularity as an elite cultural ideal.[102] In claiming "Arabness"—an Arabness anchored to sociocultural notions of Arabness forged in Zanzibar as well as in pan-Arab dialogues—elites sought a cultural identity that located prestige in new signs and genealogies of culturedness. Freed people challenged elite identification and sought to form a more inclusive notion of urbaneness by taking the name *waungwana*, but elites imagined their social singularity in many of the same ways as they had before the rapid expansion of the Zanzibari slave population. *Ustaarabu* was fixed in a Zanzibari "Arab" sensibility, signified by local social and material concepts in reference to separate, sometimes fictive, origins. It thus explicitly excluded the freed people who referenced a long history of elite self-imaging practices and claimed an elevated social position by calling themselves *waungwana*.[103]

Corporate identity was refashioned by slaves in myriad other ways—through dance groups, membership in *turuq* (Sufi orders, or "brotherhoods"), informal labor organization, and domestic congregation.[104] For example, by the 1870s, the burgeoning population of freed slaves, slaves, poorer slave-owners, and immigrants congregated opposite the elite "Stone Town" in a nebulous area called simply Ng'ambo or, literally, the "other side."[105] The social and political constitution of Ng'ambo exemplifies other ways that slaves and ex-slaves sought to redefine themselves in the context of their objectification: through the creation of a community of their own and by purchasing slaves. In the social matrix of Ng'ambo, slaves and ex-slaves sought to reconstitute themselves by investing in their own slaves and exacting some measure of control over their charges. In Ng'ambo, the poorest of slave-owners lived in close quarters with their slaves. As with the wealthy, poor slave-owners sought to use slaves to bring social benefits. According to most analysts of nineteenth-century Zanzibar, when a slave was freed, his first great investment was often in a slave.[106] Charles New wrote that, since "work is the badge of the slave," freed slaves endeavored to purchase their own slaves not only to provide financial support, but also to create for themselves a new mode of sociality. Buying a slave was a way to change one's social "badge," to be something better than a slave.[107]

The strategies of slaves and ex-slaves for self-remaking hinged on the twin abilities of self-definition and social differentiation through acts such as renaming, reclothing, and acquiring slaves. Self-definition could, however, sometimes result in the choice to stay with an owner after manumission. In such cases, place might not have changed after legal manumission, but the ability to define oneself did. It is curious how many freed slaves chose to stay with their former owners after being freed. Sometimes this choice was made out of sheer dependency. For example, "Kaiser Koor," a ten-year-old "nautch [or dancing] girl" born in Kutch, chose to remain with her former owner, Mamaji, also a Kutchi nautch dancer.[108] Some ex-slaves were more emphatic about their choices. When a thirty-year-old Yao woman (whose name is illegible in the surviving documents) was emancipated in 1873, she told the court that she had lived with her owner for twenty-three years of her own will, and that she would make up her mind as to where she went "as she pleas[ed]"—not by anyone else's direction.[109] While we cannot know why she remained with her former owner, her statement suggests that, though she was remade by another, she thought of herself as something different from her owner's projection. By choosing to stay with her former owner, she continued to define herself.

The social conditioning process of slavery created fetters more difficult to throw off than the irons that initially bound the enslaved. This was one of the psychological traumas of enslavement, a subjection through which slaves would necessarily have to negotiate a new life in Zanzibar. "Freedom" (*uhuru*) could thus be no single thing, no state simply granted to the subjected. For slaves in Zanzibar, "freedom" was reinscription, making a new self out of the objectifying parameters of slavery, creating a desirable social space within the structures of coastal social hierarchies.[110] Yet freed slaves managed their freedom through a series of self-fashioning projects that did not always entail a break with former owners. Such efforts could never wholly reconstruct the person, for even if the (ex-)slave went so far as to return to her home, a psychological bond to Zanzibar often remained. This was the case with an unnamed slave of Said bin Salim, who won a brief leave of absence from her owner in Zanzibar in order to return to her family in Digo country near Mombasa. After reaching her home, she decided never to return to Zanzibar, yet she continued to acknowledge her relationship with her owner by sending him an annual remittance of one Maria Teresa dollar.[111]

BY WAY OF CONCLUSION: HUMANITARIAN CONSEQUENCES

Since the legacies of creating symbols out of humans are far too numerous to consider here, I conclude by illustrating one outcome that would have profound repercussions: that of the concern for the African slave as the "moral purpose" of colonial annexation.[112] As I suggested earlier in this chapter, Western images of slavery in Africa bore a remarkable resemblance to slave-owner ideologies in the sense that they were bound to the conviction that slaves had no voice of their own. The negation of slaves' interests, and African interests generally, allowed Westerners to project their particular, often class-determined, values onto the continent, an imposition of voice that would be a cornerstone of evangelizing missions, antislavery crusades, and interventionist boosterism.[113] Though the apogee of the East African slave trade and colonial intervention were distanced in time—Livingstone's work captured Western imaginations decades before British or German colonial imposition in East Africa—the accumulation of antislavery rhetoric created an image of Africans as helpless children enslaved by debauched "Arabs" and in need of redemption.[114] As evidence of the deep-seated humanitarian conviction of the redeemers, when direct British intervention in East Africa was first discussed as a possibility, it was imagined as a remedy for the slave trade, not a goal in itself. As the British Consul Frederic Holmwood wrote in his annual report on Zanzibar for 1874–75, "I am convinced that half measures [to suppress the trade, i.e., by sea but not by land] will be of no avail in stopping this movement, and that, however opposed such a step may be to our traditional policy, the blessing of freedom cannot be assured to Equatorial Africa until the tree is felled at the root, and footing established in the slave-producing districts of Nyassa, by the formation of a Government settlement."[115] Among some British analysts, annexation was a solution to African problems, a moral imperative. Humanitarians believed that "order" in East Africa would not be the legacy of "Arab" colonizers on the coast but would take both the resolve and abilities of Englishmen. Only England, Sir Samuel Baker wrote in a reflection on his travels in the Lakes Region, "has the force to civilize."[116] Colonial annexation, when imagined as an effort to bring order to a continent corrupted by perpetual slaving, was thus a moral crusade, one founded on the guiding logic of the slave-owner: that slaves, like children, must become something new under foreign tutelage.[117]

For the British public, there was no stronger interest in East Africa than that of moral sentiment. Economic arguments for the possession of East Africa had to be wrapped in the cloak of redemption to win broader appeal, and even then they would only ever draw cool responses from the British government. As we saw in chapter 3, few British businesses had direct experience in East Africa, and so British policymakers believed that the economic potential of the region was unproven. Humanitarians had long pressured the British government for action against the slave trade and even the acquisition of Mombasa and the mainland.[118] This pressure spurred the British government to impose anti-slave trade treaties on Zanzibar's rulers and institute an Indian Ocean anti–slave trade patrol, but it did little to affect the Foreign Office's long-term disinterest in East

Africa. In the late 1880s, policymakers did a radical about-face. This was not the result of a newfound concern for East African slaves. Instead, the new attention paid to the East African region was born of the Foreign Office's singular desire to insure the security of more profound nodes of British interest—principally Egypt and India—in an era of rapid European imperial expansionism. As British influence in the region waned with the rapidly diminishing power of its proxy, the Sultan of Zanzibar, and East Africa became more relevant to British concerns elsewhere, Britons moved to protect real and potential imperial interests against German and French rivals. Though the Foreign Office's concerns were strategic, foreign policy and moral sentiment would decisively merge. Rationalizing annexation for itself and the public, the Foreign Office parroted the discourse of African redemption. Using humanitarian images to "clothe its African actions in the garb of philanthropy," foreign policymakers, according to Ronald Robinson, John Gallagher, and Alice Denny, "took pleasure in supposing that in the pursuit of the national interest it was also putting down the slave trade and spreading sweetness and light."[119] When East Africa became relevant to protecting greater British interests in the Mediterranean and Indian Oceans, the rhetoric of antislavery converged with a desire for colonial annexation.

The missionaries Tozer and Steere saw clearly the slippage between imperial actions and antislavery convictions. Tozer condemned "official persons" in Britain who concerned themselves with the slave trade but seemed to have no interest in slaves. Highlighting what seemed to him a horrible contradiction, he concurred with Steere that "Englishmen generally have a very much less kindly feeling towards a free negro than the Arabs have towards their slaves." "Hence," he concluded, "all the twaddle and jargon about 'inhuman traffic,' with which every official paper is bespattered, is like doctored beer, manufactured to suit the taste of the British Public."[120] Unfortunately, the rhetoric of abolition would rarely be subject to this kind of critique in the metropole. Indeed, the rhetoric of abolition would provide a palatable justification for intervention precisely because it appealed to the British public through one of their most vivid images of Africa: the wretched slave. Tozer and Steere recognized the unidimensionality of this image, perhaps because they had helped to create it. In the process of simultaneously typologizing Africans as victims and savages, redeemers, as much as the policymakers who relied on their rhetoric, obscured what slaves themselves wanted: some measure of self-determination.

The British and other Europeans had particular understandings of trajectory of human history, and the imposition of culturally specific narratives of civilization would become important to the history of East Africa's global relations. In the 1880s and 1890s, British, German, Belgian, and French interests in East Africa would substantially alter the frameworks through which East Africans negotiated relationships with the rest of the world. Yet interventionist impulses were born of geopolitical competitions, personal ambitions, and European public opinions that East Africans had little ability to affect. Here were the boundaries of East Africa's nineteenth-century remaking: despite their relationships with other regions and domestications of the world, East Africans had little control over how outsiders perceived them.[121] The images of East Africa that Westerners would develop and that would inform ideological justifications for intervention were ones that often failed to recognize both the regional meanings of East African social transformations in the latter nineteenth century and Africans' interests. As much as East Africans shaped global processes and remade their societies in relation to these processes, Western typifications of the region hinged on discursive frames of modernity, race, and civilization that held East Africans against the provincial standards of Europe. Thus, analyses of East Africa rarely acknowledged the internal logics of regional cosmopolitanisms and instead saw in them little more than debased contradictions. These frames of vision and the resulting taxonomies of East Africa that shaped Western public opinion are the focus of the final chapter.

CHAPTER 6

Picturesque Contradictions

Taxonomies of East Africa

On holiday in Zanzibar in the late 1880s, big-game hunter John C. Willoughby visited Sultan Barghash's palace at Chukwani. "I had always been under the impression that a Sultan's palace was indescribably blaze [*sic*] of pillars set with sparkling gems of incalculable value," Willoughby wrote in his memoir, "and thus if you could pick out a single loose stone and return with it to your native land, a life with such ease and comfort as results from a large revenue . . . would be your just reward." On arrival at Chukwani, Willoughby found neither the gems nor the incalculable value that he imagined. Instead, he found European chairs, chandeliers, Parisian mirrors, and colored prints from English Christmas periodicals. He was disgusted by the scene, despite the expense of the chandeliers and the opulence of much of the decor. The only things he found appealing were the "Turkish baths" and carpets—those things that most signified the Oriental exoticism he expected of Zanzibar.[1] Willoughby's presumptions, published a year before the formal acquisition of Zanzibar as a British protectorate, as well as later appraisals of Chukwani, reveal the great dissonance between the alterity Westerners hoped to find in Zanzibar and the actuality of East African cosmopolitanism. The perceptions of East Africa that were born of such dissonance and, more precisely, the efforts to explain it, were part of an analytical frame predicated on notions of race and discrete materialities. This frame, developed at the height of European and American fascination with the region, would shape the popular rhetoric of British intervention in East

Africa, and, just as important, provide perceptual building blocks for British colonial attitudes toward East Africans. Indeed, the legacies of nineteenth-century ways of seeing still inform perceptions of the East African region, and nowhere more than Zanzibar.[2]

Michael Adas's work, among other surveys of the ways in which Europeans' valuations of their own material culture (most notably new technologies) have shaped the way Westerners perceived non-Western people, points to the important place of materiality in ideologies of imperial expansion.[3] This chapter approaches imperial perceptions somewhat differently. It asks what happened when Europeans encountered their own material culture and technologies among those who were not subject to European rule and who gave new meanings to Western manufactures. To answer this question, the chapter considers how Anglophone travel-writers, missionaries, scientists, and consulate administrators referenced the cultural and material environments of East Africa to create an image of the region. The particular forms of image-making that I address arose from (1) a desire to compare East African materiality to Western ideals of "civilization," and (2) a discord between preconceived images and the cultural, economic, and social complexity that visitors like John C. Willoughby encountered. The concepts—that East Africans were internally contradicted, degenerate, and desperately needed the assistance of the West to engage successfully with modernity—that were embodied in resulting images represent a broader Western conceptualization of the world in the era of high imperialism. The internal contradiction that analysts came to see in East Africans, superficially evidenced by their mixing of "Oriental" and European furniture, umbrellas and nakedness, merry-go-rounds and veiled women, is an analytical invention born of nineteenth-century theories of difference, theories that continue to affect perceptions of Africa and much of the world.[4] Difference was the guiding conceptual tool for all of the interpretations of East Africa that I consider below. While difference is a human fact, its rationalization and the repercussions of its meaning deserve careful scrutiny. By considering nineteenth-century images of East Africa, we can perceive some of the ways in which Western analysts defined difference, represented it, and gave it coherence, meaning, and consequence for themselves and East Africans.

HIERARCHIES, IMAGES, AND EAST AFRICA IN THE WEST

The alterity Africa evidenced was not simply one of variance. By the mid–nineteenth century, many Westerners imagined difference as evidence of humanity's developmental hierarchy inscribed in slippery, imprecise, and changing ideas of race.[5] A discourse of natural human social stratification pervaded most accounts of East Africa, and this was firmly bound to the visible, therefore easily qualifiable and recordable, characteristics of populations, such as physical appearance and dress. Images of East Africa were scant before the mid-nineteenth century. The region captured the Anglophone world's fascination in the second half of the nineteenth century because it simultaneously presented the horrors of the slave trade and the romance of one of the world's last "unexplored" regions. Despite the deep histories of East Africa's global connections, to Western publics as much as to British trading houses the region seemed vast and tantalizing—what Ronald Robinson, John Gallagher, and Alice Denny called the "unopened continent."[6]

Although Britain had maintained colonies across the globe for centuries, British designs on East Africa had been mostly limited to the dreams of humanitarians intent on ending slavery in the region. In the sixteenth and seventeenth centuries the Portuguese maintained a colonial presence on the coast. But since the eighteenth-century allied coastal/Omani defeat of the Portuguese, no European power had laid claim to any substantial length of the coast north of Mozambique. The consolidation of Busaidi power at Zanzibar in the 1830s and the intimate diplomatic relationships the British developed and maintained with Busaidi rulers made any direct British intervention in the region redundant. Since the region seemed of little strategic or economic interest to the Empire, the Foreign Office chose to pursue its interests through the influence of the Sultanate of Zanzibar—a policy from which it did not waver until the end of the 1880s, when German annexation of much of Zanzibar's hinterland forced policymakers to reconsider their strategy. Though British foreign policy and public interests in the East African coast were extremely limited before the mid-nineteenth century, in the 1860s stories and images of East Africa were flooding Anglophone popular consciousness as the horrors of the slave trade and feats of "discovery" became front-page news. In the following two decades, Anglophone perceptions of East Africa would be forged on the ground in Zanzibar, Ujiji, and on the slopes of Kilimanjaro, presented through the vehicle of Western contrasts with "natives," and deduced from the images of East Africa that circulated in the West.[7]

Most mid- to late-nineteenth-century narratives of Africa shared at least one thread: that the entire continent was appallingly stunted in its evolutionary progress, that Africans were distanced from Europeans not only in space but, more importantly, in time. Temporality now seemed to set Africans apart from Westerners.[8] Africans seemed to inhabit the evolutionary past of modernity. Hegel had once famously described the African continent as "no Historical part of the world," but in the latter nineteenth century, the anthropologist Edward Tylor believed that barbarous tribes represented civilization's past, stages through which moderns had successfully, in an evolutionary sense, passed.[9] Africa seemed a great storehouse of history, an island entombed in pasts long forgotten by the rest of the world. Travel in Africa was *like* travel back in time; a contemporaneous past akin to civilization's discarded history.[10] Similar to the ways in which the Khoisan would be used as ethnological representatives of human origins—walking time capsules of the evolutionary past—East Africans resembled civilization's prehistory.[11] Theorists imagined Africans as developmentally comparable with ancients, and such evolutionary antiquity was evidenced in the material life of Zanzibaris. The distinguished raciologist Charles Pickering believed that Zanzibaris had "more than the usual proportion" of ancient Hebrew and Egyptian customs. Pickering wrote that a "Swahili," for example, immediately understood the use of an ancient Egyptian amulet he carried. Writing on the slave trade, Pickering claimed that the child-stealing that was rife among Arabs was practiced, "on much the same footing as formerly . . . by the Phoenicians."[12] Ruschenberger, an American travel-writer, described Zanzibaris in similar terms by describing clothing and the Arab character in a way that would become standard in analyses of Zanzibar. After offering a description of Arab dress, he concluded that "the costume of an Arab gentleman in the present day . . . was probably very much the same in the earliest times of which we have any record," despite the fact that such clothing was made of American textiles.[13]

Africa's retardation, many believed, resulted from the continent's disconnection from world history. For the traveler-writer Richard Burton, Africa was "the great Nineteenth Century Island," a metaphorical and physical development of the nineteenth century. The Suez Canal made Africa a physical island; its exploration wrenched it from its slumber and pitched it headlong into the contemporary world.[14] To J. Frederic Elton, a traveler who would follow Burton, Africa appeared as the "last continent unpenetrated by civilisation."[15] Harry Johnston, a contemporary of Elton, was more explicit and historical: Africa was the "new World of the nineteenth century."[16] Though such subtexts of conquest and eradication were not always explicit, most popular literature pictured Africa simultaneously as the past and, through its discovery, the future. But

Africa's future, unlike its past, had little to do with Africans themselves. Africa's future was determined by its reentrance into the flow of history occasioned by the "penetration" of Westerners. The British Consul at Zanizbar in 1875, H. Bartle Frere, hoped that through trade and the guiding hand of civilization, Africa would no longer be called the "Lost Continent."[17]

With the elaboration of geography as a key means of knowledge in the service of commerce and entertainment, this "penetration" entailed more than trade or travel; it implied a total understanding of the continent.[18] In East Africa, as elsewhere, the natural world of which humans were a part was systematized, made comprehensible in its diversity through collection, scrutinization, and categorization.[19] This turn toward scientific quantification, comparison, and categorization—in short, a more complete taxonomy—is evident in otherwise sensational travel narratives. Richard Burton, who would write four volumes on East Africa, devoted whole chapters to such seeming mundanities as the flora, fauna, and rainfall of Zanzibar. Alan Moorhead typified the seductive qualities of the comprehensive travel narratives as "exert[ing] an extraordinary power over peoples' minds." He noted that "one would have thought that there was enough here to inform, confuse, and finally satiate the most besotted student of African travels, but still the public could not have enough."[20] The desire for taxonomic knowledge of East Africa expanded in all directions, and Britons produced more of it than anyone.

By the end of the 1870s, Zanzibar and the East African mainland were emphatically on the Victorian map. After Stanley, for example, travel writers usually assumed that their readers already knew much about Zanzibar. The city could thus be quickly described with the ready clichés of sultans, ivory, cloves, and slaves, "greedy Banyans," "mongrel Swahili," and "degenerate Arabs." An overawed American arriving in Zanzibar in the early 1880s, for example, had already completely digested the image of Zanzibar in popular literature. "It's *Eastern*. It's Oriental. It's *Stanley*," exclaimed the future consul Edward Ropes Jr.[21] By 1890, the year Zanzibar formally became a British protectorate, Stanley's third account of East African travel, *In Darkest Africa*, was being read, "more universally and with deeper interest," according to a reviewer, than anything else published in the same year.[22] To appreciate the scale of this explosion of interest in East Africa, we might consider the region's coverage in a paper like the *Times* of London.[23] The number of articles relating to Zanzibar grew from virtually nil in the 1850s and 1860s to scores in any given year in the 1870s, due in no small part to Stanley's search for Livingstone.

Stanley's musings brought images of East Africa into the homes of more people than ever before. Another gauge of the fascination with East Africa after the first Stanley expedition is that when Sultan Barghash visited Europe in the summer of 1875, three years after the publication of Stanley's *How I Found Livingstone*, he attracted British attention quite out of proportion to the economic or diplomatic importance of East Africa to Britain.[24] The *Times* of London published almost daily reports on the sultan during his short visit, thirty-two in all. Perhaps more surprising, the *New York Times* covered the sultan's journeys both in England and France.[25] The fascination with the sultan was so great that by the fall a new hat design swept high-end French, British, and American markets: the Zanzibar bonnet. A domestication of the Busaidi family turban, it was a woman's felt hat wrapped in a brocaded scarf that approximated the blue, scarlet, and gold turban cloth (Swahili: *kilemba*) worn by Barghash.[26]

Magazines like the *Academy*, which ran a series of articles on Zanzibar beginning with the sultan's visit in 1875 and continuing through 1878, as well as the *Journal of the Society of the Arts, Journal of the Royal Geographical Society of London,* and *The Contemporary Review,* played important roles in disseminating information and offering forums for debate about East Africa. *Blackwood's Magazine* published both Burton's and Speke's accounts of travel across East Africa.[27] *Harper's Weekly* followed the story of Stanley's search for Livingstone closely, as did most major newspapers. Frere's writings on Zanzibar and the slave trade appeared as features in *Macmillan's Magazine.* Just as important, popular travel monographs were widely read and prompted an ever-growing audience to take an interest in East Africa. Audiences read Livingstone, Burton, Speke, and Stanley for the fantastic, for images of horrible, fascinating, and picturesque dystopias.[28] These travel narratives were laden with thick description, images, and detailed analyses. Between the 1860s and 1880s, the number of books published in which reflections on Zanzibar and East Africans were prominent mushroomed from only a few in the 1850s to scores by 1880, many of which were the most popular travelogues of the era and the standards of African travel writing, including Livingstone's *Life and Labours in Africa,* Burton's *The Lake Regions of Central Africa,* Speke's *Journal of the Discovery of the Source of the Nile,* Stanley's *How I Found Livingstone, Through the Dark Continent,* and *In Darkest Africa.*[29] Unlike narratives of West and southern Africa, the "Orient," or India, nineteenth-century descriptions of East Africa had little regional literature on which to build. East Africa was one of the last regions of the world to be systematically described by Westerners, and so writers drew from Orientalist travel narrative conventions, West African tropes of slave-trading and tribal savagery, the southern African standards of missionaries, conflict with "natives," and hunting.[30] More than any other body of literature, such travel accounts provided the basis for both Western popular and scientific knowledge of East Africa.[31]

Travel narratives were wildly popular, and from the 1860s they included an increasing number of images. These images were usually conjoined to sets of facts; thus, they were not only pleasurable, but were also evidence of the taxonomies outlined in the text. Since most East African travelogues were compilations of scientific knowledge, however fascinating in their allegories of adventure, the analyses they offered were underwritten by a concern with ordering the world, creating taxonomies of types, measuring progress, and defining concrete levels of advancement in relation to the West.[32] "Discovery" was as much about the place of the West in relation to the rest of the world as it was about East Africa.[33] What is particularly important about the image as a new mode of perception in accounts of East Africa is the kind of categorical meaning and relationships between people and the material environment that it offered to Western audiences. By ranking barbarism and semi-civilized behavior, and visually representing corresponding subjects, the assumed position of European civilization as the pinnacle of advancement revealed itself culturally, materially, and physically. Anthropological, ethnological, and other reflections on East Africa were thus manifestations of a perceived global hierarchy given dramatic form by references to and inferences from the image. Through images, East Africans became objects of Western knowledge in ways that were fundamentally distancing since, as a categorical form of knowledge, imaging was intently focused on difference, on the exotic nature of East Africans.[34]

So essential did the mass imaging of places like East Africa become to Western publishers that words began to conform to the conventions of pictures—even to act like them. The juxtapositions of places, people, and objects became "scenes," and places as well as people came to be discussed as if they were little more than pictures. This reduction, enacted through constant reference to what analysts called the "picturesque" nature of East Africa, created an exotic, consumable world—a world-as-picture—that framed people not as actors but as backdrops, figures in dramatic tableaus drawn from literary imagery.[35] Images created easily

FIG. 13.—African negro.

Figure 15. Jacob Wainwright as an object of physical
anthropology in Edward Tylor's 1880 *Anthropology.*
He is described as an "African negro," and the text is
concerned primarily with the shape of Wainwright's
nose. (Illustration from Edward Tylor, *Anthropology:
An Introduction to the Study of Man and Civilization.*
1880; repr., London: D. Appleton, 1913.)

consumable, fixed ideas about Africa that transcended class and literacy
and added a solid evidentiary underpinning to even the most superficial
analyses.[36] The efficacy of the image to reveal information about the
imaged was glaringly apparent when Zanzibari sailors arrived in Hamburg. In 1871 Sultan Majid's corvette, *Majidi,* visited the port. The crew
was not received as Zanzibaris had been previously in Europe; they were
no longer objects of simple fascination. They were now objects of scientific inquiry, documented through the image. "The opportunity offered
[by the arrival of the corvette]," the Scientific Intelligence editor of
Harper's Weekly wrote, "was embraced by the naturalists of that city to
secure photographs of the types of humanity represented in the persons of
the officers and crew." The photos resulted in a "remarkable series of
illustrations of the various races from Africa and Southern Arabia." Germany's celebrated ethnologists, Rudolf Ludwig Karl Virchow and Robert

Hartmann, commended the "accuracy" of the photographs and endorsed
their "ethopological [sic] value." The resulting publication included fifty-
four photographs accompanied by text that described the race, age,
height, color of the hair, eyes, lips, nails and other "physical peculiarities"
of each sailor.[37] The publication of the album represents a new epistemic
relationship between the West and Zanzibar. Zanzibaris had become
desirable and knowable as pictures. Pictures—including thick literary
description—not only fascinated readers, but also allowed them to make
sense of East Africa, to fit its inhabitants into elaborate taxonomies of
humanity.

Robert Hartmann's own influential ethnographic treatises, repub-
lished in several European languages, depended almost entirely on
images borrowed from travelogues.[38] These images of East Africans,
many of them sketches by artists working only from textual descriptions, provided a crucial evidentiary base for his taxonomies and suppo-
sitions about the character of each "type" presented. The materiality
and physicality of East Africans, captured and explained in image and
description, was a window into the character of places and people. In
travelogues and ethnological accounts, East Africans thus appeared more
as representative specimens than as people with names, interests, or
desires. In the last section of the chapter, I outline the specific ways in
which materiality and hierarchy were conjoined in images and analyses.
But I would like first to explore the modes of typologization that Western
analysts applied to East Africans. By doing so, we can discern the rhetorical foundation on which descriptions of East African consumerism were
constructed.

SEMI-CIVILIZED TABLEAUS

"Civilization," Rider Haggard wrote, ". . . when applied to black races,
produces effects diametrically opposite to those we are accustomed to in
white nations: it debases before it can elevate."[39] The implications of this
idea are perhaps too vast to fully address here. Yet, Haggard's evocation
of the partially civilized African highlights a forgotten turn in Victorian
theories of civilizational evolution. As a median category between civilization and barbarism, the semi-civilized—what Charles Darwin's pro-
tégé Frederic Farrar called the second "stage of humanity"—ultimately
defined both.[40] Theories of the nature of semi-civilized East Africans confirmed the difference between civilization and its proximate state.
Though evolving racial theories eventually dissolved the semi-civilized in

the twentieth century, in the late nineteenth century semi-civilization was a yardstick against which both civilization and savagery were measured. More important, the theorization of the "partially civilized" allowed for a fuller articulation of the virility of "pure" populations, of the viscosity of "purity" itself. In their almost unanimous abhorrence of "Swahili," "mongrel Arabs," and other semi-civilized East Africans, Western analysts defined cultural virtues in biological terms, as the genetic heritage of specific races.[41] Where civilization became equated with purity, in the second half of the nineteenth century, degeneracy was equated with the semi-civilized, the hybrid.[42]

Hybridity was a mid-nineteenth-century invention closely connected to the idea of the semi-civilized. It first emerged as a biological theory of the erosion of pure types through their combination. Hybridity therefore implied not just the crossing of two unlike types but that the mixing of pure types resulted in degeneration of their descendants. Many Victorian theorists, like John Jackson, imagined the hybrid person as a "fermenting monstrosity" internally conflicted, a "blot on creation" whom nature "hastens with all possible expedition to reduce to annihilation."[43] Like hybridity, the concept of the semi-civilized was rooted in the idea that two essentially unlike things combine to form something qualifiably different from its progenitors. When a little civilization was given to the savage, he became semi-civilized, which in the latter nineteenth century did not imply progress toward civilization but internal contradiction.[44] According to most analysts of East Africa, the African-Arab hybrids of Zanzibar inherited both their African and Arab biological vices. Analysts did not assume that Zanzibaris were half-civilized, but that "half" was evidence of the inability of Zanzibaris to become civilized on their own. Many presumed that, like the hybrid, the semi-civilized person had no chance for autonomous civilization because her "semi-ness" forfeited progress, except in the most minimal ways. Just as physical hybrids were often theorized as infertile, so Zanzibaris had become sterile in their cultural evolution;[45] their "semi-ness" locked them in stasis.

The notion of the semi-civilized was also an attempt to make sense of the diverse histories of consumer desire, economy, marriage, and migration that were so clearly evident in East Africa. By the time G. F. Scott Eliot published his treatise on "the Suahili" in the early 1890s, the relation of purity to civilization, as well as purity's distinction from cultural and/or racial mongrelity, had been heavily theorized. He wrote that a "Suahili" boy, "who is usually not removed by a single generation from savagery cannot be expected to show the truthfulness, honesty, unselfishness, and purity which, as we know, always and invariably characterise European youths who have been brought up in Christian teaching, and represent in their instincts about twenty centuries of hereditary civilisation."[46] Eliot's assumptions represent the accumulation of several decades of racial theorizing that presumed civilization to be, in part, biologically determined. If civilization were instinctual, a result of genetic purity, then, without European intervention, Africans had little chance of attaining the virtues Western analysts saw in themselves. The obsession with purity and its virtues even led some analysts to the conclusion, by the 1870s, that British humanitarian efforts should be trained on those "pure" Africans untouched by civilization, for it would seem they were the greatest hope for Africa's progress.[47] While few British administrators in Zanzibar or government policymakers at home agreed that efforts should be primarily directed toward "pure" Africans, most concluded that East Africans were so adversely affected by the slave trade and their failed attempts at auto-civilization that they needed the paternal hand of European guidance.

East Africans and their material environment provided images of contrasts that demonstrated to many Western observers the incongruity of combination. While civilization could be defined by what it had progressed beyond, semi-civilized peoples were recognizable for what they had not attained. Thus, discussions of the semi-civilized Zanzibari were concerned with defining the shades of difference between Zanzibar and civilization, usually through the absence of one or another Western material or moral virtue.[48] The American Consul Speer described Zanzibar in this way: there were "no actors, theatres, painters, no coopers, public mills, no cloth factories, no fancy gardeners, no steam machinery, no post office, no author, no lawyers, real estate agents, no (native) doctors [i.e., no "natives" trained in Western medicine], no speech makers, printing press, no taxes, politicians, banks and no proper money."[49] Aside from the fact that much of this is false—for example, Zanzibaris owned steam-powered sugar mills, and there were several standard currencies in the city (Barghash had even minted his own by this time)—the fact that Zanzibar was only defined by what it was not suggests that semi-civilization was not so much a stage of attaining half-civilization as it was a state of having only the most negligible civilized veneer. The semi-civilized and degraded nature of Zanzibar was apparent everywhere an observer turned. Human and object alike evidenced the degeneracy of semi-civilized society. The author W. Cope Devereux took his readers down a "dirty, narrow street, lined with wigwam shops, where slave food is the principle article sold. Here there is a medley of putrid shark, decayed vegetables, rank meat, sour ghee, and diseased and villainous-looking mongrel Arabs and high-hipped negro women . . . the atmosphere so tainted, the whole so disgusting that we were very glad to find ourselves even in the slave market."[50] Devereux's picture of decay is indicative of the way literary "scenes" worked as metaphors for the very nature of Zanzibari society. The entire scene breathes of horrible degeneracy; the rank meat, sour ghee, and decayed vegetables were matched by the villainous-looking "mongrel Arabs." The superficiality of the material environment was imagined to evidence the character of Zanzibaris.

In Western accounts of East Africa, clothing was primary evidence for the categorization of character. Through clothes, analysts and readers could read race, attitude, social place, and character. Rebecca Wakefield introduced the population of Zanzibar to her readers by describing it as a "strange mixture." "There first meets you," she wrote, "the dignified Arab, dressed in long costly robes and bright turban." Next, "the fairer and intelligent looking Hindoo; then a number of more than half naked Sawahili slaves."[51] The picture reveals an index of humanity that necessarily begins with lighter-skinned, clothed, free people and ends with the African as naked, enslaved, and neither dignified nor intelligent. The American adventurer J. Ross Browne devoted much space to the hierarchization of Zanzibaris through material differentiation. At the horse-racing grounds, he found

> [t]he Banyans, with their tall red turbans; the Hindus, with their loose pantaloons and long black beards, the Parsees, with their square calico hats and tight coats; the Persians, few in number, but conspicuous, with their rich flowery costumes and flashy silk turbans; and here and there a dusky Belooche, gave a picturesque and animated appearance to the scene. For the most part, however, this heterogeneous concourse of people consisted of different tribes of Arabs, from the sultan and his officers down to the darkest Sowhelian or half-breed.[52]

In reflections such as these, objects typified and identified people, and taxonomic description reduced them to their material trappings. People were given internal coherency inferred from their clothing and then fitted into a racial structure.

Anglophone writers imagined diversities as evidencing a graphic, classlike hierarchy, from the ostensibly "pure" Banyan (Hindu western Indian) *down* to the "half-breed." Charles Pickering, who began his research into the races of mankind at Zanzibar not long after Browne's departure, was more explicit about this hierarchy. The Banyans of Kutch, he surmised, were "obviously pure," and thus distinct from the various mongrels of Zanzibar.[53] Devereux described a Zanzibari "Arab" named "Bullhead" [Bilad], the interpreter on his ship, in venomous terms. "These half-breed Arabs," he begins his description, "are generally roguish; a species of low cunning outcasts, possessing the subtlety of the Asiatic, the treachery of the Arab, and cowardice of the negro; and would do anything for a few dollars." Here the "half-breed's" genealogy reveals not just genetic history, but a history of incorporating all of the inadequacies of his corporate ancestry. The nature of such mixed people was evidenced in their materiality. "Our ruffian," Devereux continues, "I will describe: He wears a large white turban, on a little grisly cocoanut-looking [sic] skull; bleared right eye, left blind; face, a dirty black, indented by small-pox. . . . Extended nostrils, thick lips, and short neck; a light soiled cotton garment comes below the knees, and over it a bad imitation of a Zouave jacket, white, with a dash of blue."[54] Like his mongrel heritage and complexion, his jacket is an imitation, and his unseemly "halfness" is matched by his appearance: he is soiled, grisly. There is, in fact, nothing pure about him. The inadequacies of his genealogy and materiality are reflected by each other. What Devereux's description points up is that images of Zanzibar were often taxonomic: human types could be easily recognized and defined, while race and materiality were intimately aligned.

This kind of typologization of Zanzibaris was guided by a profound faith in essential differences. Diametrically opposed to the "fine-looking" Banyan was the "modern Msuahili," whom Charles New described as "a medley of almost everything oriental, and . . . perhaps not without a spice of something occidental in his blood." In such taxonomies, semi-civilized people became the explicit focus of attention because they defined the opposite ends of the spectrum most clearly. New describes the Swahili as the progeny of the "Arabs of various tribes, Hindoos, Belooch, etc., [who] have been so long resident upon the coast, and have so inter-married with the natives, that a race of half-castes has arisen; hybrids, or creoles, widely differing from each other according to their various parentage, yet coming under the one designation, Wasuahili." It is thus halfness, more than specific heritage, that defined the Swahili for New. He continues with a more precise physical categorization, and draws a direct line between semi-civilization and barbarism: "Every physical type is to be found among [the Swahili], from the high Asiatic of the noble Arab to the lowest negro type of the people who come from the regions of the Lake Nyassa." Here race, geography, and character are tightly bound. The "lowest type" is from the interior of Africa; the "high" noble is Asiatic.[55] This rhetorical conflation of geography, color, intellect, and ability was a hallmark of the science of race that was merging with popular discourse when New wrote his treatise.[56]

From the early 1870s, popular accounts of Zanzibar such as New's employed a more scientifically inflected language in which skin color and culture were inseparable. Expeditions of discovery were fitted out with not only barometers and survey apparatuses, but also mandates to document the "types" of people whom they encountered. For instance, in 1873 the British Association for the Advancement of Science appointed a joint committee of geographers and anthropologists to draw up general instructions for anthropological investigation. The first of the committee's actions was to give the Cameron Expedition from Zanzibar to the Lakes, "detailed notes and queries on general anthropology, physical anthropology, religions, myths, customs, language, war-customs, iron-manufacture, ornamentation, etc."—"drawn up," the report on the expedition's outfitting read, "by the members of the committee and others who are recognised as authorities in their respective branches of anthropology." Finally, Vernon Cameron was furnished with a set of the famous physician Paul Broca's tables, "for estimating the colour and the skin and hair" of peoples encountered.[57]

Victorian racio-cultural theories of semi-civilization had already written Zanzibar out of modernity. Africans, Indians, Arabs, Islam, Hinduism—all these categories were defined as antithetical to modern society. "An Arab government," Charles New wrote in his analysis of Zanzibar, "is necessarily a Muhammadan government, and Muhammadanism carries with it two essential concomitants enough to bear down any nation or people, viz., *polygamy* and *slavery.* Where such a system exists, progress is impossible. It lays an embargo upon all civilization. Sapping, as it does, the foundation of all morality, it destroys the physical energy, enervates the mental power, and hangs like a dead weight upon every people who are its victims."[58] In this rhetoric, Sultan Barghash himself—despite his cosmopolitan vision— became the object of parody, an example of the contradiction of Muslims and modernity. When Barghash sailed one of his steamships to Jiddah in order to make the hajj, Bishop Tozer wrote mockingly, with a surprising ignorance of Islam, that Barghash was, "a modernizer that might well make Mahomet turn in his coffin."[59] Richard Burton laid the "debased nature" of all East Africans squarely on the shoulders of semi-civilized coastal residents who were, he charged, "degenerating from a more civilised Arab history rather than a people advancing towards cultivation."[60]

Contemporary Western common sense dictated that the hybrid was weak, morally and physically inferior, and incapable of real civilization on his own. As a result, Western reflections often singled out the "half-caste" for ridicule. In places like West and South Africa, reflections on the person of partial European ancestry were usually contemptuously framed.[61] In East Africa, Westerners faced the conceptual problem of mixedness in a population that was not only a confusing amalgamation of people from all over the world, but that enthusiastically incorporated objects from the West. By consuming Western goods, Zanzibaris seemed to both compress the cultural distance between themselves and Westerners and complicate material definitions of civilization. As a result, the disparagement of East African desire for Western goods developed a defensive tone in Western analyses. In the literature on East Africa, Anglophone authors were particularly critical of what they perceived as reflections of their civilization in the semi-civilized "native."

OBJECTS OF CIVILIZATION

"Scenes" were not pleasurable when, as John C. Willoughby found, the familiar merged with the exotic, that is, when the analyst faced the hybrid. In their "halfness," semi-civilized people were neither properly civilized nor picturesquely alien. Joseph Osgood wrote of a Zanzibari wedding crowd dressed in diverse styles typical of "half-civilized" peoples: "This one wears a soldier's cap and a worn out military coat; . . . that one a white turban this one a civet skin, . . . and that ludicrous collection of skins and cloth, rags, and colors, adorns the indispensable buffoon of the procession."[62] In their ostensibly European, Arab, and African clothing the crowd appeared discordant, neither like Europeans, Arabs, nor Africans. Clelia Weeks wrote that semi-civilization was also exemplified in the way in which "the Arab enjoys music." This consisted, she explained, of putting one music box on top of another and setting both to play at once. Unable to properly appreciate the music, the Arab seemed to experience European music only as discordance.[63] Much like a Zanzibari in a European soldier's cap or an "Arab" enjoying two music boxes playing at once, the African with an umbrella—a sign of Victorian, middle-class sensibility and taste—seemed an outrageous combination to Western visitors. A guide sent to Vernon Cameron's caravan from the famous king Mirambo carried an umbrella while marching, and this humored as much as it incensed Cameron. "He kept it open the whole day," Cameron wrote, "continually spinning it round and round in a most ludicrous fashion; and when we came to some jungle he added to the absurdity of his appearance by taking off his only article of clothing—his loin-cloth—and placing it on his head after having carefully folded it. The sight of a perfectly naked negro walking under an umbrella was," he concluded, "too much for my gravity, and I fairly exploded with laughter."[64] The "negro" and the umbrella were two things essentially different and incommensurate: one rude, the other a symbol of middle-class sensibility. The umbrella was, therefore, out of place in the "negro's" hands.

Umbrellas and other symbols of Western gentility in the hands of Africans often offended the sensibility of Westerners. In the mass use of the umbrella, Zanzibari fashion appeared to Western analysts as incongruous, a world turned upside-down. Though wealthy Zanzibaris were undoubtedly frustrated by the popular appropriation of the umbrella as a status symbol, Westerners' inability to come to terms with a consumer culture in which freed slaves carried umbrellas laid bare the exclusionary conceptual foundation of Western modernity. Ropes's letters home evidence a perception of the Zanzibari consumption of umbrellas as an inversion of global hierarchies: "It strikes me rather queerly," he wrote, "to see a half naked nigger carrying an umbrella." A few days later, unable to come to terms with the use of umbrellas in the city, he again wrote, "[it] strikes me queerly" that "all the people[,] even negroes carry *umbrellas.*" He later draws a more detailed sketch of the sheer incommensurability of the fact: "They carry [umbrellas] for sun or rain . . . even if they have only a little breech cloth on, or work all day in the sun bare headed."[65] For Ropes, the umbrella in Zanzibar contradicted the "proper" place and use of such consumer objects. To accept the marginalized poor, and even slaves, into the category of metropolitan gentility was, for Ropes, anarchy. It was the opposite of Western imaginings of modernity; it was disorder. To Americans and Europeans, the mass consumption of umbrellas in Zanzibar suggested a Zanzibari cognizance of Western modernity and yet Zanzibaris' utter inability to approximate it. Ropes, like Willoughby, assailed Zanzibari "Arab taste." He wrote that, "amid all of His Highnesses [sic] [Sultan Barghash's] splendor you would recognize a yellow painted chair or a piece of cheap German crockery alongside of something worth perhaps a thousand dollars." Such poor taste was indicative of the incommensurability of semi-civilized sensibilities and civilization. "Arabs," he concluded, "have no idea of things."[66] For Ropes, taste was an objective quality that only Westerners seemed to understand. Even someone with the vast resources of the sultan did not comprehend the logic of civilized taste. Willoughby described a reception hosted by Barghash as "an odd mixture of tawdry pomp, semi-barbaric splendour, and downright shoddiness."[67] Willoughby thought the reception and Barghash's palace at Chukwani were strange, incongruous mixes, shoddy and spurious attempts at civility.

About the same time that Ropes wrote of the sultan's ignorance of taste, the *Pall Mall Gazette* (London) carried a story on Germany's increasing interest in East Africa. The author credited the Germans with understanding the importance of indulging the absurdities of semi-civilized desires, of the "necessity . . . to Humour the tastes of semi-civilized consumers." Though Germans seemed to understand Zanzibari tastes, Western imports in Zanzibar nonetheless appeared inauthentic among the semi-civilized. The author of the *Gazette* article singled out Barghash's steam-powered merry-go-rounds for ridicule.[68] By disparaging the sultan's merry-go-rounds and the royal family's enjoyment of them, the author reveals his inability to imagine Arabs appreciating an object so quintessentially Western. Like a "negro" with an umbrella, the scene of the sultan and his wives on a merry-go-round was out of place and thus comical.

East African consumerism, described through the tropes of a barefoot African carrying an umbrella and the sultan with merry-go-rounds, seemed to challenge European images of themselves, of their uniqueness. Middle- to upper-class Victorians writing about Zanzibar defined themselves through a rhetoric concerned with "virtue," which encompassed material, cultural, and spiritual ideals. Though many believed that non-Westerners should engage in certain Western patterns of consumption and accept Western worldviews, Westerners were often entirely unprepared to confront what they imagined as modernisms in East Africa when Africans seem to have adopted them on their own. Dorothy Hammond and Alta Jablow suggest that such transgressors of a Victorian imagined cultural integrity, "contravened the clear-cut distinctions the British had drawn and intended to maintain between themselves and the Africans."[69]

In the second half of the nineteenth century, Western analysts sought ways to interpret what they saw as cultural hybridity recognizable in African appropriations of European or other imported goods.[70] Ludwig Ritter von Höhnel, who traveled extensively in the interior in the 1880s, acutely perceived a discordance between Western objects and the "native." He described Miriali, governor of the Kilimanjaro district, dressed in a scarlet "Arab bernouse" covered in gold tinsel. Over this he wore a red American general's coat worked with gold lace, a collar of vulture's feathers, and tied a Maasai colobus skin band just below each knee. To this Miriali added a broad-brimmed straw hat trimmed with bright red cloth and two long white ostrich feathers. Around his body he wore an additional eleven yards of red cloth *(bendera)*. At Miriali's request, members of the Count Samuel Teleki expedition took a picture of him and his men. Thereafter, he went to change clothes and returned without the regalia, as von Höhnel puts it most tellingly, "as a black man, pure and simple."[71] Without the Western clothes—symbols of his cosmopolitanness and superior access to foreign consumer goods—Miriali was a simple black man again, no longer confusingly mixed or ridiculous in von Höhnel's eyes. He was now pure. Though Miriali wanted a picture with his men to depict him in his imported finery, it is only when he took off the hybrid outfit and wrapped himself in more everyday cloth that he seemed to von Höhnel a black man, pure and simple.

Like von Höhnel, May French-Sheldon, a.k.a. Bibi Bwana ("Bébé Bwana")—the first Western woman to lead a caravan across East Africa—visited Kilimanjaro. There she encountered a man, who met her

tricked out in a pair of German military trousers, with side stripes, a white knitted shirt with a brilliant pin on the bosom, a celluloid high collar, a cravat of the most flaming color, a striped woolen Scotch shooting-coat, a flamboyant pocket-handkerchief and a pair of Russia-leather shoes, exposing blue silk clocked socks. His fine head was disfigured by wearing a black silk pot hat, which was canted backwards, bonnet fashion, by the long porcupine quill ear ornaments thrust through the rims of his ears. He carried an English walking-stick with a huge silver knob, and held in his hands a pair of kid gloves.

"This clown," French-Sheldon told her readers, was Miriali. She continued that he had "ridiculously bedecked himself" in the finery to honor his extraordinary guest, the "Bibi Bwana," or "Mrs. Sir."[72] Yet she could not contain her contempt for his clothes. "It is a shame a man like Mireali *[sic]*," she concluded, "should be so imposed upon by those [visitors who gave or sold him European clothes] who should have known better." Such clothes were inappropriate for him. French-Sheldon could not bear the contradiction, the ludicrousness of the chief in sundry European fashions. As soon as she was able to gain a private word she asked him, "Mireali, why do you wear these clothes?" She added, "They make you look like a goat." "I want to see you in your own native cloth and see you as Mireali, the great African sultan that you are," she told him.[73]

According to French-Sheldon's wishes, in the morning Miriali "presented himself with an enormous cloth . . . wound around him, and thrown over his shoulders in the most graceful and artistic manner, trailing regally behind him, carrying a long spear," which he complemented with his "picturesque coterie of wives and followers, all in native costumes." He finally appeared as French-Sheldon wanted him to: "He looked truly majestic as he advanced with his picturesque cortege," she explained to her readers, "and I could not help recalling some of the old pictures of Roman senators."[74] Miriali's incorporation of Western clothes into his regalia seemed horribly out of place, for what French-Sheldon expected of an African chief was his picturesqueness, reminiscent of antiquity, not the trappings of civilization. Mongrelization, hybridity, and semi-civilized fashion were neither picturesque nor desirable. For von Höhnel and French-Sheldon, Africa needed to present itself as black, pure and simple.

A desired cultural and material dissonance between the West and Africa was explicit in most accounts of East Africa, but Henry Morton Stanley offered his readers the most damning critique of the incommensurability of Western objects with African environments. He mocked Bishop Tozer for wearing his vestments of office in Zanzibar. "[T]his High Church . . . prelate in his crimson robe of office, and in the queerest of all head-dresses," Stanley explained, "seen stalking through the streets of Zanzibar, or haggling over the price of a tin-pot at a tinker's stall, is the most ridiculous sight I have seen anywhere outside of a clown show." The bishop's clothes seemed patently out of place, and Stanley declared, "I as a white man solemnly protest against the absurdity." A "picture" akin to the bishop, "in his priestly robes and a paper cap, in a tinker's stall," Stanley wrote, "is the King of Dahomey in a European hat with his body naked, promenading pompously about in this exquisite full dress." The bishop's clothes were as out of place in Africa as a European hat on an African's head. Stanley concluded that, "Whatever the Bishop in his blissful innocence may think of the effect which it produces in the minds of the heathen, I can inform him, that to the Arabs and Wanguana who have settled in Unyanyembe he is only an object of supreme ridicule."[75] This final point, the bishop's attempts to impress "natives" by donning his full attire, highlights Western residents' desire to define their uniqueness in and through East Africa in the latter nineteenth century. At the same time, Stanley's exception, "as a white man," to the fact that another white man presented himself in such a way as to become the object of "native" ridicule is further indicative of Victorian desires to firmly distinguish between Europeans as a group and "others," and to impress upon Africans the hierarchical distance between African and Western societies. Modernity, after all, was comparative.

Western diplomatic missions in Zanzibar were particularly keen to impress East Africans with Western material culture. After Seyyid Said, out of deference for the British, refused to fire a salute in honor of the U.S. Independence Day, the American consul and the entire American community of Zanzibar decided to take action.[76] One long-time American expatriate explained to the U.S. secretary of state that the lack of salute, "lowered the US in the opinion of a semi-barbarous people like that of Zanzibar, whose estimate of a foreign nation is formed from seeing the display of its physical power."[77] With no other reason than to impress upon East Africans the importance and ingenuity of Americans, the secretary of state arranged for the U.S. Navy to dispatch one of its most impressive, steam-powered warships, the *Susquehanna*, to Zanzibar. While in port, the commodore in charge of the vessel admitted anyone on board who was interested, showing them the mechanics of the engine and other spectacles of the ship.[78] The British soon followed the Americans in a show of material know-how, as would the French and other European nationalities. So while Western visitors felt conflicted about Africans consuming things like music boxes or hats, they nonetheless wished for positive recognition of Western goods, even African envy of such objects. More than any other British consul, Playfair meditated on this singular point of impressing the "native" with the material fruits of "civilization." He recorded his dream to "make one more effort to arouse [Sultan Seyyid Majid of Zanzibar] from his fatal apathy": "I would show him what civilization is in the hope that he may be induced to desire a share in it for himself," he mused.[79] Playfair thought that the "native" should not only desire Western civilization but also appreciate Westerners for their advancement. Bishop Tozer similarly wished to indoctrinate select "mission boys" in Zanzibar into civilization. He wrote that if a convert ever became a viable candidate for the clergy, care "will be taken during a long course of training to imbue him with English tastes and habits, to surround him with the artificial wants of our nineteenth century, and to cut him off from all his former associations and sympathies." He would not be semi-civilized, like an African in European clothes, but fully remade, cut off from all former associations through European tutelage. The "giant strength of heathenism," Tozer believed, could only be overcome "by the green withes of a modern education and the new rope of western civilization."[80]

Policymakers, missionaries, and travelers expressed their desire that the East African "native" should want to be like them. While these same people often had no desire for a black or brown mirror image of the West—Tozer himself made only a hypothetical exception for a particularly apt candidate—they desperately wanted East Africans to revere Western goods. While missionaries and administrators alike had no interest in Zanzibaris simply acquiring English things, resettled freed-slave colonies provided an example of how Africans could be remade and taught to properly appreciate Western goods and ideas under European tutelage. Returning to Zanzibar from freed-slave settlements in the Seychelles, Captain W. F. Prideaux, a member of the British diplomatic corps in Zanzibar, wrote that "[t]he Africans . . . take pride in assuming European costume as soon as their means permit them to do so. Altogether, it is impossible not to feel that they have risen several degrees higher in the scale of civilization than those who have been left within the range of Eastern influence" (i.e., on Zanzibar and the coast).[81] Real civilization had to be taught by those who inherited it, and this could be accomplished only under direct European control. In the British imagination there was no auto-civilization. By this logic, Western goods could only be used properly under the direction of those who produced or understood them. The friction between European desires to expand Western commerce with Africa and indignation at the way Africans used Western goods would not be resolved by colonial intervention. For as power relations changed in the 1890s, Europeans increasingly depended on certain goods to define themselves as something different than, and superior to, the colonized.

CONCLUSION: VISCERALITIES

Depictions of Zanzibar were allegories of the West's internal coherence and its senior relation to all East Africans. Westerners created images of East Africa that drew on longer traditions of Orientalism and African travel narratives and also fashioned new tropes of Africa as evolutionarily stunted and in need of guidance. British policymakers, facing the encroachment of other Europeans on what they considered their historic sphere of influence, made claims to East Africa in a bid to secure larger strategic interests. Their justification for the colonial possession of East Africa, however, drew on the rhetorical creation of Africans as in need of humanitarian intervention. For even in areas where Britons had only marginal pecuniary interest, and the British public knew little of its government's strategic and political concerns, the notion of East African degeneration under "Arab" influence, framed in hierarchical, classist terms resonant with British experiences, underwrote the general acceptance of colonial acquisition. For metropolitan publics, the images propagated, or sometimes only confirmed, by travel writers and other analysts became what Patrick Brantlinger calls a popular "enabling factor" of imperial expansion.[82] Writing about this sudden interest in the European acquisition of East Africa at the end of the 1880s, Joseph Thomson, much like Tozer and Steere, bemoaned the fervor of colonization evident in the daily newspapers, "full of the exciting incidents of the race for 'new colonies,' as the mangrove swamps and sterile wastes were pleasingly called."[83] Some, like Thomson, recognized the great fiction of the "civilizing mission" despite their own prejudices. They had seen East Africa, understood, and even contributed to the horrible simplification of "native" life offered to and desired by the home public.

By the 1880s, the idea of "Arab"-ruled Zanzibar's unfitness for the modern age without proper tutelage had firmly taken root.[84] Many analysts of East Africa had come to agree that only European intervention could stop African degeneration, a devolution theorized in racial discourse and proven in images of East African material life. Writing in the months that followed Barghash's death, Thomson, who had been both the guest of the sultan and had served him, confirmed that from the mid-1880s Barghash had been treated by Britain and Germany "as a barbarous chief, and as an obstacle to civilizing influences."[85] To a changing Western notion of civilization, inflected by shifting geopolitical concerns, Zanzibari cosmopolitanism seemed inadequate for the task of midwifing Zanzibar's integration into the modern world. The deprivations of the entire East African region, compounded by the "Arab" presence on the coast, seemed only remediable by humanitarian European guidance.

This compulsion to civilize, when paired with a definition of East Africa as degraded by semi-civilized slave traders and thus lost to the modern world without European intervention, offered colonization a compelling discursive underpinning. Before his death in 1888, Barghash had seen the handwriting on the wall. He had attempted to curry favor with Britain and use its power in the region to ensure the security and longevity of his sultanate. As the geopolitical climate changed in the last years of his life, Barghash's efforts were no longer paying political dividends. More than a decade before the carving up of his realm began, Barghash had recognized the limits of his diplomatic abilities in an age of empire. During his 1875 visit to Britain, he was routinely asked, "Is there anything that you can suggest that will benefit your country?" His response was always the same: "I want nothing but the good will of England."[86] That good will was limited.

By interpreting European goods in East Africa as out of place, Europeans transposed their ideas of essential Africanness or Arabness onto East Africans. In disparaging East African uses of Western imports, Westerners reified their preconceived images of Europeanness and Africanness as different and incommensurate. Shoring up the boundaries of Europeanness, particularly in a moment of rapid global integration, was a psychological defense of significant proportions, since the proof of European superiority lay in such quintessential difference. Western analysts thus engaged in an interpretive process similar to that of East Africans, but they reached broad conclusions that starkly contrasted with Zanzibari self-images. While East Africans domesticated imported goods, giving them meanings related to Western ones but also distinct from them, Europeans delocalized East African meanings by insisting on interpretations shaped by Victorian elite social frames. African domestications not only contradicted the emblematic Africa expected by many visitors, but the disjuncture between presumptions of how Africa should appear and the reality of life in Zanzibar revealed disconcerting images to Westerners in East Africa and, through the books they authored, readers at home. Though divergent understandings of objects need not have been of great relevance to either Zanzibaris or Westerners, Western interpretations of Zanzibari consumerism became part of a taxonomical regime that would define the rhetoric and logics of colonialism in the region.

As testimony to the deep-seated presumptions of cultural ideal types, the trope of out-of-placeness is discernable in mainstream Western interpretations of East Africa and much of the world more than a century after the colonization of Africa. Western assumptions of contradiction in the mixing of "modern," "Western," "African," and "Oriental" bodies and things are still evident in everyday reflections. The irony of a Zanzibari on a mobile phone, a Malaysian woman with her head covered using an ATM terminal, or Afghani men praying next to their motorcycles (the first a postcard and the other images published in the *Economist*)—even though the people pictured do not themselves perceive any contradiction— is the cognitive inheritance of Victorian theories of difference. The perception of essential difference between the West and "the rest," evidenced in the "paradoxical" juxtaposition of Western goods with "traditional" people, forces both the West and "the rest" to exist as autonomous, spatial-cultural realms despite complex historical intermeshings that challenge the idea that they are, or ever were, separate or distinct. The notion that Western things in non-Western environments are contradictory or ironic reveals the desire of Westerners to assume a cultural and material tradition entirely distinct from (and superior to) the rest of the world. Sadly, Westerners have not fully addressed their visceral reactions to an African wearing a *Titanic* T-shirt or their sense of paradox when a veiled woman is pictured drinking a Pepsi.

Conclusion

This study has attempted to shed light on a vast archive of interconnectivity and socioeconomic experience that constitutes the world in mundane ways. I began with the supposition that global relations consist of reciprocities that trouble unilinear accounts of global integration. My strategy has been to start with place-based actions and perceptions of the world and then trace the repercussions of these out to distant places and people. The overlapping scales, strategies, and meanings that I have described here suggest not only differences in the ways East Africans related to people from elsewhere but also shifting perceptions of East Africans. Mutsamuduans and Zanzibaris attempted to strategically manipulate outsiders' perceptions of them, but changes in Western geopolitical concerns and worldviews in the latter nineteenth century made East African visions of global relationships increasingly irrelevant to the interests of the imperial powers that were rapidly colonizing much of the world. By the 1880s, East African cosmopolitanisms faced Western competitive interests and moral discourses rooted in perceptions of difference and bound to projects of global domination that East Africans could not significantly alter. Colonial imposition would shape East Africa's global relationships in profound ways, and yet East Africa's precolonial refashionings left legacies both in the world economy and in the self-definitions of people from Zanzibar to Buganda, eastern Congo, and Lake Malawi. Colonization created new and shifting structures of interaction, but its processes were grafted onto routes of relation forged in the nineteenth century and continually reshaped in their shadow.[1]

I began by suggesting that the circumstances of East Africa's global relationships can elucidate larger processes of interrelation and raise epistemological questions of import to the theorization of globality. Though each chapter has addressed particular themes in specific locales, three broad conclusions warrant additional reflection because they are relevant beyond the contexts that I have narrated. The first and most evident point is that contemporary globality has myriad forgotten antecedents. Not to be mindful of this is to dispossess "peripheries" of their global historical relevance. Tylor's "civilized moderns" were not the only ones to travel the world, develop knowledges of it, and attempt to understand and characterize their place in it. East Africans too were cognizant of "events and their consequences far and wide over the world." For instance, when Count Teleki and Ludwig Ritter von Höhnel had difficulties engaging porters for an ascent of Kilimanjaro, Miriali intervened, warning the men to treat Europeans well since, "all Europe watched what was going on at Kilimanjaro."[2] East Africans did not simply react to global change; they affected the world in important ways. This is not to say that East African images of and actions in the world were more important than those of others—only that East Africans maintained particular visions of global relation that were lost in Western theorizations of Africa. Colonialism did not wrench East Africa from its isolation or introduce the benefits of the modern world. Instead, it superimposed a particular vision of universal interrelation over East Africa's global relationships, while excluding Africans from many of the social, economic, and political rights championed by theorists of modernity.[3]

The notion that contemporary globality has precedent also begs the question of comparison. It may seem futile to measure nineteenth-century globality against the present. Configurations of relation are, after all, always unique to the moment. Yet historical comparison does offer the possibility of locating analogies to, and discontinuities from, the past in the world we have inherited. The rapidity of significant change during the late twentieth and early twenty-first centuries has been astounding. Capital, people, and information move faster than ever before. There are more people on earth, material consumption is greater, and the natural environment is being altered in decisive ways. Perhaps more important, there seems to have been a discernible shift in consciousness over the last two decades. Our very way of seeing the world has changed, and this has had repercussions that transcend and shape the material and digital realities that more commonly gain our attention.[4] But just as the past is not always what it seems, the present is not always as unprecedented as we tend to believe.

We should remain mindful of the fact that change, be it in perception or relation, is relative. Has the Internet had as much impact on the world as the telegraph did? Comparatively, the time-space compression effected by the telegraph when it reduced the amount of time to communicate between London and Zanzibar from months to minutes was greater, though less democratized, than the advent of the Internet, which came long after the telephone. Air travel has compressed time-space as well, though not always more than did the train. Much like air travel, railways reduced travel times to just fractions of what they had been. My point here is not that the Internet and the proliferation of airlines are reruns of history. My suggestion is that we must appreciate the cognitive experiences of heightened time-space compression in their real (historical) times. The telegraph and train had profound effects on consciousness that produced senses of global intermeshing similar to those in our time.[5] Assertions that global economic integration in the late nineteenth century was profound and that global consciousness was as acute in the early twentieth century as it is now may seem inconsequential.[6] But if, as Stuart Hall argues, the confidence that everything is destined to be sped up, displaced, transformed, and reshaped is a hallmark of modernity, then the shift in consciousness that has given birth to the discourse of "globalization" may represent a new manifestation of an older cognitive process rather than an epochal horizon.[7]

Globalization consciousness, in accordance with the precepts of modernity, seems to be largely confirming many of the historical silences routinized in the nineteenth and twentieth centuries. For while the lived experiences of people in the North Atlantic (though certainly not them only), according to Michel-Rolph Trouillot, have come to challenge the conceptual boundaries of human interaction, presuming the novelty of present border crossings reaffirms isolationist interpretations of human history. In the breaching of "traditional" boundaries, the historical boundedness of geographical, cultural, or biological entities is reconfirmed. Like the Swahili "mongrel" of nineteenth-century accounts—evidencing a mixing of neatly distinguished African, Arab, Indian, and European—hybridity in the present reifies the unlike types brought into dynamic tension. Perhaps as a result of new "mixtures," modernity's fate will be the dissolution of its categories occasioned by the collapse of the boundaries it fortified. More than likely, however, new configurations of difference will replace the particular realms of isolation we inherited from nineteenth-century theorists, as the popular reception of Samuel Huntington's thesis that civilizations and their cultures represent *the* defining differences among human societies suggests. In a time of globalization, a Zanzibari using a high-tech device such as a mobile phone is still seen, from a Western photographer's perspective, as a historical paradox. It is my hope that archaeologies of historical globality can counterbalance the contemporary experience of paradox, irony, and wonder occasioned by changing patterns of global interconnectivity.

The second point I wish to make is that meaning is fragile and contingent. The meanings we give objects are relative and can easily transcend spatial, social, and gendered boundaries. British men's handkerchiefs became part of women's fashion in East Africa, while wealthy Parisian women wore bonnets that approximated the aesthetics of Sultan Barghash's familial turban. Further, the divergent meanings of globally circulating consumer goods must always be considered in accounts of the global economy because these meanings affect demand and trade. The use of brass wire for personal adornment in East Africa, in contrast to its uses in the United States, was important not only for the local social relationships it addressed. East African demand for particular kinds of brass wire also determined the shape of trade, the success of Americans in the Zanzibari market, and even the production techniques and working lives of New Englanders. Having said this, I admit that I have not done justice to the multifarious and changing meanings given to globally circulating goods. The meanings ascribed to merekani cloth in Zanzibar, for instance, were often different from those given merekani in the Lake Malawi region.[8] Even in Mutsamudu, where the manipulation of British symbols had much to do with perceptions of British abilities, there is no evidence to suggest that the meanings Britons and Mutsamuduans gave any object were the same. In fact, Britons regularly protested that Mutsamuduans did not really understand the cultural significance of British objects. For Mutsamuduans, however, the meaning of English things was tied to political, social, and economic strategies, not to British ideals of class, status, or order.

The third point that I want to make is that globality is never unidimensional or unidirectional; thus, it cannot be understood as a single process called "globalization" that spreads from the West to "the rest." The contemporary world has inherited a genealogical tree with innumerable, overlapping branches. Like any genealogical tree, where we choose to begin and end tracing our lineages determines the lines of import and the overall image we produce. For example, tracing out the lines of interrelation that connected East Africa to wider networks before colonialism offers a picture different from that developed through a focus on the "rise of the West" or the "core" of the world-system. The other genealogies we can discern through East Africa are no less our history. No matter how counterintuitive they seem in historiographical hindsight, these other lineages of globality reveal the multi-dimensionality of translocal dialogue. To appreciate the multi-dimensionality of global integration, we must look at the interests and the repercussions of acting on these interests for everyone, even seemingly marginal people. The scenes outlined in this book reveal that the minutiae of negotiated trans-actions and consumer desire on the part of people considered marginal to global systems were, at times, as important to patterns of global integra-tion as were state regulation and production. The histories we write need to be continually rethought in light of such mutuality.

Global integration has offered opportunities for some, but I do not mean to suggest that it is a panacea. Contemporary globalization, like modernization, is no cure for the inequalities patently visible across the planet. My point in these pages has only been that because of their greater autonomy in setting the parameters of global relationships before colonization, East Africans developed certain advantageous positions of exchange and adjusted quickly to both new economic opportunities as well as new technologies. East Africans sought to engage transregional networks on terms that they imagined would be the most beneficial to them. Precolonial Africa was not "merrie"—as the narratives of the enslaved and those whose lives were destroyed by the conflict, disease, and famine of the nineteenth century testify—but military subjugation, direct (if only loose) control of producers, and the protection of home markets during the colonial era gave Europeans, for the first time, deci-sive trade advantages.

Perceptions of Africa have also had long-term effects. While Africans are no longer seen as biologically incompatible with modernity, many still assume that there is something essentially different about African economies that should be altered. Indeed, it is still commonly believed that only external intervention in the everyday lives of Africans, using principles in which many economists have dogmatic faith (e.g., liberal-ization, privatization, and openness to short-term, speculative capital), can pull Africans into the flow of "real time" and instill in them proper economic postures. Effectively, emphasis is shifted away from Western protectionism and African producers' inability to access large foreign markets to the liquidation of what few protections Africans have for their own economies.[9] Westerners, under the guise of "development," still desire total access to African resources while allowing African producers only the most circumscribed access to Western markets.[10] Africans are faced with enormous difficulties in renegotiating their relationships to the world market as a result of constraints that international governing bodies seem largely unwilling, and African leaders disinterested or unable, to address adequately.[11] The demands for "trade, not aid" that have become the mantra of African trade representatives and their supporters seem to fall on deaf ears.

The perceptual legacies of nineteenth-century Western analyses also place other burdens on contemporary East Africa, particularly in tourism-oriented Zanzibar, where the history of sultans, harems, Stanley, Livingstone, and the slave trade seems to be the only one it possesses. It is picturesque alterity, a confirming distance, that travelers seek and international organizations attempt to "conserve" in contemporary Zanzibar.[12] This history is, moreover, one on which Zanzibar has come to depend as a result of the economic benefits promised by tourism. Fictive pasts are reflected in the archaic Zouave jackets of hotel employees' uniforms, the tour guide's stories of harem intrigues, and the Anglican altar said to have been built on the site of the slave whipping post. These images both confirm and reenact nineteenth-century myths and bind Zanzibar to a history it never owned. The East African coast's economy has, in part, come to depend on a past that it has little choice but to create in relation to the alterity that Western tourists and funding agencies expect. It is a hallmark of tourism in an age of globality that foreigners visit East Africa to experience a world subdued by its past, a world of strange difference largely disconnected from time. In 2002 Jacqueline Rance wrote that arriving at Lamu, a popular tourist destination north of Mombasa, "gives one the sense of being 500 years back in time." "This is precisely what visitors love and want," she continued, "to escape from the rushing Western world and its systems, and taste antiquity."[13] This is the world we have inherited. What we have lost is a world never as predictable as we imagine, never as disconnected, never as isolated as we commonly believe.

Notes

INTRODUCTION

1. Michel-Rolph Trouillot, "The Perspective of the World: Globalization Then and Now," in *Beyond Dichotomies: Histories, Identities, Cultures, and the Challenge of Globalization*, ed. E. Mudimbe-Boyi (Albany, NY: State University of New York Press, 2002), 6–7.

2. Frederick Cooper, "What Is the Concept of Globalization Good For? An African Historian's Perspective," *African Affairs* 100 (2001): 189–213. As J. Lorand Matory suggests, we should not allow descriptions of contemporary globalization "to reduce the past to a one-dimensional foil"; see *Black Atlantic Religion: Tradition, Transnationalism, and Matriarchy in the Afro-Brazilian Candomblé* (Princeton, NJ: Princeton University Press, 2005), 9.

3. Benjamin Barber, *Jihad vs. McWorld: How Globalism and Tribalism Are Reshaping the World* (New York: Ballantine Books, 1995); Thomas Friedman, *The Lexus and the Olive Tree: Understanding Globalization* (New York: Anchor Books, 2000); Samuel Huntington, *The Clash of Civilizations and the Remaking of World Order* (New York: Simon and Schuster, 1997); Bernard Lewis, *What Went Wrong? The Clash Between Islam and Modernity in the Middle East* (New York: Harper Perennial, 2002). Mahmood Mamdani terms these reflections on incommensurate differences "culture talk"; see *Good Muslim, Bad Muslim: America, the Cold War, and the Roots of Terror* (New York: Random House, 2004).

4. Martin Lewis and Kären Wigen, *The Myth of Continents: A Critique of Metageography* (Berkeley and Los Angeles: University of California Press, 1997).

5. Michel Foucault, *Power/Knowledge: Selected Interviews and Other Writings, 1972–1977*, ed. C. Gordon (New York: Pantheon, 1980); Michel Rolph-Trouillot, *Silencing the Past: Power and the Production of History* (Boston: Bea-

con Press, 1995); Arif Dirlik, *Postmodernity's Histories: The Past as Legacy and Project* (Lanham, MD: Rowman and Littlefield, 2000).

6. Seteney Shami suggests that excavating alternative pasts is an important intellectual exercise because it allows us to challenge the "teleological certainty" of the present; see "Prehistories of Globalization: Circassian Identities in Motion," *Public Culture* 12, no. 1 (2000): 177–204. For thoughtful critiques of the discourse of globalization, see Gayatri Chakravorty Spivak, "Cultural Talks in the Hot Peace: Revisiting the 'Global Village,'" in *Cosmopolitics: Thinking and Feeling Beyond the Nation,* ed. Pheng Cheah and Bruce Robbins (Minneapolis: University of Minnesota Press, 1998), 329; and Richard Kilminster, "Globalization as an Emergent Concept," in *The Limits of Globalization,* ed. Alan Scott (London: Routledge, 1997), 257–83; James Mittelman, *Whither Globalization? The Vortex of Knowledge and Ideology* (London: Routledge, 2005).

7. Thus, this book responds to Anna Tsing's charge to study the *landscape* of circulation as well as the *flow;* see "The Global Situation," *Current Anthropology* 15, no. 3 (2000): 346–47.

8. Maghan Keita argues that Africa's importance to global history remains underestimated; see "Africa and the Construction of a Grand Narrative in World History," in *Across Cultural Boundaries: Historiography in Global Perspective,* ed. E. Fuchs and B. Stuchtey (Lanham, MD: Rowman and Littlefield, 2002), 285–308.

9. Steven Feierman, "African Histories and the Dissolution of World History," in *Africa and the Disciplines: Contributions of Research in Africa to the Social Sciences and the Humanities,* ed. Robert H. Bates, V. Y. Mudimbe, and Jean O'Barr (University of Chicago Press, 1993), 167–212; Joseph C. Miller, "History and Africa/Africa and History," *American Historical Review* 104, no.1 (1999): 1–32.

10. Walter Rodney, *How Europe Underdeveloped Africa* (Washington, DC: Howard University Press, 1989); Edward Alpers, *Ivory and Slaves in East Central Africa* (London: Heinemann, 1975); Abdul Sheriff, *Slaves, Spices, and Ivory in Zanzibar* (London: James Currey, 1987).

11. Nicholas Thomas frames the argument this way: "Exchange relations demand closer scrutiny if they are in fact the origins of subsequent exploitation and asymmetry." See "The Cultural Dynamics of Peripheral Exchange," in *Barter, Exchange and Value: An Anthropological Approach,* ed. C. Humphrey and S. Hugh-Jones (Cambridge: Cambridge University Press, 1992), 23.

12. Africa's production for world markets has been the focus of most studies of precolonial African economic history. See, in addition to the works listed in note 10, A. G. Hopkins, *An Economic History of West Africa* (New York: Columbia University Press, 1973); Immanuel Wallerstein, "The Three Stages of African Involvement in the World-Economy," in *The Political Economy of Contemporary Africa,* ed. Peter Gutkind and Immanuel Wallerstein (Beverly Hills: Sage, 1976), 35–63; J. Forbes Munro, *Africa and the International Economy, 1800–1960* (Totowa, NJ: Rowman and Littlefield, 1976); D. Crummey and C. Stewart, eds., *Modes of Production in Africa: The Precolonial Era* (Beverly Hills, CA: Sage, 1981); Ralph Austen, *African Economic History* (London:

Heinemann, 1987); Juhani Koponen, *People and Production in Late Precolonial Tanzania: History and Structures* (Jyväskylä: Finnish Society for Development Studies, 1988). For exceptions to this trend, see below.

13. John Iliffe, *A Modern History of Tanganyika* (Cambridge: Cambridge University Press, 1981); Jean and John Comaroff, *Of Revelation and Revolution,* 2 vols. (Chicago: University of Chicago Press, 1991–97); Jonathon Glassman, *Feasts and Riot: Revelry, Rebellion, and Popular Consciousness on the Swahili Coast, 1856–1888* (Portsmouth, NH: Heinemann, 1995); Jane Guyer, ed., *Money Matters: Instability, Values, and Social Payments in the Modern History of West African Communities* (Portsmouth, NH: Heinemann, 1995); Joseph C. Miller, *Way of Death: Merchant Capitalism and the Angolan Slave Trade, 1730–1830* (Madison: University of Wisconsin Press, 1988); Timothy Burke, *Lifebuoy Men, Lux Women: Commodification, Consumption, and Cleanliness in Modern Zimbabwe* (Durham, NC: Duke University Press, 1996); Emmanuel Akyeampong, *Drink, Power, and Cultural Change: A Social History of Alcohol in Ghana, c. 1800 to Recent Times* (Portsmouth, NH: Heinemann, 1996); Justin Willis, *Potent Brews: A Social History of Alcohol in East Africa, 1850–1999* (Athens: Ohio University Press, 2002).

14. See, for instance, Jean Baudrillard, *The System of Objects* (New York: Verso, 1996); and *The Consumer Society* (London: Sage, 1998); Mary Douglas and Baron Isherwood, *The World of Goods: Towards an Anthropology of Consumption* (1979; repr. London: Penguin, 1995); D. Howes, ed., *Cross-Cultural Consumption: Global Markets, Local Realities* (London: Routledge, 1996); Daniel Miller, *Acknowledging Consumption: A Review of New Studies* (New York: Routledge, 1995).

15. Joseph Miller, in his consideration of imports at Luanda, predicted that "[i]mports are likely to prove more momentous for Africa's history than its better publicized exports." He developed this point further in *Way of Death*, exemplifying the ways in which the uses of commodities reconfigured social relationships as well as relationships of production. See Miller, "Imports at Luanda, Angola 1785–1823," in *Figuring African Trade*, ed. G. Liesegang, H. Pasch, and A. Jones (Berlin: Dietrich Reimer Verlag, 1986), 164.

16. David Richardson, "West African Consumption Patterns and Their Influence on the Eighteenth-Century English Slave Trade," in *The Uncommon Market: Essays in the Economic History of the Atlantic Slave Trade*, ed. A. Gemery and J. Hogendorn (New York: Academic Press, 1979), 308, 310.

17. Philip Curtin, *Economic Change in Precolonial Africa: Senegambia in the Era of the Slave Trade* (Madison: University of Wisconsin Press, 1975); Joseph Inikori, *Africans and the Industrial Revolution in England: A Study in International Trade and Economic Development* (Cambridge: Cambridge University Press, 2002); Miller, *Way of Death*; John Thornton, "The Role of Africans in the Atlantic Economy, 1450–1650: Modern Africanist Historiography and the World-Systems Paradigm," *Colonial Latin American Historical Review* 3, no. 2 (1994): 125–40; R. Nielsen, "The History and Development of Wax-Printed Textiles Intended for West Africa and Zaire," in *The Fabrics of Culture: The Anthropology of Clothing and Adornment*, ed. J. Cordwell and R. Schwarz (The Hague: Mouton, 1979), 467–98. The situation was even more complex in the

case of currency. See, for example, Guyer, *Money Matters*, and Jan Hogendorn and Marion Johnson's work on the shell trade, *The Shell Money of the Slave Trade* (Cambridge: Cambridge University Press, 1986).

18. Daniel Headrick, *Tools of Empire: Technology and European Imperialism in the Nineteenth Century* (New York: Oxford University Press, 1981), 106–7; Hopkins, *Economic History*.

19. See Jane Guyer, "Wealth in People, Wealth in Things: Introduction," *Journal of African History* 36, no. 1 (1995): 83–88. For the intersections of things, wealth, people, and global economies, see also C. Piot's, "Of Slaves and the Gift: Kabre Sale of Kin During the Era of the Slave Trade," *Journal of African History* 37, no. 1 (1996): 31–49. For a pioneering analysis of the ways in which market factors and the politics of social relationships work in dynamic tension, see Sara Berry, *No Condition Is Permanent: The Social Dynamics of Agrarian Change in Sub-Saharan Africa* (Madison: University of Wisconsin Press, 1993).

20. Douglas and Isherwood, *World of Goods;* Arjun Appadurai, ed., *The Social Life of Things* (Cambridge: Cambridge University Press, 1986); Ray Porter and John Brewer, *Consumption and the World of Goods* (London: Routledge, 1993); T. H. Breen, *The Marketplace of Revolution: How Consumer Politics Shaped American Independence* (Oxford: Oxford University Press, 2004).

21. Pierre Bourdieu, *Distinction: A Social Critique of the Judgment of Taste* (London: Routledge, 1984); Grant McCracken, *Culture and Consumption: New Approaches to the Symbolic Character of Consumer Goods and Activities* (Bloomington: Indiana University Press, 1988); Baudrillard, *Consumer Society*.

22. J. Tobin, ed., *Re-made in Japan: Everyday Life and Consumer Taste in a Changing Society* (New Haven, CT: Yale University Press, 1992); Benjamin Orlove, ed., *The Allure of the Foreign: Imported Goods in Postcolonial Latin America* (Ann Arbor: University of Michigan Press, 1997); A. Raz, *Riding the Black Ship: Japan and Tokyo Disneyland* (Cambridge, MA: Harvard University Press, 1999); M. Alfino, J. Caputo, and r. Wynyard, eds., *McDonaldization Revisited: Critical Essays on Consumer Culture* (Westport, CT: Praeger, 1998); David Howes, ed., *Cross-Cultural Consumption: Global Markets, Local Realities* (London: Routledge, 1996); James Watson, ed., *Golden Arches East: McDonald's in East Asia* (Stanford, CA: Stanford University Press, 1997). See also Michel de Certeau, *The Practice of Everyday Life* (Berkeley and Los Angeles: University of California Press, 1984).

23. George Ritzer, *The McDonaldization of Society* (Thousand Oaks, CA: Pine Forge, 1995); A. Haugerud, M. P. Stone, and P. Little, eds., *Commodities and Globalization: Anthropological Perspectives* (Oxford: Rowman and Littlefield, 2000).

24. On the notion of domestication see Howes, *Cross-Cultural Consumption*. The idea of domestication is similar to what Eckhardt Fuchs terms "transcultural transfer," or the movement of ideas and their interpolation into different cultural systems. Through the realm of historiography, he and several co-contributors show how culturally specific historical writings shape and are shaped by cultural transfers. See Fuchs, "Introduction: Provincializing Europe: Historiography and a Transcultural Concept," in Fuchs and Stuchtey, *Across Cultural Boundaries*, 1–28.

CHAPTER 1: SIMILITUDE AND GLOBAL RELATIONSHIPS

1. For historical examples, see Marshal Sahlins, "Cosmologies of Capitalism: The Trans-Pacific Sector of 'The World System,'" in *Culture in Practice: Selected Essays* (New York: Zone Books, 2000), 415–70; Benjamin Orlove, ed., *The Allure of the Foreign: Imported Goods in Postcolonial Latin America* (Ann Arbor: University of Michigan Press, 1997); Jean Comaroff and John Comaroff, *Of Revelation and Revolution*, vol. 2 (Chicago: University of Chicago Press, 1997); Nicholas Thomas, *Entangled Objects: Exchange, Material Culture, and Colonialism in the Pacific* (Cambridge: Cambridge University Press, 1991); Richard White, *The Middle Ground: Indians, Empires, and Republics in the Great Lakes Region, 1650–1815* (Cambridge: Cambridge University Press, 1991). For more contemporary examples, see Karen Hansen, *Salaula: The World of Secondhand Clothing and Zambia* (Chicago: University of Chicago Press, 2000); A. Haugerud, P. Stone, and P. Little, eds., *Commodities and Globalization: Anthropological Perspectives* (Lanham, MD: Rowman and Littlefield, 2000); A. Barker, ed., *Consuming Russia: Popular Culture, Sex, and Society Since Gorbachev* (Durham, NC: Duke University Press, 1999); G. Gemunden, *Framed Visions: Popular Culture, Americanization, and the Contemporary German and Austrian Imagination* (Ann Arbor: University of Michigan Press, 1998); David Howes, ed., *Cross-Cultural Consumption: Global Markets, Local Realities* (London: Routledge, 1996); J. Zha, *China Pop: How Soap Operas, Tabloids, and Bestsellers Are Transforming a Culture* (New York: New Press, 1995).

2. Aviad Raz, *Riding the Black Ship: Japan and Tokyo Disneyland* (Cambridge, MA: Harvard University Press, 1999); and "Domesticating Disney," *Journal of Popular Culture* 33, no. 4 (1999): 73–97.

3. Anthony King, ed., *Culture, Globalization and the World-System* (London: Macmillan, 1991); Ulf Hannerz, "Notes on the Global Ecumene," *Public Culture* 1, no. 2 (1989): 66–75; J. Nederveen Pieterse, "Globalization as Hybridization," in *Global Modernities*, ed. M. Featherstone (London: Sage, 1995),45–68; Brian Larkin, "Indian Films and Nigerian Lovers: Media and the Creation of Parallel Modernities," *Africa* 67, no. 3 (1997): 406–39; Michel de Certeau, *The Practice of Everyday Life*, trans. Steven Randall (Berkeley and Los Angeles: University of California Press, 1984).

4. M. Alfino, J. Caputo, and R. Wynyard, eds., *McDonaldization Revisited: Critical Essays on Consumer Culture* (Westport, CT: Praeger, 1998); J. Tobin, ed., *Re-Made in Japan: Everyday Life and Consumer Taste in a Changing Society* (New Haven, CT: Yale University Press, 1992).

5. James Watson, "China's Big Mac Attack," *Foreign Affairs* (May–June 2000), 120–34; James Watson, ed., *Golden Arches East: McDonald's in East Asia* (Stanford, CA: Stanford University Press, 1997). For an exploratory consideration of the possibilities of cultural reinterpretation, see Ulf Hannerz, "Scenarios for Peripheral Cultures," in King, *Culture, Globalization and the World-System*, 107–28.

6. Michael Taussig, *Mimesis and Alterity: A Particular History of the Senses* (New York: Routledge, 1993), 250.

7. "Memorandum, Political Department, Bombay, 18 May 1862," AA12/8,

Zanzibar National Archives, Zanzibar (hereafter ZNA). See also A. Bourde, "Un Comorien adventureux au XIXe siecle: L'extraordinaire voyage du Prince Abudin," in *Méditerranée et Océan Indien. Travaux de Sixième Colloque International d'Histoire Maritime* (Venice: S. E. V. P. E. N., 1970), 265–92.

8. Rigby to Sunley, 5 June 1860, AA2/4, ZNA.

9. Ibid.

10. Robert L. Playfair was the first to recognize that Prince Abdullah was the "notorious" Prince Abudin. Playfair to Anderson, 15 November 1863, AA3/18, ZNA.

11. "Account of the Voyage from Johanna to London, Made by the Princes Mohammed and Abdalla," (ca. 1863), FO 19/8, Public Record Office, London (hereafter PRO).

12. Three months after Palmerston discontinued their stipends they were still in London, though now only petitioning Palmerston for passage home. Prince Abdullah to Viscount Palmerston, London, 19 September 1863, and same to same, 10 December 1863, FO 19/8, PRO.

13. Sunley to Russell, 7 March 1866, AA1/5, ZNA; Jean Martin, *Comores: Quatre îles entre pirates and planteurs,* vol. 2 (Paris: l'Harmattan, 1983), 12–13.

14. The political resident at Aden identified him as "Amir Seyed Mahamed bin Sultan Abdulla, Prince of Johanna" in 1866. He had arrived from Istanbul on a French steamer. Political Resident, Aden to Secretary to Government Bombay, 2 November 1866, FO 19/8, PRO.

15. Letter from Alloue, Sultan of Johanna, to Admiral of Mauritius, 1254 Hegira [Hijra], 25 Thani (September 1838), ADM 1/5945, PRO. Sultan Alawi was deposed by the father of the then-current sultan, Salim, who was a cousin to Abdullah on his father's side; Sunley to Russell, 7 March 1866, AA1/5, ZNA; Pelly to Kinlock, 4 October 1861, AA12/8, ZNA. According to the consul, Prince Mahmud, Abdullah's uncle, with whom he traveled to London, was the popular choice for sultan in the 1860s; Sunley to Russell, 7 March 1866, AA1/5, ZNA.

16. Memorandum, Political Department, Bombay, 18 May 1862, AA12/8, ZNA.

17. Rigby to Sunley, 5 June 1860, AA2/4, ZNA. Rigby's letter was one of the first to urge the Government to warn against giving money to Nzwanians "[w]hen they are not deserving of it, and do not need it." Rigby to Secretary of the Government, Bombay, 1 June 1861, AA12/8, ZNA.

18. For an ethnographic reflection on the internal social dynamics of mimesis in Comorian societies over several centuries, see Iain Walker, "Mimetic Structuration: Or, Easy Steps to Building an Acceptable Identity," *History and Anthropology* 16, no. 2 (2005): 187–210. Walker suggests that while Comorians may have initially used strategic mimicry to negotiate relationships with outsiders, it would become a "general social praxis" locally that continues to shape social relationships within Comorian society (192).

19. Homi Bhabha, "Of Mimicry and Man: The Ambivalence of Colonial Discourse," in *The Location of Culture* (New York: Routledge, 1994), 85–92. Simon Gikandi has written about a similar strategy of the appropriation of the instruments of colonial rule in an attempt to partially transcend the "colonization of consciousness"; see his "The Embarrassment of Victorianism: Colonial Sub-

jects and the Lure of Englishness," in *Victorian Afterlife*, ed. J. Kucich and D. Sadoff (Minneapolis: University of Minnesota Press, 2000), 163. Similitude is also distinct from, but tactically akin to, what Detienne and Vernant call *mètis*, or the ability to manipulate hostile forces—too powerful to be confronted directly—to one's advantage. Bayart calls this tactic "trickery" and points to its ubiquity in postcolonial African politics. See M. Detienne and J.-P. Vernant, *Les ruses de l'intelligence: La mètis des Grecs* (Paris: Flammarion, 1974); and Jean-François Bayart, "Africa in the World: A History of Extraversion," *African Affairs* 99, no. 395 (2000): 259, n. 99. Echoing the reception literature outlined above, Iain Walker broadens the definition of mimesis to refer to a "mechanism" for incorporating foreign influences and practices into local praxis by which domesticated influences ultimately "come to have an autonomy from their object." Walker suggests that mimesis, like the processes of cultural domestication that I outline in chapter 4, is "a strategy for the construction of social identities based on images of the Other" ("Mimetic Structuration," 192, 204–5).

20. On the scholarly and familial networks that bound the Comoros to the East African coast, the Hadramawt, and ports across the Indian Ocean, see Anne Bang, *Sufis and Scholars of the Sea: Family Networks in East Africa, 1860–1925* (London: RoutledgeCurzon, 2003); and Engseng Ho, *The Graves of Tarim: Genealogy and Mobility across the Indian Ocean* (Berkeley and Los Angeles: University of California Press, 2006). In a famous incident in the early nineteenth century, ten Nzwanians sailed on the hajj but wrecked off Ras Hafun, on the Horn of Africa. There they found passage to Muscat and took a vessel to Penang, Malaysia. From Penang they went to Bombay, Calcutta, and Cape Town without ever completing the hajj. See Rev. Elliot, "A Visit to the Island of Johanna," *United Service Journal* 1 (1830): 144.

21. See William Jones, "Remarks on the Island of Hinzuan, or Johanna," *Asiatick Researches* 5 (1807): 93; *A Letter from a Gentleman on Board an Indianman to his Friend in London giving an account of the Island of Johanna in the year 1784* (London: John Stockdale, 1789), 12.

22. J. Ross Browne, *Etchings of a Whaling Cruise* (Cambridge, MA: Belknap Press of Harvard University Press, 1968), 279.

23. J. Richards, "A Cruize through the Mozambique Channel," *Nautical Magazine and Naval Chronicle*, July 1849, 342. William Bernard's earlier account says only the king's house had this ornament; see his *Narrative of the Voyages and Services of the Nemesis, from 1840 to 1843*, (London: Henry Colburn, 1844). James Prior described the king's house using similar terms; see his *Voyage along the Eastern Coast of Africa, to Mosambique, Johanna, and Quiloa; to St. Helena . . . in the Nisus Frigate* (London: Sir Richard Phillips and Co., 1819), 48.

24. A. de Horsey, "On the Comoro Islands," *Journal of the Royal Geographical Society* 34 (1864): 262. Sunley describes these visits in greater detail, putting the number at sixty-two—the majority of which were American—in 1852; see Sunley to Secretary of State, 1858, AA1/5, ZNA. See also Gary W. Clendennen and Peter M. Nottingham, *William Sunley and David Livingstone: A Tale of Two Consuls* (Madison: University of Wisconsin, African Studies Program, 2000).

Notes to Pages 20–23

25. John Ovington, *A Voyage to Suratt in the Year 1689*, in *India in the Seventeenth Century*, vol. 1., ed. J. P. Guha (New Delhi: Associated Publishing House, 1976), 51–52. On Comorian economic and political connections to Mozambique Island, see Edward Alpers, "A Complex Relationship: Mozambique and the Comoro Islands in the Nineteenth and Twentieth Centuries," *Cahiers d'Études Africaines* 161 (2001): 73–95.

26. Cornwall, *Observations on Several Voyages to India*, in *A New General Collection of Voyages and Travels*, vol. 3, ed. Thomas Astley (London: Printed for Thomas Astley, 1750), 392.

27. Théophile Frappaz, *Les Voyages du Lieutenant de vaisseau Frappaz dans les mers des Indes*, ed. Raymond Decary (Tananarive, Madagascar: Pitot de la Beaujardiére, 1939), 86.

28. Ovington, *Voyage to Suratt*, 52.

29. Jones, "Island of Hinzuan," 78.

30. Richards, "Mozambique Channel," 340.

31. *Letter to a Gentleman*, 10–11. W. Owen, *Narrative of Voyages to Explore the Shores of Africa, Arabia, and Madagascar*, vol. 1 (New York: J. & J. Harper, 1833), 115. On the uses and commonness of engraved breastplates and badges, see Elliot, "Island of Johanna," 145–47. While the uses of engraved gorgets in places like early colonial Australia signified the restrictions placed on native people, gorgets operated much more ambiguously in Mutsamudu. See Chris Healy's cogent analysis of the repressive uses of breastplates in colonial Australia, "Chained to Their Signs: Remembering Breastplates," in *Body Trade: Captivity, Cannibalism and Colonialism in the Pacific*, ed. B. Creed and J. Hoorn (New York: Routledge, 2001), 24–35.

32. *Letter to a Gentleman*, 10–11. Owen reported that a Lord Rodney was a captain of the port, interpreter, and master of ceremonies. See Owen, *Narrative of Voyages*, 115.

33. Henry Rooke, *Travels to the Coast of Arabia Felix; and from thence by the Red-Sea and Egypt, to Europe* (London: Printed for R. Blamire, 1784), 45.

34. Jones, "Island of Hinzuan," 87–88, 95.

35. Anton P. Hove, *Tours for Scientific and Economical Research made in Guzerat, Kattiawar, and the Conkuns, in 1787–88* (Bombay: Bombay Education Society Press, 1855), 1.

36. Council of Chiefs of Johanna, 1862, Letter to Lord Russell from the Below, Johanna, 17 October 1862, FO19/8, fol. 73, PRO. Since this letter was drafted in relation to Prince Abdullah's visit to England, it is possible that he forged it. Alternatively, the undersigned might have backed Abdullah's uncle's claim to the throne and thus were willing to sign their names to an appeal to the British for intervention. Unfortunately, the intention of the mission is not clear from the remaining documentation.

37. Prior, *Voyage along the Eastern Coast of Africa*, 55; personal communication, Martin Ottenheimer, March 1997.

38. H. Plumer, "Journal of a Voyage from London to Madras [ca. 1769]," MS, Bell Library, University of Minnesota, Minneapolis.

39. Jones, "Island of Hinzuan," 78; "Bishop Tozer's Journals and Letters,"

bk. 3, 15 August 1864, Johanna, CB1/1B, ZNA; Rooke, *Travels to the Coast of Arabia Felix*, 50. On completing his conversation with the English surveyors, the sultan offered them coconut milk in English tumblers with which to drink "healths"; see Owen, *Narrative of Voyages*, 117. Prior, *Voyage along the Eastern Coast of Africa*, 47–48; Pelly to Klinlock, 4 October 1861, AA12/8, ZNA; Pelly, "Miscellaneous Observations upon the Comoro Islands," *Transactions of the Bombay Geographical Society* (1860–62): 91. Shinzwani was also written in Arabic characters. Richards, "Mozambique Channel," 344; Prior, *Voyage along the Eastern Coast of Africa*, 47–48.

40. Owen, *Narrative of Voyages*, 119.

41. Prior, *Voyage along the Eastern Coast of Africa*, 47–48.

42. Browne, *Etchings of a Whaling Cruise*, 251–53.

43. Henry Grose, *A Voyage to the East Indies* (London: Printed for S. Hooper, 1772), 21.

44. Jones, "Island of Hinzuan," 90.

45. Prior, *Voyage along the Eastern Coast of Africa*, 47–48.

46. Elliot, "Island of Johanna," 149.

47. Jones, "Island of Hinzuan," 101.

48. Prior, *Voyage along the Eastern Coast of Africa*, 49–50.

49. William Bernard, *Narrative of the Voyages and Services of the Nemesis, from 1840 to 1843* (London: Henry Colburn, 1844), 141.

50. Ibid.

51. Grose, *Voyage to the East Indies*, 21.

52. Ovington, *Voyage to Suratt*, 50.

53. Grose, *Voyage to the East Indies*, 25.

54. *Letter to a Gentleman*, 11–12.

55. Much of this shipment was pillaged en route by a French cruiser. Capt. Thomlinson, June 1809, quoted in H. Salt, *A Voyage to Abyssinia* (London: F. C. and J. Rivington, 1814), 77–78.

56. Bernard, *Narrative of the Voyages*, 130.

57. Prior, *Voyage along the Eastern Coast of Africa*, 54.

58. Thomlinson, in Salt, *Voyage to Abyssinia*, 78.

59. Bernard, *Narrative of the Voyages*, 134–35. The Malagasy rebel Ramanetaka was reported to have received assistance from the French. His primary base of support, however, was Mwali (138).

60. Ibid., 140.

61. Ibid., 148.

62. When the English flag was run up, the sultan smiled, "and appeared to take far greater pride in that unstained ensign, than in his own independent flag, or his own precarious authority," or so Hall believed. "Great," Bernard wrote, "were the rejoicings of the whole people of the town; in fact, the day had been one of continued excitement to all parties." The excitement was no doubt less for the British flag itself than for what it symbolized in this instance: repelling an impending invasion. See Bernard, *Narrative of the Voyages*, 147–49.

63. Rooke, *Travels to the Coast of Arabia Felix*, 40–41.

64. Prior, *Voyage along the Eastern Coast of Africa*, 63.

65. Browne, *Etchings of a Whaling Cruise*, 274–75.

66. Prior, *Voyage along the Eastern Coast of Africa*, 47–48.

67. Owen, *Narrative of Voyages*, 117; Rooke, *Travels to the Coast of Arabia Felix*, 50.

68. Elliot, "Island of Johanna," 148.

69. Ibid., 152.

70. Browne, *Etchings of a Whaling Cruise*, 251–53.

71. Owen, *Narrative of Voyages*, 118.

72. Jones, "Island of Hinzuan," 100.

73. "Sales at Johanna," 21 March 1838, MSS 24, Emmerton Family Papers, Peabody-Essex Museum, Salem, MA (hereafter PE). .

74. Sunley to Earl of Clarendon, 15 June 1858, AA1/5, ZNA; Pelly to Kinlock, 4 October 1861, AA12/8, ZNA.

75. Rooke, *Travels to the Coast of Arabia Felix*, 47. It is doubtful that the crew intended to sell the girl in India, as it seems they were simply teasing with the would-be purchaser by offering the girl at a price beyond his means. It was more common for Nzwanians to buy concubines in the Ottoman realm or in Zanzibar.

76. Prior, *Voyage along the Eastern Coast of Africa*, 55.

77. Sultan Alloue of Johanna to Sir William Nicolay, Governor of Mauritius, September 1839, ADM 1/5945, PRO.

78. In this vein, see Jonathan Friedman's discussion of early nineteenth-century Hawaiian self-renaming and consumption of diverse imported European goods. He describes Hawaiian consumer strategies as the "accumulation of western identity via acts of consumption of both goods and names." I would add that perhaps such "western identity" might have been used for multiple ends. See Jonathan Friedman, "Being in the World: Globalization and Localization," *Theory, Culture, and Society* 7, nos. 2–3 (1990): 326.

79. Bernard, *Narrative of the Voyages*, 147–49.

80. Though all four of the Comoros Islands were colonized by the French, Comorians played important roles as cultural brokers across East Africa in the years immediately preceding and following European colonial intervention. In the late 1860s, David Livingstone, impressed with a group of Nzwanians he had traveled with on an earlier trip, hired several Nzwanians on his last journey across eastern Africa. See Donald Simpson, *Dark Companions: The African Contribution to the European Exploration of East Africa*. (London: Paul Elek, 1975). In 1888, Comorians took leading roles in the Bushiri Rebellion on the *Mrima* (mainland coast opposite Zanzibar Island). The most prominent among the Comorians was a man by the name of Jahazi, who spoke English and had served under Stanley in the Congo. According to Jonathon Glassman, Jahazi's experience as a cultural broker for Europeans and the knowledge of ordinance gained during his time with Stanley would prove useful to Bushiri. See his *Feasts and Riot: Revelry, Rebellion, and Popular Consciousness on the Swahili Coast, 1856–1888* (Portsmouth, NH: Heinemann, 1995), 232.

81. As Robert Young has reminded us, globalization has not always entailed "irresistible totalization"; see *Postcolonialism: An Historical Introduction* (London: Blackwell, 2001), 2.

CHAPTER 2: THE SOCIAL LOGICS OF NEED

1. I follow Jean Baudrillard's definition of consumption throughout: "the virtual totality of all objects and messages ready-constituted as a more or less coherent discourse. If it has any meaning at all, consumption means an activity consisting of the systematic manipulation of signs." For Baudrillard, consumption's motivational force is more psychical than physical. To become an object of consumption, an object must first become a sign, usually external, "to a relationship that it now merely signifies." In deriving consistency and meaning from an abstract and systematic relationship to all other sign-objects, the object of consumption becomes part of a series in which it is given value. See Jean Baudrillard, *The System of Objects* (New York: Verso, 1996), 199–200.

2. Economists tend to speak of "preference" in place of "desire," and this, as both J. Marks and J. Troyer suggest, often ends in a reification of physical utility in the valuation of goods. See J. Marks, ed., *The Ways of Desire: New Essays in Philosophical Psychology on the Concept of Wanting* (Chicago: Precedent, 1986), 7–8; J. Troyer, "Rationality and Maximization," in *Ethics: Foundations, Problems, and Applications*, ed. E. Morscher and R. Stranzinger (Vienna: Verlag Hölder-Pichler-Tempsky, 1981), 211–15; E. Sternberg, *The Economy of Icons: How Business Manufactures Meaning* (Westport, CT: Praeger, 1999), 4. For Baudrillard, the needs that desire produces are very rarely the utilitarian objects of classical economics. Likewise, he suggests that commodities are more than Marxian containers of hidden relationships. Instead, objects are signifiers employed in creating and recreating differing relationships among people. See Jean Baudrillard, *The Consumer Society* (London: Sage, 1998); Arjun Appadurai, "Commodities and the Politics of Value," in *The Social Life of Things: Commodities in Cultural Perspective*, ed. Arjun Appadurai (Cambridge: Cambridge University Press, 1986), 3–63. To paraphrase Alfred Gell, consumption is thus a process of converting purchasing power (exchange-value) into a "socially coherent definition of the self" in relation to others; see his "Newcomers to the World of Goods: Consumption among the Muria Gonds," in Appadurai, ed., *The Social Life of Things*, 113.

3. The second largest city on the coast, Mombasa had a permanent population of about ten thousand people. The estimates diverge radically between visitors, but among those who lived in Mombasa, the numbers do not range much beyond ten thousand in the first half of the century. After mid-century, however, the population grew exponentially. See F. Berg, "Mombasa Under the Busaidi Sultanate" (Ph.D. diss., University of Wisconsin, 1971); J. Krapf, *Travel, Researches and Missionary Labours During Eighteen Years Residence in East Africa* (Boston: Ticknor and Fields, 1860); Richard Burton, *The Lake Regions of Central Africa*, 2 vols. (London: Longman, 1860); Charles Guillain, *Documents sur l'histoire, la geographie et le commerce de la Afrique Orientale*, vols. 2–3 (Paris: A. Bertrand, 1856).

4. Muhammad Abdulaziz, ed. and trans., *Muyaka: Nineteenth-Century Swahili Popular Poetry* (Nairobi: Kenya Literature Bureau, 1994), 153–54. See also Berg, "Mombasa"; Guillain, *Documents* 3:262–63; Burton, *Lake Regions* 2:78.

5. According to Berg, the name Mombasa even began to replace the local term for the city—Mvita—in popular use under Busaidi rule ("Mombasa," 33).

6. Demanding the repayment of debts was not always easy in Mazrui Mombasa. The records of the short-lived English Consulate in the mid-1820s are replete with accounts of creditors being harangued, jailed, or otherwise molested when they attempted to call in their debts. See Lt. J. Emery, "A Journal of British Establishment at Mombasa from 1824 to 1826," ADM 52/3940, Public Record Office, London (hereafter PRO). The formation of a body of rights for merchants that was enforced by the Busaidi *Liwali* (governor) changed this situation. Krapf argues that "Banians" (Hindus, generally from the northwestern Indian subcontinent) were allowed much more freedom in the realms of brokerage and investment under the Busaidis as the enforcement of debt laws made it easier for lenders to collect, thus making investments much less risky. The Busaidi government also curtailed practices like the throwing of Indians into the sea on *siku ya mwaka* (solar new year's day), as well as other crimes that were previously allowed against Indians. See Charles New, *Life, Wanderings, and Labours in Eastern Africa* (1873; repr., London: Frank Cass, 1971), 65. See also Owen's discussion of the rights of "Banyans" in the 1820s–30s. W. F. W. Owen, *Narrative of Voyages to Explore the Shores of Africa, Arabia, and Madagascar*, vol. 2 (London: Richard Bentley, 1833), 150–51.

7. This also gave Mombasa at least three currencies in common with Zanzibar and western India. In 1861, Robert Thornton exchanged rubles in Mombasa. He wrote that a ruble, plus three *pice*, could be exchanged for MT$1; see the entry for 16 June 1861, *Journal of Robert Thornton*, Thornton Papers, Rhodes House, Oxford University; Abdul Sheriff, *Slaves, Spices, and Ivory in Zanzibar* (London: Heinemann, 1987), xix; Richard Burton, *Zanzibar; City, Island, and Coast*, vol. 2 (London: Tinsley Brothers, 1872), 46; Krapf, "Letter to Captain Graham, Mombas, 1 May 1845," in "Krapf of East Africa," *East and West Review* 3 (1937): 267–68; Krapf, *A Dictionary of the Suahili Language* (London: Trubner, 1882), 271, 113.

8. If a slave killed another slave, the owner of the offender was fined only MT$50. Krapf, *Dictionary*, 66, 155.

9. Frederick Cooper, *Plantation Slavery on the East Coast of Africa* (New Haven, CT: Yale University Press, 1972).

10. Note the accord here with Glassman's argument that new outlets for agricultural produce—the demand for cash crops, specifically—gave greater opportunities for previously excluded people, like small-scale farmers, to engage a larger system of commodification and signs. See Jonathon Glassman, *Feasts and Riot: Revelry, Rebellion, and Popular Consciousness on the Swahili Coast, 1856–1888* (Portsmouth: Heinemann, 1995), chap. 1; Jean Baudrillard, *Jean Baudrillard: Selected Writings*, ed., M. Poster (Palo Alto, CA: Stanford University Press, 1988), 49.

11. The wealthy of Mombasa also invested heavily in mosque construction and renovation under the Busaidis. According to Berg, twenty-eight mosques were built or restored by Arabs in the Busaidi era, and ten were either built or repaired by Swahili (Berg, "Mombasa," 154). Mosques offer further examples of the extension of the person into the realm of the symbolic and the desire for

recognition. According to Berg, while the means by which wealth was acquired was, over time, forgotten, the mosque—sometimes even its name—continued to reflect the wealth and generosity of the social group with which it was associated; see Berg, "Mombasa," 164; and F. Berg, "The Swahili Community of Mombasa, 1500–1900," *Journal of African History* 9, no. 1 (1968): 35–56. My research confirms that, of the mosques renovated or built under the Busaidis, most are identified with the groups that built them, even if they no longer exist as coherent social units in Mombasa (interviews with Said Muhammad Antar, August 1998 and December 1999, Mombasa Old Town; Abdullah Muhammad, January 2000, Mombasa Old Town).

12. A good example of both the material changes and rapid increase in wealth in nineteenth-century Mombasa is the increase in imported European porcelain evident in the archaeological record. George Abungu's archaeological analysis of the Ndia Kuu Mosque in Mombasa Old Town revealed wares from China, India, the Persian Gulf, and Portugal at the earliest levels (from the mid-sixteenth century). In the nineteenth century, however, English, Dutch, and other Western European wares began to supersede not only their Asian counterparts, but also all local ceramics. Abungu shows that local ceramics predominated up to the nineteenth century, but, by the end of the century, very few locally made ceramics were found in the middens. The only local shards were those from cooking pots and water jars; all bowls, plates, and cups were imported. See George Abungu, "Islam on the Kenyan Coast: An Archaeological Study of Mosques" (Master's thesis, University of Cambridge, 1986), 27–28. See also Richard Wilding, "Ceramics of the Lamu Archipelago" (Ph.D. diss., University of Nairobi, 1977); Judy Aldrick, "The Painted Plates of Zanzibar," *Kenya Past and Present* 12 (1997): 26–28.

13. Krapf, *Dictionary*, 3, 59, 253 (subsequent citations of this work are given parenthetically in the text and notes by the abbreviation *D* and the page number). This ability of the previously excluded to engage in local signifying practices would become an even more pervasive social phenomenon during the later part of the nineteenth century as the patron-client and master-slave relationships that defined much of earlier Mombasan social intercourse were reconfigured because of new methods of accumulation and the abolition of slavery. See Frederick Cooper, *From Slaves to Squatters: Plantation Labour and Agriculture in Zanzibar and Coastal Kenya, 1890–1925* (New Haven, CT: Yale University Press, 1980). See also chapter 5.

14. Shaykh al-Amin bin 'Ali al Mazrui, *The History of the Mazru'i Dynasty of Mombasa*, ed. and trans., James M. Ritchie (Oxford: Oxford University Press, 1995), 80. Some of Muyaka's most famous verses were political propaganda, particularly his exchanges with Zahidi Mngumi and other Lamuans in the early nineteenth century; see Ann Biersteker and Ibrahim Noor Shariff, eds., *Mashairi ya Vita vya Kuduhu: War Poetry in Kiswahili Exchanged at the Time of the Battle of Kuduhu* (East Lansing: Michigan State University Press, 1995). Throughout this chapter I depend on Mohamed Abdulaziz's compilation of Muyaka's work instead of the less comprehensive collection of William Hichens and Mbarak Hinawy, *Diwani ya Muyaka* (Johannesburg: University of Witswatersrand Press, 1940).

15. On Muyaka's verse in Zanzibar, see Edward Steere, *Swahili Tales, as Told by the Natives of Zanzibar* (London: Bell and Daldy, 1870), xiii. In the example given by Steere, Muyaka's verses on the *vita vya kiduhu* (Lamu-Mombasa/Pate battle) were recalled in Zanzibar nearly fifty years after their composition.

16. To standardize Krapf's spellings—that is, translate them into modern, standard Swahili—would obscure both their dialectical provenance and Krapf's interpretations. As far as Muyaka's work is concerned, I have used Abdulaziz's meticulous translations as a guide, but the final interpretations are my own.

17. In his collection of Swahili words, ideas, songs, and poetry, Krapf was particularly interested in Swahili metaphysical definitions of the self. While ironically never evangelizing to the people whose language he studied most closely, he believed that his research into Mombasan notions of the mind, soul, and body offered a springboard to address the belief systems of the non-Muslim populations of the mainland.

18. Krapf completed his dictionary in the early 1850s, but it was not published until after his death in 1882. The dictionary reflects translation work he began in the mid-1840s. Krapf's letter to Richard Waters (2 September 1844, Mombas [*sic*]) is one of the few documents in which Krapf speaks of his work in compiling the dictionary, though only in passing. Even in his introduction to the dictionary Krapf says very little about its compilation. See Personal Papers, Journals, Richard Waters Papers, MH 14 Peabody-Essex Museum, Salem, MA. Muyaka's verses, by the time they were collected by Mwalimu Sikujua bin Abdullah (a younger contemporary of Muyaka's), and transliterated by Rev. W. E. Taylor of the East African Christian Missionary Society, were also several decades old. For a full treatment of W. E. Taylor and the verses he transliterated, see Ann Biersteker, *Kujibizana: Questions of Language and Power in Nineteenth and Twentieth Century Poetry in Kiswahili* (East Lansing: Michigan State University Press, 1996).

19. According to Krapf, there had been other agencies, like the *mtima*. By the mid-nineteenth century, these had been superseded by the three dominant agencies that I outline here. We might also include *thámiri:* "thought," "conscience." But, since *thámiri* refers to functions that can be duplicated by the other agencies discussed here, I leave it aside (*D*, 370). The older agencies could still be found in specialized language, like poetic verse, which accented the classical. On *mtima,* which could mean self, spirit, or heart in "old Kisuahili" as well as in "Kisegua, Kiniassa, and Kisamb," see *D*, 255; and Abdulaziz, *Muyaka*, 181, 226. More recently, *dhati* (borrowed from Arabic), has taken on a meaning that is more primary than any of the agencies I discuss here. Johnson defined it in the 1930s as "essence," the "innermost self." See F. Johnson, *A Standard Swahili-English Dictionary* (Nairobi: Oxford University Press, 1939), 74. The *Kamusi ya Kiswahili Sanifu* offers a similar contemporary definition, though more akin to what Krapf calls the *nafsi.* The *Kamusi* also defines *dhati* as *asili,* which implies an over-arching "essence" closer to Johnson's definition. See Taasisi ya Uchunguzi wa Kiswahili, *Kamusi ya Kiswahili Sanifu* (Dar es Salaam: Oxford University Press, 1997), 44; *Kamusi Project: Internet Living Swahili Dictionary* (2001; http://www.yale.edu/swahili/). The word *dhati* does not appear in Krapf's work or in Steere's dictionary of nineteenth-century Zanzibar Swahili, which suggests that it

might not have come into general usage until the end of the nineteenth or the early twentieth century. See Edward Steere, *A Handbook of the Swahili Language, as Spoken at Zanzibar* (1870; repr., London: Society for Promoting Christian Knowledge, 1894).

20. It could likewise be the core or center of a thing: the heart of a coconut, or the heart of a *kanzu* (i.e., the slit that reaches from the neck to the mid-chest of a man's long shirt). *Roho* might also mean the pit of the throat, but it doesn't seem to have this connotation in its surviving literary uses.

21. *Joyo* meant both "heart" and "avarice" (*D*, 120).

22. Sayyid Abdulla ibn Ali ibn Nassir, *Al-Inkishafi: Catechism of a Soul*, ed. and trans., J. de Vere Allen (Nairobi: East African Literature Bureau, 1977); S. Partington, *Animation of the Soul: A Translation of the KiSwahili, Islamic Epic Al-Inkishafi* (Mombasa: Mombasa Academy, 1999).

23. Abdulaziz, *Muyaka*, 188–89.

24. Ibid., 192–93.

25. Ibid., 268–69.

26. Ibid., 244–45.

27. The collective self was termed the *nafsi*, taken from the Arabic for "self" or "soul" (*D*, 272); cf. Johnson, *Standard Swahili-English Dictionary*, 328.

28. An *mbéko*, or present given to a person who may become useful in the future, could also affect the roho and through it bodily actions or decisions. To "put a good *mbéko*" on a person meant to leave them with a good memory that the giver hoped would translate into some advantage in the future (*D*, 214, 75, 310).

29. The punishment for thieves (and adulterers) was a public affair that allowed all Mombasans the opportunity to chastise the criminal. Accused persons were stripped nearly naked, led through the streets of the town with their hands tied behind their backs, and beaten along the way (*D*, 108, 273). Getting away with theft, however, could be easy for those with the power of *kilimato*, or the ability to see in all directions and cause people to fall asleep before robbing them (*D*, 146).

30. In contemporary Mombasa, the person with "the eye" (*mato/macho*, literally "the eyes," but translated in the singular) is not only desirous, but also has the power to destroy anyone who possesses the object of the eye's longing. For example, if someone with the eye sees somebody else carrying a loaf of bread that the eye wants, the power of the eye makes the bread poisonous to its possessor. The person takes the bread home, never knowing that it has been infected with the poison of the eye, and those who eat the bread become ill or die.

31. "To cry avariciously": *ku lia joyo* (*D*, 187, 279).

32. *Roho ku-i-pa mbelle* (*D*, 185).

33. Because of their overindulgence, both gluttons and drunkards were not respectable: they had no shame. Without shame to regulate desire and longings, they became outcasts and objects of satire and ridicule (*D*, 236,382). But even among gluttons, a social distinction was made between the *mláfi* and the *mlaji*. Whereas both were insatiable and ate too much food at once, the *mlaji* did not go about asking for food from others. They may both *kúla kua pupa*—have eaten quickly so that they may consume more than others—but the *mláfi* was

despicable for his begging, while the *mlaji* was only reviled for his *buba,* or undue haste, what Krapf called a "morbid anxiety to finish a business" (*D,* 401, 331 [*pupa*], 29).

34. Abdulaziz, *Muyaka,* 108–9.

35. Ibid., 332–33.

36. Ibid., 258–59.

37. In Lacanian formulations, a central element of the definition of desire as a condition is that it cannot be satiated because the object of desire is not any material thing, but the state represented by certain object—wealth, respectability, or cultural refinement, for example. See Jacques Lacan, *Freud's Papers on Technique,* trans. John Forrester (New York: W. W. Norton, 1988); P. Fuery, *Theories of Desire* (Carlton: Melbourne University Press, 1995).

38. In contemporary, standard Swahili the word *kifuli* means a "lock." Krapf, who may have gotten the orthography wrong, only uses this word for "shade," which would be *kivule* in contemporary, standard Swahili. Krapf does not give a definition for the English word *lock.*

39. When a roho was killed, it was euphemistically said to be "dug" (*D,* 372).

40. Krapf says that physicians were powerless to change the fate of the roho: "When the roho is called, there is no recourse" (*D,* 258).

41. Mijikenda people (whom Krapf calls *Nyika*) in the Mombasa area shared the concept of the *koma.* Burton, *Zanzibar,* 2: 87. Playfair describes the *koma* of Mijikenda as the "shade" of an ancestor to whom one can appeal in times of trouble. Playfair to Havelock, 9 April 1864, L/P&S/9/41, British Library, India Office Library, London (hereafter IOL). In Mombasa, a horrible fate awaited the *koma* of the wicked. An angel, *mukari wanakirri,* could torment the *koma* in its grave by keeping it conscious of itself. This was called the "punishment of the grave" (*D,* 266).

42. "Hence the Suahilis carefully remove the peeled bark of sugar-cane [from their houses] before they go to bed. The natives are also much afraid of large black cats, because, in their superstitious opinion, they are very apt to fetch the *kifuli ja rokho*" (*D,* 276). Even once it became a *koma,* the kifuli had means. If a woman became sexually involved during the mourning months after her husband's death, upon being washed in the sea at the end of mourning—along with her bed, plates, pots, and mats—the *koma* of her dead husband could attack and kill her (412).

43. In Krapf's dictionary, only *sháuku* appears as a term for "want," and its implication was exclusively romantic (Krapf alternatively defines it as "lust" [329]).

44. Most other terms, like *u'ju, dáka, madáka, makhtaji, ngóa* (*ku timiza ngoayakwe,* "to satisfy one's desire") connoted mild longings in senses that were not entirely limited to material objects. See also 398, 354, 191, 197, 279.

45. It follows that an *mtashi* was a desirous person, someone who wants a thing (Abdulaziz, *Muyaka,* 332).

46. As a reflection of aspiration, if a person saw his possessions as insufficient—not "large" enough—one might say: *mtu huyu adaka kitu kikuba, kituchakwe ni kidogo;* "This person wants something big, their thing [now] is [too] small" (*D,* 355). In contemporary usage, the noun and verb are reversed: that is,

kutamani is the verb and *tamaa* is the noun. It is unclear if this reversal has happened over time or if this inversion was an error on Krapf's part in compiling his
dictionary.

47. A European ship was considered a *tamásha*, spectacular in itself and for
what it brought. It was a curiosity, an oddity (D, 356).

48. *Hatta ku ona vibaya moyonimoyoni*, "until one experiences pains in
one's heart" (D, 176).

49. *Chakúla hiki kina-ni-kináisha rohoni* (D, 149). Another example is
nadaka nefasi, "I desire according to my own wishes." When combined with
marithawa—"abundance," "plenty," "according to one's wish"—we get *kulla
kitu kua nefasiyakwe*, "delight or wish of the spirit"; *nimekúla marithawa*, "I
have eaten to my fill and with delight" (203). It is this satiation which Muyaka,
in a famous refrain, satirically idealizes as satisfaction: *ai, things and the one who
receives them, when the two meet* (Abdulaziz, *Muyaka*, 1992).

50. *Ku eza*: v.; "to be able, to have power over, to be equal" (D, 60).

51. European porcelain was often called *sahani ya Mris* or *Moris*: "the
Maurician plate," since it initially came from Mauritius. Ibid., 320.

52. See also, L. Donley, "House Power: Swahili Space and Symbolic Markers," in *Structural and Symbolic Archaeology*, ed. Ian Hodder (Cambridge: Cambridge University Press, 1982), 63–73; "The Social Uses of Swahili Space and
Objects" (PhD diss., Cambridge University, 1984).

53. This jewelry consisted of silver rings on the feet (MT$10 each), a *kekee ya
mkono* on each hand (MT$2 each), the *shamili la shikio* in each ear (MT$2), a
mkuffu (necklace, from MT$1 to MT$2). This might be augmented by a *koa la
fetha*, a silver ring adorning the upper arms at MT$15 each (D, 87).

54. Emery described similar practices twenty years earlier. See Emery, "A
Journal of British Establishment at Mombasa."

55. This ceremony, the *yongóa*, was reportedly specific to the Thelatha
Twaifa of Mombasa. Across the bay at Jomvu, people represented their wealth in
a similar public display, punctuated by piling up fifty to sixty bags of corn and
dancing on them (D, 430).

56. Likewise, *ku la ngoa yakwe* meant to "[lit.] 'eat' [i.e., satisfy] one's
desires" (D, 187).

57. *Mabaniani hawali vitu vema, hawajilishi maliyao, ni wegni joyo, ni
mabáhili.*

58. Even more indicative of the repercussions of the miser's breaking of social
norms is the punishment of a defaulting member of a *kikóa*, or rotating dinner
party among friends. To save the expense and trouble of cooking, Mombasans,
particularly in times of famine or before the rainy season, organized parties. If
one defaulted, that is, feasted like Famau at the tables of others and offered them
nothing in return, s/he could be offered the proverb, "He who eats at the ban-
quet, but doesn't repay [the host] has his/her head shaved clean." Partners who
shied from duty had their heads shaved, making them recognizable for their fail-
ings and open to public ridicule (D, 144).

59. Gell, "Newcomers to the World of Goods," 113. There was a distinction
between people who had *real* wealth, and those who were *fáhari*, or wanton. To
be *fahari* was to live "above one's position"; *ku ji-fania fáhari* was like *ku-ji-fania*

utágiri, to live "like the wealthy but without their means" (*D,* 61). To live richly and yet to be of meager means was to be reckless, unruly, and careless.

60. One did not have to be a patron to lose possessions and the respect they brought to their owners. One might lose cash, possessions, food, slaves, and so on through gambling. The people of Jomvu, just across the bay from Mombasa, were "said to have been passionately fond of gambling," according to Krapf. It was through gambling (playing dice) that they, by Krapf's reckoning, "ruined themselves" (*D,* 297).

61. Abdulaziz, *Muyaka,* 274–75. We might also read Muyaka to mean that, as suggested earlier, distribution is a delicate social process.

62. Ibid., 162–65.

63. William Taylor, *African Aphorisms; or Saws from Swahililand* (London: Society for Promoting Christian Knowledge, 1891), 16; cf. Abdulaziz, *Muyaka,* 85.

64. *Mguame kale ulikua na jaha (= witu wingi) na Nasibu ika endeme, ulipo ukituma raha kua makamo ya mfalume, sasa unabeha mujinimuetu, kuheme (= kuhami).*

65. In figurative speech, if one was said to have "[formerly] eaten wheat"— that most costly and ostentatious of foods—the implication was that they were disgraced by a fall from wealth. One who "ate wheat" was once rich, but now must be content with little (*D,* 278).

66. Playing on the Mgwame trope, Muyaka uses the fallen man as a meta-phorical device to publicly condemn the actions of Maalam bin Mwinyi Shafi al-Kilindini, the Kilindini sheikh who struck a compromise with Sayyid Said to give Mombasa over to the Busaidis. "The destroyer of the country is a child of the land, always assess the foreigner well; Mngwame is at the market; he sells mat-ting bags for slips of palm-leaf" (Abdulaziz, *Muyaka,* 151–52). According to sev-eral sources, Maalam al-Kilindini facilitated Sayyid's invasion of 1837 by dis-tributing gifts to key Swahili and Mijikenda in return for their capitulation. As a result, Said's forces landed at Kilindini and took Mombasa with little resistance. (See Berg, "Mombasa," 78; Krapf, *Travels,* 435–36; Guillain, *Documents,* 2:602–5.) Steere offered a commonly heard perspective on the Kilindini actions: *Wakilindini si watu ni punda milia, Walikuza nti yao kwa reali mia;* "Kilindini people are not human, they are zebras, They sold their country for 100 dollars" (*Swahili Tales,* xi). Whereas, of the defeated Mazrui, Mombasans said: *Masrúe ni kikondo, wafa kiunguana:* "the Mazrui were like sheep, they died nobly in the fashion of gentlemen [when they were expelled by Seyyid Said]" (*D,* 163). Though the sentence is in the present tense, Krapf interpreted it as a direct refer-ence to the Busaidi invasion.

67. *Ji-tukánisha kua watu.* Richly symbolic in its use to describe Mgwame's actions, the phrase, "to cause oneself to be despised," was commonly used to refer to the act of going naked in public.

68. Nassir, *Al-Inkishafi.*

69. Lacan terms this anxiety *amphanisis:* the fear of losing the signifiers of being; see Fuery, *Theories of Desire,* 24. This—what Lacan calls the "fading" of the subject when those things that reflect their personhood back onto them are taken away—was the psychological terror of poverty.

70. Abdulaziz, *Muyaka*, 308–9.

71. Ibid., 284–85.

72. Burton, *Lake Regions*, 2:398.

73. Abdulaziz, *Muyaka*,180–81.

74. Ibid., 172–73. Many of Muyaka's verses were replies to disparaging comments made by women. He was self-conscious about his appearance, and thus his public addresses to women focused on the themes of (1) their inability to see beneath his outward appearance and (2) what he called their use of clothing to deceive men (173, fn. 2).

75. Abdulaziz, *Muyaka*, 252–53.

76. Ibid., 109–10, 252–53.

77. See Roland Barthes, *The Fashion System* (New York: Hill and Wang, 1983); P. Bourdieu, *Distinction: A Social Critique of the Judgment of Taste* (London: Routledge, 1984); G. Faurschou, "Obsolescence and Desire: Fashion and the Commodity Form," in *Postmodernism—Philosophy and the Arts*, ed., H. Silverman (New York: Routledge, 1990), 234–59; Grant McCracken, *Culture and Consumption: New Approaches to the Symbolic Character of Consumer Goods and Activities* (Bloomington: Indiana University Press, 1988). In extreme cases, as in the contemporary United States, objects can lose sign-value so quickly that they must be replaced soon after their purchase; vide the American advertising tropes, "This Year's Model" or "Fall Fashions."

78. See Fuery, *Theories of Desire*, 186.

CHAPTER 3: THE GLOBAL REPERCUSSIONS OF CONSUMERISM

1. In using the phrase "world-system theory," I do not mean to imply that there is unity among theorists of world-systems beyond a concentration on systemic interaction and a belief that systems exist. Christopher Chase-Dunn and Thomas Hall sum up the field as a concern with *systemness:* how events in one locale have consequences for social structures in another. See Chase-Dunn and Hall, *Rise and Demise: Comparing World-Systems* (Boulder, CO: Westview Press,1997), 17. According to Immanuel Wallerstein, the general "claim to strength" of the world-systems perspective is that it makes sense out of seeming coincidences that in fact link far corners of the globe; see his "Feudalism, Capitalism, and the World-System in the Perspective of Latin America and the Caribbean: Comments on Stern's Critical Tests," *American Historical Review* 94, no. 4 (October 1988): 884–85.

2. See especially Immanuel Wallerstein, *The Modern World-System*, 3 vols. (New York: Academic Press, 1974–1989); *Historical Capitalism; with Capitalist Civilization* (New York: Verso, 1995), and "The Three Stages of African Involvement in the World-Economy," in *The Political Economy of Contemporary Africa*, ed. Peter Gutkind and Immanuel Wallerstein (Beverly Hills, CA: 1976), 30–57.

3. The language of core/periphery categorization has become so normalized that its genesis and assumptions are rarely acknowledged in globalization literature. See, for instance, Kevin Cox's introduction to a recent anthology on economic globalization, *Spaces of Globalization: Reasserting the Power of the*

Local, ed. Kevin Cox (New York: Guilford Press, 1997), 1. Other social scientists working in a historical vein, such as Andre Gunder Frank, have attacked the conclusions of world-system analysts but have not challenged the idea of "cores" as the determining features of global systems; see his *ReOrient: Global Economy in the Asian Age* (Berkeley and Los Angeles: University of California Press, 1998). At the same time, some world-systems theorists, such as Chase-Dunn and Hall, have argued that it is a mistake to assume that all relations among "less" and "more developed" societies entail exploitation or processes of underdevelopment (*Rise and Demise*, 36).

4. Many historians and anthropologists have criticized the monocausal, analytical logic at the heart of Immanuel Wallerstein's model of the world-system, a logic that only explains change in the "periphery" by reference to the system's center, or "core." See Steve Stern, "Feudalism, Capitalism, and the World-System in the Perspective of Latin America and the Caribbean," *American Historical Review*, 93, no. 4 (October 1988): 829–72, and the ensuing debate between Stern and Wallerstein in the same volume. Over two decades ago, R. Robertson and F. Lechner suggested that contemporary theory *must* account for the trajectories of global integration in a "multidimensional fashion"; see their "Modernization, Globalization and the Problem of Culture in World-Systems Theory," *Theory, Culture, and Society* 2, no. 3 (1985): 113. Peter Geschiere, Richard Kilminster, and Arif Dirlik have recently extended this critique to contemporary globalization studies, arguing that the ability of the local to shape global relationships is still too easily overlooked. Geschiere suggests that only detailed analysis of exchanges "may effectively debunk a terminology, still coming so easily to many colleagues, that serves to depict people in the 'periphery' as only receivers or as re-actors"; see Peter Geschiere, "Historical Anthropology: Questions of Time, Method and Scale," *Interventions* 3, no. 1 (2001): 37; Richard Kilminster, "Globalization as an Emergent Concept," in *The Limits of Globalization*, ed. Alan Scott (London: Routledge, 1997), 269; Arif Dirlik, *Postmodernity's Histories: The Past as Legacy and Project* (Lanham, MD: Rowman and Littlefield, 2000). 160. Good examples of how global systems can look from local perspectives include Marshal Sahlins' imaginative essay, "Cosmologies of Capitalism: The Trans-Pacific Sector of 'The World System,'" in *Culture in Practice: Selected Essays* (New York: Zone Books, 2000), 415–70; April Lee Hatfield, *Atlantic Virginia: Intercolonial Relations in the Seventeenth Century* (Philadelphia: University of Pennsylvania Press, 2004); and Donald Wright, *The World and a Very Small Place in Africa.* (Armonk, NY: M. E. Sharpe, 1997).

5. Wallerstein, "Three Stages," 35. Wallerstein recognized that linkages between regions in the world economy are reciprocal, but he argued that in these linkages we find the "underlying determinants of social actions at a more local level" (35). I suggest that linkages, because of the reciprocities they convey, reveal both the negotiation of various social actions *and* the imposition of economic constraints. Also working through a sociological optic, Anthony Giddens and Roland Robertson moved in a somewhat different direction by stressing the dialogic processes and multicausality inherent in global integration. See Anthony Giddens, *The Consequences of Modernity* (Stanford, CA: Stanford University Press, 1990), and *Modernity and Self-Identity: Self and Society in the Late Mod-*

ern Age (Stanford, CA: Stanford University Press, 1991); Roland Robertson, *Globalization: Social Theory and Global Culture* (London: Sage, 1992).

6. C. A. Bayly, in *The Birth of the Modern World, 1780–1914* (Malden, MA: Blackwell, 2004), takes a multicausal approach to a diversity of global transformations. Frederick Cooper offers a sharp critique of the tendency among globalization theorists to derive historical conclusions from "idealized versions of the 'globalized present' " in ways that occlude past contingencies, choices, decisions, and constraints. Cooper argues that globalization models, like modernization theory (we might add dependency, world-systems, and neoliberal approaches), reduce great diversities of phenomena to singular conceptual frames that may reveal important constants but at the same time obscure myriad historical processes. This "singular notion of change" has undermined the utility of most social science theories of global integration. See Frederick Cooper, "What Is the Concept of Globalization Good for? An African Historian's Perspective," *African Affairs* 100, no. 399 (2001): 205, 212. For other important efforts to bring historiography into dialog with globalization studies, see Barry K. Gills and William R. Thompson, eds., *Globalization and Global History* (New York: Routledge, 2006); A. G. Hopkins, *Global History: Interactions Between the Universal and the Local* (New York: Palgrave Macmillan, 2006); A. G. Hopkins, ed., *Globalization in World History* (New York: W. W. Norton, 2002); Bruce Mazlish and Akira Iriye, eds., *The Global History Reader* (New York: Routledge, 2005); Patrick Manning, *Navigating World History: Historians Create a Global Past* (New York: Palgrave Macmillan, 2003); Philip Pomper, Richard H. Elphick, and Richard T. Vann, *World History: Ideologies, Structures, and Identities* (Malden, MA: Blackwell, 1998).

7. Perhaps more than any other field, economic anthropology has directly addressed the cultures and social meanings of exchange. See, for instance, Jane Guyer, ed., *Money Matters: Instability, Values, and Social Payments in the Modern History of West African Communities* (Portsmouth, NH: Heinemann, 1995); Caroline Humphrey and Stephen Hugh-Jones, eds., *Barter, Exchange, and Value: An Anthropological Approach* (Cambridge: Cambridge University Press, 1992); Nicholas Thomas, *Entangled Objects* (Cambridge, MA: Harvard University Press, 1991); Parker Shipton, *Bitter Money: Cultural Economy and Some African Meanings of Forbidden Commodities* (Washington, DC: American Anthropological Association, 1989).

8. David Richardson, "West African Consumption Patterns and Their Influence on the Eighteenth-Century English Slave Trade," in *The Uncommon Market: Essays in the Economic History of the Atlantic Slave Trade,* ed. Henry Gemery and Jan Hogendorn (New York: Academic Press, 1979), 303–30; see also Emmanuel Akyeampong, *Drink, Power, and Cultural Change: A Social History of Alcohol in Ghana, c. 1800 to Recent Times* (Portsmouth, NH: Heinemann, 1996); Stanley Alpern, "What Africans Got for Their Slaves," *History in Africa* 22 (1995): 5–43; George Metcalf, "A Microcosm of Why Africans Sold Slaves: Akan Consumption Patterns in the 1770s," *Journal of African History* 28, no. 3 (1987): 377–94.

9. Richardson, "West African Consumption Patterns," 308. Philip Curtin's work on the Senegambia in the eighteenth and early nineteenth centuries argued

a similar point. French industries were unable to copy Indian manufactured cloth—even though they attempted to counterfeit the Indian textiles, stamping them with look-alike marks—and were thus dependent on Indian manufacturers until the 1830s. Moreover, Curtin argued that the economy of slave supply in the Western Sudan did not respond to external market conditions, and even at the height of the slave trade, the external market did not fully determine the economic orientation of Senegambian states. He concluded that until the end of the slave trade, the terms of trade favored Africans. See Curtin, *Economic Change in Precolonial Africa: Senegambia in the Era of the Slave Trade* (Madison: University of Wisconsin Press, 1975), 312–13.

10. Richardson, "West African Consumption Patterns." Joseph Miller's work has also demonstrated that a focus on African imports can shed valuable light on the changing dynamics of Africa's regional and global economic relationships as well as shifting social and productive relationships within many African societies. See, in particular, "Imports at Luanda, Angola 1785–1823," in *Figuring African Trade*, eds. Gerhard Liesegang, Helma Pasch, and Adam Jones (Berlin: D. Reimer, 1986), 163–246, and *Way of Death: Merchant Capitalism and the Angolan Slave Trade, 1730–1830* (Madison: University of Wisconsin Press, 1988).

11. Richard Roberts, "West Africa and the Pondicherry Textile Industry," in *Cloth and Commerce: Textiles in Colonial India*, ed. Tirthankar Roy (Thousand Oaks, CA: Sage, 1996), 142–74. Roberts also notes that colonial conquest in the Western Sahel depended on French abilities to adapt to West African economies.

12. Miller, "Imports at Luanda," 196–97. Marion Johnson argued that before colonialism, global trade not only did not destroy local industry in West Africa, but it actually spurred local production in some areas. West African weavers imported large amounts of British-spun cotton yarn in the late nineteenth century and even exported cloth to Brazil and Barbados. See Marion Johnson, "Technology, Competition, and African Crafts," in *The Imperial Impact: Studies in the Economic History of Africa and India*, ed. C. Dewey and Anthony G. Hopkins (London: Athlone Press, 1978), 259–69; See also, Jean and John Comaroff, *Of Revelation and Revolution*, 2 vols. (Chicago: University of Chicago Press, 1991–1997), 2:ch.5, esp. fn. 59; Ruth Nielsen, "The History and Development of Wax-Printed Textiles Intended for West Africa and Zaire," in *The Fabrics of Culture: The Anthropology of Clothing and Adornment*, ed. Justine Cordwell and Ronald Schwarz (The Hague: Mouton, 1979), 467–98.

13. The notion of mutual effect is, of course, not unique to this analysis; it has become a central concern of colonial historiography. Frederick Cooper summarizes this stance: "Recognition of the much greater power of the Europeans in the colonial encounter does not negate the importance of African agency in determining the shape the encounter took." See his "Conflict and Connection: Rethinking Colonial African History," *American Historical Review* 99, no. 5 (1994): 1529. Micro-focused accounts of the dynamics of colonial interfaces have begun to reveal how seemingly marginal actors can, at times, significantly affect more powerful ones. For instance, Jean and John Comaroff have explored the cultural complexities of what has been termed "reciprocal determination" in Tswana-European encounters. Though reciprocity does not amount to equity, the Comaroffs and others demonstrate that inequity does not arrest the possibilities

of mutual determination and adaptation within a variety of constraining circumstances. See Jean and John Comaroff, *Revelation and Revolution;* and A. Gupta, "History, Rule, Representation: Scattered Speculations on *Of Revelation and Revolution,* Volume II," *Interventions* 3, no. 1 (2001): 40–46. See also, Timothy Mitchell, ed. *Questions of Modernity* (Minneapolis: University of Minnesota Press, 2000), 2; Frederick Cooper and Laura Stoler, eds., *Tensions of Empire: Colonial Cultures in a Bourgeois World* (Berkeley and Los Angeles: University of California Press, 1997); Stuart Hall, "The West and the Rest: Discourse and Power," in *Modernity: An Introduction to Modern Societies,* ed. Stuart Hall (Oxford: 1997), 184–227; Edward Said, *Culture and Imperialism* (New York: Vintage, 1993). For a fascinating example of the colonizer's domestication of the tastes and values of the colonized see Marcy Norton, "Tasting Empire: Chocolate and the Internalization of Mesoamerican Aesthetics," *American Historical Review* 111, no. 3 (2006), 660–91.

14. See Frederick Cooper, "Africa in a Capitalist World," in *Crossing Boundaries: Comparative History of Black People in Diaspora,* ed. D. Clark Hine and J. McLeod (Bloomington: Indiana University Press, 1999), 394, and "Africa and the World Economy," in *Confronting Historical Paradigms: Peasants. Labor, and the Capitalist World System in Africa and Latin America,* ed. Frederick Cooper et al. (Madison: University of Wisconsin Press, 1993), 84–201.

15. Richard White, *The Middle Ground: Indians, Empires, and Republics in the Great Lakes Region, 1650–1815* (Cambridge: Cambridge University Press, 1991). On institutional analysis, see Lauren Benton, "From the World-Systems Perspective to Institutional World History: Culture and Economy in Global Theory," *Journal of World History* 7, no. 2 (1996): 261–95; and *Law and Colonial Cultures: Legal Regimes in World History, 1400–1900* (New York: Cambridge University Press, 2002); Douglas North, *Institutions, Institutional Change and Economic Performance* (New York: Cambridge University Press, 1990). On the encounter approach, see Alfred Crosby, *The Columbian Exchange: Biological and Cultural Consequences of 1492* (Westport, CT: Greenwood, 1972); Jerry Bentley, *Old World Encounters: Cross-Cultural Contacts in Pre-Modern Times* (New York: Oxford University Press, 1993).

16. "The Copal Trade at Zanzibar," *Journal of the Society of Arts* 22 (July 1874): 752–53. On the relation of caravan traffic to planting seasons, see Stephen J. Rockel, "'A Nation of Porters': The Nyamwezi and the Labour Market in Nineteenth-Century Tanzania," *Journal of African History* 41, no. 2 (2000): 173–95, and *Carriers of Culture: Labor on the Road in Nineteenth-Century East Africa* (Portsmouth, NH: Heinemann, 2006).

17. Joseph Thomson, *To the Central African Lakes and Back: The Narrative of the Royal Geographical Society's East Central African Expedition, 1878–80* (London: S. Low, Marston, Searle & Rivington, 1881), 35–36.

18. Richard Burton, *The Lake Regions of Central Africa: A Picture Exploration,* vol. 2 (London: Longman, 1860), 400.

19. Thomson, *Central African Lakes,* 35–6.

20. Harry Johnston, *The Kilima-njaro Expedition: A Record of Scientific Exploration in Eastern Equatorial Africa* (London: Kegan Paul, Trench, 1886), 45.

21. Burton, *Lake Regions*, 2:396.

22. Henry M. Stanley, *How I Found Livingstone: Travels, Adventures, and Discoveries in Central Africa* (New York: Charles Scribner's' Sons, 1887), 24; J. R. Harding, "Nineteenth-Century Trade Beads in Tanganyika," *Man* (July 1962): 104–6.

23. Stanley, *How I Found Livingstone*, 473.

24. For instance, B. Frank Fabens had to send two hundred bales of drills back to Salem when he could find no buyers for them. At seven hundred to eight hundred yards per bale, this was a very large consignment of cloth. See Fabens to Michael Shepard, August 16, 1844, MH 23, Shipping Papers, Correspondence (1843–46), box 12, fol. 3, Peabody-Essex Museum, Salem, MA (hereafter PE).

25. Invoice of Merchandise shipped on board the Brig Cherokee, Salem, 24 February 1840, MH 23, Michael Shepard Papers, box 2, fol. 6, PE; Ward to Shepard, 25 March 1850, Consular Papers, vol. B, Letter Book, MSS 47, Charles Ward Papers, PE; *Bombay Gazette*, pt. 1, January to December 1875, V/11/2200, India Office Library, British Museum, London (hereafter IOL).

26. Ward to Shepard, 25 March 1850, MSS 47, Charles Ward Papers, Consular Papers, vol. B, Letter Book, PE; Ward to Shepard, 16 May 1846, MH 23, Shipping Papers, Correspondence (1843–46), PE.

27. A few years later, Richard Burton, the only European traveler to publish a detailed description of East African consumer interests, wrote that the muskets exported to East Africa had to have a black butt and an elephant on the lock, otherwise they would never survive in the market. He also wrote that they had to be inexpensive, not exceeding three or four shillings. See Burton, *Zanzibar: City, Island, and Coast* vol. 2 (London: Tinsley Brothers, 1872), 412; Jelly to [obscure], 17 April 1845, MS MH 14, Richard Waters Papers, PE. East Africans had very specific demands for gunpowder as well. When Americans tried to sell glazed powder in Zanzibar, they incurred significant losses when it was refused on the mainland; Fabens to Shepard, 27 September 1846, and Ward to Shepard, 16 May 1846, MH 23, Shipping Papers, Correspondence (1843–46), PE.

28. Ward to Shepard, 24 September 1849, MSS 47, Charles Ward Papers, Consular Papers, vol. B, PE.

29. Ward to Shepard, 25 March 1850, MSS 47, Charles Ward Papers, Consular Papers, vol. B, PE. Another American wrote that a consignment of wire received in Zanzibar was about one-third too thick and as a result could find no buyers in town. Fabens to Shepard, 16 August 1844, MH 23, Shipping Papers, Correspondence (1843–46), box 12, fol. 3, PE.

30. Moreover, the coils had to weigh between nine and ten pounds or else they were very difficult to sell. Ward to Shepard, 5 February 1849, MSS 47, Charles Ward Papers, Consular Papers, vol. B, PE; Fabens to Shepard, 29 August 1844, MH 23, Shipping Papers, Correspondence (1843–46), PE; Ward to Shepard, 3 December 1850, PE MSS 47, Charles Ward Papers, Consular Papers, vol. B, PE.

31. Jelly to West, August 30, 1837, MH 235, J. A. West Papers, box 1, fol. 3, PE.

32. Burton, *Lake Regions*, 2:397.

33. "Report by Lewis Pelly on the tribes, trade and resources of the Gulf lit-

toral, 1863," 18, IOL Mss Eur/F126/48, reprinted as "Remarks on the Tribes and Resources around the Shoreline of the Persian Gulf," *Transactions of the Bombay Geographical Society*, 17 (1863–64): 32–103. Many thanks to Edward Alpers for locating the original version of this report. For detailed descriptions of these turban cloths, see "Marchandises d'importation propres au Commerce de la Côte de Zanguébar [ca. 1860]," Océan Indien 5/23, no.7, Centre des Archives d'Outre-Mer, Aix-en-Provence (hereafter CAOM). I am grateful to Chris Hayden for locating this and other French archival material.

34. Hamerton to Malet [ca. 1852], A3/11, Zanzibar National Archives, Zanzibar, Tanzania (hereafter ZNA). At the end of the decade, Burton called for further British attempts to replicate the American cloth (*Lake Regions*, 2:388). Despite its unpopularity elsewhere, Usambara consumers apparently preferred the Manchester cloth in the late 1870s. See Keith Johnston, "Notes of a Trip from Zanzibar to Usambara, in February and March, 1879," *Proceedings of the Royal Geographical Society and Monthly Record of Geography*, 1, no. 9 (1879): 545.

35. Rigby, "Return of the Imports at the Port of Zanzibar in the Year 1859," AA2/4, ZNA.

36. Burton, *Lake Regions* 2:398.

37. Richard Thornton, Letters, 3 June 1861, MSS. Afr. s. 27, Rhodes House, Oxford; Charles New, *Life, Wanderings, and Labours in Eastern Africa* (1873; rprt., London: Frank Cass, 1971), 452. For more on caravan leaders, see Rockel, *Carriers of Culture*.

38. Burton, *Lake Regions*, 2:390.

39. James Grant, *A Walk Across Africa, or Domestic Scenes from My Nile Journey* (Edinburgh: William Blackwood and Sons, 1864), 87.

40. Johnston, *Kilima-njaro Expedition*, 46.

41. See Jonathon Glassman, *Feasts and Riot: Revelry, Rebellion, and Popular Consciousness on the Swahili Coast, 1856–1888* (Portsmouth, NH: Heinemann, 1995), 49–51; May French-Sheldon, *Sultan to Sultan: Adventures among the Masai and Other Tribes of East Africa* (London: Saxon, 1892), 194.

42. Lt. Ludwig Ritter von Höhnel, *Discovery of Lakes Rudolf and Stefanie*, vol. 1 (London: Longmans, Green, 1894), 104–5.

43. Thomson, *Central African Lakes*, 56.

44. Here I second Christopher Chase-Dunn's critique of the notion that world-systems are necessarily constituted by a division of labor in which a core exports manufactured goods and a periphery exports raw materials; see his *Global Formation: Structures of the World-Economy* (Cambridge, MA: Blackwell, 1989).

45. Burton, *Lake Regions*, 2:396.

46. Ibid., 2:410. Johnston, *Kilima-njaro Expedition*, 45; Charles Pickering, *The Races of Man and the Geographical Distribution* (London: George Bell and Sons, 1876), 202.

47. Burton, *Lake Regions*, 2:418. Additionally, Zanzibari smiths made brass and copper bracelets for export to Ugogo; see Vernon Cameron, *Across Africa* (New York: Harper & Brothers, 1877), 78. For an important overview of the southern Somalia cloth industry, see Edward Alpers, "*Futa Benaadir*: Continuity and Change in the Traditional Cotton Textile Industry of Southern Somalia, c. 1840–1980," in *Actes du Colloque Entreprises et Entrepreneurs en Afrique*

(XIXe et XXe siècles), ed. Catherine Coquery-Vidrovitch and Alain Forest (Paris: L'Harmattan, 1983), 1:77–98.

48. Burton, *Zanzibar*, 1:224.

49. Burton, *Lake Regions*, 2:399.

50. Ibid., 2:397–99.

51. W. S. W. Ruschenberger, *A Voyage Round the World; Including an Embassy to Muscat and Siam, in 1835, 1836, and 1837* (Philadelphia: Carey, Lea & Blanchard, 1839), 38; Colonel Sykes, "Notes on the Possessions of the Imaum of Muskat, on the Climate and Productions of Zanzibar," *Journal of the Royal Geographical Society* 23 (1853): 108; Burton, *Zanzibar*, 1:350.

52. New, *Life, Wanderings, and Labours*, 63, 270. Zanzibaris imported raw, uncleaned cotton from western India for use in the weaving industry, while they exported local bombax to Nyamwezi, where it was used as a substitute for cotton. At Ujiji, weavers used bombax to spin a kind of yarn that Burton described as of a better quality than that spun from Unyanyembe cotton (*Lake Regions*, 2:418).

53. A sample of this local indigo cloth was sent to Bombay in 1862 to ascertain its value. It was later sent on to the Chamber of Commerce, Calcutta. See Brooke to Stewart, Bombay, 16 June 1862, AA12/8, ZNA. American merchants sent samples of Zanzibari indigo to Lowell mills, but the mills never used it.

54. Much of this discussion is taken from P. H. Northway, "Salem and the Zanzibar-East African Trade, 1825–1845," *Essex Institute Historical Collections* 90 (1954): 123–53, 261–73, 361–88; and Cyrus Brady, *Commerce and Conquest in East Africa* (Salem: Essex Institute, 1950).

55. P. L. Simmonds, "The Gums and Resins of Commerce," *American Journal of Pharmacy,* (March 1857): 80, 134.

56. Burton, *Zanzibar*, 1:266.

57. Northway, "Salem and the Zanzibar-East African Trade," 128–31, 153.

58. This kind of global consciousness was not out of the ordinary in Salem. Salemites prided themselves on their knowledge of places like Canton and Zanzibar. See Winifred Barr Rothenberg, "The Invention of American Capitalism: The Economy of New England in the Federal Period," in *Engines of Enterprise: An Economic History of New England,* ed. Peter Temin (Cambridge, MA: Harvard University Press, 2000), 69–108; Northway, "Salem and the Zanzibar-East African Trade," 372.

59. Mansfield, "Navigation and Commerce of the United States at this port of Zanzibar during the quarter ending June 30, 1858," roll 2, vols. 4–5, United States Consulate Records, Zanzibar, National Archives, Washington, DC (microfilm; hereafter USCZ).

60. "Invoice of goods shipped on board the Brig Rolla, 1843," MH 14, Richard P. Waters Papers: Ships Papers (*Rolla*), box 1 fol. 4, PE.

61. Ruschenberger, *Voyage Round the World*, 47. In southern Somalia, merekani counterfeits could even be detected by smell (personal communication, Edward Alpers, May 2006).

62. Hamerton to [obscure], 26 March 1847, AA1/3, ZNA. British firms, like that of Newman, Hunt, and Christopher, operated in Zanzibar in the 1820s and 30s, but the entrance of American cloths pushed them out of the market.

63. Speer to Seward, 25 June 1862, roll 2, vols. 4-5, USCZ.

64. Brady, *Commerce and Conquest in East Africa*, 116.

65. Abbott to Webster, 12 March 1851, roll 1, vols. 1-3, USCZ.

66. Burton, *Zanzibar*, 1:72, 382-3; J. T. Last, "A Voyage to the Masai People Living Beyond the Borders of Nguru Country," *Proceedings of the Royal Geographical Society and Monthly Record of Geography*, 5, no. 7 (1883): 518. Merekani was even used as a form of tributary payment. The Governor of Pangani, according to Krapf, paid tribute to Kimweri ye Nyumbai of Shambaa in the form of two hundred yards of Lowell sheeting (Krapf, *Travel, Researches and Missionary Labours During Eighteen Years Residence in East Africa* [Boston: Ticknor and Fields, 1860], 375).

67. Grant, *Walk Across Africa*, 87.

68. For a thorough discussion of the importance of commodification processes to the political economy of nineteenth-century East Africa, see Glassman, *Feasts and Riot*, ch. 1; see also Edward Alpers, *Ivory and Slaves: Changing Patterns of International Trade in East Central Africa to the Later Nineteenth Century* (Berkeley and Los Angeles: University of California Press, 1975); Abdul Sheriff, *Slaves, Spices and Ivory in Zanzibar: Integration of an East African Commercial Empire into the World Economy, 1770-1873* (London: James Currey, 1991); Juhani Koponen, *People and Production in Late Precolonial Tanzania: History and Structures* (Helsinki: Finnish Society for Development Studies, 1988); Philip Curtin et al., *African History* (New York: Longman, 1995), ch. 13.

69. Pingree to Waters, 13 May 1843, MH 14, Waters Papers, box 1, fol. 2, PE.

70. Northway, "Salem and the Zanzibar-East African Trade," 367.

71. Ibid. 375.

72. The mill boasted a board of directors that included many of Salem's most prominent Zanzibar exporters. Waters would later become the director of the Naumkeag Bank as well; see Northway, "Salem and the Zanzibar-East African Trade," 273.

73. *Annual Report of the Engineer to the Naumkeag Steam Cotton Company, Salem (Mass.)* (Salem: Tri-Weekly Gazette Press, 1848), 7.

74. Rudolph Dick, *Nathaniel Griffin (1796-1876) of Salem—and His Naumkeag Steam Cotton Company* (New York: The Newcomen Society in North America, 1951), 11-13, and "Pequot Mills: The Naumkeag Steam Cotton Company of Salem, Mass.," *Cotton History Review* 1, no. 4 (1960): 109-17; Peter Temin, "The Industrialization of New England, 1830-1880," in Temin, ed., *Engines of Enterprise*, 109-52.

75. Northway, "Salem and the Zanzibar-East African Trade," 128-31.

76. On the details of this trade see, "Marchandises d'importation propres au Commerce de la Côte de Zanguébar, [ca.1860]" Océan Indien 5/23, no. 7, CAOM; and "Lois & coutumes de Douaner Commerce sous les divers pavillons, [ca.1860]" Océan Indien 5/23, no.2, CAOM.

77. Rigby, "Return of Merchant Shipping arrivals at the Port of Zanzibar during the last five years," AA2/4, ZNA. All of this was direct trade between the United States and Zanzibar, not ships involved in the "carrying trade," or intra-Indian Ocean exchange.

78. Ibid. For purposes of comparison, the amount of cloth imported into

Zanzibar in 1859 was more than the total projected annual production of the Naumkeag Mill during its first year of operation (1848); see *Annual Report of the Engineer*, 7.

79. Rigby, "Return of the Imports at the Port of Zanzibar in the year 1859," AA2/4, ZNA; "New England's Cotton Trade," *New York Times*, August 29, 1875, 5.

80. FO 54/22, Public Record Office, Kew (hereafter PRO).

81. Ropes, "Report on the Commerce of Zanzibar, 5 October 1865, roll 2, vols. 4–5, USCZ.

82. Ropes, "Report [on Zanzibar], 1865," roll 2, vol. 5, USCZ.

83. For the dramatic increase in Bombay textile exports to East Africa beginning in 1861, see Abdul Sheriff's table (appendix A) in *Slaves, Spices, and Ivory*, 249–52. Of course, the increase in cotton production in India would further spur this trade. On the globalization of cotton production during and after the U.S. Civil War, see Sven Beckert, "Emancipation and Empire: Reconstructing the Worldwide Web of Cotton Production in the Age of the American Civil War," *American Historical Review* 109, no. 5 (2004): 1405–38.

84. Webb, "Report on the Trade of the Zanzibar Coast for the two years, ending this day [30 September 1873]," roll 3, vols. 6–7, USCZ.

85. Bachelder, "Report on the Trade of Zanzibar for the year ending June 30, 1880," roll 3, vols. 6–7, USCZ.

86. Edward Ropes Jr. "Trade Report on Zanzibar June 30th '83—June 30th '84," in *The Zanzibar Letters of Edward D. Ropes, Jr., 1882–1892*, ed. Norman Bennett (Boston: Boston University Press, 1973), 121. This was taken from the American Consul Cheney's report, "Trade in Zanzibar for the year 1883–4," roll 3, vols. 6–7, USCZ.

87. Pratt, "Trade Report of Zanzibar, July 1, 1886 to June 30, 1887," roll 4, vol. 8, USCZ.

88. Edward Alpers, "Gujarat and the Trade of East Africa, 1500–1800," *International Journal of African Historical Studies* 9, no. 1 (1976): 22–44. Gujarati traders' concentration had largely shifted to Mozambique by the turn of the nineteenth century. See Pedro Machado, "Gujarati Indian Merchant Networks in Mozambique, 1777–c.1830" (PhD diss., University of London, School of Oriental and African Studies, 2005). For earlier examples of the relationships between Indian cloth manufacturing and East African consumers, see also Michael Pearson, *Port Cities and Intruders: the Swahili Coast, India, and Portugal in the Early Modern Era* (Baltimore, MD: Johns Hopkins University Press, 1998); and Jeremy Prestholdt, "As Artistry Permits and Custom May Ordain: The Social Fabric of Material Consumption in the Swahili World," Northwestern University Program for African Studies Working Paper no. 3 (Evanston, IL: Program of African Studies, Northwestern University, 1998).

89. Frere to Granville, 7 May 1873, FO 84/1391, PRO; T. Postans, "Some account of the present state of the trade between the port of Mandvie in Cutch, and the East Coast of Africa," *Transactions of the Bombay Geographical Society* 3 (1839–40): 170, 174.

90. Marianne Young, *Cutch, or Random Sketches of Western India* (London: Smith, Elder, 1838), 12, 14.

91. M. Reda Bhacker, *Trade and Empire in Muscat and Zanzibar: Roots of British Domination* (New York: Routledge, 1992), 160.

92. James Christie, *Cholera Epidemics in East Africa: An account of the several diffusions of the disease in that country from 1821 till 1872, with an outline of the geography, ethnology, and trade connections of the regions through which the epidemics passed* (London: Macmillan, 1876), 356.

93. Playfair to Earl Russell, 20 December 1863, AA3/21, ZNA.

94. Playfair to Earl Russell, 1 January 1865, FO 54/22, PRO.

95. "Report on the External Commerce of the Presidency of Bombay for the Year 1863–64," V/17/290, IOL. In saying "export destination" I mean to distinguish between Indian and non-Indian reported destinations. The annual reports on trade do not do so. Instead, they simply list the port to which a cargo was sent. Many Bombay textiles sent to Surat or Kutch might have found their way to East Africa, but I have chosen not to speculate on this indirect trade.

96. "Report on the External Commerce of the Presidency of Bombay for the Year 1866–67," V/17/293, IOL. This was not always constant, however, since by 1870 these percentages had fallen somewhat.

97. "Report on the External Commerce of the Presidency of Bombay for the Year 1863–64," V/17/290, IOL.

98. "Annual Report on the Trade and Navigation of the Presidency of Bombay for the Year 1874–75," V/17/301, IOL.

99. Though the first mechanized mills in India were founded in Pondicherry, these employed European, not Indian, capital. See Roberts, "West Africa and the Pondicherry Textile Industry"; Rajnarayan Chandavarkar, *The Origins of Industrial Capital in India: Business Strategies and the Working Classes in Bombay, 1900–1940* (New York: Cambridge University Press, 1994), 26, 247.

100. Chandavarkar, *Origins of Industrial Capital in India*, 56.

101. Ropes, *Zanzibar Letters*, 34, fn.113; Holmans to MacKinnon, 1 June 1879, MacKinnon Papers, PPMS1/Corr 1, box 22, fol. 88, School of Oriental and African Studies Library, University of London.

102. Ropes, *Zanzibar Letters*, 20.

103. Cheney, "Trade in Zanzibar for the Year 1883–84," roll 3, vols. 6–7, USCZ. Steamers were only one sector of the trans–Indian Ocean trade. On the all-important dhow trade of the western Indian Ocean, see Erik Gilbert, *Dhows and Colonial Economy in Zanzibar, 1860–1970* (Columbus: Ohio University Press, 2005).

104. "Annual Statement of Trade and Navigation for the Bombay Presidency for the Year 1881–82," V/17/311, IOL. At this time, the total exports of Indian manufactured goods were increasing, but the increases in the textile trade were particularly marked.

105. "Annual Statement of Trade and Navigation for the Bombay Presidency for the Year 1887–88," V/17/317, IOL.

106. See, for example, the "Annual Statement of Trade and Navigation for the Bombay Presidency for the Year 1881–82," V/17/311, IOL.

107. Ibid. Again, I have excluded Bombay exports to other Indian ports in this tabulation. This number includes almost ten million yards of unbleached sheetings (52.6 percent of the total Indian-produced sheetings exported from Bombay),

more than two million yards of other unbleached cloth (28.8 percent of the total), as well as the majority of drills, jeans, and chadders exported from Bombay. Zanzibar also imported nearly nine million yards of British-manufactured colored cloth from Bombay, bringing the total annual Bombay export trade in textiles to East Africa up to *twenty-two million yards*. Zanzibar was the single largest market for Bombay-exported umbrellas, glassware, and furniture as well.

108. "Annual Report of the Trade and Navigation of the Bombay Presidency for the Year 1889–90," V/17/319, IOL.

109. Ibid. Mozambique imported nearly 25 percent of Bombay's unbleached cloth exports. This made eastern Africa the single largest market by far for the Bombay textile industry's export trade.

110. French-Sheldon, *Sultan to Sultan,* 225. Merekani, in particular, was still popular in Maasai country in the 1880s (Last, "A Voyage to the Masai People," 531).

111. Chandavarkar, *Origins of Industrial Capital in India,* 239; D. Mazumdar, "Labor Supply in Early Industrialization: The Case of the Bombay Textile Industry," *Economic History Review* 26, no. 3 (1973): 477–96.

112. Even colonial conquest did not negate the effects Africans could have on economic systems through consumer demand. See, in particular, Christopher Steiner's analysis of European textile production for West African consumers under colonialism, "Another Image of Africa: Toward an Ethnohistory of European Cloth Marketed in West Africa, 1873–1960," *Ethnohistory* 32, no. 2 (1985): 91–110. See also Timothy Burke's groundbreaking study, *Lifebuoy Men, Lux Women: Commodification, Consumption, and Cleanliness in Modern Zimbabwe* (Durham, NC: Duke University Press, 1996).

113. For important interventions that challenge discrete historical trajectories, be they national, regional, or continental, in contemporary globalization discourse, see J. Lorand Matory, *Black Atlantic Religion: Tradition, Transnationalism, and Matriarchy in the Afro-Brazilian Candomblé* (Princeton, NJ: Princeton University Press, 2005); Bayly, *The Birth of the Modern World;* Michel-Rolph Trouillot, *Global Transformations: Anthropology and the Modern World* (New York: Palgrave Macmillan, 2003); Martin Lewis and Kären Wigen, *The Myth of Continents: A Critique of Metageography* (Berkeley and Los Angeles: University of California Press, 1997); and Michael Geyer and Charles Bright, "World History in a Global Age," *American Historical Review* 100, no. 4 (1995): 1034–60. Of course, building an archive of human interrelation beyond the categories of nation-state and continent lies at the heart of the world/global/transnational history project.

114. Vinay Lal, *Empire of Knowledge: Culture and Plurality in the Global Economy* (London: Pluto Press, 2002).

CHAPTER 4: COSMOPOLITANISM AND CULTURAL DOMESTICATION

1. Johannes Fabian, *Time and the Other: How Anthropology Makes Its Object* (New York: Columbia University Press, 2002).

2. Edward Tylor, *Anthropology: An Introduction to the Study of Man and Civilization* (1880; repr., London: D. Appleton, 1913), 439.

3. Enrique Dussel, *The Invention of the Americas: Eclipse of "the Other" and the Myth of Modernity* (New York: Continuum, 1995); and *The Underside of Modernity*, ed. and trans. E. Mendieta (Atlantic Highlands, NJ: Humanities Press, 1997).

4. Stuart Hall describes modernity's "others" as its "constitutive outside." See Stuart Hall and Sarat Maharaj, *Modernity and Difference*, ed. Sarah Campbell and Gilane Tawadros (London: Institute of International Visual Arts, 2001). Susan Friedman offers a particularly rich reading of the history of binary definitions of modernity in "Definitional Excursions: The Meanings of Modern/ Modernity/Modernism," *Modernism/Modernity* 8, no. 3 (2001): 503. See also Michel-Rolph Trouillot, "The Otherwise Modern: Caribbean Lessons from the Savage Slot," in Bruce M. Knauft, ed., *Critically Modern: Alternatives, Alterities, Anthropologies* (Bloomington, IN: Indiana University Press, 2002), 220–40; John Jervis, *Transgressing the Modern: Explorations in the Western Experience of Otherness* (Oxford: Blackwell, 1999); Peter J. Taylor, *Modernities: A Geohistorical Interpretation* (Minneapolis: University of Minnesota Press, 1999).

5. Mary Louise Pratt, *Imperial Eyes: Travel Writing and Transculturation* (New York: Routledge, 1992). See also Jean and John Comaroff, *Of Revelation and Revolution*, vol. 2 (Chicago: University of Chicago Press, 1997); Frederick Cooper and Laura Stoler, *Tensions of Empire: Colonial Cultures in a Bourgeois World* (Berkeley and Los Angeles: University of California Press, 1997); Timothy Mitchell, "The Stage of Modernity," in *Questions of Modernity*, ed. Timothy Mitchell (Minneapolis: University of Minnesota Press, 2000), 1–34; Stuart Hall, "The West and the Rest: Discourse and Power," in *Modernity: An Introduction to Modern Societies*, ed. Stuart Hall et al. (Oxford: Blackwell, 1997), 184–227; V. Erlmann, *Music, Modernity, and the Global Imagination: South Africa and the West* (New York: Oxford University Press, 1999).

6. Timothy Mitchell has summarized this operation succinctly: staging the modern has always required the nonmodern. Modernity, he argues, is not possible without those defined against it (Mitchell, *Questions of Modernity*, xxvi). Whereas the English word *modern* previously meant simply "contemporary," in the early nineteenth century it began to take on connotations of both time and value: *modern* meant "improved," something that had progressed beyond an earlier time. See Raymond Williams, *Keywords: A Vocabulary of Culture and Society* (London: Fontana, 1976), 174.

7. See Mitchell, *Questions of Modernity*; Carol A. Breckenridge, ed., *Consuming Modernity: Public Culture in a South Asian World* (Minneapolis: University of Minnesota Press, 1995).

8. Arjun Appadurai, *Modernity at Large: Cultural Dimensions of Globalization* (Minneapolis: University of Minnesota Press, 1998). See also Mike Featherstone, Scott M. Lash, and Roland Robertson, eds., *Global Modernities* (London: Sage, 1995); Sanjay Subrahmanyam, "Hearing Voices: Vignettes of Early Modernity in South Asia, 1400–1750," *Daedalus* 127, no. 3 (1998): 75–104; Dilip Gaonkar, "On Alternative Modernities," and L. Lee, "Shanghai Modern: Reflections on Urban Culture in China in the 1930s," in *Public Culture* 11, no. 1 (1999) 75–108; Charles Piot, *Remotely Global: Village Modernity in West Africa* (Chicago: University of Chicago Press, 1999); "Special Issue: Multiple

Modernities," *Daedalus* 129, no. 1 (2000), especially N. Göle, "Snapshots of Islamic Modernities," 91–115. For recent descriptions of East African modernities, see Pat Caplan and Farouk Topan, eds., *Swahili Modernities: Culture, Politics, and Identity on the East Coast of Africa* (Trenton, NJ: Africa World Press, 2004); and Stephen J. Rockel, *Carriers of Culture: Labor on the Road in Nineteenth-Century East Africa* (Portsmouth, NH: Heinemann, 2006), 23.

9. John Comaroff, "Governmentality, Materality, Legality, Modernity," in Jan-Georg Deutsch, Peter Probst, and Heike Schmidt, eds., *African Modernities* (Portsmouth, NH: Heinemann, 2002), 130, fn. 40. Arif Dirlik draws a similar critique of Gunder Frank's five-thousand-year world-system. By universalizing capitalist development, Gunder Frank poses it as the fate of humankind rather than the product of a particular history. See Arif Dirlik, "Is There History After Eurocentrism? Globalism, Postcolonialism, and the Disavowal of History," *Cultural Critique* 42 (Spring 1999): 15. Mitchell is perhaps the most direct in his assessment. For him, the vocabulary of "alternative modernities" reinforces a fundamentally singular modernity, only modified by certain local circumstances (*Questions of Modernity*, xiii). See also Jonathan Friedman, "Modernity and Other Traditions," in Bruce M. Knauft, ed., *Critically Modern: Alternatives, Alterities, Anthropologies* (Bloomington, IN: Indiana University Press, 2002), 287–314.

10. Dirlik, "Is There History After Eurocentrism?" 15; Jan-Georg Deutsch, Peter Probst, and Heike Schmidt, "Cherished Visions and Entangled Meanings," in Jan-Georg Deutsch, Peter Probst, and Heike Schmidt, eds., *African Modernities* (Portsmouth, NH: Heinemann, 2002), 1–17.

11. As Dipesh Chakrabarty suggests, Victorian elite discourses created and enforced the circumstances by which knowledge and perception either came through or referred back to them. Modernity is among the most powerful of these discourses; see *Provincializing Europe: Postcolonial Thought and Historical Difference* (Princeton, NJ: Princeton University Press, 2000).

12. Michael Geyer and Charles Bright, "World History in a Global Age," *American Historical Review* 100, no. 4 (1995): 1047; C. A. Bayly, *The Birth of the Modern World, 1780–1914* (Malden, MA: Blackwell, 2004).

13. Carol Breckenridge, Sheldon Pollock, Homi Bhabha, and Dipesh Chakrabarty, "Cosmopolitanisms," in *Cosmopolitanism*, ed. Carol Breckenridge, Sheldon Pollock, Homi Bhabha, and Dipesh Chakrabarty (Durham, NC: Duke University Press, 2002), 11. Scott Malcomson has similarly defined cosmopolitanisms as involving "individuals with limited choices deciding to enter into something larger than their immediate cultures." See "The Varieties of Cosmopolitan Experience," in *Cosmopolitics: Thinking and Feeling Beyond the Nation* (Minneapolis: University of Minnesota Press, 1998), 40.

14. Zanzibar imported several tons of sugar every year from the United States, France, India, and Singapore, both in loaf and refined granule form. See, for example, Christopher Rigby, "Return of the Imports at the Port of Zanzibar for the Year 1859," AA2/4, Zanzibar National Archives (hereafter ZNA). On the Manila project, see Capt. Sandwith Drinker in H. Eilts, "Ahmad bin Na'aman's Mission to the United States in 1840, The Voyage of Al-Sultanah to New York City," *Essex Institute Historical Collections* 98 (October 1962): 272.

15. Ward to Buchanan, 13 March 1847, U.S. Consulate, Zanzibar (hereafter USCZ), roll 1, vols. 1–3. American and European merchants alike in Zanzibar developed a "deep concern" about the Sultan's mercantile pursuits, particularly his direct trade with the West, because he imported all goods duty-free. See Peters and Pollock to Sultan Sayyid Said, 20 February 1847, AA1/3, ZNA; Hamerton to [obscure], 3 January 1847, AA1/3, ZNA.

16. Eilts, "Ahmad bin Na'aman's Mission," 271.

17. A. Jiddawi, "Extracts from an Arab Account Book, 1840–1854," *Tanganyika Notes and Records* 31 (1951): 27.

18. Ibid., 29.

19. Eilts, "Ahmad bin Na'aman's Mission," 252; Jiddawi, "Arab Account Book," 29; Letter from William H. Feely, 14 March 1845, MH-14, Richard P. Waters Papers, PE.

20. For recent definitions of consumerism in varying contexts see C. Carson, "The Consumer Revolution in Colonial British America: Why Demand?" in *Of Consuming Interests: The Style of Life in the Eighteenth Century*, ed. Cary Carson, Ronald Hoffman, and Peter J. Albert (Charlottesville: University of Virginia, 1994), 486, fn. 5; Peter Stearns, *Consumerism in World History: The Global Transformation of Desire* (New York: Routledge, 2001), ix.

21. Rigby to Wood, 1 May 1860, L/P&S/9/37, India Office Library, British Library (hereafter IOL).

22. Jean and John Comaroff, *Of Revelation and Revolution*, 2:89.

23. This kind of transatlantic travel was common in the early to mid-nineteenth century. For example, American merchant ships often employed Zanzibaris and Comorians for multiple journeys. See, for example, the contracts of "Malbruke, Hammadee, & Oulede," to work on the bark *Arthur Pickering* in Consular Certificate, Mansfield, 14 December 1858, MH 23, West Papers, PE.

24. Possibly Michael Shepard, a Salem businessman whose firm had agents at Zanzibar, or a member of his family.

25. J. Ross Browne, *Etchings of a Whaling Cruise* (1846; repr., Cambridge, MA: Belknap Press of Harvard University Press, 1968), 412–13, 345.

26. M. Guillain, *Documents sur l'histoire, la géographie et le commerce de l'Afrique Orientale*, illustrated volume (Paris: Bertrand, 1856). By 1891, the sultan was handing out autographed photographs to visitors. See M. French-Sheldon, *Sultan to Sultan: Adventures among the Masai and other Tribes of East Africa* (London: Saxon, 1892).

27. Clelia Weeks, "Zanzibar," *Harper's New Monthly Magazine* 38 (December–May, 1868–1869), 313.

28. Rebecca Wakefield, *Memoirs of Mrs. Rebecca Wakefield, Wife of the Rev. T. Wakefield*, ed. R. Brewin (London: Hamilton, Adams, 1879), 112–13.

29. Bhabha, quoted in a question addressed to James Clifford, in Lawrence Grossberg, Cary Nelson, and Paula A. Treichler, eds., *Cultural Studies* (New York: Routledge, 1992), 114.

30. Joseph Osgood, *Notes of Travel* (Salem, MA: George Creamer, 1854), 29–30; Judy Aldrick, "The Painted Plates of Zanzibar," *Kenya Past and Present* 12 (1997): 26–28.

31. Wakefield, *Memoirs*, 93–94, 108; Weeks, "Zanzibar," 307.

32. Emily Ruete [Sayyida Salme], *Memoirs of an Arabian Princess*, reprinted in *An Arabian Princess Between Two Worlds: Memoirs, Letters Home, Sequels to the Memoirs, Syrian Customs and Usages*, ed. E. Van Donzel (New York: E. J. Brill, 1993), 164–65.

33. Jean Baudrillard, *Jean Baudrillard: Selected Writings*, ed. Mark Poster (Stanford, CA: Stanford University Press, 1988), 44.

34. The consumer's "need" for the vase is often directly related to its essential place within a standard assortment of goods. We can think of contemporary American homes in similar terms. A "complete set" for the living room often includes a couch or sofa, easy chair, television, coffee table, entertainment center, bookcase, and pictures on the wall. The absence of any one of these can seem disorienting, and thus each is desired for its importance in completing the culturally defined set; see Baudrillard, *Selected Writings*, 196.

35. Ruete, *Memoirs of an Arabian Princess*, 164–65.

36. Elizabeth and Henry Jacob, *A Quaker Family in India and Zanzibar, 1863–1865*, ed. Y. Bird (York, UK: William Sessions, 2000), 165.

37. Edward Steere, "On East African Tribes and Languages," *Journal of the Anthropological Institute of Great Britain and Ireland* 1 (1872): cxlvi.

38. Waters Journal, 14 April 1837, MH 14, Richard P. Waters Papers, PE.

39. Browne, *Whaling Cruise*, 441.

40. Jacob and Jacob, *Quaker Family*, 165.

41. On Captain Hassan, see Captain Henry Hart to the Vice Admiral Sir John Gore, 10 February 1834, F/4/1475, Board's Collections, vol. 1475, IOL; W. Ruschenberger, *A Voyage Round the World: Including an Embassy to Muscat and Siam, in 1835, 1836, and 1837* (Philadelphia: Carey, Lea & Blanchard, 1839), 37.

42. Ruschenberger, *Voyage Round the World*, 28–29.

43. James Clifford, *Routes: Travel and Translation in the Late Twentieth Century* (Cambridge, MA: Harvard University Press, 1997); Ulf Hannerz, "The World in Creolization," *Africa* 57, no. 4 (1987): 546–59.

44. See, for instance, the story of Juma Nasibu, one of the porters in Dodgshun's caravan to Ujiji in 1877–79, who had been in England for three years, where he had spent several months in school. He used this experience to his advantage and found employment with the Cameron expedition and later worked at the British Consulate. See Norman Bennett, ed., *From Zanzibar to Ujiji: The Journal of Arthur W. Dodgshun, 1877–1879* (Boston: Boston University Press, 1969), 35, 55, fn. 113. Charles Pickering wrote that he met many "Soahili" in Bombay who came to India as free sailors; see *The Races of Man and Their Geographical Distribution* (London: George Bell and Sons, 1876), 192. See also Sultan Majid's protest of the constant English harassment of Zanzibari shipping under the pretense that the African crews must be slaves; Saeed bin Majid to Chuchill, December 1868, L/P&S/9/48, IOL; and "Return of Slaves emancipated by Lieut. Col. Playfair, from the date of his assuming charge of British Consulate Zanzibar [n.d.]," A12/3, ZNA.

45. Ship's Register, British Consulate: Free African Register, AA12/13, ZNA; Janet Ewald, "Crossers of the Sea: Slaves, Freedmen, and Other Migrants in the

Northwestern Indian Ocean, c. 1750–1914," *American Historical Review* 105, no. 1 (2000): 69–91.

46. Kirk to Secretary of the India Office, 23 April 1869, L/P&S/9/48, IOL.

47. Ludwig Ritter von Höhnel, *Discovery of Lakes Rudolf and Stefanie*, vol. 1 (London: Longmans, Green, 1894), 11–12.

48. Browne, *Whaling Cruise*, 350.

49. For Wainwright's journal, see Jacob Wainwright, "Tagebuch von Jacob Wainwright über den Transport von Dr. Livingston's Leiche, 4 Mai 1873–18, Februar 1874," *Petermann's Mittheilungen* 20 (1874): 187–93.

50. Joseph Thomson, *To the Central African Lakes and Back: The Narrative of the Royal Geographical Society's East Central African Expedition, 1878–80* (London: S. Low, Marsten, Searle & Rivington, 1881), 34. Hugh Peter Kayamba, son of Sultan Kimweri of Wakilindi, likewise studied in England before returning to Zanzibar to teach at St. Andrew's College (Universities Mission to Central Africa). Kayamba was a Muslim, but converted to Christianity and studied at UMCA schools before traveling to England. See M. Kayamba, "The Story of Martin Kayamba Mdumi, M. B. E. of the Bondei Tribe," in *Ten Africans*, ed. Marjory Perham (London: Faber and Faber, 1936), 173–99.

51. Muhammad bin Khamis accompanied the sultan's envoy to England in 1842 and had been previously "taken to England to be educated" by one "Mr. Hunt"; Hamerton to Secret Committee, 9 February 1842, L/P&S/9/12, IOL. The renowned geographer William Cooley depended on Muhammad bin Khamis's information for his *Inner Africa Laid Open, in an Attempt to Trace the Chief Lines of Communication Across That Continent South of the Equator* (London: Longman, Brown, Green, and Longmans, 1852). Browne, *Whaling Cruise*, 344–45; cf. J. Osgood, *Notes of Travel*, 45; Richard Burton, *Zanzibar: City, Island, and Coast* (London: Tinsley Brothers, 1872), 1:286.

52. Burton later wrote of Muhammad's proposal and dismissed it as if the very prospect of an African leading an exploration party were richly ironic (*Zanzibar* 2:287).

53. W. Ruschenberger, *Voyage Round the World*, 37.

54. Even new spirits, or *pepo*, came into existence. Grant wrote that the Zanzibari freed slaves in his employ described a great variety of *pepo*, including several of English and Ethiopian provenance. See James Grant, *A Walk Across Africa, or Domestic Scenes from My Nile Journey* (Edinburgh: William Blackwood and Sons, 1864), 259. Alpers has analyzed a mid-nineteenth century *pepo* of which a detailed description exists. Gongoni binti Gongoni was a female *pepo* whose genealogy linked her to Pemba, Tumbatu (on Zanzibar Island), and southern Arabia. See Edward Alpers, " 'Ordinary Household Chores': Ritual and Power in a Nineteenth-Century Swahili Women's Spirit Possession Cult," *International Journal of African Historical Studies* 17, no. 4 (1984): 695.

55. See Anne McClintock, *Imperial Leather: Race, Gender and Sexuality in the Colonial Conquest* (New York: Routledge, 1995); and T. Richards, *The Commodity Culture of Victorian England: Advertising and Spectacle, 1851–1914* (Stanford, CA: Stanford University Press, 1990).

56. James Clifford, "Traveling Cultures," in Grossberg, Nelson, and Treichler, eds., *Cultural Studies*, 114–15.

57. Swahili was the language of communication in most environments throughout the nineteenth century—with some exceptions, such as among Indian businessmen, in state correspondence, or in some religious matters.

58. Grant McCracken fleshes out this distinction between systems of fashion and patina in *Culture and Consumption* (Bloomington: Indiana University Press, 1988), 16.

59. Glassman argues that the ever-wider distribution of what were previously "prestige" goods gave relatively poor people an opportunity to, "contest the precise meanings of what had once been exclusive markers of status and political power." See Jonathon Glassman, *Feasts and Riot: Revelry, Rebellion, and Popular Consciousness on the Swahili Coast, 1856–1888* (Portsmouth, NH: Heinemann, 1995), 37.

60. Ruete [Salme], *Memoirs of an Arabian Princess*. His sons would follow this tradition. See Kirk to Gonne, 13 April 1869, and Letter from Suliman bin Ali Secretary to His Highness Seyd Majid Sultan of Zanzibar to Churchill, April 1869, L/P&S/9/48, IOL.

61. Laura Fair gives a particularly rich account of changes in fashion among non-elites in *Pastimes and Politics in Zanzibar: Culture, Community and Identity in Post-Abolition Urban Zanzibar.* (Athens: Ohio University Press, 2001), and "Remaking Fashion in the Paris of the Indian Ocean: Dress, Performance, and the Cultural Construction of a Cosmopolitan Zanzibari Identity," in *Fashioning Africa: Power and the Politics of Dress*, ed. Jean Allman (Bloomington: Indiana University Press, 2004), 13–30.

62. See A. Coombes and A. Brah, "Introduction: The Conundrum of 'Mixing'"; and Nicholas Thomas, "Technologies of Conversion: Cloth and Christianity in Polynesia," in *Hybridity and Its Discontents: Politics, Science, Culture*, ed. A. Coombes and A. Brah (New York: Routledge, 2000), 1–16 and 198–215. Jean and John Comaroff argue that Western clothes offered an "experimental language" for the creation of new identities (*Of Revelation and Revolution*, 2:235).

63. Ruete, *Memoirs of an Arabian Princess*, 259.

64. Pierre Bourdieu, *Distinction: A Social Critique of the Judgment of Taste* (Cambridge, MA: Harvard University Press, 1984). Bourdieu challenges the Veblenian notion of consumer demand as engaging in competition with one's neighbors in an attempt to either keep up with or outdo them. Since there are elements of competitiveness in much inter- as well as intragroup consumer demand, we might think of demand as addressing inclusion, differentiation, and uniqueness alternately.

65. For the role of actual and metaphorical clothing in the discourses of slave-making and unmaking, see Jonathon Glassman, "The Bondsman's New Clothes: The Contradictory Consciousness of Slave Resistance on the Swahili Coast," *Journal of African History* 32, no. 2 (1991): 277–312; and Fair, *Pastimes and Politics*. On the idea of consumption as constituting of "social citizenship," see Don Slater, *Consumer Culture and Modernity* (Cambridge, MA: Blackwell, 1997), 4–5.

66. Ruete, *Memoirs of an Arabian Princess*, 157.

67. On the Mrima, many Shirazi sought to affect an "Arab" identity in the

latter nineteenth century in order to, as Glassman suggests, not only equate themselves with Omanis from overseas but also distinguish themselves from newcomers (Glassman, *Feasts and Riot*, 63).

68. Playfair, "Administration Report of the Zanzibar Political Agency, for the Year Ending 31 May, 1864," L/P&S/9/41, IOL. Of these, 62.5 percent were French imports, 31 percent were British re-exports from Bombay, and 6.5 percent were German (from Hamburg).

69. Baudrillard suggests that the advent of mirrors as central features of home decor in eighteenth- and nineteenth-century Europe reflects an expansion of consumers' consciousnesses, a new obsession with self-replication. See Jean Baudrillard, *The System of Objects* (New York: Verso, 1996), 22–23.

70. Burton, *Lake Regions* 2:400; Hines to Secretary of State, 25 October 1864, roll 2, vols. 4–5, USCZ; Sykes, "Notes on the Possessions of the Imaum of Muskat, on the Climate and Productions of Zanzibar, and on the Prospects of African Discovery from Mombas," *Journal of the Royal Geographical Society* 23 (1853): 107–8.

71. Edward Ropes, *The Zanzibar Letters of Edward D. Ropes, Jr., 1882–1892*, ed. Norman Bennett (Boston: Boston University Press, 1973), 18.

72. H. Cotterill, ed., *Travels and Researches among the Lakes and Mountains of Eastern and Central Africa: From the Journals of the Late J. Frederic Elton* (London: John Murray, 1879), 66.

73. Barghash sat for several photographic portraits and, according to Harry Johnston, he sent one of these to Paris with instructions for it to be enlarged, doubled, and converted from an image of him in sitting position to him standing. H. Johnston, *The Kilima-njaro Expedition: A Record of Scientific Exploration in Eastern Equatorial Africa* (London: Kegan Paul, Trench, 1886), 31–32.

74. Thomson, *Central African Lakes*, 22–23.

75. Capt. Atkins Hamerton, quoted in John M. Gray, *History of Zanzibar, from the Middle Ages to 1856* (London: Oxford University Press, 1962), 205; C. Devereux, *A Cruise on the "Gorgon"; or, Eighteen Months on H. M. S. "Gorgon," Engaged in the Suppression of the Slave Trade on the East Coast of Africa* (London: Bell and Daldy, 1869), 296–97.

76. On the changing relation of the Barghash state to its subjects, see Randall Pouwels, "Islam and Islamic Leadership in the Coastal Communities of Eastern Africa, 1700 to 1914" (PhD diss., University of California, Los Angeles, 1979), part 3.

77. Barghash imported a printing press and began publishing Ibadhi jurisprudence volumes in 1880. Valerie J. Hoffman, "Muslim-Christian Encounters in Nineteenth-Century Zanzibar," *MIT Electronic Journal of Middle Eastern Studies. Special Issue: Islam and Arabs in East Africa* (Fall 2005, http://web.mit.edu/cis/www/mitejmes/intro.htm, accessed July 19, 2007), 63; Johnston, *Kilima-njaro Expedition*, 33–34.

78. Kirk to Wedderburn, 1 January 1872, L/P&S/9/49, IOL.

79. Henry M. Stanley, *Through the Dark Continent*, vol. 1 (New York: Harper Brothers, 1878), 43.

80. Johnston, *Kilima-njaro Expedition*, 29.

81. Henry M. Stanley, *In Darkest Africa* (London: Sampson Low, 1890), 60.

82. Speer, *Report on Zanzibar,* 1862, roll 2, vols. 4–5, USCZ.

83. Playfair justified Barghash's banishment by arguing that he was "most intolerant of anything like civilizing influences and in his communications with Europeans he was habitually haughty even as to insolence." Playfair to Gonne, 19 April 1865,L/P&S/9/42, IOL.

84. Abdul Sheriff and Javed Jafferji, *Zanzibar Town: An Architectural Exploration* (Zanzibar: Gallery Publications, 1998), 76.

85. "On the Track of the Germans in East Africa," *Pall Mall Gazette,* 6182, vol. 41, 3 June 1885.

86. Beehler, *The Cruise of the Brooklyn* (Philadelphia: J. B. Lippincott, 1885), 174.

87. According to oral tradition, the doors were carved by Indian artisans brought to Zanzibar specifically for this purpose; interview with Muhammad Rashid, Beit al Ajaib, August 2000; Abdul Sheriff, ed., *The History and Conservation of Zanzibar Stone Town* (Athens: Ohio University Press, 1995), 52.

88. Battle has suggested that Barghash's House of Wonders was, "an expression of domination, the city is the arena of display." See S. Battle, "The Old Dispensary: An Apogee of Zanzibari Architecture," in Sheriff, ed., *Zanzibar Stone Town,* 94–96.

89. Johnston, *Kilima-njaro Expedition,* 31–32; John Willoughby, *East Africa and Its Big Game: The Narrative of a Sporting Trip from Zanzibar to the Borders of the Masai* (London: Longmans, Green, 1889), 15–16.

90. On the sultan's visit to the Crystal Palace, see the *Times* (London), 18 June 1875, as well as thirty other articles in the same paper covering his entire stay in England. See also the *New York Times,* multiple articles from 10 June to 9 August 1875; L. Sabunji, *Tanzih al-absar wa-al-afkar fi rihlat Sultan Zanjabar, jama'ahu Zahir ibn Sa'id* (Muscat: Wizarat al-Turath al-Qawmi wa-al-Thaqafah, 1988); Kirk to Earl of Derby, 17 May 1875, L/P&S/9/51, IOL.

91. "Queen's Jubilee—Mr. T. Tohan *[sic]* of Zanzibar, Gift of an Hospital and £15,000 to Celebrate in Zanzibar," *Times* (London), 2 March 1887, 11, col. F.

92. Battle, "Old Dispensary," 95.

93. Ibid., 91.

94. Ibid., 96.

95. See especially F. Siravo, *Zanzibar: A Plan for the Historic Stone Town* (Zanzibar: Gallery Publications, 1996).

96. Frere to Granville, 14 January 1873, AA1/10, ZNA.

97. Johnston, *Kilima-njaro Expedition,* 30.

98. Thomson, *Central African Lakes,* 28.

99. "The Sultan of Zanzibar," *New York Times* (reprinted from the *Standard*), 17 July 1875, 2.

100. Ropes, *Zanzibar Letters,* 15; P. Le Charmetant, *D'Alger à Zanzibar* (Paris: Libr. Tardieu, 1882), 131–37.

101. See Robert Lyne, *An Apostle of Empire, being the Life of Sir Lloyd William Matthews* (London: G. Allen & Unwin, 1936), 46; Reginald Coupland, *The Exploitation of East Africa, 1856–1890* (London: Faber and Faber, 1939), 241–42; Ropes, *Zanzibar Letters,* 15, fn. 51.

102. Ropes, *Zanzibar Letters*, 15.

103. Willoughby, *East Africa and Its Big Game*, 16; Johnston, *Kilima-njaro Expedition*, 31, 35; Ropes, *Zanzibar Letters*, 10, 13, 31.

104. Thomson, *Central African Lakes*, 26.

105. Beehler, *Cruise of the Brooklyn*, 178–79.

106. Burton wrote of coastal elites "priding themselves" on the public use of umbrellas (*Lake Regions* 1:34). See Glassman's discussion of the use of umbrellas at Saadani in *Feasts and Riot*, 157.

107. Burton, *Zanzibar* 1:109; Burton, *Lake Regions* 1:386–87.

108. "Annual Statement of Trade and Navigation of the Presidency of Bombay for the Year 1881–82," V/17/311, IOL.

109. This notion of a cultural code that is "more than the sum of its parts" is borrowed from Jean and John Comaroff's reflections in *Of Revelation and Revolution* 2:245.

110. "Introduction," and Dipesh Chakrabarty, "Witness to Suffering: Domestic Cruelty and the Birth of the Modern Subject in Bengal," in Mitchell, *Questions of Modernity*, xv and 49–86.

111. Robert Young has argued that the resurrection of another Victorian idea—*hybridity*—as a means of postcolonial critique has severe limitations because it necessarily conjoins divisive bio-categories to contemporary theory. Young writes, "[Hybridity] may be used in different ways, given different inflections and apparently discrete references, but it always reiterates and reinforces the dynamics of the same conflictual economy whose tensions and divisions it reenacts in its own antithetical structure." See Robert Young, *Colonial Desire: Hybridity in Theory, Culture and Race* (New York: Routledge, 1995), 27.

112. Michael Geyer and Charles Bright argue that contests over the terms of global integration and how the identities of individuals, social groups, and societies should be defined was a hallmark of the twentieth-century world. See their "World History in a Global Age," *American Historical Review*, 100, no. 4 (1995): 1058.

113. As Jonathon Glassman demonstrates, imported concepts such as race and nation—much like the objects described above—were domesticated to speak to specific, twentieth-century Zanzibari concerns; see "Slower Than a Massacre: The Multiple Sources of Racial Thought in Colonial Africa," *American Historical Review*, 109, no. 3 (2004): 720–54.

CHAPTER 5: SYMBOLIC SUBJECTION AND SOCIAL REBIRTH

1. Jonathon Glassman, "The Bondsman's New Clothes: The Contradictory Consciousness of Slave Resistance on the Swahili Coast," *Journal of African History* 32, no. 2 (1991): 277–312.

2. On the relation of the ending of the overseas slave trade to the prices and availability of slaves in Zanzibar, see Frederick Cooper, *Plantation Slavery on the East Coast of Africa* (New Haven, CT: Yale University Press, 1977); Abdul Sheriff, *Slaves, Spices, and Ivory in Zanzibar* (London: Heinemann, 1990); Jonathon Glassman, *Feasts and Riot: Revelry, Rebellion, and Popular Consciousness on the Swahili Coast, 1856–1888* (Portsmouth, NH: Heinemann, 1995).

3. The percentage of slaves born on the African mainland was probably lower for the larger population, though people born on the mainland were undoubtedly in the majority. See "List of Slaves unlawfully held in slavery by British Indian Subjects at Zanzibar and its dependencies, who have been emancipated at the Consulate [1860]," A12/3, ZNA. Of the 259 additional slaves emancipated by the British consul between 1863 and 1874, only three were born in Zanzibar; see "Return of Slaves emancipated by Lieut. Col. Playfair, from the date of his assuming charge of British Consulate Zanzibar [n.d.]," A12/3, ZNA. See also James Christie, "Slavery in Zanzibar as It Is," in *The East African Slave Trade*, ed. Edward Steere (London: Harrison, 1871); and Sheriff, *Slaves, Spices, and Ivory*, 230.

4. Edward Steere, *Swahili Tales, as Told by the Natives of Zanzibar* (London: Bell and Daldy, 1870), 497. The place of the enslaved in regimes of consumption is conspicuously absent in studies of both consumption and slavery. Jane Guyer has suggested a rethinking of the boundaries between personhood and "thingness"; see "Wealth in People, Wealth in Things," *Journal of African History* 36, no. 1 (1995): 83–88. Rey Chow poignantly highlighted consumer studies' neglect of commodified people in her critique of Appadurai's *The Social Life of Things*: "By centering the politics of commoditization of *things* in exchange, [Appadurai] anthropomorphizes things but avoids blurring the line between things and people, and thus preserves the safe boundaries of an old, respectable humanism. However, the most critical implication of his theory begins precisely where he stops . . . *persons, like things, have commodified lives.*" Chow, "Where Have All the Natives Gone?" in *Displacements: Cultural Identities in Question*, ed. A. Bammer (Bloomington: Indiana University Press, 1994), 125–51. See also Appadurai, "The Thing Itself," *Public Culture* 18, no. 1 (2006): 15–21.

5. R. Thornton, "Notes Towards a Theory of Objects and Persons," *African Anthropology* 4, no. 1 (1997): 41.

6. Homi Bhabha calls slavery a place of "not there," following Toni Morrison's assertion of a "stressed, dislocatory absence" integral to narratives of slavery. See Bhabha, "Fireflies Caught in Molasses: Questions of Cultural Translation," in *October: The Second Decade, 1986–1996*, ed. Rosalind Krauss (Cambridge, MA: MIT Press, 1997), 222; S. Miers and I. Kopytoff, "African 'Slavery' as an Institution of Marginality," in *Slavery in Africa: Historical and Anthropological Approaches*, ed. S. Miers and I. Kopytoff (Madison: University of Wisconsin Press, 1977), 3–81.

7. Speer, "Report on Zanzibar, 1862," roll 2, vols. 4–5, United States Consulate Records, Zanzibar (hereafter USCZ). Gissing's report from Mombasa, claimed that the Chagga sold each other "very freely": Gissing to Kirk, 10 May 1884, AA10/1, ZNA. See also C. Piot's survey of the blurred categories between people, even members of a kin group, and exchangeable things: "Of Slaves and the Gift: Kabre Sale of Kin During the Era of the Slave Trade," *Journal of African History* 37, no. 1 (1996): 31–49.

8. See, in particular, Marcia Wright, *Strategies of Slaves and Women in East Central Africa* (Bloomington: University of Indiana Press, 1989), passim; see also Case No. 3 of 1875, in the Vice-Admiralty Court at Zanzibar, L/P&S/9/51, British Library, India Office Library, London (hereafter IOL); W. J. Rampley,

Matthew Wellington: Sole Surviving Link with Dr. Livingstone (London: Society for Promoting Christian Knowledge, [ca. 1930]); Edward Alpers, "The Story of Swema: Female Vulnerability in Nineteenth-Century East Africa," in *Women and Slavery in Africa*, ed. Claire Robertson and Martin Klein (Madison: University of Wisconsin Press, 1983), 185–219; and "Representations of Children in the East African Slave Trade," paper presented at the Avignon Conference on Slavery and Forced Labour, "Children in Slavery," Avignon, France, May 2004; Rebecca Wakefield, *Memoirs of Mrs. Rebecca Wakefield, Wife of the Rev. T. Wakefield*, ed R. Brewin (London: Hamilton, Adams, 1879), 203.

9. Rigby, Consular Court, Zanzibar, A3/11, ZNA. As in most of such British consular court cases, the slave was asked to testify. In the Kadhi's court, a slave was allowed to testify against another slave, but not against his master. Speer, "Report on Zanzibar, 1862," roll 2, vols. 4–5, USCZ.

10. The myth that slaves were better off in slavery than in their home societies was likewise common in slave societies in the Western Hemisphere.

11. This notion of slaves as childlike subordinates was common in many African societies. See, for example, Miers and Kopytoff, *Slavery in Africa*, on the concept of slaves as kin/children and the social absorption of enslaved people.

12. Karl Schmidt, *Sansibar: Ein ostafrikaniches Culturbild* (Leipzig: Brodhaus, 1888), 46, quoted in Cooper, *Plantation Slavery*, 78.

13. In the agricultural sector, as Cooper notes, the increasing economic importance of slaves did not entirely dissolve their social value or political salience. "Whether the clove industry prospered or stagnated," Cooper argued in his study of plantation slavery in East Africa, "the slaves' labor helped provide subsistence while their presence conveyed prestige" (*Plantation Slavery*, 78). As evidence of the kind of social capital slave-owners commanded, Glassman suggests that owners' prestige and wealth could be further enhanced when slaves achieved renown in the caravan trade or in local dance societies. Even among concubines, for whom bearing the son of their owner brought the prestige and protection of birthing a free-born child, the status of slavery meant a necessary social reliance on the graces of their master (*Feasts and Riot*, 80, 90); see also Margaret Strobel, *Muslim Women in Mombasa, 1890–1975* (New Haven, CT: Yale University Press, 1979), 49–50; Claire Robertson and Martin Klein, eds., *Women and Slavery in Africa* (Madison: University of Wisconsin Press, 1983).

14. Emily Ruete [Sayyida Salme], *Memoirs of an Arabian Princess*, reprinted in *An Arabian Princess between Two Worlds: Memoirs, Letters Home, Sequels to the Memoirs, Syrian Customs and Usages*, ed. E. Van Donzel (New York: E. J. Brill, 1993), 150. On the symbolic uses of slaves elsewhere, see S. Marmon, "Domestic Slavery in the Mamluk Empire: A Preliminary Sketch," in *Slavery in the Islamic Middle East*, ed. S. Marmon (Princeton, NJ: Markus Weiner, 1999), 1–24; M. Ennaji, *Serving the Master: Slavery and Society in Nineteenth Century Morocco* (New York: St. Martin's Press, 1998).

15. James Christie, *Cholera Epidemics in Africa* (London: Macmillan, 1876), 382; "The Story of Rashid bin Hassani of the Bisa tribe, Northern Rhodesia," recorded by W. F. Baldock, in *Ten Africans*, by Margery F. Perham (London: Faber and Faber, 1936), 81–120.

16. Hamerton to Secret Department, 2 January 1842, L/P&S/9/12, IOL; Christie, *Cholera Epidemics*, 328.

17. Great Britain, Foreign Office, *Correspondence Respecting Sir Bartle Frere's Mission* (London: Harrison and Sons, 1873), 49.

18. Clelia Weeks, "Zanzibar," *Harper's New Monthly Magazine* 38 (December–May, 1868–69): 312. When the sultan introduced his eldest daughter to French-Sheldon, he remarked, "See how a Sultan dresses his daughter!" See May French-Sheldon, *Sultan to Sultan: Adventures among the Masai and Other Tribes of East Africa* (London: Saxon, 1892), 93. As further evidence of the analogies between slavery, childhood, and the status of wife, all three addressed the male head of the household in the same fashion: *shikamoo*, "I grasp your ankles" (Glassman, *Feasts and Riot*, 94).

19. See, for example, New's description of women dressed up with expensive jewelry and clothing in order to "meet the taste and take the eye of the purchaser!" Charles New, *Life, Wanderings, and Labours in Eastern Africa* (1873; repr. London: Frank Cass, 1971), 29–30. Traders also often shaved parts of the enslaveds' heads to mark their condition; see "Translations of two papers found . . . dated 20 Rabia il Akher 1282, Zanzibar," AA3/25, ZNA. This strategy of subjection and presentation for sale was common in many other slave societies. See, for example, Saidiya Hartman's *Scenes of Subjection* (Oxford: Oxford University Press, 1997), and Walter Johnson's ethnography of the Southern slave market, *Soul By Soul: Life in the Antebellum Slave Market* (Cambridge, MA: Harvard University Press, 1999), chaps. 4–5.

20. J. Holman, *Travels in Madras, Ceylon, Maurutius, Cormoro Islands, Calcutta, Etc.* (London: Routledge, 1840), 50.

21. Joseph Osgood, *Notes of Travel* (Salem, MA: George Creamer, 1854), 50.

22. On slave names, see "List of slaves unlawfully held in slavery by British Indian Subjects," A12/3, ZNA.

23. Hamerton to Secret Department, Zanzibar, 2 January 1842, L/P&S/9/12, IOL; Speer, "Report on Zanzibar, 1862," roll 2, vols. 4–5, USCZ. For a further discussion of *wapambe*, see Glassman, *Feasts and Riot*, 130, 132–33.

24. Ruete, *Memoirs of an Arabian Princess*, 157.

25. Ibid., 315. See also C. Devereux, *A Cruise in the "Gorgon" or Eighteen Months on H. M. S. "Gorgon," Engaged in the Suppression of the Slave Trade on the East Coast of Africa* (London: Bell and Daldy, 1869), 70.

26. Devereux, *Cruise in the "Gorgon,"* 414.

27. Ruete, *Memoirs of an Arabian Princess*, 251–52; see also Ennaji, *Serving the Master*.

28. In slave-holding ideology, slaves had no "words," no political voice apart from that of their masters. Krapf recorded a phrase that sums up this ideology succinctly: *Watuma hawana kalima wa nafsizao*: lit., "slaves have no words for their interests"; that is, "slaves cannot speak for themselves." See Johann Krapf, *A Dictionary of the Suahili Language* (London: Trubner, 1882), 269.

29. Cooper also writes of an Ethiopian slave of the sultan at Zanzibar, Feruzi, who resettled in Malindi after manumission and enhanced his public standing by building a mosque (*Plantation Slavery*, 250); see also W. Ruschenberger, *A Voyage Round the World* (Philadelphia, PA: Carey, Lea and Blanchard, 1839), 49.

30. Ruete, *Memoirs of an Arabian Princess*, 287.

31. Orlando Patterson, *Slavery and Social Death: A Comparative Study* (Cambridge, MA: Harvard University Press, 1982). On social death as part of a process of slavery, see Frederick Cooper, "The Problem of Slavery in African Studies," *Journal of African History* 20, no. 1 (1979): 103–25.

32. Johann Krapf, *Travel, Researches and Missionary Labours During Eighteen Years Residence in East Africa* (Boston: Ticknor and Fields, 1860), 229.

33. The metaphor of Africa as diseased found particular currency, given the older notion of Africa as "the white man's grave." See "My First Slaver: A Tale of the Zanzibar Coast," *Colburn's United Service Magazine* (July 1880): 356. The association of Africa with sickness and affliction is still salient. A *Wall Street Journal* reviewer of Ryszard Kapuscinki's *The Shadow of the Sun* (2001) touted the book as a "highly detailed . . . introduction to Africa's afflictions." The quotation appears above the title on the front cover of the paperback edition.

34. These final written words of Livingstone are emblazoned on his tombstone in Westminster Abbey. See H. Waller, *The Last Journals of David Livingstone, in Central Africa, from 1865 to His Death* (Hartford, CT: R. W. Bliss, 1875), 447.

35. "My First Slaver," 356.

36. On the role of missionary societies in disseminating information about Africa to a mass audience, see S. Thorne, " 'The Conversion of Englishmen and the Conversion of the World Inseparable': Missionary Imperialism and the Language of Class in Early Industrial Britain," in *Tensions of Empire*, ed. Frederick Cooper and Laura Stoler (Berkeley and Los Angeles: University of California Press, 1997), 238–62. On Queen Victoria's speech addressing the East African slave trade, see E. Hutchinson, *The Slave Trade of East Africa* (London: Sampson Low, Marston, Low, and Searle, 1874), 78.

37. Katrin Bromer, ed. and trans., *The Jurisdiction of the Sultan of Zanzibar and the Subjects of Foreign Nations* (Würzburg: Ergon Verlag, 2001), 20–21. *Mateka* were alternatively called "slaves of the [British] Consul," *watumwa wa balozi*. See Ludwig Ritter von Höhnel, *Discovery of Lakes Rudolph and Stefanie* (London: Longmans, Green, 1894), 1:15; Glassman, *Feasts and Riot*, 108; R. Githige, "The Issue of Slavery: Relations between the CMS and the State on the East African Coast Prior to 1895," *Journal of Religion in Africa* 16, no. 3 (1986): 209–25.

38. Frederick Cooper, Thomas Holt, and Rebecca Scott, "Introduction," in *Beyond Slavery: Explorations of Race, Labor, and Citizenship in Postemancipation Societies*, ed. Cooper, Holt, and Scott (Chapel Hill: University of North Carolina Press, 2000), 7.

39. The function of popular anti–slave trade rhetoric in Britain as a foil for the inhumanities of the factory system was first recognized by David Brion Davis and was later taken up in Frederick Cooper's analyses of East African slavery. Abolitionism existed before industrialization, but it took on new urgency at the end of the eighteenth century. See Cooper, *Plantation Slavery;* and, "Conditions Analogous to Slavery: Imperialism and Free Labor Ideology in Africa," in Cooper, Holt, and Scott, eds., *Beyond Slavery*, 107–51.

40. Frederick Cooper, *From Slaves to Squatters* (New Haven, CT: Yale Uni-

versity Press, 1980), 26; see also E. P. Thompson, *The Making of the English Working Class* (London: Gollancz, 1963).

41. Speer wrote that he frequently visited the slave market because it was the place "of most animation in this city (always excepting the nigger dances)"; see Speer, "Report on Zanzibar, 1862," roll 2, vol. 4–5, USCZ. Some, like Charles Pickering, closely studied the slave market in an attempt to create a detailed taxonomy of African physiognomies; see his *The Races of Man and Their Geographical Distribution* (London: George Bell and Sons, 1876), 198–206. In Brazil, the United States, and elsewhere, visits to the slave market were common features of travel narratives. See Hartman, *Scenes of Subjection;* Johnson, *Soul By Soul.*

42. J. Cotterill, ed., *Travels and Researches among the Lakes and Mountains of Eastern and Central Africa: From the Journals of the Late J. Frederic Elton* (London: John Murray, 1879), 42–44.

43. "The Slave Market at Zanzibar," *The Illustrated London News*, 8 June 1872.

44. Ibid. While in Zanzibar, J. Holman visited the slave market every day and wrote almost exclusively about the women he encountered there; see his *Travels in Madras;* James Kirkman, ed., "The Zanzibar Diary of John Studdy Leigh, Part 1," *International Journal of African Historical Studies* 13, no. 2 (1980): 285–86.

45. Much as in the United States, the body of the enslaved woman in the Zanzibari market became the singular icon of abolitionist literature; see Gwen Bergner, "Myths of Masculinity: The Oedipus Complex and Douglass's 1845 Narrative," in *The Psychoanalysis of Race,* ed. Christopher Lane (New York: Columbia University Press, 1998), 255.

46. Cotterill, *Travels and Researches,* 38–39.

47. Weeks, "Zanzibar," 311. Richard Burton called slaves in the market "hardly human"; see his *Zanzibar: City, Island, and Coast,* 2 vols. (London: Tinsley Brothers, 1872), 1:351–52.

48. Waller, *Last Journals of David Livingstone,* 25.

49. Kirk, "Memorandum [ca. 1869]," L/P&S/9/48, IOL.

50. Kirk to Gonne, 21 September 1869, L/P&S/9/48, IOL. Compare this with Kingsley's account of a visit to Ireland, where he meditated on the "human chimpanzees" he saw there. "To see white chimpanzees is dreadful; if they were black, one would not feel it so much"; quoted in M. Biddiss, "Introduction," in *Images of Race,* ed. M. Biddiss (Surrey: Leicester University Press, 1979), 30.

51. Kirk to Gonne, 4 October 1869, L/P&S/9/48, IOL.

52. Weeks wrote of a white slave woman owned by Bibi Aisha using similar terms ("Zanzibar," 312). Kirk freed an additional three Circassian women in 1869; see "Return of Slaves emancipated by Lieut. Col. Playfair, from the date of his assuming charge of British Consulate Zanzibar [n.d.]," A12/3, ZNA.

53. On Persian slaves exported from Bundar Abbas, see Hamerton to Palmerston, 10 February 1848, AA1/3, ZNA.

54. On the trade of Indian women to Zanzibar, see Hennell to the Secretary of the Bombay Government, 31 August 1841, FO 54/5, Public Record Office, London.

55. Kirk to Wedderburn, 8 April 1871, L/P&S/9/49, IOL.

56. Devereux, *Cruise in the "Gorgon,"* 121.

57. George L. Sulivan, *Dhow Chasing in Zanzibar Waters on the Eastern Coast of Africa* (London: S. Low, Marsten, Low & Searle, 1873), 178–79.

58. Devereux, *Cruise in the "Gorgon,"* 121.

59. Captain Philip Colomb, *Slave-Catching in the Indian Ocean: A Record of Naval Experiences* (1873; repr. London: Dawsons of Pall Mall, 1968), 438.

60. Seward to Gonne, 15 October 1866, L/P&S/9/43, IOL.

61. Ibid.

62. Frere to Earl Granville, 7 May 1873 (Enclosure in no. 53, *Memorandum on Disposal of Liberated Slaves*); Great Britain, Foreign Office, *Correspondence Respecting Sir Bartle Frere's Mission,* 119.

63. G. Ward, ed., *Letters of Bishop Tozer and his Sister together with some other records of the Universities' Mission from 1863–1873* (London: Office of the Universities' Mission to Central Africa, 1902), 229–31; Joseph Thomson, *To the Central African Lakes and Back* (London: S. Low, Marsten, Searle & Rivington, 1881), 21. This predisposition to dress "houseboys" in kanzus and fezzes became common in the early years of British colonial rule in Kenya. See Margaret Jean Hay, "Changes in Clothing and Struggles over Identity in Colonial Western Kenya," in *Fashioning Africa: Power and the Politics of Dress,* ed. Jean Allman (Bloomington: Indiana University Press, 2004), 67–83.

64. Ward, *Letters of Bishop Tozer,* 136–37; Captain Prideaux to the Earl of Derby, 2 January 1875, L/P&S/9/51, IOL.

65. While this redressing would mark the redeemed as "superior" to some raw slaves, it was not uncommon to see men for sale in the slave market wearing fezzes given them on arrival. Moreover, though the kanzu was worn by freed people as a sign of their status, the slaves of the elite also wore kanzus. Ward, *Letters of Bishop Tozer,* 82–83.

66. Ibid., 103–4.

67. As the missionaries gained more slaves, they continued to dress them uniformly. Girls were given pink frocks, and the consul sent cloth jackets for the boys (ibid., 120).

68. Wakefield, *Memoirs of Mrs. Rebecca Wakefield,* 127.

69. Ward, *Letters of Bishop Tozer,* 132.

70. The practice of "buying" children through African missions continued long after the end of the slave trade. See J. Nederveen Pieterse, *White on Black: Images of Africa and Blacks in Western Popular Culture* (New Haven, CT: Yale University Press, 1992), 72–73; Wakefield, *Memoirs of Mrs. Rebecca Wakefield,* 122–23.

71. Willoughby, *East Africa and Its Big Game* (London: Longmans, Green, 1889), 33. A testament to the enduring paternalism of redeemers toward freed slaves is Rampley's c. 1930 reference to Livingstone as the "great master" of the freed slaves who worked for him and their becoming orphans after his death; see Rigby to Stewart, 22 February 1862, AA12/8, ZNA; Rampley, *Matthew Wellington,* 30, 33.

72. Miers and Kopytoff, *Slavery in Africa;* Marcia Wright, *Strategies of Slaves and Women in East Central Africa* (Bloomington: University of Indiana Press, 1989). Glassman argues that on the nineteenth-century East African coast

the ideas of slavery and freedom *(uhuru)* were not necessarily discrete categories in peoples' minds. "Uhuru was not a status one was born with," Glassman suggests, "but was rather a condition bestowed on a slave, by the master or some other powerful patron." Thus, when one "was granted uhuru, one exchanged bonds with the master for a new type of bond with one's benefactor" *(Feasts and Riot,* 113).

73. Glassman, *Feasts and Riot;* Cooper, Holt, and Scott, "Introduction," 5.

74. Burton, *Zanzibar* 1:179–80.

75. Political Agent of Zanzibar to Secretary of the Government, Bombay, 17 March 1866, AA3/25, ZNA. AA3/25 contains a considerable amount of information about Mabruki's case.

76. Simmel, quoted in Jean and John Comaroff, *Of Revelation and Revolution* 2:273.

77. Devereux, *Cruise in the "Gorgon,"* 107–8.

78. "Depositions of various male and female African slaves found in possession of Kanoo Munjee a Banian, British Subject, residing at Zanzibar," 5 February 1860, AA3/11, ZNA.

79. Burton, *The Lake Regions of Central Africa,* 2 vols. (London: Longman, 1860), 1:34; and *Zanzibar* 1:109, 386–87.

80. Laura Fair, *Pastimes and Politics: Culture, Community, and Identity in Post-Abolition Urban Zanzibar, 1890–1945* (Athens: Ohio University Press, 2001), chap. 2.

81. On slaves' conviction that return was impossible, see Sulivan, *Dhow Chasing in Zanzibar Waters,* 186.

82. On theft, see, for example, Consular Court Zanzibar, Criminal case no.7, 18 December 1867, AA7/1, ZNA.

83. Burton, *Zanzibar* 1:343–44.

84. Devereux, *Cruise in the "Gorgon,"* 107; New, *Life, Wanderings, and Labours,* 59.

85. Rashid was only officially freed on the death of his master, Bibi Zem Zem, Sultan Barghash's sister. See "Story of Rashid bin Hassani" (also discussed in Cooper, *Plantation Slavery,* 232). J. Willoughby's gunbearer, "Faas," turned down an offer of manumission when Willoughby sought to buy his freedom. He told Willoughby that he preferred to remain a slave because he would always be assured of a home when unable to find employment as a porter. See Willoughby, *East Africa and Its Big Game,* 259. Glassman records several similar circumstances that confirm the centrality of social dependence to slavery on the East African coast. He goes so far as to suggest that even slave rebels did not seek "independence" but community and the ability to determine their place within it *(Feasts and Riot,* 107).

86. Ruete [Salme] wrote that the Circassian concubines in her household were well aware of their social value and therefore refused to eat with Ethiopian or East African concubines. This refusal to eat with others of differing social standing was common in Zanzibar: adults did not eat with children, men often only ate with other men, and the elite did not share meals with those they deemed less respectable. In response to their haughtiness, the children of Ethiopian concubines derisively called the children of Circassian mothers "Highness" (Ruete, *Memoirs of an Arabian Princess,* 174, 176).

87. Ward, *Letters of Bishop Tozer*, 117–18.

88. Livingstone was impressed with Wainwright and requested his company in his subsequent travels. Wainright later escorted Livingstone's body to London and was invited to Livingstone's funeral in Westminster Abbey as a "representative of Africa." Thereafter he toured England, speaking to various congregations with the support of the CMS. Matthew Wellington, whose birth name was Chengwimbe, also took on a new name at the Nasik mission. Though missionaries gave him the name "Matthew," he chose "Wellington" (Rampley, *Matthew Wellington*).

89. Fred Morton, *Children of Ham: Freed Slaves and Fugitive Slaves on the Kenya Coast, 1873 to 1907* (Boulder, CO: Westview Press, 1990), 52–55.

90. Ibid., 59.

91. Ibid., 57, fn. 24.

92. See August Nimtz, *Islam and Politics in East Africa* (Minneapolis: University of Minnesota Press, 1980); Cooper, *Plantation Slavery;* Glassman, *Feasts and Riot;* Mohamed el Zein, *The Sacred Meadows* (Evanston, IL: Northwestern University Press, 1974).

93. Glassman argues that the appropriation of the title *mwungwana* (the singular of *waungwana*) was common among porters and other free-born, upcountry people in coastal East Africa. The term implied an urbaneness, an association with coastal culture (*Feasts and Riot,* 62).

94. Edward Steere, *Handbook of the Swahili Language as Spoken at Zanzibar* (1870; repr., London: Society for Promoting Christian Knowledge, 1894), 406.

95. Krapf, *Dictionary,* 269, 406. Steere's dictionary of the Zanzibari dialect reiterates Krapf's definition, emphasizing that *uungwana* meant civilized ("as opposed to *-shinzi*") and free ("as opposed to *-tumwa*"). See Steere, *Handbook of the Swahili Language,* 406.

96. Krapf, *Dictionary,* 259, 269, 390. Elsewhere Krapf wrote that Europeans, Arabs, and Indians were called "Unguana," "in opposition to the Blacks and slaves, or Watoto wa Hami [children of Ham]." See Johann Krapf, "The East Africa Mission," *Church Missionary Record* 1, no. 17 (1846): 38.

97. Krapf, *Dictionary,* 312. Krapf's explanation is as follows: "*huyu Muarabu ni punguani si Muarabu kamili,* this man is only a half-caste Arab, not a full Arab; that is, his father is an Arab, but his mother is or was a slave. *Mtu huyu ni punguani,* or *yuna punguani kua mamai si muunguana kamili anatangamana na maji ya kitumoa, aliepunguka uunguana,* this man is free but his freedom is defective on account of his mother who was a slave, and was liberated."

98. John H. Speke, *Journal of the Discovery of the Source of the Nile* (New York: Harper and Brothers, 1868), xxvi.

99. Thomson, *Central African Lakes,* 91–92; Glassman, *Feasts and Riot.* *Waungwana* was such a common self-identifying term for Swahili-speaking porters that a variant of Swahili spoken in eastern Congo was popularly known as *Kiungwana.*

100. Consular Court Proceeding, 13 January 1860, AA3/11, ZNA.

101. Much like *uungwana,* these terms were also deployed by ex-slaves and the poor to further their own social interests.

102. For a discussion of the cultural and semantic transition among elites from *uungwana* to *ustaarabu*, see Randall Pouwels, *Horn and Crescent* (Cambridge: Cambridge University Press, 1987), passim.

103. Glassman suggests that even *ustaarabu* was quickly appropriated by slaves and others, which gave rise to the term *mtumwa mstaarabu* (*Feasts and Riot*, 92).

104. Strobel, *Muslim Women in Mombasa;* and Glassman, *Feasts and Riot;* David Sperling, "The Frontiers of Prophecy: Healing, the Cosmos and Islam on the East African Coast in the Nineteenth Century," in *Revealing Prophets*, ed. D. Anderson and D. Johnson (London: James Currey, 1995), 83–101; Edward Alpers, " 'Ordinary Household Chores,' " *International Journal of African Historical Studies* 17, no. 4 (1984): 677–702.

105. Cooper, *Plantation Slavery*, 229; Garth Myers, "The Early History of the 'Other Side' of Zanzibar Town," in *The History and Conservation of Stone Town Zanzibar,* ed. Abdul Sheriff (Athens: Ohio University Press, 1995), 30–45; "Reconstructing Ng'ambo: Town Planning and Development on the Other Side of Zanzibar" (PhD diss., University of California, Los Angeles, 1993); and Johann Ludwig Krapf, *'Memoir on the East African Slave Trade': Ein unveröffentlichtes Dokument aus dem Jahr 1853* (Vienna: Afro-Pub, 2002). When Rigby emancipated more than four thousand slaves owned by Indians in Zanzibar, almost all moved to Ng'ambo and took jobs such as water-carriers and produce-sellers (Grant, *A Walk Across Africa,* 12).

106. Osgood, *Notes of Travel,* 50–51; Colomb, *Slave-Catching,* 371.

107. New, *Life, Wanderings, and Labours,* 64.

108. Ibid.

109. "Return of Slaves emancipated by Lieut. Col. Playfair, from the date of his assuming charge of British Consulate Zanzibar [n.d.]," A12/3, ZNA.

110. Glassman, "Bondsman's New Clothes."

111. Burton, *Zanzibar* 2:111.

112. P. J. Cain and A. G. Hopkins, *British Imperialism, 1688–2000* (London: Longman, 2000). "Moral purpose" is D. Hammond and A. Jablow's phrase, taken from *The Africa That Never Was* (New York: Twayne, 1970), 50.

113. This notion of Africans as a tabula rasa carried over into colonial discourse. The African character, was, according to one colonialist, "a blank sheet whereon we may write at will, without the necessity of first deleting old impressions"; see Pieterse, *White on Black,* 88.

114. Krapf, who was prescient in many ways, articulated in 1845 what would become the popular ideology of colonialism: "The great question . . . is whether the moral Government of God will at this period bring the African mankind into closer connection with the rest of the world, or whether he will postpone it until the occidental Christendom is more aroused to a sense of the great duties which Christians have to fulfill"; see Johann Krapf, "Letter to Capt. Graham, Mombas, 1st May, 1845," in "Krapf of East Africa," *East and West Review* 3 (1937): 263, 265, 268. On the history of antislavery rhetoric and images of Africa, see Philip Curtin, *The Image of Africa: British Ideas and Actions, 1780–1850* (Madison: University of Wisconsin Press, 1973); Patrick Brantlinger, "Victorians and Africans: The Genealogy of the Myth of the Dark

Continent," *Critical Inquiry* 12, no. 1 (1985): 166–203; R. Austen and W. Smith, "Images of Africa and British Slave-Trade Abolition: The Transition to an Imperialist Ideology, 1787–1807," *African Historical Studies* 2, no. 1 (1969): 69–83.

115. "Administration Report of the Political Agent and Consul-General at Zanzibar for the Year 1873 and 1874," L/P&S/9/51, IOL; Churchill to H. M. Secretary to the Secretary of State for India, India Office, London, 22 August 1868, L/P&S/9/48, IOL. The correspondence between British Consul John Kirk and William Mackinnon—the commercial magnate who would receive coastal Kenya as a semi-private trusteeship—is likewise steeped in an idealistic rhetoric based on encouraging trade and achieving greater British control for the express goal of liberating Africans from slavery and a host of other vices. While Mackinnon had more economic interests in East Africa than any Briton, he was a devout Christian and believed deeply in the moral necessity of intervention as the only means to the humanitarian ends of abolition and civilization. PPMS1/Corr 1, Mackinnon Papers, School of Oriental and African Studies Library, University of London. See also John S. Galbraith, *Mackinnon and East Africa, 1878–1895: A Study in the "New Imperialism."* (Cambridge: Cambridge University Press, 1972).

116. Samuel Baker, *The Albert N'yanza, Great Basin of the Nile, and Explorations of the Nile Sources* (London: Macmillan, 1866), 445. Consul John Kirk, was more direct: "It is an uphill work keeping orientals straight. I would far sooner govern the country offhand and have done with it"; quoted in E. Ropes Jr., *The Zanzibar Letters of Edward D. Ropes, Jr., 1882–1892*, ed. Norman Bennett (Boston: Boston University Press, 1973), 30, fn. 101.

117. For the ideology of colonization as the moral answer to the slave trade/slavery, see Cooper, "Conditions Analogous to Slavery," 116; Frere, in a letter to the British Parliament, wrote that "as far as physical comfort, security, and chance of rising in the world goes, [being a slave in Zanzibar] is better than anything to which he could have aspired in his own country"; see Great Britain, Foreign Office, *Correspondence Respecting Sir Bartle Frere's Mission*, 148–9; Speke, *Journal of the Discovery*, xxvi; Weeks, "Zanzibar," 311; Ward, *Letters of Bishop Tozer*, 136–37.

118. Ronald Robinson, John Gallagher, and Alice Denny, *Africa and the Victorians: The Climax of Imperialism* (Garden City, NY: Anchor Books, 1968), 47.

119. Ibid, 24.

120. Ward, *Letters of Bishop Tozer*, 226.

121. Sultan Barghash's 1875 European tour and the autobiography of Sayyida Salme binti Said/Emily Ruete (Barghash's half sister), *Memoirs of an Arabian Princess*, were the most significant attempts by East Africans to shape European images of the region.

CHAPTER 6: PICTURESQUE CONTRADICTIONS

1. John C. Willoughby, *East Africa and Its Big Game: The Narrative of a Sporting Trip from Zanzibar to the Borders of the Masai* (London: Longmans, Green, 1889), 11–12.

2. William Bissell, "Engaging Colonial Nostalgia," *Cultural Anthropology,* 20, no. 2 (2005): 215–48.

3. Michael Adas, *Machines as the Measure of Man: Science, Technology, and Ideologies of Western Dominance* (Ithaca, NY: Cornell University Press, 1989), 3–4.

4. Breckenridge et. al. call this desire to separate and purify never-autonomous realms a core concern of modern Western consciousness. See Carol Breckenridge, Sheldon Pollock, Homi Bhabha, and Dipesh Chakrabarty, eds. *Cosmopolitanism* (Durham, NC: Duke University Press, 2002), 12. India has a similar history of being described as essentially contradictory: its ancient temples paradoxically stand next to modern factories. See Dipesh Chakrabarty, *Provincializing Europe: Postcolonial Thought and Historical Difference* (Princeton, NJ: Princeton University Press, 2000), 49.

5. As Disraeli famously declared before the House of Commons in 1849, "Race implies difference, difference implies superiority, and superiority leads to dominance." Quoted in Biddiss, "Introduction," in *Images of Race,* ed. M. Biddiss (Surrey: Leicester University Press, 1979), 16. On the correlation of civilization and race, see, for example, L. H. Morgan, *Ancient Society: Researches in the Lines of Human Progress from Savagery through Barbarism to Civilization* (New York: H. Holt, 1878); Philip Curtin, *The Image of Africa* (Madison: University of Wisconsin Press, 1973).

6. Ronald Robinson, John Gallagher, and Alice Denny, *Africa and the Victorians: The Climax of Imperialism* (Garden City, NY: Anchor Books, 1968), 18.

7. Johannes Fabian, "Remembering the Other: Knowledge and Recognition in the Exploration of Central Africa," *Critical Inquiry* 26, no. 1 (1999): 49–69.

8. Bernard McGrane develops this distinction between hierarchies of knowledge and temporality in *Beyond Anthropology* (New York: Columbia University Press, 1989). See also H. Alan C. Cairns, *Prelude to Imperialism: British Reactions to Central African Society, 1840–1890* (London: Routledge & Kegan Paul, 1965).

9. Hegel is quoted in Anne McClintock, *Imperial Leather: Race, Gender and Sexuality in the Colonial Conquest* (New York: Routledge, 1995), 40; Tylor, *Anthropology: An Introduction to the Study of Man and Civilization* (1880; repr., London: D. Appleton, 1913), 401; see also Nicholas Thomas, *Out of Time: History and Evolution in Anthropological Discourses* (Ann Arbor: University of Michigan Press, 1989); Curtis Keim, *Mistaking Africa: Curiosities and Inventions of the American Mind* (Boulder, CO: Westview Press, 1999). Western authors applied this notion that societies traveled along varying evolutionary time-lines to much of the world in the latter nineteenth century. The Americo-Hawaiian biographer William Armstrong wrote in his reflections on King David Kalakua's life that Hawaiians could not simply adopt the "self-rule of the Anglo-Saxons," for it was an "evolution" of political habits and customs that Anglo-Saxons had slowly developed over time; see his *Around the World with a King: The Circumnavigation of His Majesty King David Kalakua* (1903; repr., Tokyo: Charles E. Tuttle, 1977), 11. For a valuable genealogy of "civilization" discourse, see Bruce Mazlish, *Civilization and Its Contents* (Stanford, CA: Stanford University Press, 2004).

10. This interpretation of non-Westerners as temporally distinct in anthropological discourse is more fully considered in Fabian's, *Time and the Other: How Anthropology Makes Its Object* (New York: Columbia University Press, 2002). Such temporal designations of difference still find their way into our vocabulary of alterity. The recourse to ideas like "intrinsic ansynchrony" as a hallmark of the Third World is just one example that closely resembles nineteenth-century definitions of cultural dissimilarity. See J. Nederveen Pieterse, "Globalization as Hybridization," in *Global Modernities*, ed. Mike Featherstone et. al. (London: Sage, 1995), 69–90. Thomas Friedman rehashed this concept of a place out-of-time in his reference to Iraq as a nation that has been, "on a vacation from history" (*Charlie Rose*, June 3, 2004). Even more absurdly, Tim Butcher of the BBC, reporting from the Democratic Republic of Congo, recently wrote that, "the hands of the Congolese clock are not just standing still, they are spinning backwards"; see "Re-Charting the Mighty Congo," BBC, 1 January, 2005, http://news.bbc.co.uk.

11. In Hammond and Jablow's words, Africa became a "reservoir" of antiquity in the nineteenth century. See D. Hammond and A. Jablow, *The Africa That Never Was: Four Centuries of British Writing about Africa* (New York: Twayne, 1970), 90. Some analysts were explicit in their regard of Africans as unchanging through centuries. Charles Mackay wrote that "in all the record of history, from Moses downwards, the negro has been the same"; see "The Negro and Negrophilists," *Blackwood's Edinburgh Magazine* 99 (1866): 587. Emblematic of the legacies of this way of seeing, a recent CNN International report on the lives of Botswanan "Bushman" removed from their ancestral homes in the Kalahari referred to one of the interviewees, Maswe Gkiiwe, as a "throwback to a bygone era" (12 December 2006).

12. Charles Pickering, *The Races of Man and Their Geographical Distribution* (London: George Bell and Sons, 1876), 196.

13. W. Ruschenberger, *A Voyage Round the World* (Philadelphia, PA: Carey, Lea, and Blanchard, 1839), 29.

14. Richard Burton, *Zanzibar: City, Island, and Coast*, 2 vols. (London: Tinsley Brothers, 1872), 1:118.

15. H. Cotterill, ed., *Travels and Researches among the Lakes and Mountains of Eastern and Central Africa: From the Journals of the Late J. Frederic Elton* (London: John Murray, 1879), 23.

16. Harry Johnston, *The Kilima-njaro Expedition. A Record of Scientific Exploration in Eastern Equatorial Africa* (London: Kegan Paul, Trench, 1886), 550.

17. "Zanzibar, A Commercial Power," *MacMillan's Magazine*, 32 (May–October 1875): 288.

18. It is an extraordinary fact that between 1848 and 1877 the number of subscribers to the Royal Geographical Society of Britain grew from about six hundred to three and a half thousand. It is also telling of East Africa's relation to the new field of geography that Sir H. Bartle Frere became the president of the Royal Geographical Society after serving as British consul in Zanzibar. See R. C. Bridges, "Europeans and East Africans in the Age of Exploration," *Geographical Journal* 139, no. 2 (1973): 220–32; Timothy Young, *Travellers in Africa: British Travelogues, 1850–1900* (New York: Manchester University Press, 1988); Frere,

228

Notes to Pages 151–152

"A Few Remarks on Zanzibar and the East Coast of Africa," *Proceedings of the Royal Geographical Society of London*, 17, no. 5 (1872–73): 343–54.

19. Michel Foucault, *The Order of Things: An Archaeology of the Human Sciences* (New York: Vantage, 1994), chaps. 5 and 10; Pratt, *Imperial Eyes: Travel Writing and Transculturation* (New York: Routledge, 1992); J. Sheehan, "Culture," in *The Nineteenth Century*, ed. T. C. W. Blanning (Oxford: Oxford University Press, 2000), 126–57.

20. Alan Moorhead, quoted in Hammond and Jablow, *Africa That Never Was*, 51–52.

21. Edward Ropes, *The Zanzibar Letters of Edward D. Ropes, Jr., 1882–1892*, ed. Norman Bennett (Boston: Boston University, 1973), 6.

22. Quoted in T. Richards, *The Commodity Culture of Victorian England* (Stanford, CA: Stanford University Press, 1990), 136. See also Felix Driver, "Henry Morton Stanley and His Critics: Geography, Exploration, and Empire," *Past and Present* 133 (November 1991): 134–66. Zanzibar now also hosted the embassies of not only the United States, the United Kingdom, France, and Germany, but also Portugal, Italy, Belgium, and Austria. See Pratt, "Trade Report of Zanzibar, July 1 1886 to June 30, 1887," roll 4, vol. 8, USCZ.

23. Changes in the French popular press were very similar to those in the British and U.S. presses. According to W. Schneider, before 1870 information about Africa was available to a small elite in France, but thereafter events made it into the popular press and information about Africa was widely consumed; see *An Empire for the Masses: The French Popular Image of Africa, 1870–1900* (Westport, CT: Greenwood Press, 1982), 5.

24. During Barghash's European tour, H. Bartle Frere described East Africa as "almost a blank in the [British] commercial map of the world" ("Zanzibar A Commercial Power," 288). Interest in East Africa and the new science of discovery had, at least before the 1880s, very little relation to metropolitan mercantilism. Bridges claims, in fact, that membership in an organization like the Royal Geographical Society, which financed Burton and Speke among others, was made up mostly of the bureaucratic bourgeoisie, not the commercial middle class (Bridges, "Europeans and East Africans," 220–32).

25. The *Academy* even published a piece on the sultan's piano-playing abilities: "Sultan of Zanzibar a Good Pianist," *Academy* 8 (July–December 1875): 181.

26. Messrs. Ballard and Halley, "New York Fashions," *Harper's Bazaar*, 11 September 1875.

27. Richard Burton, "Zanzibar, and Two Months in East Africa," *Blackwood's Edinburgh Magazine* (February, March, and May 1858): 200–224, 276–90, 572–89. The only extensive travelogue of East Africa published in the West before Burton's *Lake Regions*, was Guillain's detailed, three-volume *Documents*. It came complete with a supplementary volume made up of maps and images reproduced from photographs (see chap. 4). In the 1860s, Carl Claus von der Decken's *Reisen in Ost Afrika* offered an extensive treatise on the East African coastal region, including a great number of images, many adapted from Guillain's photographs.

28. The writings of explorers or explorer-missionaries like Livingstone would

also spur a new patriotic spirit in Britain in the second half of the nineteenth century. See John MacKenzie, *Propaganda and Empire: The Manipulation of British
Public Opinion, 1880–1960* (London: Manchester University Press, 1984). Their
narratives continue to influence perceptions of and engagements with Africans.
For instance, Kelly James, author of *Dancing with the Witchdoctor: One
Woman's Stories of Mystery and Adventure in Africa* (New York: William Mor-
row, 2001), credits Burton with stirring in her a burning desire to see Africa.

29. Richard Thornton, for example, read Burton's work during his stay in
Mombasa; see the entry for 22 June 1861, Richard Thornton Journals, MSS. Afr.
s. 49, Rhodes House Library, Oxford.

30. In the blending of diverse narrative traditions with the verve of the "discovery" of the Nile's source, Hammond and Jablow suggest that East African
exploration narratives represent the apogee of nineteenth-century travel literature. On the standardization of regional genres, see Hammond and Jablow,
Africa That Never Was, 51.

31. McGrane, *Beyond Anthropology,* 115.

32. The relation of geography and political economy to definitions of civilization is still strikingly present. Though analyses like F. Fernández-Armesto's
Civilizations: Culture, Ambition, and the Transformation of Nature (New York:
Simon and Schuster, 2001) attempt to pluralize the idea of civilization, they are
often bound to a nineteenth-century concept of civilization that defines it as an
essential bundle of characteristics held by a particular population and, presumably, absent in other peoples. In Fernández-Armesto's narrative, geography and
economy determine civilization in ways similar to Victorian analysts' parameters
for definitions of civilized populations. Fernández-Armesto offers both a "Check-
list of Civilization" and a section explicating "The Civilizing Ingredient."

33. For instance, John Stuart Mill's seminal reflection on civilization in 1836
(reprinted in 1859) was explicit in its methodology for defining the idea of civilization: civilization, he argued, was the "direct converse or contrary" of barbarism. At its core, Mill believed civilization to entail improvement and advancement; see *Dissertations and Discussions: Political, Philosophical, and Historical.*
vol. 1 (1859; repr. New York: Haskell House, 1973), 160–205. Mill concludes
that civilization is what is necessarily accepted when a people throws off the
bonds of savagery. Mill was one of contemporary Britain's most liberal thinkers,
arguing against the grain that diversity in character had nothing to do with inherent natural, differences. See also Mill, *Principles of Political Economy* (London:
Longmans, 1871); Robert Young, *Colonial Desire: Hybridity in Theory, Culture
and Race* (New York: Routledge, 1995), 83

34. In this regard, see P. Landau and D. Kaspin, *Images and Empires: Visuality and Colonial and Postcolonial Africa* (Berkeley and Los Angeles: University of
California Press, 2002); J. Ryan, *Picturing Empire: Photography and the Visualization of the British Empire* (London: Reacktion, 1997).

35. On the concept of the "world-as-picture," see Timothy Mitchell, *Questions of Modernity* (Minneapolis: University of Minnesota Press, 2000); and
Colonising Egypt (Berkeley and Los Angeles: University of California Press,
1991).

36. A poignant example of this is "The Slave Trade and Those Interested,"

published in the *Phrenological Journal and Science of Health,* January 1874, 38–39, which juxtaposed the politics of British interests in East Africa with sketches of physical types, drawn by H. Bartle Frere's son. See also MacKenzie, *Propaganda and Empire;* V. G. Kiernan, *The Lords of Human Kind: European Attitudes towards the Outside World in the Imperial Age* (London: Serif, 1995); R. Hallet, "Changing European Attitudes to Africa," in *Cambridge History of Africa,* vol. 5, ed. J. Flint (Cambridge: Cambridge University Press, 1976), 458–96.

37. The article added that "[a]mong the Arabian tribes there are several which cannot be distinguished from the fairest Indo-Germanic, with the exception, of course, of the clothing and customs"; *Harper's Weekly,* 16 December 1871, 1175.

38. See, in particular, Robert Hartmann, *Die Völker Afrikas* (Leipzig: F. A. Brockhaus, 1879); and *Abyssinien und die übrigen Gebiete de Ostküste Afrikas* (Leipzig: G. Freytag, 1883).

39. Rider Haggard, *King Solomon's Mines* [1885], quoted in McClintock, *Imperial Leather,* 241.

40. Frederic Farrar, "Aptitudes of Races," *Transactions of the Ethnological Society of London* 5 (1867): 116.

41. I use the term *race* here in its broader, nineteenth-century sense, encompassing nation and place of birth: *vide* the Irish race, English race, African race. For the larger context of purity and race in Victorian discourse, see J. DeVere Brody, *Impossible Purities: Blackness, Femininity, and Victorian Culture* (Durham, NC: Duke University Press, 1998).

42. Robert Young suggests that the word *hybrid* first came into the discourse of classificatory human types sometime between 1843 and 1861; see Young, *Colonial Desire,* 6.

43. John Jackson, "Race in Legislation and Political Economy," *Anthropological Review* 4 (1866): 125. For Jackson, half-castes, whom he believed became fully degenerate after four generations, were the clear proof of the existence of discrete races. Other theorists, like J. Prichard, entirely rejected the application of hybridity to humanity, suggesting instead that race was the mislabeling of variety within a unitary human species. See Young, *Colonial Desire,* 10.

44. Lauren Benton and John Muth typify representations of hybridity as "a collection of conflicting traits and impulses" in "On Cultural Hybridity: Interpreting Colonial Authority and Performance," *Journal of Colonialism and Colonial History* 1, no. 1 (2000): 17.

45. Steere claimed that mixed-race Zanzibaris had "limited progeny." This notion of mixed-race peoples being sterile was common in Anglophone theorizations of hybridity in the nineteenth century. See, for example, Paul Broca's influential, *On the Phenomena of Hybridity in the Genus Homo* (London: Longman, Green, Longman and Roberts, 1864).

46. G. F. Scott Eliot, *A Naturalist in Mid-Africa* (London: A. D. Innes, 1896), 353–54.

47. "East African Slave Trade," *Quarterly Review* 133 (July and October 1872): 541–42. E. C. Hore, in an article published in the *Journal of the Royal*

Anthropological Institute less than a year before the first German attempts at colonizing East Africa, wrote of "real samples" of the "native African" in the deep interior. These were isolated tribes who, because of their insulation from the semi-civilized coast, maintained a "certain amount of social order and tranquility." These pure Africans, Hore believed, should be the focus of British efforts. "There is an opportunity," he concluded, "in these comparably undisturbed tribes . . . to test the effects upon the African race of Christian civilization—before the disturbing influences of fortune-hunters overwhelm such germs of civilization as they possess." In their purity, isolated tribes were imagined to contain the seeds of civilization which, without proper cultivation, would soon be spoiled by the mongrel nature of the coastal traders. See E. C. Hore, "On the Twelve Tribes of Tanganyika," *Journal of the Royal Anthropological Institute of Great Britain and Ireland* 12 (1883): 3, 4, 20.

48. Hammond and Jablow, *Africa That Never Was*, 64.

49. Speer, "Report on Zanzibar, 1862," roll 2, vols. 4–5, USCZ.

50. W. Cope Devereux, *A Cruise in the "Gorgon"* (London: Bell and Daldy, 1869), 103.

51. Rebecca Wakefield, *Memoirs of Mrs. Rebecca Wakefield*, ed. R. Brewin (London: Hamilton, Adams, 1879), 102–3.

52. J. Ross Browne, *Etchings of a Whaling Cruise* (Cambridge, MA: Belknap Press of Harvard University Press, 1968), 421–22.

53. Kutch had for centuries been an important player in the trans–Indian Ocean trade. It absorbed populations, goods, and ideas from across the entire Indian Ocean and, as a result, the notion that Kutchis were "pure" in the sense of biological boundedness is particularly problematic. Pickering's description exemplifies not just the fiction of purity, but its malleability as a hierarchical category; see Pickering, *Races of Man*, 271; Ruschenberger, *Voyage Round the World*, 35.

54. Devereux, *Cruise in the "Gorgon,"* 63–64.

55. Charles New, *Life, Wanderings, and Labours in Eastern Africa* (1873; repr. London: Frank Cass, 1971), 56.

56. New's account provides strong support for Robert Young's claim that by the end of the 1860s race was not only a determining factor in human difference, but it no longer required empirical evidence (Young, *Colonial Desire*, 140). Philip Curtin has likewise suggested that new racial doctrines of the mid–nineteenth century were positively received by the educated public since they accorded well with national xenophobias. See Curtin, *Image of Africa*; D. Lorimer, *Colour, Class, and the Victorians: English Attitudes to the Negro in the Mid-Nineteenth Century* (Leicester, UK: Leicester University Press, 1978).

57. A. Fox, "Report on Anthropology, at the Meeting of the British Association for the Advancement of Science for 1872 at Brighton," *Journal of the Anthropological Institute of Great Britain and Ireland* 2 (1873): 360–61.

58. New, *Life, Wanderings, and Labours*, 34.

59. G. Ward, ed., *Letters of Bishop Tozer and his Sister* (London: Office of the Universities' Mission to Central Africa, 1902), 225.

60. Burton, *Zanzibar* 1:81.

61. Hammond and Jablow, *Africa That Never Was*, 99. The case of the West African "half-caste" was, according to Hammond and Jablow, roughly the same

in British conception before colonization: "The half-caste was as difficult and uncomfortable a by-product of empire as the Westernized African, and the novelists were as censorious of him. There is neither humor nor sympathy in the portrayals, rather a shuddering withdrawal as from something repulsive and disquieting. The 'taint of the tar-brush' was a stigma, eliciting the same reaction of hostility as the Westernized African, and for the same reasons. In regard to the half-caste there was an additional factor involving the racist imperative to maintain the purity of blood lines" (110).

62. Joseph Osgood, *Notes of Travel* (Salem, MA: George Creamer, 1854), 41.

63. Clelia Weeks, "Zanzibar," *Harper's New Monthly Magazine* 38 (December–May, 1868–69): 317.

64. Vernon Cameron, *Across Africa* (New York: Harper & Brothers, 1877), 151.

65. Ropes, *Zanzibar Letters*, 14.

66. Ibid., 36–37.

67. Willoughby, *East Africa and Its Big Game*, 18.

68. "On the Track of the Germans in East Africa," *Pall Mall Gazette* 6182, vol. 41, 3 June 1885.

69. We are also reminded here of Hammond and Jablow's observation that British imperialists "had vested political, economic, and psychological interests in maintaining . . . contrasts" (*Africa That Never Was*, 99); see also Pickering, *Races of Man*, 197; Hore, "Twelve Tribes of Tanganyika," 4.

70. On the process of what Patrick Brantlinger calls "imperialization," or the formation of a popular imperialist consciousness, see "Victorians and Africans: The Genealogy of the Myth of the Dark Continent," *Critical Inquiry* 12, no. 1 (1985): 167.

71. Ludwig Ritter von Höhnel, *Discovery of Lakes Rudolf and Stefanie*, vol. 1 (London: Longmans, Green, 1894), 1:180–81.

72. May French-Sheldon, *Sultan to Sultan: Adventures among the Masai and Other Tribes of East Africa* (London: Saxon, 1892), 356–58.

73. Ibid., 358.

74. Ibid., 359–60.

75. Stanley, *How I Found Livingstone: Travels, Adventures, and Discoveries in Central Africa* (New York: Charles Scribner's Sons, 1887), 19–20.

76. Ward to Department of State, 13 July 1850, roll 1, vols. 1–3; Ward to Seyyid Said, 5 July 1850, roll 1, vols. 1–3; Jelly, Masury, and McMullan to Ward, 8 July 1850, roll 1, vols. 1–3, all in USCZ.

77. Abbott to Webster, 12 March 1851, roll 1, vol. 1–3, USCZ.

78. Ward to Webster, 14 June 1852, roll 1, vols. 1–3, USCZ; Mansfield to Cass, 18 April 1859, roll 2, vols. 4–5, USCZ; Ropes to Cass, 20 October 1859, roll 2, vols. 4–5, USCZ; same to same, 25 December 1859, roll 2, vols. 4–5, USCZ.

79. Playfair continued, "I would show him railways, roads and irrigational [sic] works; I would point out the difference between the cleanliness of Indian towns and the hideous filth of Zanzibar; I would show him what the introduction of European capital and skill has done in India—and having done this, surely there is reason to hope for some good result"; Playfair to Gonne, 19 April 1865, L/P&S/9/42, IOL.

80. Ward, *Letters of Bishop Tozer*, 194.

81. Captain Prideaux to the Earl of Derby, 2 January 1875, L/P&S/9/51, IOL.

82. Patrick Brantlinger, *Rule of Darkness: British Literature and Imperialism, 1830–1914* (Ithaca, NY: Cornell University Press, 1988), x. Edward Said first argued that while economic and political factors were essential to colonization, the creation of a canon of particular knowledge about the Orient culturally enabled Western expansion; see his *Orientalism* (New York: Vintage Books, 1979).

83. Joseph Thomson, "East Africa as It Was and Is," *Contemporary Review* 55 (January 1889): 46. See also Mill, *Dissertations and Discussions*, 170.

84. Holmwood, "Administration Report of the Political Agent and Consul-General at Zanzibar for the Years 1873 and 1874," L/P&S/9/51, IOL.

85. Thomson, "East Africa," 46. On hearing of Barghash's death in April of 1888, Ropes wrote to his father—the former American consul—using the harshest of terms: "like the case of our American Indians . . . it is best that he & they be exterminated" (Ropes, *Zanzibar Letters*, 94).

86. "The Sultan of Zanzibar," *New York Times* (reprinted from the *Standard*), 17 July 1875, 2.

CONCLUSION

1. Histories of interconnectivity in the Indian Ocean cast a particularly long shadow over the courses of colonialism in the region. For examples of this in the spheres of economy and social relations, see Gilbert's study of the longevity of the regional dhow trade and Mazrui and Shariff's survey of contests over Swahili as an identity marker: Erik Gilbert, *Dhows and Colonial Economy in Zanzibar: 1860–1970* (Columbus: Ohio University Press, 2005); Alamin Mazrui and Ibrahim Noor Shariff, *The Swahili: Idiom and Identity of an African People* (Trenton, NJ: Africa World Press, 1994).

2. Ludwig Ritter von Höhnel, *Discovery of Lakes Rudolf and Stefanie*, vol. 1 (London: Longmans, Green, 1894), 182–83.

3. On the colonial propensity to claim a universal modernity while denying it to Africans, see, for instance, Simon Gikandi, "Reason, Modernity, and the African Crisis," and Jan-Georg Deutsch, Peter Probst, and Heike Schmidt, "Cherished Visions and Entangled Meanings," in *African Modernities: Entangled Meanings in Current Debate,* ed. Jan-Georg Deutsch, Peter Probst, and Heike Schmidt (Portsmouth, NH: Heinemann, 2002), 135–57 and 1–17 respectively.

4. Arjun Appadurai, *Modernity at Large: Cultural Dimensions of Globalization* (Minneapolis: University of Minnesota Press, 1998).

5. Stephen Kern, *The Culture of Time and Space, 1880–1918* (Cambridge, MA: Harvard University Press, 2003). In J. Lorand Matory's words, "Gross quantitative increase does not a qualitative difference make"; see *Black Atlantic Religion: Tradition, Transnationalism, and Matriarchy in the Afro-Brazilian Candomblé* (Princeton, NJ: Princeton University Press, 2005), 270. For an inter-

esting example of analogous Roman experiences of heightened global consciousness see Roland Robertson and David Inglis, "The Global *Animus*: In the Tracks
of World Consciousness," in Barry K. Gills and William R. Thompson, eds.,
Globalization and Global History (New York: Routledge, 2006), 33–47.

6. See M. Yahuda, "China's Win-Win Globalization," *YaleGlobal Online*, 19
February 2003, www.yaleglobal.yale.edu; Jo-Anne Pemberton, *Global Metaphors: Modernity and the Quest for One World* (London: Pluto Press, 2001);
K. O'Rourke and J. Williamson, "When Did Globalization Begin?" National
Bureau of Economic Research Working Paper 7632 (2000), and *Globalization
and History: The Evolution of a Nineteenth-Century Atlantic Economy* (Cambridge, MA: Harvard University Press, 1999). For a comparison of the movement
of capital in the late nineteenth and twentieth centuries, see M. Clemens and
J. Williamson, "Where Did British Capital Go? Fundamentals, Failures, and the
Lucas Paradox: 1870–1913," National Bureau of Economic Research Working
Paper 8028 (2000), http://papers.nber.org/papers/w8028. For concerted efforts to
bring historiographies of global relationships to bear on contemporary debates,
see especially Michael Geyer and Charles Bright, "World History in a Global
Age," *American Historical Review* 100, no. 4 (1995): 1034–60; A. G. Hopkins,
Globalization in World History (New York: W. W. Norton, 2002), and *Global
History: Interactions Between the Universal and the Local* (New York: Palgrave
Macmillan, 2006), as well as Michael D. Bordo, Alan Taylor, and Jeffrey G.
Williamason, eds., *Globalization in Historical Perspective* (Chicago: University
of Chicago Press, 2003); Jürgen Osterhammel and Niels P. Petersson, *Globaliza-
tion: A Short History*, trans. Dona Geyer (Princeton, NJ: Princeton University
Press, 2005); Bruce Mazlish and Akira Iriye eds., *The Global History Reader*
(New York: Routledge, 2005); and Gills and Thompson, *Globalization and
Global History*.

7. Stuart Hall, "Introduction," in *Modernity: An Introduction to Modern
Societies*, ed. Stuart Hall et al. (Oxford: Blackwell, 1996), 17. Frederick Cooper
reminds us that the "annihilation of space by time" is a nineteenth-century idea
born of the expansion of capitalism; see "What Is the Concept of Globalization
Good For? An African Historian's Perspective," *African Affairs* 100 (2001):
189–213. If anything, the profound change in the recent past has been the global
internalization and manipulation of certain precepts of modernity—for example,
that "modern things" and "a modern time" exist. As Arjun Appadurai suggests
in *Modernity at Large,* though the meanings and manifestations of the modern
may be diverse, the notion of the modern has become nearly universal. See also
James Ferguson, *Expectations of Modernity: Myths and Meanings of Urban Life
on the Zambian Copperbelt* (Berkeley and Los Angeles: University of California
Press, 1999); Bruce M. Knauft, "Critically Modern: An Introduction," in Bruce
M. Knauft, ed., *Critically Modern: Alternatives, Alterities, Anthropologies*
(Bloomington, IN: Indiana University Press, 2002), 1–56.

8. The traders who delivered such goods affected these meanings, as did consumers' ideas about foreign or regional locales. See the example of "Zanzibari"
guns as the designation of lower-quality muskets in contrast to guns associated
with specific European nations in Jonathon Glassman, *Feasts and Riot* (Portsmouth, NH: Heinemann, 1995), 50–1.

9. According to a recent Oxfam report, a one percent increase in Africa's share of world exports would equal approximately five times the amount of aid and debt relief annually provided to the continent. Kevin Watkins and Penny Fowler, "Rigged Rules and Double Standards: Trade, Globalisation, and the Fight against Poverty," http://www.maketradefair.com/assets/english/report_english.pdf, 8. The difficulties that African producers face thus do not stem from dependency in its strictest sense but from a deep inequality of market access. John Lonsdale, "Globalization, Ethnicity and Democracy: A View from 'the Hopeless Continent,'" in Hopkins, *Globalization in World History*, 194–219.

10. In response to these imbalances of trade, Samir Amin argues for greater freedom on the part of each society or nation to negotiate its own relationships—or "terms of interdependence"—with world markets. Only then, he suggests, will "peripheral" economies have a greater opportunity for "growth"; see *Capitalism in an Age of Globalization* (New York: New Press, 2001). For a cogent Foucauldian analysis of postwar development discourse, see Arturo Escobar, *Encountering Development: The Making and Unmaking of the Third World* (Princeton, NJ: Princeton University Press, 1995). See also J. Nederveen Pieterse, "Dilemmas of Development Discourse: The Crisis of Developmentalism and the Comparative Method," *Development and Change* 22, no. 1 (1991): 5–29.

11. Joseph Stiglitz, *Globalization and Its Discontents* (New York: W. W. Norton, 2002). Where Africans have loosened constraints on trade—in the informal sector, for instance—they have succeeded in exploiting certain comparative advantages. The enormous success of Meruans (Kenya) in the interstate *qat* (Swahili: *miraa, marungi*) trade is a telling example of African initiatives in creating and maintaining global production and supply chains reaching from Kenya to Somalia, the Middle East, Europe, and North America. See Jean-François Bayart, "Africa in the World: A History of Extraversion," *African Affairs* 99, no. 395 (2000): 240.

12. William C. Bissell, "Engaging Colonial Nostalgia," *Cultural Anthropology* 20, no. 2 (2005): 215–48, and "City of Stone, Space of Contestation: Urban Conservation and the Colonial Past in Zanzibar," 2 vols. (PhD diss., University of Chicago, 1999).

13. Rance, "Letter from Lamu," *Coast Express* (Kenya), 6 December 2002.

Selected Bibliography

Many contributions to larger works (chapters) are cited in the notes only, but entries are included here for most of those larger works. Some journal articles that are infrequently cited are not included here but cited only in the notes.

MANUSCRIPT SOURCES

France

CENTRE DES ARCHIVES D'OUTRE-MER, AIX-EN-PROVENCE
Océan Indien 5/23, nos. 2 and 7; Océan Indien 15/64

Tanzania

ZANZIBAR NATIONAL ARCHIVES, ZANZIBAR
A3/11, A12/3, AA1/3, AA1/5, AA1/10, AA2/4, AA3/11, AA3/18, AA3/21, AA3/25, AA7/1, AA10/1, AA12/1A, AA12/8, AA12/13, CB1/1B

United Kingdom

BRITISH LIBRARY, INDIA OFFICE LIBRARY, LONDON
F/4/1475, L/P&S/9/12, L/P&S/9/37, L/P&S/9/41, L/P&S/9/42, L/P&S/9/43, L/P&S/9/48, L/P&S/9/49, L/P&S/9/51, V/11/2200, V/17/290 to V/17/320

PUBLIC RECORDS OFFICE, LONDON
ADM 52/3940, ADM 1/5945, FO 19/8, FO 54/5, FO 54/22, FO 84/1391

RHODES HOUSE, OXFORD UNIVERSITY
Thornton Papers, MSS. Afr. s. 27

SCHOOL OF ORIENTAL AND AFRICAN STUDIES LIBRARY,
UNIVERSITY OF LONDON
MacKinnon Papers, PPMS 1

United States

BELL LIBRARY, UNIVERSITY OF MINNESOTA, MINNEAPOLIS
Plumer, K. "Journal of a Voyage from London to Madras" [ca. 1769]
NATIONAL ARCHIVES, WASHINGTON, DC
United States Consulate Records, Zanzibar, (microfilm) Rolls 1 to 4, Vols. 1–8
PEABODY-ESSEX MUSEUM, SALEM, MA
MSS 24, Emmerton Family Papers; MSS 47, Charles Ward Papers; MH 14, Richard P. Waters Papers; MH 23, Michael Shepard Papers; MH 235 J. A. West Papers

PUBLISHED MATERIAL AND THESES

Abdulaziz, Muhammad., ed. and trans. *Muyaka: Nineteenth Century Swahili Popular Poetry.* Nairobi: Kenya Literature Bureau, 1994.
Abu-Lughod, Janet. "The World-System Perspective in the Construction of Economic History." *History and Theory* 34, no. 2 (1995): 86–98.
Abungu, George. "Islam on the Kenyan Coast: An Archaeological Study of Mosques." Master's thesis, University of Cambridge, 1986.
Adas, Michael. *Machines as the Measure of Man: Science, Technology, and Ideologies of Western Dominance.* Ithaca, NY: Cornell University Press, 1989.
Akyeampong, Emmanuel. *Drink, Power, and Cultural Change: A Social History of Alcohol in Ghana, c.1800 to Recent Times.* Portsmouth, NH: Heinemann, 1996.
Aldrick, Judy. "The Painted Plates of Zanzibar." *Kenya Past and Present* 12 (1997): 26–28.
Alfino, M., J. Caputo, and R. Wynyard, eds. *McDonaldization Revisited: Critical Essays on Consumer Culture.* Westport, CT: Praeger, 1998.
Allman, Jean, ed. *Fashioning Africa: Power and the Politics of Dress.* Bloomington: Indiana University Press, 2004.
Alpern, S. "What Africans Got for Their Slaves." *History in Africa* 22 (1995): 5–43.
Alpers, Edward A. "Representations of Children in the East African Slave Trade." Paper presented at the Avignon Conference on Slavery and Forced Labour, "Children in Slavery," Avignon, France, May 2004.
———. "A Complex Relationship: Mozambique and the Comoro Islands in the Nineteenth and Twentieth Centuries." *Cahiers d'Études Africaines* 161 (2001): 73–95.
———. "Indian Ocean Africa: The Island Factor." *Emergences: Journal for the Study of Media and Composite Cultures* 10, no. 2 (2000): 373–86.
———. " 'Ordinary Household Chores': Ritual and Power in a Nineteenth-

Century Swahili Women's Spirit Possession Cult." *International Journal of African Historical Studies* 17, no. 4 (1984): 677–702.

———. "The Story of Swema: Female Vulnerability in Nineteenth-Century East Africa," in *Women and Slavery in Africa*, ed. Claire Robertson and Martin Klein. Madison: University of Wisconsin Press, 1983, 185–219.

———. "*Futa Benaadir:* Continuity and Change in the Traditional Cotton Textile Industry of Southern Somalia, c. 1840–1980," in *Actes du Colloque Entreprises et Entrepreneurs en Afrique (XIXe et XXe siècles)*, ed. Catherine Coquery-Vidrovitch and Alain Forest. Tome 1. Paris: L'Harmattan, 1983, 77–98.

———. "Gujarat and the Trade of East Africa, 1500–1800." *International Journal of African Historical Studies* 9, no. 1 (1976): 22–44.

———. *Ivory and Slaves: Changing Patterns of International Trade in East Central Africa to the Later Nineteenth Century.* Berkeley and Los Angeles: University of California Press, 1975.

Amin, Samir. *Capitalism in an Age of Globalization.* New York: New Press, 2001.

Annual Report of the Engineer to the Naumkeag Steam Cotton Company, Salem (Mass.). Salem, MA: Tri-Weekly Gazette Press, 1848.

Appadurai, Arjun. *Modernity at Large: Cultural Dimensions of Globalization.* Minneapolis: University of Minnesota Press, 1998.

———. "Disjuncture and Difference in the Global Cultural Economy." *Public Culture* 2, no. 2 (1990): 1–24.

———, ed. *The Social Life of Things: Commodities in Cultural Perspective.* Cambridge: Cambridge University Press, 1986.

Arnoldi, Mary Jo, Christraud M. Gear, and Kris Hardin, eds. *African Material Culture.* Bloomington: Indiana University Press, 1996.

Atkins, Keletso. *The Moon Is Dead! Give Us Our Money! The Cultural Origins of an African Work Ethic, Natal, South Africa, 1843–1900.* Portsmouth, NH: Heinemann, 1993.

Audi, R. "The Concept of Wanting." *Philosophical Studies* 24, no. 1 (1973): 1–21.

Austen, Ralph. *African Economic History.* London: Heinemann, 1987.

———, and W. Smith. "Images of Africa and British Slave-Trade Abolition: The Transition to an Imperialist Ideology, 1787–1807." *African Historical Studies* 2, no. 1 (1969): 69–83.

Baker, Samuel. *The Albert N'yanza, Great Basin of the Nile, and Explorations of the Nile Sources.* London: Macmillan, 1866.

Bammer, A. *Displacements: Cultural Identities in Question.* Bloomington: Indiana University Press, 1994.

Bang, Anne. *Sufis and Scholars of the Sea: Family Networks in East Africa, 1860–1925.* London: RoutledgeCurzon, 2003.

Barber, Benjamin. *Jihad vs. McWorld: How Globalism and Tribalism Are Reshaping the World.* New York: Ballantine Books, 1995.

Barker, A., ed. *Consuming Russia: Popular Culture, Sex, and Society Since Gorbachev.* Durham, NC: Duke University Press, 1999.

Barnard, Lieut. Frederick Lamport. *A Three Years Cruise in the Mozambique Channel.* 1848; repr., London: Dawsons of Pall Mall, 1969.

Barnes, Ruth, ed. *Textiles in Indian Ocean Societies.* London: RoutledgeCurzon, 2005.

Barth, Fredrik. *Models of Social Organization.* Royal Anthropological Institute Occasional Paper No. 23. London: Royal Anthropological Institute, 1966.

Barthes, Roland. *The Fashion System.* New York: Hill and Wang, 1983.

———. *Empire of Signs.* New York: Hill and Wang, 1982.

Baudrillard, Jean. *The Consumer Society.* London: Sage, 1998.

———. *The System of Objects.* New York: Verso, 1996.

———. *Jean Baudrillard: Selected Writings.* Ed. Mark Poster. Stanford, CA: Stanford University Press, 1988.

———. *For a Critique of the Political Economy of the Sign.* St. Louis: Telos Press, 1981.

———. *The Mirror of Production.* St. Louis: Telos Press, 1975.

Bayly, C. A. *The Birth of the Modern World, 1780–1914.* Malden, MA: Blackwell, 2004.

Beckert, Sven. "Emancipation and Empire: Reconstructing the Worldwide Web of Cotton Production in the Age of the American Civil War." *American Historical Review* 109, no. 5 (2004): 1405–38.

Beehler, W. *The Cruise of the Brooklyn.* Philadelphia: J. B. Lippincott, 1885.

Bennett, Norman, ed. *From Zanzibar to Ujiji. The Journal of Arthur W. Dodgshun, 1877–1879.* Boston: Boston University Press, 1969.

———, and George Brooks, eds. *New England Merchants in Africa: A History Through Documents, 1802 to 1865.* Boston: Boston University Press, 1965.

Bentley, Jerry. *Old World Encounters: Cross-cultural Contacts in Pre-modern Times.* New York: Oxford University Press, 1993.

Benton, Lauren. *Law and Colonial Cultures: Legal Regimes in World History, 1400–1900.* New York: Cambridge University Press, 2002.

———. "From the World-Systems Perspective to Institutional World History: Culture and Economy in Global Theory." *Journal of World History* 7, no. 2 (1996): 261–95.

Berg, Frederick. "Mombasa Under the Busaidi Sultanate." PhD diss., University of Wisconsin, 1971.

———. "The Swahili Community of Mombasa, 1500–1900." *Journal of African History* 9, no. 1 (1968): 35–56.

Bermingham, A., and J. Brewer, eds. *The Consumption of Culture, 1600–1800.* New York: Routledge, 1995.

Bernard, William D. *Narrative of the Voyages and Services of the Nemesis, from 1840 to 1843.* London: Henry Colburn, 1844.

Berry, Sara. *No Condition Is Permanent: The Social Dynamics of Agrarian Change in Sub-Saharan Africa.* Madison: University of Wisconsin Press, 1993.

Bhabha, Homi. "Fireflies Caught in Molasses: Questions of Cultural Translation." In *October: The Second Decade, 1986–1996.* Cambridge, MA: MIT Press, 1997.

———. *The Location of Culture.* New York: Routledge, 1994.

Biddiss, M., ed. *Images of Race.* Surrey: Leicester University Press, 1979.

Biersteker, Ann. *Kujibizana: Questions of Language and Power in Nineteenth and Twentieth Century Poetry in Kiswahili.* East Lansing: Michigan State University Press, 1996.

———, and Ibrahim Noor Shariff, eds. *Mashairi ya Vita vya Kuduhu: War Poetry in Kiswahili Exchanged at the Time of the Battle of Kuduhu.* East Lansing: Michigan State University Press, 1995.

Bissell, William C. "Engaging Colonial Nostalgia." *Cultural Anthropology* 20, no. 2 (2005): 215–48.

———. "City of Stone, Space of Contestation: Urban Conservation and the Colonial Past in Zanzibar." 2 vols. PhD diss., University of Chicago, 1999.

Blanning, T. C. W., ed. *The Nineteenth Century.* Oxford: Oxford University Press, 2000.

Blaut, James. *The Colonizer's Model of the World: Geographical Diffusionism and Eurocentric History.* New York: Guilford Press, 1993.

Bordo, Michael D., Alan Taylor, and Jeffrey G. Williamason, eds. *Globalization in Historical Perspective.* Chicago: University of Chicago Press, 2003.

Boteler, Thomas. *Narrative of a Voyage of Discovery to Africa and Arabia.* 2 vols. London: R. Bentley, 1835.

Bourde, A. "Un Comorien adventureux au XIXe siecle: L'extraordinaire voyage du Prince Abudin." In *Méditerranée et Océan Indien. Travaux de Sixième Colloque International d'Histoire Maritime.* Venice: S. E. V. P. E. N., 1970.

Bourdieu, Pierre. *Distinction: A Social Critique of the Judgment of Taste.* Cambridge, MA: Harvard University Press, 1984.

Brady, Cyrus. *Commerce and Conquest in East Africa.* Salem: Essex Institute, 1950.

Brah, Avtar, and Annie E. Coombes, eds. *Hybridity and Its Discontents: Politics, Science, Culture.* New York: Routledge, 2000.

Brantlinger, Patrick. *Rule of Darkness: British Literature and Imperialism, 1830–1914.* Ithaca, NY: Cornell University Press, 1988.

———. "Victorians and Africans: The Genealogy of the Myth of the Dark Continent." *Critical Inquiry* 12, no. 1 (1985): 166–203.

Braudel, Fernand. *Civilization and Capitalism, Fifteenth–Eighteenth Century.* 3 vols. New York: Harper and Row, 1979–85.

Breckenridge, Carol A., ed. *Consuming Modernity: Public Culture in a South Asian World.* Minneapolis: University of Minnesota Press, 1995.

Breckenridge, Carol A., Sheldon Pollock, Homi Bhabha, and Dipesh Chakrabarty, eds. *Cosmopolitanism.* Durham, NC: Duke University Press, 2002.

Breen, Timothy H. *The Marketplace of Revolution: How Consumer Politics Shaped American Independence.* Oxford: Oxford University Press, 2004.

———. " 'Baubles of Britain': The American and Consumer Revolutions of the Eighteenth Century." In *Of Consuming Interests: The Style of Life in the Eighteenth Century,* ed. C. Carson. Charlottesville: University Press of Virginia, 1994.

———. "An Empire of Goods: The Anglicization of Colonial America, 1690–1776." *Journal of British Studies* 25, no. 4 (1986): 467–99.

Brewer, John, and Roy Porter, eds. *Consumption and the World of Goods.* London: Routledge, 1993.

Bridges, R. C. "Europeans and East Africans in the age of exploration." *Geographical Journal* 139, no. 2 (1973): 220–32.

Broca, Paul. *On the Phenomena of Hybridity in the Genus Homo.* London: Longman, Green, Longman, and Roberts, 1864.

Brody, J. DeVere. *Impossible Purities: Blackness, Femininity, and Victorian Culture.* Durham, NC: Duke University Press, 1998.

Bromer, Katrin, ed. and trans. *The Jurisdiction of the Sultan of Zanzibar and the Subjects of Foreign Nations.* Würzburg: Ergon Verlag, 2001.

Browne, J. Ross. *Etchings of a Whaling Cruise.* Cambridge, MA: Belknap Press of Harvard University Press, 1968.

Burke, Timothy. *Lifebuoy Men, Lux Women: Commodification, Consumption, and Cleanliness in Modern Zimbabwe.* Durham, NC: Duke University Press, 1996.

Burton, Richard. *Zanzibar: City, Island, and Coast.* 2 vols. London: Tinsley Brothers, 1872.

———. *The Lake Regions of Central Africa: A Picture Exploration.* 2 vols. London: Longman, 1860.

———. "The Lake Regions of Central Equatorial Africa." *Journal of the Royal Geographical Society* 29 (1859): 1–464.

———. "Zanzibar, and Two Months in East Africa." *Blackwood's Edinburgh Magazine* (February, March, and May 1858).

Cairns, H. Alan C. *Prelude to Imperialism: British Reactions to Central African Society, 1840–1890.* London: Routledge & Kegan Paul, 1965.

Cameron, Vernon. *Across Africa.* New York: Harper and Brothers, 1877.

Caplan, Pat, and Farouk Topan, eds. *Swahili Modernities: Culture, Politics, and Identity on the East Coast of Africa.* Trenton, NJ: Africa World Press, 2004.

Castell, Manuel. *The Rise of the Network Society.* Malden, MA: Blackwell, 1997.

Certeau, Michel de. *The Practice of Everyday Life.* Trans. Steven Randall. Berkeley and Los Angeles: University of California Press, 1984.

Chakrabarty, Dipesh. *Provincializing Europe: Postcolonial Thought and Historical Difference.* Princeton, NJ: Princeton University Press, 2000.

Chandavarkar, Rajnarayan. *The Origins of Industrial Capital in India: Business Strategies and the Working Classes in Bombay, 1900–1940.* New York: Cambridge University Press, 1994.

Charmetant, P. *D'Alger à Zanzibar.* Paris: Libr. Tardieu, 1882.

Chase-Dunn, Christopher, and Thomas Hall. *Rise and Demise: Comparing World-Systems.* Boulder, CO: Westview Press, 1997.

———. *Global Formation: Structures of the World-Economy.* Cambridge, MA: Blackwell, 1989.

Chaudhuri, K. N. *Trade and Civilisation in the Indian Ocean: An Economic History from the Rise of Islam to 1750.* New York: Cambridge University Press, 1985.

Cheah, Pheng, and Bruce Robbins. *Cosmopolitics: Thinking and Feeling Beyond the Nation.* Ed. Pheng Cheah and Bruce Robbins. Minneapolis: University of Minnesota Press, 1998.

Christie, James. *Cholera Epidemics in East Africa. An account of the several diffusions of the disease in that country from 1821 till 1872, with an outline of the geography, ethnology, and trade connections of the regions through which the epidemics passed.* London: Macmillan, 1876.

Clendennen, Gary W., and Peter M. Nottingham. *William Sunley and David Livingstone: A Tale of Two Consuls.* African Studies Program. Madison: University of Wisconsin, 2000.

Clifford, James. *Routes: Travel and Translation in the Late Twentieth Century.* Cambridge, MA: Harvard University Press, 1997.

———. "Traveling Cultures." In *Cultural Studies,* ed. Lawrence Grossberg, Carrie Nelson, and Paula Treichler, 96–116. New York: Routledge, 1992.

Clunas, Craig. "Modernity Global and Local: Consumption and the Rise of the West." *American Historical Review* 104, no. 5 (1999): 1497–1511.

Colomb, Captain Philip. *Slave-Catching in the Indian Ocean: A Record of Naval Experiences.* 1873; repr., London: Dawsons of Pall Mall, 1968.

Comaroff, Jean, and John Comaroff. "Revelations upon *Revelation*: After Shocks, Afterthoughts." *Interventions* 3, no. 1 (2001): 100–26.

———. *Of Revelation and Revolution.* 2 vols. Chicago: University of Chicago Press, 1991–97.

Cooley, William. *Inner Africa Laid Open, in an Attempt to Trace the Chief Lines of Communication Across that Continent South of the Equator.* London: Longman, Brown, Green, and Longmans, 1852.

Coombes, Annie E. *Reinventing Africa: Museums, Material Culture and Popular Imagination in Late Victorian and Edwardian England.* New Haven, CT: Yale University Press, 1994.

Cooper, Frederick. "What Is the Concept of Globalization Good For? An African Historian's Perspective," *African Affairs* 100 (2001): 189–213.

———. "Africa in a Capitalist World." In *Crossing Boundaries: Comparative History of Black People in Diaspora,* ed. Darlene Clark Hine and Jacqueline McLeod. Bloomington: Indiana University Press, 1999.

———. "Conflict and Connection: Rethinking Colonial African History." *American Historical Review* 99, no. 5 (1994): 1516–45.

———. "Africa and the World Economy." In *Confronting Historical Paradigms: Peasants, Labor, and the Capitalist World System in Africa and Latin America,* ed. Frederick Cooper, Allen Isaacman, and Florencia E. Mallon. Madison: University of Wisconsin Press, 1993.

———. *From Slaves to Squatters: Plantation Labour and Agriculture in Zanzibar and Coastal Kenya, 1890–1925.* New Haven, CT: Yale University Press, 1980.

———. "The Problem of Slavery in African Studies." *Journal of African History* 20, no. 1 (1979): 103–25.

———. *Plantation Slavery on the East Coast of Africa.* New Haven. CT: Yale University Press, 1977.

Cooper, Frederick, Thomas Holt, and Rebecca Scott, eds. *Beyond Slavery: Explorations of Race, Labor, and Citizenship in Postemancipation Societies.* Chapel Hill: University of North Carolina Press, 2000.

Cooper, Frederick, and Ann Laura Stoler. "Introduction." In *Tensions of Empire: Colonial Cultures in a Bourgeois World*, 1–56. Berkeley and Los Angeles: University of California Press, 1997.

Cornwall. *Observations on Several Voyages to India*. In *A New General Collection of Voyages and Travels*, vol. 3, ed. T. Astley. London: Printed for Thomas Astley, 1750.

Cotterill, H., ed. *Travels and Researches among the Lakes and Mountains of Eastern and Central Africa. From the Journals of the Late J. Frederic Elton.* London: John Murray, 1879.

Coupland, Reginald. *East Africa and Its Invaders*. Oxford: Oxford University Press, 1961.

———. *The Exploitation of East Africa, 1856–1890*. London: Faber and Faber, 1939.

Creed, B., and J. Hoorn, eds. *Body Trade: Captivity, Cannibalism and Colonialism in the Pacific*. New York: Routledge, 2001.

Crosby, Alfred, *The Columbian Exchange: Biological and Cultural Consequences of 1492*. Westport, CT: Greenwood Press, 1972.

Crummey, D., and C. Stewart, eds. *Modes of Production in Africa: The Precolonial Era*. Beverly Hills, CA: Sage, 1981.

Curtin, Philip. *Economic Change in Precolonial Africa: Senegambia in the Era of the Slave Trade*. Madison: University of Wisconsin Press, 1975.

———. *The Image of Africa: British Ideas and Actions, 1780–1850*. Madison: University of Wisconsin Press, 1973.

Curtin, Philip, Steven Feierman, Leonard Thompson, and Jan Vansina. *African History: From Earliest Times to Independence*. New York: Longmans, 1995.

Deutsch, Jan-Georg, Peter Probst, and Heike Schmidt, eds. *African Modernities: Entangled Meanings in Current Debate*. Portsmouth, NH: Heinemann, 2002.

Deutsch, Jan-Georg, and Brigitte Reinwald, eds. *Space on the Move: Transformations of the Indian Ocean Seascape in the Nineteenth and Twentieth Century*. Berlin: Klaus Schwarz Verlag, 2002.

Devereux, W. Cope. *A Cruise in the "Gorgon"; or Eighteen Months on H. M. S. "Gorgon," Engaged in the Suppression of the Slave Trade on the East Coast of Africa*. London: Bell and Daldy, 1869.

Dick, Rudolph. "Pequot Mills: The Naumkeag Steam Cotton Company of Salem, Mass." *Cotton History Review* 1, no. 4 (1960): 109–17.

———. *Nathaniel Griffin (1796–1876) of Salem—and His Naumkeag Steam Cotton Company*. New York: The Newcomen Society in North America, 1951.

Dirlik, Arif. *Postmodernity's Histories: The Past as Legacy and Project*. Lanham, MD: Rowman and Littlefield, 2000.

———. "Is There History After Eurocentrism? Globalism, Postcolonialism, and the Disavowal of History." *Cultural Critique* 42 (Spring 1999): 1–34.

Donley, Linda. "Life in the Swahili Town Reveals the Symbolic Meanings of Spaces and Artifact Assemblages." *African Archaeological Review* 5 (1986): 181–92.

———. "The Social Uses of Swahili Space and Objects." PhD diss., Cambridge University, 1984.

———. "House Power: Swahili Space and Symbolic Markers." In *Structural and Symbolic Archaeology*, ed. Ian Hodder, 63–73. Cambridge: Cambridge University Press, 1982.

Douglas, Mary, and Baron Isherwood. *The World of Goods: Towards an Anthropology of Consumption*. 1979; repr. London: Penguin, 1995.

Driver, Felix. "Henry Morton Stanley and His Critics: Geography, Exploration, and Empire." *Past and Present* 133 (November 1991): 134–66.

Dussel, Enrique. *The Underside of Modernity*. Ed. and trans. E. Mendieta. Atlantic Highlands, NJ: Humanities Press, 1997.

———. *The Invention of the Americas: Eclipse of "the Other" and the Myth of Modernity*. New York: Continuum, 1995.

"East African Slave Trade." *Quarterly Review* 133 (July and October 1872): 521–57.

Eilts, H. "Ahmad bin Na'aman's Mission to the United States in 1840: The Voyage of Al-Sultanah to New York City." *Essex Institute Historical Collections* 98 (April–July 1962): 219–279.

Eliot, G. F. Scott. *A Naturalist in Mid-Africa*. London: A. D. Innes, 1896.

Elliot, Rev. "A Visit to the Island of Johanna." *United Service Journal and Naval Military Magazine* pt. 1 (1830): 144–52.

Ennaji, Mohammed. *Serving the Master: Slavery and Society in Nineteenth Century Morocco*. New York: St. Martin's Press, 1998.

Erlmann, Veit. *Music, Modernity, and the Global Imagination: South Africa and the West*. New York: Oxford University Press, 1999.

Escobar, Arturo. *Encountering Development: The Making and Unmaking of the Third World*. Princeton, NJ: Princeton University Press, 1995.

Evans, D. *An Introductory Dictionary of Lacanian Psychoanalysis*. New York: Routledge, 1997.

Ewald, Janet. "Crossers of the Sea: Slaves, Freedmen, and other Migrants in the Northwestern Indian Ocean, c. 1750–1914." *American Historical Review* 105, no. 1 (2000): 69–91.

Fabian, Johannes. *Time and the Other: How Anthropology Makes Its Object*. New York: Columbia University Press, 2002.

———. "Remembering the Other: Knowledge and Recognition in the Exploration of Central Africa." *Critical Inquiry* 26 (1999): 49–69.

Fair, Laura. *Pastimes and Politics: Culture, Community, and Identity in Post-Abolition Urban Zanzibar, 1890–1945*. Athens: Ohio University Press, 2001.

Faurschou, G. "Obsolescence and Desire: Fashion and the Commodity Form." In *Postmodernism—Philosophy and the Arts*. Ed. H. Silverman, 234–59. New York: Routledge, 1990.

Featherstone, Mike, ed. *Cultural Theory and Cultural Change*. London: Sage, 1992.

———, ed. *Global Culture: Nationalism, Globalization and Modernity*. London: Sage, 1990.

Featherstone, Mike, Scott Lash, and Ronald Robertson, eds. *Global Modernities*. London: Sage, 1995.

Feierman, Steven. "African Histories and the Dissolution of World History." In *Africa and the Disciplines: Contributions of Research in Africa to the Social*

Sciences and the Humanities, ed. Robert H. Bates, V. Y. Mudimbe, and Jean O'Barr. Chicago: University of Chicago Press, 1993, 167–212.

Ferguson, James. *Expectations of Modernity: Myths and Meanings of Urban Life on the Zambian Copperbelt*. Berkeley and Los Angeles: University of California Press, 1999.

Fernández-Armesto, F. *Civilizations: Culture, Ambition, and the Transformation of Nature*. New York: Simon and Schuster, 2001.

Fine, B., and E. Leopold. *The World of Consumption*. London: Routledge, 1993.

Forty, A. *Objects of Desire: Design and Society since 1750*. London: Thames and Hudson, 1986.

Foster, Helen Bradley. *New Raiments of Self: African-American Clothing in the Antebellum South*. Routledge: New York, 1997.

Foucault, Michel. *The Order of Things: An Archaeology of the Human Sciences*. New York: Vantage, 1994.

———. *Power/Knowledge: Selected Interviews and Other Writings, 1972–1977*. Ed. C. Gordon. New York: Pantheon, 1980.

Frappaz, Théophile. *Les Voyages du Lieutenant de vaisseau Frappaz dans les mers des Indies*. Ed. R. Decary. Tananarive: Pitot de la Beaujardiére, 1939.

French-Sheldon, May. *Sultan to Sultan: Adventures among the Masai and Other Tribes of East Africa*. London: Saxon, 1892.

Friedman, Jonathan. *Cultural Identity and Global Process*. London: Sage, 1994.

———. "Being in the World: Globalization and Localization." *Theory, Culture, and Society* 7, no. 2 (1990): 311–28.

Friedman, Susan. "Definitional Excursions: The Meanings of Modern/Modernity/Modernism." *Modernism/Modernity* 8, no. 3 (2001): 493–513.

Friedman, Thomas. *The Lexus and the Olive Tree: Understanding Globalization*. New York: Anchor Books, 2000.

Fuchs, Eckhardt, and Benedikt Stuchtey, eds. *Across Cultural Boundaries: Historiography in Global Perspective*. Lanham, MD: Rowman and Littlefield, 2002.

Fuery, P. *Theories of Desire*. Carlton: Melbourne University Press, 1995.

Gaonkar, Dilip P. "On Alternative Modernities." *Public Culture* 11, no. 1 (1999): 1–18.

Gemunden, G. *Framed Visions: Popular Culture, Americanization, and the Contemporary German and Austrian Imagination*. Ann Arbor: University of Michigan Press, 1998.

Geschiere, Peter. "Historical Anthropology: Questions of Time, Method and Scale." *Interventions* 3, no. 1 (2001): 31–39.

Geyer, Michael, and Charles Bright. "World History in a Global Age." *American Historical Review* 100 no. 4 (1995): 1034–60.

Giddens, Anthony. *Modernity and Self-identity: Self and Society in the Late Modern Age*. Stanford, CA: Stanford University Press, 1991.

Gilbert, Erik. *Dhows and Colonial Economy in Zanzibar: 1860–1970*. Columbus: Ohio University Press, 2005.

Gills, Barry K., and William R. Thompson. *Globalization and Global History*. New York: Routledge, 2006.

Githige, R. "The Issue of Slavery: Relations between the CMS and the State on the East African Coast Prior to 1895." *Journal of Religion in Africa* 16, no. 3 (1986): 209–25.

Glassman, Jonathon. "Slower Than a Massacre: The Multiple Sources of Racial Thought in Colonial Africa," *American Historical Review* 109, no. 3 (2004): 720–54.

———. *Feasts and Riot: Revelry, Rebellion, and Popular Consciousness on the Swahili Coast, 1856–1888.* Portsmouth, NH: Heinemann, 1995.

———. "The Bondsman's New Clothes: The Contradictory Consciousness of Slave Resistance on the Swahili Coast." *Journal of African History* 32, no. 2 (1991): 277–312.

Goldberg, David T. *Racist Culture: Philosophy and the Politics of Meaning.* Cambridge, MA: Blackwell, 1994.

Grant, James. *A Walk Across Africa, or Domestic Scenes from My Nile Journey.* Edinburgh: William Blackwood and Sons, 1864.

Grose, Henry. *A Voyage to the East Indies.* London: Printed for S. Hooper, 1772.

Guillain, Charles. *Documents sur l'histoire, la geographie et le commerce de la Afrique Orientale.* 3 vols. Paris: Bertrand, 1856.

Gundara, J. "Aspects of Indian Culture in Nineteenth Century Zanzibar." *South Asia,* n.s., 3, no. 1 (1980): 14–27.

Gupta, Akhil. "History, Rule, Representation: Scattered Speculations on *Of Revelation and Revolution,* Volume II." *interventions* 3, no. 1 (2001): 40–46.

Guyer, Jane, ed. *Money Matters: Instability, Values, and Social Payments in the Modern History of West African Communities.* Portsmouth, NH: Heinemann, 1995.

———. "Wealth in People, Wealth in Things." *Journal of African History* 36, no. 1 (1995): 83–88.

Hall, Stuart, et al., eds. *Modernity: An Introduction to Modern Societies.* Oxford: Blackwell, 1996.

Hallet, R. "Changing European Attitudes to Africa." In *Cambridge History of Africa,* vol. 5, ed. J. Flint, 458–96. Cambridge: Cambridge University Press, 1976.

Hammond, Dorothy, and Alta Jablow, *The Africa That Never Was: Four Centuries of British Writing about Africa.* New York: Twayne, 1970.

Hannerz, Ulf. *Transnational Connections.* London: Routledge, 1996.

———. "Notes on the Global Ecumene." *Public Culture* 1, no. 2 (1989): 66–75.

———. "The World in Creolization." *Africa* 57, no. 4 (1987): 546–59.

Harding, J. R. "Nineteenth-Century Trade Beads in Tanganyika." *Man,* July 1962, 104–6.

Hartman, Saidiya. *Scenes of Subjection.* Oxford: Oxford University Press, 1997.

Hartmann, Robert. *Abyssinien und die übrigen Gebiete de Ostküste Afrikas.* Leipzig: G. Freytag, 1883.

Hatfield, April Lee. *Atlantic Virginia: Intercolonial Relations in the Seventeenth Century.* Philadelphia: University of Pennsylvania Press, 2004.

Haugerud, Angelique, Margaret Priscilla Stone, and Peter D. Little, eds. *Commodities and Globalization: Anthropological Perspectives.* Lanham, MD: Rowman and Littlefield, 2000.

Hayman, Philip, "My First Slaver: A Tale of the Zanzibar Coast." *Colburn's United Service Magazine* (July 1880).

Headrick, Daniel. *Tools of Empire: Technology and European Imperialism in the Nineteenth Century*. New York: Oxford University Press, 1981.

Hichens, William, and Mbarak Hinawy, eds. *Diwani ya Muyaka*. Johannesburg: University of Witswatersrand Press, 1940.

Ho, Engseng. *The Graves of Tarim: Genealogy and Mobility across the Indian Ocean*. Berkeley and Los Angeles: University of California Press, 2006.

———. "Empire through Diasporic Eyes: A View from the Other Boat," *Comparative Studies in Society and History* 46, no. 2 (2004): 210–46.

Hogendorn, Jan, and Marion Johnson. *The Shell Money of the Slave Trade*. Cambridge: Cambridge University Press, 1986.

Höhnel, Ludwig Ritter von. *Discovery of Lakes Rudolf and Stefanie*. vol. 1. London: Longmans, Green, 1894.

Holman, J. *Travels in Madras, Ceylon, Maurutius, Comoro Islands, Calcutta, Etc.* London: Routledge, 1840.

Hopkins, A. G. *Global History: Interactions Between the Universal and the Local*. New York: Palgrave Macmillan, 2006.

———, ed. *Globalization in World History*. New York: W. W. Norton, 2002.

———. *An Economic History of West Africa*. New York: Columbia University Press, 1973.

Hore, E. C. "On the Twelve Tribes of Tanganyika." *Journal of the Royal Anthropological Institute of Great Britain and Ireland* 12 (1883): 2–21.

Horsey, A. de. "On the Comoro Islands." *Journal of the Royal Geographical Society* 34 (1864): 258–63.

Hove, Anton P. *Tours for Scientific and Economical Research Made in Guzerat, Kattiawar, and the Conkuns, in 1787–88*. Bombay: Bombay Education Society Press, 1855.

Howes, David, ed. *Cross-Cultural Consumption: Global Markets, Local Realities*. London: Routledge, 1996.

Humphrey, Caroline, and S. Hugh-Jones, eds. *Barter, Exchange, and Value: An Anthropological Approach*. Cambridge: Cambridge University Press, 1992.

Huntington, Samuel. *The Clash of Civilizations and the Remaking of World Order*. New York: Simon and Schuster, 1997.

———. *The Clash of Civilizations? The Debate*. New York: Foreign Affairs, 1993.

Hutchinson, E. *The Slave Trade of East Africa*. London: Sampson Low, Marston, Low, and Searle, 1874.

Iliffe, John. *A Modern History of Tanganyika*. Cambridge: Cambridge University Press, 1981.

Jackson, John. "Race in Legislation and Political Economy." *Anthropological Review* 4 (1866): 113–35.

Jacob, Elizabeth, and Henry Jacob. *A Quaker Family in India and Zanzibar, 1863–1865*. Ed. Y. Bird. York: Ebor Press, 2000.

Jameson, Fredric, and Masao Miyoshi, eds. *The Cultures of Globalization*. Durham, NC: Duke University Press, 1998.

Jenkins, Keith, ed. *The Postmodern History Reader*. New York: Routledge, 1997.

Jiddawi, A. "Extracts from an Arab Account Book, 1840–1854." *Tanganyika Notes and Records* 31 (July 1951): 25–31.

Johnson, F. *A Standard Swahili-English Dictionary.* Nairobi: Oxford University Press, 1939.

Johnson, Marion. "Technology, Competition, and African Crafts." In *The Imperial Impact: Studies in the Economic History of Africa and India,* ed. C. Dewey and Anthony G. Hopkins, 259–69. London: Athlone Press, 1978.

Johnson, Walter. *Soul By Soul: Life in the Antebellum Slave Market.* Cambridge, MA: Harvard University Press, 1999.

Johnston, Harry. *The Kilima-njaro Expedition. A Record of Scientific Exploration in Eastern Equatorial Africa.* London: Kegan Paul, Trench, 1886.

Jones, William. "Remarks on the Island of Hinzuan, or Johanna." *Asiatick Researches* 5 (1807): 77–107.

Kamusi Project: Internet Living Swahili Dictionary. http://www.yale.edu/swahili/.

Kapferer, Bruce, ed. *Transaction and Meaning: Directions in the Anthropology of Exchange and Symbolic Behavior.* Philadelphia, PA: Institute for the Study of Human Issues, 1976.

Keim, Curtis. *Mistaking Africa: Curiosities and Inventions of the American Mind.* Boulder, CO: Westview Press, 1999.

King, Anthony, ed. *Culture, Globalization and the World-System.* London: Macmillan, 1991.

Kirkman, James, ed. "The Zanzibar Diary of John Studdy Leigh, Part 1." *International Journal of African Historical Studies* 13, no. 2 (1980): 281–312.

Knauft, Bruce M., ed. *Critically Modern: Alternatives, Alterities, Anthropologies.* Bloomington, IN: Indiana University Press, 2002.

Koponen, Juhani. *People and Production in Late Precolonial Tanzania: History and Structures.* Jyväskylä: Finnish Society for Development Studies, 1988.

Krapf, Johann Ludwig. *'Memoir on the East African Slave Trade': Ein unveröffentlichtes Dokument aus dem Jahr 1853.* Vienna: Afro-Pub, 2002.

———. "Letter to Captain Graham, Mombas, 1st May, 1845." In "Krapf of East Africa." *East and West Review* 3 (1937): 259–69.

———. *A Dictionary of the Suahili Language.* London: Trubner, 1882.

———. *Travel, Researches and Missionary Labours During Eighteen Years Residence in East Africa.* Boston: Ticknor and Fields, 1860.

———. "The East Africa Mission." *Church Missionary Record* 1, no. 17 (1846): 38.

Kristeva, Julia. *Revolution in Poetic Language.* New York: Columbia University Press, 1984.

Kucich, J., and D. Sadoff, eds. *Victorian Afterlife.* Minneapolis: University of Minnesota Press, 2000.

Lacan, Jacques. *Freud's Papers on Technique.* Trans. John Forrester. New York: W. W. Norton, 1988.

Landau, Paul, and Deborah Kaspin. *Images and Empires: Visuality and Colonial and Postcolonial Africa.* Berkeley and Los Angeles: University of California Press, 2002.

Larkin, Brian. "Indian Films and Nigerian Lovers: Media and the Creation of Parallel Modernities." *Africa* 67, no. 3 (1997): 406–39.

Law, Robin, ed. *From Slave Trade to "Legitimate" Commerce: The Commercial Transition in Nineteenth-Century West Africa*. New York: Cambridge University Press, 1995.

Lee, L. O. "Shanghai Modern: Reflections on Urban Culture in China in the 1930s." *Public Culture* 11, no. 1 (1999): 75–108.

Lee, M. *Consumer Culture Reborn: The Cultural Politics of Consumption*. London: Routledge, 1993.

A Letter to a Gentleman on Board an Indiaman to his Friend in London giving an account of the Island of Johanna in the year 1784. London: John Stockdale, 1789.

Lewis, Bernard. *What Went Wrong? The Clash Between Islam and Modernity in the Middle East*. New York: Perennial, 2002.

Lewis, Martin, and Kären Wigen. *The Myth of Continents: A Critique of Metageography*. Berkeley and Los Angeles: University of California Press, 1997.

Liesegang, Gerhard, Helma Pasch, and Adam Jones, eds. *Figuring African Trade*. Berlin: Dietrich Reimer Verlag, 1986.

LiPuma, E. *Encompassing Others: The Magic of Modernity in Melanesia*. Ann Arbor: University of Michigan Press, 2000.

Loeb, Lori Anne. *Consuming Angels: Advertising and Victorian Women*. New York: Oxford University Press, 1994.

Lorimer, Douglas A. *Colour, Class, and the Victorians: English Attitudes to the Negro in the Mid-Nineteenth Century*. Leicester, UK: Leicester University Press, 1978.

Lyne, Robert. *An Apostle of Empire, Being the Life of Sir Lloyd William Matthews*. London: George Allen & Unwin, 1936.

Machado, Pedro. "Gujarati Indian Merchant Networks in Mozambique, 1777–c. 1830." PhD diss., University of London, School of Oriental and African Studies, 2005.

Mackay, Charles. "The Negro and Negrophilists." *Blackwood's Edinburgh Magazine* 99 (1866): 581–97.

MacKenzie, John. *Propaganda and Empire: The Manipulation of British Public Opinion, 1880–1960*. London: Manchester University Press, 1984.

Maier, C. "Consigning the Twentieth Century to History: Alternative Narratives for the Modern Era." *American Historical Review* 105, no. 3 (2000): 1–46.

Marks, J., ed. *The Ways of Desire: New Essays in Philosophical Psychology on the Concept of Wanting*. Chicago: Precedent, 1986.

Marmon, S. "Domestic Slavery in the Mamluk Empire: A Preliminary Sketch." In *Slavery in the Islamic Middle East*, ed. S. Marmon, 1–24. Princeton, NJ: Markus Weiner, 1999.

Martin, Jean. *Comores: Quatre îles entre pirates and planteurs*. Tome 2. Paris: l'Harmattan, 1983.

Marx, Karl. *Capital: A Critique of Political Economy*. 3 vols. Trans. B. Fowkes. Harmondsworth: Penguin, 1977.

Matory, J. Lorand. *Black Atlantic Religion: Tradition, Transnationalism, and Matriarchy in the Afro-Brazilian Candomblé*. Princeton, NJ: Princeton University Press, 2005.

———. "The English Professors of Brazil: On the Diasporic Roots of the Yorùbá

Nation." *Comparative Studies of Society and History* 41, no. 1 (1999): 72–103.

Mazlish, Bruce. *Civilization and Its Contents.* Stanford, CA: Stanford University Press, 2004.

Mazlish, Bruce, and Akira Iriye, eds. *The Global History Reader.* New York: Routledge, 2005.

Mazlish, Bruce, and Ralph Buultjens, eds. *Conceptualizing Global History.* Boulder, CO: Westview Press, 1993.

Mazrui, Alamin, and Ibrahim Noor Shariff. *The Swahili: Idiom and Identity of an African People.* Trenton, NJ: Africa World Press, 1994.

Mazru'i, Shaykh al-Amin bin 'Ali al. *The History of the Mazru'i Dynasty of Mombasa.* Ed. and trans. James M. Ritchie. Oxford: Oxford University Press, 1995.

Mazumdar, D. "Labor Supply in Early Industrialization: The Case of the Bombay Textile Industry." *Economic History Review* 26, no. 3 (1973): 477–96.

Mbembe, Achille. *On the Postcolony.* Berkeley and Los Angeles: University of California Press, 2001.

McClintock, Anne. *Imperial Leather: Race, Gender and Sexuality in the Colonial Conquest.* New York: Routledge, 1995.

McCracken, Grant. *Culture and Consumption: New Approaches to the Symbolic Character of Consumer Goods and Activities.* Bloomington: Indiana University Press, 1988.

McGrane, Bernard. *Beyond Anthropology.* New York: Columbia University Press, 1989.

McKendrick, Neil, John Brewer, and J. H. Plumb, eds. *The Birth of a Consumer Society.* London: Europa Press, 1982.

Metcalf, George. "A Microcosm of Why Africans Sold Slaves: Akan Consumption Patterns in the 1770s." *Journal of African History* 28, no. 3 (1987): 377–94.

Middleton, John. *The World of the Swahili: An African Mercantile Civilization.* New Haven, CT: Yale University Press, 1992.

Miers, Suzanne, and Igor Kopytoff, eds. *Slavery in Africa: Historical and Anthropological Approaches.* Madison: University of Wisconsin Press, 1977.

Mill, John Stuart. *Dissertations and Discussions: Political, Philosophical, and Historical.* Vol. 1. 1859; repr., New York: Haskell House, 1973.

Miller, Daniel, ed. *Worlds Apart: Modernity through the Prism of the Local.* New York: Routledge, 1995.

———, ed. *Acknowledging Consumption: A Review of New Studies.* New York: Routledge, 1995.

———. *Material Culture and Mass Consumption.* London: Routledge, 1987.

Miller, Joseph C. "History and Africa/Africa and History." *American Historical Review* 104, no. 1 (1999): 1–32.

———. *Way of Death: Merchant Capitalism and the Angolan Slave Trade, 1730–1830.* Madison: University of Wisconsin Press, 1988.

Minturn, R. *From New York to Delhi, by way of Rio de Janeiro, Australia, and China.* New York: D. Appleton, 1858.

Mitchell, Timothy, ed. *Questions of Modernity*. Minneapolis: University of Minnesota Press, 2000.

———. *Colonising Egypt*. Berkeley and Los Angeles: University of California Press, 1991.

Mittelman, James. *Whither Globalization? The Vortex of Knowledge and Ideology*. London: Routledge, 2005.

———, ed. *Globalization: Critical Reflections*. London, 1996.

Morgan, L. H. *Ancient Society: Researches in the Lines of Human Progress from Savagery through Barbarism to Civilization*. New York: H. Holt, 1878.

Morton, Fred. *Children of Ham: Freed Slaves and Fugitive Slaves on the Kenya Coast, 1873 to 1907*. Boulder, CO: Westview Press, 1990.

Mudimbe, Valentin. *The Invention of Africa*. Bloomington: Indian University Press, 1988.

Mudimbe-Boyi, Elisabeth, ed. *Beyond Dichotomies: Histories, Identities, Cultures, and the Challenge of Globalization*. Albany, NY: State University of New York Press, 2002.

Munro, J. Forbes. *Africa and the International Economy, 1800–1960*. Totowa, NJ: Rowman and Littlefield, 1976.

Myers, Garth. "Reconstructing Ng'ambo: Town Planning and Development on the Other Side of Zanzibar." PhD diss., University of California, Los Angeles, 1993.

Nassir, Sayyid Abdulla ibn Ali ibn. *Al-Inkishafi: Catechism of a Soul*, ed. and trans., J. de Vere Allen. Nairobi: East African Literature Bureau, 1977.

Neubauer, D. "Assaying the Frontiers of Globalization: Explorations in the New Economy." *American Studies* 41, nos. 2–3 (2000): 13–31.

New, Charles. *Life, Wanderings, and Labours in Eastern Africa*. 1873; repr., London: Frank Cass, 1971.

Nielsen, Ruth. "The History and Development of Wax-Printed Textiles Intended for West Africa and Zaire." In *The Fabrics of Culture: The Anthropology of Clothing and Adornment*, ed. J. Cordwell and R. Schwarz, 467–98. The Hague: Mouton, 1979.

Nimtz, August. *Islam and Politics in East Africa*. Minneapolis: University of Minnesota Press, 1980.

North, Douglas. *Institutions, Institutional Change and Economic Performance*. New York: Cambridge University Press, 1990.

Northrup, David. *The African Discovery of Europe, 1450–1850*. Oxford: Oxford University Press, 2002.

Northway, P. H. "Salem and the Zanzibar-East African Trade, 1825–1845." *Essex Institute Historical Collections* 90 (1954): 123–53, 261–73, and 361–88.

Norton, Marcy. "Tasting Empire: Chocolate and the Internalization of Mesoamerican Aesthetics." *American Historical Review* 111, no. 3 (2006): 660–91.

Orlove, Benjamin, ed. *The Allure of the Foreign: Imported Goods in Postcolonial Latin America*. Ann Arbor: University of Michigan Press, 1997.

O'Rourke, K., and J. Williamson. "When Did Globalization Begin?" National Bureau of Economic Research Working Paper 7632, 2000. Online at http://papers.nber.org/papers/w7632.pdf.

———. *Globalization and History: The Evolution of a Nineteenth-Century Atlantic Economy.* Cambridge, MA: Harvard University Press, 1999.

Osgood, Joseph. *Notes of Travel; or, Recollections of Majunga, Zanzibar, Muscat, Aden, Mocha, and Other Eastern Ports.* Salem, MA: George Creamer, 1854.

Ovington, John. *A Voyage to Suratt in the Year 1689.* Vol. 1 of *India in the Seventeenth Century,* ed. J. P. Guha. New Delhi: Associated Publishing House, 1976.

Owen, W. F. W. *Narrative of Voyages to Explore the Shores of Africa, Arabia, and Madagascar.* 2 vols. New York: J. & J. Harper, 1833.

Parry, J., and M. Bloch, eds. *Money and the Morality of Exchange.* Cambridge: Cambridge University Press, 1989.

Partington, S. *Animation of the Soul: A Translation of the KiSwahili, Islamic Epic Al-Inkishafi.* Mombasa: Mombasa Academy, 1999.

Patterson, Orlando. *Slavery and Social Death: A Comparative Study.* Cambridge, MA: Harvard, 1982.

Pelly, Lewis. "Remarks on the Tribes and Resources around the Shoreline of the Persian Gulf." *Transactions of the Bombay Geographical Society* 17 (1863–64): 32–103.

———. "Miscellaneous Observations upon the Comoro Islands." *Transactions of the Bombay Geographical Society* 16 (June 1860–December 1862): 88–98.

Pemberton, Jo-Anne. *Global Metaphors: Modernity and the Quest for One World.* London: Pluto Press, 2001.

Perham, Margery F. *Ten Africans.* London: Faber and Faber, 1936.

Pickering, Charles. *The Races of Man and Their Geographical Distribution.* London: George Bell and Sons, 1876.

Pieterse, J. Nederveen. *White on Black: Images of Africa and Blacks in Western Popular Culture.* New Haven, CT: Yale University Press, 1992.

———. "Dilemmas of Development Discourse: The Crisis of Developmentalism and the Comparative Method." *Development and Change* 22, no. 1 (1991): 5–29.

Piot, Charles. "Of Hybridity, Modernity, and Their Malcontents." *interventions* 3, no. 1 (2001).

———. "Of Slaves and the Gift: Kabre Sale of Kin During the Era of the Slave Trade." *Journal of African History* 37, no. 1 (1996): 31–49.

Pomper, Philip, Richard H. Elphick, and Richard T. Vann. *World History: Ideologies, Structures, and Identities.* Malden, MA: Blackwell, 1998.

Postans, T. "Some account of the present state of the trade between the port of Mandvie in Cutch, and the East Coast of Africa." *Transactions of the Bombay Geographical Society* 3 (1839/40): 169–76.

Pouwels, Randall. *Horn and Crescent: Traditional Islam on the East African Coast, 800–1900.* Cambridge: Cambridge University Press, 1987.

———. "Islam and Islamic Leadership in the Coastal Communities of Eastern Africa, 1700 to 1914." PhD diss., University of California, Los Angeles, 1979.

Pramar, V. "Wooden Architecture of Gujerat." PhD diss., University of Baroda, 1980.

Pratt, Mary Louise. *Imperial Eyes: Travel Writing and Transculturation.* New York: Routledge, 1992.

Prior, James. *Voyage along the Eastern Coast of Africa, to Mosambique, Johanna, and Quiloa; to St. Helena . . . in the Nisus Frigate.* London: Sir Richard Phillips, 1819.

Rampley, W. J. *Matthew Wellington: Sole Surviving Link with Dr. Livingstone.* London: Society for Promoting Christian Knowledge, [ca. 1930].

Rance, J. "Letter from Lamu." *Coast Express* (Kenya), 6 December 2002.

Raz, Aviad. *Riding the Black Ship: Japan and Tokyo Disneyland.* Cambridge, MA: Harvard University Press, 1999.

Richards, J. "A Cruize through the Mozambique Channel." *Nautical Magazine and Naval Chronicle,* July 1849, 337–44.

Richards, T. *The Commodity Culture of Victorian England: Advertising and Spectacle,1851–1914.* Stanford, CA: Stanford University Press, 1990.

Richardson, David. "West African Consumption Patterns and Their Influence on the Eighteenth-Century English Slave Trade." In *The Uncommon Market: Essays in the Economic History of the Atlantic Slave Trade.* Ed. A. Gemery and J. Hogendorn. New York: Academic Press, 1979.

Riggins, Stephen Harold, ed. *The Socialness of Things: Essays in the Socio-Semiotics of Objects.* Berlin: Mouton de Gruyter, 1994.

Ritzer, George. *The McDonaldization of Society.* Thousand Oaks, CA: Pine Forge, 1995.

Roberts, Richard. "West Africa and the Pondicherry Textile Industry." In *Cloth and Commerce: Textiles in Colonial India,* ed. Tirthankar Roy, 142–74. Thousand Oaks, CA: Sage, 1996.

———. *Two Worlds of Cotton: Colonialism and the Regional Economy in the French Soudan, 1800–1946.* Stanford, CA: Stanford University Press, 1996.

———. *Warriors, Merchants, and Slaves: The State and the Economy in the Middle Niger Valley, 1700–1914.* Stanford, CA: Stanford University Press, 1987.

Robertson, Claire, and Martin Klein, eds. *Women and Slavery in Africa.* Madison: University of Wisconsin Press, 1983.

Robertson, Roland. *Globalization: Social Theory and Global Culture.* London: Sage, 1992.

———, and F. Lechner. "Modernization, Globalization and the Problem of Culture in World-Systems Theory." *Theory, Culture & Society* 2, no. 3 (1985): 103–18.

Robinson, Ronald, John Gallagher, and Alice Denny. *Africa and the Victorians: The Climax of Imperialism.* Garden City, NY: Anchor Books, 1968.

Rockel, Stephen J. *Carriers of Culture: Labor on the Road in Nineteenth-Century East Africa.* Portsmouth, NH: Heinemann, 2006.

———. "'A Nation of Porters': The Nyamwezi and the Labour Market in Nineteenth-Century Tanzania." *Journal of African History* 41, no. 2 (2000): 173–95.

Rodney, Walter. *How Europe Underdeveloped Africa.* Washington, DC: Howard University Press, 1989.

Rooke, Henry. *Travels to the Coast of Arabia Felix; and from thence by the Red-Sea and Egypt, to Europe.* London: Printed for R. Blamire, 1784.

Ropes, Edward D., Jr. *The Zanzibar Letters of Edward D. Ropes, Jr., 1882–1892.* Ed. Norman Bennett. Boston: Boston University Press, 1973.

Ruete, Emily [Sayyida Salme]. *Memoirs of an Arabian Princess.* In *An Arabian Princess between Two Worlds: Memoirs, Letters Home, Sequels to the Memoirs, Syrian Customs and Usages,* ed. E. Van Donzel, 143–406. New York: E. J. Brill, 1993.

Ruschenberger, W. *A Voyage Round the World; Including an Embassy to Muscat and Siam, in 1835, 1836, and 1837.* Philadelphia, PA: Carey, Lea, and Blanchard, 1839.

Rutz, Henry, and Benjamin Orlove, eds. *The Social Economy of Consumption.* Lanham, MD: University Press of America, 1989.

Ryan, J. *Picturing Empire: Photography and the Visualization of the British Empire.* London: Reacktion, 1997.

Sabunji, L. *Tanzih al-absar wa-al-afkar fi riḥlat Sultan Zanjabar, jama'ahu Zahir ibn Sa'id.* Muscat: Wizarat al-Turath al-Qawmi wa-al-Thaqafah, 1988.

Sacleux, Charles. *Dictionnaire Swahili-Français.* Paris: Institut d'ethnologie, 1939.

Sahlins, Marshal. "Cosmologies of Capitalism: The Trans-Pacific Sector of 'The World System.'" In *Culture in Practice: Selected Essays,* 415–70. New York: Zone Books, 2000.

Said, Edward. *Covering Islam.* New York: Vintage, 1999.

———. *Culture and Imperialism.* New York: Vintage, 1993.

———. *Orientalism.* New York: Vintage Books, 1979.

Salt, Henry. *A Voyage to Abyssinia.* London: F. C. and J. Rivington, 1814.

Schmidt, Karl. *Sansibar: Ein ostafrikaniches Culturbild.* Leipzig: Brodhaus, 1888.

Schneider, William H. *An Empire for the Masses: The French Popular Image of Africa, 1870–1900.* Westport, CT: Greenwood Press, 1982.

Scott, Alan, ed. *The Limits of Globalization.* London: Routledge, 1997.

Shami, Seteney. "Prehistories of Globalization: Circassian Identity in Motion." *Public Culture* 12, no. 1 (2000): 177–204.

Sheriff, Abdul, ed. *The History and Conservation of Zanzibar Stone Town.* Athens: Ohio University Press, 1995.

———. *Slaves, Spices, and Ivory in Zanzibar: Integration of an East African Commercial Empire into the World Economy, 1770–1873.* London: James Currey, 1987.

Sheriff, Abdul, and Javed Jafferji. *Zanzibar Town: An Architectural Exploration.* Zanzibar: Gallery Publications, 1998.

Siravo, F. *Zanzibar: A Plan for the Historic Stone Town.* Zanzibar: Gallery Publications, 1996.

Smith, Woodruff D. *Consumption and the Making of Respectability, 1600–1800.* New York: Routledge, 2002.

Speke, John H. *Journal of the Discovery of the Source of the Nile.* New York: Harper and Brothers, 1868.

Sperling, David. "The Frontiers of Prophecy: Healing, the Cosmos and Islam on the East African Coast in the Nineteenth Century." In *Revealing Prophets,* ed. D. Anderson and D. Johnson, 83–101. London: James Currey, 1995.

Stanley, Henry M. *In Darkest Africa.* London: Sampson Low, 1890.

———. *How I Found Livingstone: Travels, Adventures, and Discoveries in Central Africa.* New York: Charles Scribner's Sons, 1887.

———. *Through the Dark Continent.* 2 vols. New York: Harper and Brothers, 1878.

Stearns, Peter. *Consumerism in World History: The Global Transformation of Desire.* Routledge: New York, 2001.

Steere, Edward. *A Handbook of the Swahili Language, as Spoken at Zanzibar.* 1870; repr., London: Society for Promoting Christian Knowledge, 1894.

———. "On East African Tribes and Languages." *Journal of the Anthropological Institute of Great Britain and Ireland* 1 (1872): 143–54.

———, ed. *The East African Slave Trade.* London: Harrison, 1871.

———. *Swahili Tales, as Told by the Natives of Zanzibar.* London: Bell and Daldy, 1870.

Sternberg, E. *The Economy of Icons: How Business Manufactures Meaning.* Westport, CT: Praeger, 1999.

Stiglitz, Joseph. *Globalization and Its Discontents.* New York: W. W. Norton, 2002.

Strobel, Margaret. *Muslim Women in Mombasa, 1890–1975.* New Haven, CT: Yale University Press, 1979.

Subrahmanyam, Sanjay. "Hearing Voices: Vignettes of Early Modernity in South Asia, 1400–1750." *Daedalus* 127, no. 3 (1998): 75–104.

"Sultan of Zanzibar a Good Pianist." *Academy* 8 (July–December 1875): 181.

Sykes, Colonel. "Notes on the Possessions of the Imaum of Muskat, on the Climate and Productions of Zanzibar, and on the Prospects of African Discovery from Mombas." *Journal of the Royal Geographical Society* 23 (1853).

Taasisi ya Uchunguzi wa Kiswahili (Chuo Kikuu cha Dar es Salaam). *Kamusi ya Kiswahili Sanifu.* Dar es Salaam: Oxford University Press, 1997.

Taussig, Michael. *Mimesis and Alterity: A Particular History of the Senses.* New York: Routledge, 1993.

———. "History as Commodity in Some Recent American (Anthropological) Literature." *Critique of Anthropology* 9, no. 1 (1989): 7–23.

Taylor, Peter J. *Modernities: A Geohistorical Interpretation.* Minneapolis: University of Minnesota Press, 1999.

Taylor, William. *African Aphorisms; or Saws from Swahililand.* London: Society for Promoting Christian Knowledge, 1891.

Temin, Peter, ed. *Engines of Enterprise: An Economic History of New England.* Cambridge, MA: Harvard University Press, 2000.

Thomas, Nicholas. *Entangled Objects: Exchange, Material Culture, and Colonialism in the Pacific.* Cambridge, MA: Harvard University Press, 1991.

———. *Out of Time: History and Evolution in Anthropological Discourses.* Ann Arbor: University of Michigan Press, 1989.

Thompson, E. P. *The Making of the English Working Class.* London: Gollancz, 1963.

Thomson, Joseph. "East Africa as It Was and Is." *The Contemporary Review* 55 (January–June 1889): 41–51.

———. *To the Central African Lakes and Back: The Narrative of the Royal Geographical Society's East Central African Expedition, 1878–80.* London: S. Low, Marston, Searle & Rivington, 1881.

Thornton, John. "The Role of Africans in the Atlantic Economy, 1450–1650: Modern Africanist Historiography and the World-Systems Paradigm." *Colonial Latin American Historical Review* 3, no. 2 (1994): 125–40.

Thornton, R. "Notes Towards a Theory of Objects and Persons." *African Anthropology* 4, no. 1 (1997): 36–51.

Tobin, Joseph J., ed. *Re-Made in Japan: Everyday Life and Consumer Taste in a Changing Society.* New Haven, CT: Yale University Press, 1992.

Tomlinson, Alan, ed. *Consumption, Identity, and Style.* London: Routledge, 1990.

Tomlinson, John. *Globalization and Culture.* Chicago: University of Chicago Press, 1999.

Trouillot, Michel-Rolph. *Global Transformations: Anthropology and the Modern World.* New York: Palgrave Macmillan, 2003.

———. *Silencing the Past: Power and the Production of History.* Boston: Beacon Press, 1995.

Troyer, J. "Rationality and Maximization." In *Ethics: Foundations, Problems, and Applications,* ed. E. Morscher and R. Stranzinger, 211–15. Vienna: Verlag Hölder-Pichler-Tempsky, 1981.

Tsing, Anna. "The Global Situation." *Cultural Anthropology* 15, no. 3 (2000): 327–60.

Tylor, Edward. *Anthropology: An Introduction to the Study of Man and Civilization.* 1880; repr., London: D. Appleton, 1913.

Veblen, Thorstein. *The Theory of the Leisure Class.* London: Allen and Unwin, 1924.

Wagnleitner, Reinhold. *Coca-Colonization and the Cold War: The Cultural Mission of the United States in Austria after the Second World War.* Trans. Diana M. Wolf. Chapel Hill: University of North Carolina Press, 1994.

Wainwright, Jacob. "Tagebuch von Jacob Wainwright über den Transport von Dr. Livingston's Leiche, 4. Mai 1873–18, Februar 1874." *Petermanns Mittheilungen* 20 (1874): 187–93.

Wakefield, Rebecca. *Memoirs of Mrs. Rebecca Wakefield, Wife of the Rev. T. Wakefield.* Ed. R. Brewin. London: Hamilton, Adams, 1879.

Walker, Iain. "Mimetic Structuration: Or, Easy Steps to Building and Acceptable Identity." *History and Anthropology* 16, no. 2 (2005): 187–210.

Waller, Horace. "Two Ends of the Slave Stick." *Contemporary Review,* April 1889, 532–33.

———. *The Last Journals of David Livingstone, in Central Africa, from 1865 to His Death.* Hartford, CT: R.W. Bliss, 1875.

Wallerstein, Immanuel. *Historical Capitalism; with Capitalist Civilization.* New York: Verso, 1995.

———. *The Modern World-System.* 3 vols. New York: Academic Press, 1974–89.

———. "The Three Stages of African Involvement in the World-Economy." In

The Political Economy of Contemporary Africa, ed. Peter Gutkind and Immanuel Wallerstein, 30–57. Beverly Hills, CA: Sage, 1976.

Ward, G., ed., *Letters of Bishop Tozer and His Sister together with Some Other Records of the Universities' Mission from 1863–1873.* London: Office of the Universities' Mission to Central Africa, 1902.

Waters, Malcolm. *Globalization.* London: Routledge, 2001.

Watson, James. "China's Big Mac Attack." *Foreign Affairs* 79 (May–June 2000): 120–34.

———, ed. *Golden Arches East: McDonald's in East Asia.* Stanford, CA: Stanford University Press, 1997.

Weeks, Clelia. "Zanzibar." *Harper's New Monthly Magazine* 38 (December–May, 1868–1869): 306–18.

White, Shane. "A Question of Style: Blacks in and around New York City in the Late Eighteenth Century." *Journal of American Folklore* 102, no. 403 (1989): 23–44.

Wilding, Richard. "Ceramics of the Lamu Archipelago." PhD diss., University of Nairobi, 1977.

Williams, Raymond. *Keywords: A Vocabulary of Culture and Society.* London: Fontana, 1976.

Willis, Justin. *Potent Brews: A Social History of Alcohol in East Africa, 1850–1999.* Athens: Ohio University Press, 2002.

———. *Mombasa, the Swahili and the Making of the Mijikenda.* Oxford: Clarendon Press, 1993.

Willoughby, John. *East Africa and Its Big Game: The Narrative of a Sporting Trip from Zanzibar to the Borders of the Masai.* London: Longmans, Green, 1889.

Wilson, Rob, and Wimal Dissanayake, eds. *Global/Local: Cultural Production and the Transnational Imagery.* Durham, NC: Duke University Press, 1996.

Wright, Marcia. *Strategies of Slaves and Women in East Central Africa.* Bloomington: University of Indiana Press, 1989.

Xiao bin Tang, ed. *Chinese Modern: The Heroic and the Quotidian.* Durham, NC: Duke University Press, 2000.

Young, Marianne. *Cutch, or Random Sketches of Western India.* London: Smith, Elder, 1838.

Young, Robert. *Postcolonialism: An Historical Introduction.* London: Blackwell, 2001.

———. *Colonial Desire: Hybridity in Theory, Culture and Race.* New York: Routledge, 1995.

Young, Timothy. *Travellers in Africa: British Travelogues, 1850–1900.* New York: Manchester University Press, 1988.

Zein, Mohamed el. *The Sacred Meadows.* Evanston, IL: Northwestern University Press, 1974.

Zha, J. *China Pop: How Soap Operas, Tabloids, and Bestsellers Are Transforming a Culture.* New York: New Press, 1995.

Index

Page references in *italics* refer to illustrations.

Index

Pratt, Mary Louise, 88
Pratt, Seth A. (American consul), 78
Prichard, J., 230n43
Prideaux, Captain W. F., 167
Primitiveness: modernity and notion of, 88; Western projections of, 115
Prior, Sir James, 22, 23, 24, 183n23; and Bombay Jack, 30–31; on Mutsamuduan clothing, 28
Purity: in Victorian discourse, 156, 230n41, 231nn47,53; in Western consciousness, 226n4. *See also* Hybridity

Qurrah Idris (Qualla), 98

Race: Disraeli and, 226n5; and hybridity, 232n61; nineteenth-century concepts of, 154–56, 158–67, 230n41; and slavery, 128–30; in Victorian discourse, 230n41, 231n56
Racial science, 231n56; emergence of, 160–1
Railways: global impact of, 173; in Zanzibar, 105
Rajab (Zanzibari), 94–96, 101
Ramadan, business during, 63
Ramanetaka (Malagasy rebel), 185n59
Raz, Aviad, 14
Reciprocity, British sense of, 31
Renier, Admiral, 26
Richards, J., 21, 23
Richardson, David, 6–7, 61, 62
Rigby, Colonel, 17, 182n17; emancipation of slaves, 224n105
Roberts, Richard, 61, 62, 198n11
Robertson, Roland, 196n5
Robinson, Ronald, 145, 149
Roho (soul), 35, 38, 41–45, 57, 58, 191n20; constitution of self, 41–42; death of, 192nn39,40; and desire, 41–45, 46, 58; *kifuli* of, 44–45, 192nn38, 42; *kijito* of, 42–43; Krapf on, 41; loss of control over, 43–44; relationship to body, 41, 44; of thieves, 42
Rolla (merchant ship), 74
Rooke, Major, 27
Ropes, Edward, Jr., 78, 151; and Barghash, 113, 233n85; on umbrellas, 162
Royal Geographical Society, membership of, 227n18, 228n24
Ruete, Emily. *See* Salme binti Said, Sayyida

Sahel, Western, colonial conquest in, 198n11
Sahlins, Marshal, 196n4
Said, Edward, 233n82

Said al-Busaidi, Seyyid (Sultan of Zanzibar), 35, 36, 232n79; capture of Mombasa, 194n66; décor of, 101, 110; diplomatic relations of, 166; mercantile pursuits of, 91–92, 209n15; portraits of, 95; slave manumission by, 136; status codes and, 101; trade mission to United States, 91–93
Salem (Massachusetts): commerce with East Africa, 10, 59, 63, 73–78, 200n24; commerce with Zanzibar, 73–78, 204n78; global consciousness in, 202n58; Indian Ocean trade of, 72–73; Naumkeag Steam Cotton Company, 76, 85, 203n72, 204n78; transition from mercantilism, 78; Whipple Gum Copal Factory, 73; Zanzibari travelers to, 94–95
Salim (Sultan of Nzwani), 182n15
Salme binti Said, Sayyida (Emily Ruete), 96, 97, 101–2, 225n121; on concubines, 222n86; on jewelry, 104; on slaves, 121, 123
Samuli (beads), 65
Schneider, W., 228n23
Self, Mombasan concepts of, 38–58, 87
Self-definition: East African, 117; through objects, 34–35, 45–58, 87, 100, 101–5, 117, 134–43
Self-perception, Western modes of, 88, 91
Semi-civilization: and East Africans, 157–70; Western concept of, 155–61
Senegambia, textile trade in, 197n9
Servants, colonial, clothing of, 221n63
Seward, G. Edward (British Consul), 131–32
Sewji, Jairam, 104
Shamy, Seteney, 178n6
Sháuku (want), 192n43
Shewane, Sayyida, 123
Shinzwani (language of Nzwani), 19, 185n39
Sidi Bombay, 135
Similitude: and aesthetics, 27–31; in asymmetrical power relationships, 18; in global relations, 9; and *mètis*, 183n19; Mutsamuduan strategy of, 13–14, 20–32, 171; Prince Abdullah's use of, 15–18
Simmel, Georg, 135
Slave market, Zanzibari, 126–28, 127, 220nn41,44; Burton on, 220n47
Slave narratives, Zanzibari, 119–20
Slave-owners, Zanzibari, 119–24; exslave, 142; ideology of, 132; poor, 121, 142; social capital of, 119; wealthy, 122–23

Text:	10/13 Sabon
Display:	Sabon
Compositor:	BookMatters, Berkeley
Indexer:	Roberta Engleman
Printer and binder:	Maple-Vail Manufacturing Group